SALIENCE IN SECOND LANGUAGE ACQUISITION

Salience in Second Language Acquisition brings together contributions from top scholars of second language acquisition (SLA) in a comprehensive volume of the existing literature and current research on salience. In the first book to focus exclusively on this integral topic, the editors and contributors define and explore what makes a linguistic feature salient in sections on theory, perpetual salience, and constructed salience. They also provide a history of SLA theory and discussion on its contemporary use in research. An approachable introduction to the topic, this book is an ideal supplement to courses in SLA, and a valuable resource for researchers and scholars looking for a better understanding of the subject.

Susan M. Gass is University Distinguished Professor in the Second Language Studies Program at Michigan State University, USA. She has served as President of the American Association for Applied Linguistics and of the International Association of Applied Linguistics. She is the recipient of numerous awards and is the current co-editor of *Studies in Second Language Acquisition*.

Patti Spinner is Associate Professor in the Second Language Studies Program at Michigan State University, USA.

Jennifer Behney is Assistant Professor of Italian and Second Language Acquisition in the Department of Foreign Languages and Literatures at Youngstown State University, USA.

Second Language Acquisition Research Series
Susan M. Gass and Alison Mackey, Series Editors

To view all of the books in this series, please visit: www.routledge.com/Second-Language-Acquisition-Research-Series/book-series/LEASLARS

Recent Monographs on Theoretical Issues

The Psychology of the Language Learner – Revisited (2015)
Dörnyei/Ryan

The Second Language Learning Processes of Students with Specific Learning Difficulties (2017)
Kormos

Salience in Second Language Acquisition (2018)
Gass/Spinner/Behney

Recent Monographs on Research Methodology

SLA Research and Materials Development for Language Learning (2016)
Tomlinson

Stimulated Recall Methodology in Applied Linguistics and L2 Research, Second Edition (2017)
Gass/Mackey

Understanding, Evaluating, and Conducting Second Language Writing Research (2017)
Polio/Friedman

The Second Language Learning Processes of Students with Specific Learning Difficulties (2017)
Kormos

Of Related Interest

Second Language Acquisition
An Introductory Course, Fourth Edition (2013)
Gass/Behney/Plonsky

Second Language Research
Methodology and Design (2005)
Mackey/Gass

SALIENCE IN SECOND LANGUAGE ACQUISITION

Edited by
Susan M. Gass, Patti Spinner
and Jennifer Behney

NEW YORK AND LONDON

First published 2018
by Routledge
711 Third Avenue, New York, NY 10017

and by Routledge
2 Park Square, Milton Park, Abingdon, Oxon, OX14 4RN

Routledge is an imprint of the Taylor & Francis Group, an informa business

© 2018 Taylor & Francis

The right of Susan M. Gass, Patti Spinner, and Jennifer Behney to be identified as the authors of the editorial material, and of the authors for their individual chapters, has been asserted in accordance with sections 77 and 78 of the Copyright, Designs and Patents Act 1988.

All rights reserved. No part of this book may be reprinted or reproduced or utilized in any form or by any electronic, mechanical, or other means, now known or hereafter invented, including photocopying and recording, or in any information storage or retrieval system, without permission in writing from the publishers.

Trademark notice: Product or corporate names may be trademarks or registered trademarks, and are used only for identification and explanation without intent to infringe.

Every effort has been made to contact copyright-holders. Please advise the publisher of any errors or omissions, and these will be corrected in subsequent editions.

Library of Congress Cataloging-in-Publication Data
A catalog record for this book has been requested

ISBN: 978-1-138-22567-1 (hbk)
ISBN: 978-1-138-22568-8 (pbk)
ISBN: 978-1-315-39902-7 (ebk)

Typeset in Bembo
by Apex CoVantage, LLC

To the salient little ones in our lives

CONTENTS

Acknowledgements   x
List of Illustrations   xi
List of Contributors   xiv

1 Salience in Second Language Acquisition and Related Fields   1
 Susan M. Gass, Patti Spinner, and Jennifer Behney

PART I
Salience in SLA Theory   **19**

2 Salience in Usage-Based SLA   21
 Nick Ellis

3 Detectability in Feature Reassembly   41
 Donna Lardiere

4 The Role of Salience in Linguistic Development:
 A Contrarian View   64
 William O'Grady, Kitaek Kim, and Chae-Eun Kim

PART II
Perceptual Salience in SLA   87

5 The L2 Acquisition of Italian Tense: The Role of Salience   89
   Jennifer Behney, Patti Spinner,
   Susan M. Gass, and Lorena Valmori

6 The Effect of Perceptual Salience on Processing L2 Inflectional
   Morphology   107
   Hannelore Simoens, Alex Housen, and Ludovic De Cuypere

7 The Role of Salience in the Acquisition of Hebrew as a Second
   Language: Interaction With Age of Acquisition   131
   Robert DeKeyser, Iris Alfi-Shabtay, Dorit Ravid, and
   Meng Shi

8 Salience and Novel L2 Pattern Learning   147
   Kim McDonough and Pavel Trofimovich

PART III
Constructed Salience in SLA   165

9 Enhancing the Input to Promote Salience of the L2:
   A Critical Overview   167
   Ronald P. Leow and Alexandra Martin

10 Salience, Cognitive Effort, and Word Learning: Insights from
   Pupillometry   187
   Kelli Ryan, Phillip Hamrick, Ryan T. Miller, and
   Christopher A. Was

11 Effects of Contextual and Visual Cues on Spoken Language
   Processing: Enhancing L2 Perceptual Salience Through
   Focused Training   201
   Debra M. Hardison

PART IV
Salience in Context   221

12 Salience of Noun–Adjective Agreement in L2 Latin   223
    John Sarkissian and Jennifer Behney

13 Measuring Lexical Alignment During L2 Chat Interaction:
    An Eye-Tracking Study   244
    Marije Michel and Bryan Smith

14 Task Modality, Noticing, and the Contingency of
    Recasts: Insights on Salience From Multiple Modalities   269
    Nicole Ziegler

    Afterword: The Role of Salience in Second
    Language Research   291
    Patti Spinner, Jennifer Behney, and Susan M. Gass

Index   *298*

ACKNOWLEDGEMENTS

Even though it is our names that appear on the cover of this book as editors, there are many individuals whose contributions must be acknowledged. First of all, we acknowledge the authors who responded quickly to comments and to the requested changes to their papers. Many authors and outside scholars served as readers for papers in the volume and we are grateful for their timely reviews and perceptive comments. Alison Mackey read the papers as well as our own introduction and afterword and provided feedback that saved us from embarrassing errors.

Our research assistant Xuehong He (better known as Stella) was of enormous help in the final stages of putting all the papers together. Her keen eye found problems that might have otherwise gone unnoticed.

And, finally, many thanks to Rebecca Novack and Kathrene Binag who saw this project through from the beginning to end. We are, of course, pleased to see the end.

Susan M. Gass, East Lansing, Michigan
Patti Spinner, East Lansing, Michigan
Jennifer Behney, Youngstown, Ohio

ILLUSTRATIONS

Figures

4.1	Sample picture used for eye-tracking task (Clackson et al., 2011)	68
4.2	Sample protocol used to elicit a subject RC	69
4.3	Sample protocol used to elicit an indirect object RC	70
4.4	Sample protocol used to elicit a direct object RC	71
4.5	Sample protocol used to elicit an oblique RC	72
4.6	A sample picture, adapted from Song, O'Grady, Cho, and Lee (1997)	79
6.1	Salience by conditions of grammaticality and explicitness	121
7.1	Interaction between salience level and age of acquisition	137
10.1	Scatterplot depicting relationships between recognition test accuracy for hits and mean pupil dilation in the training phase by group. Each dot represents a single participant. The gray region around the regression lines indicates the 95% confidence interval.	195
11.1A	L1 Japanese: Mean percentage of target word needed for identification in pretest and posttest per modality (AV, A-only) and condition (sentence, excised word)	208
11.1B	L1 Japanese: Mean percentage of target word needed for identification in pretest and posttest by modality and initial consonant category (collapsed across condition)	209
11.2	L1 Japanese: Mean duration in gates of word candidates proposed for stimuli *riot* (pretest) and *robot* (posttest) in AV and A-only sentence presentations	210
11.3A	L1 Korean: Mean percentage of target word needed for identification in pretest and posttest per modality (AV, A-only) and condition (sentence, excised word)	211

xii Illustrations

11.3B	L1 Korean: Mean percentage of target word needed for identification in pretest and posttest by modality and initial consonant category (collapsed across condition)	212
11.4	L1 Korean: Mean duration in gates of word candidates proposed for stimuli *razor* (pretest) and *lighter* (posttest) in AV and A-only sentence presentations	213
11.5A	L1 English: Mean percentage of target word needed for identification per modality (AV, A-only) and condition (sentence, excised word)	214
11.5B	L1 English: Mean percentage of target word needed for identification per modality, condition, and initial consonant category	215
13.1	Example experimental task: reconstruct middle part of an abstract	252
13.2	Design of the study	252
13.3	Experimental setup showing the task (reconstruct the middle part of an abstract) on the left and chat window of the interaction between participants 3 and 4 on the right (including superimposed eye-gazes)	254
13.4	Screenshot of participant 1 paying attention to participant 6's earlier writing of 'to find the groups' while writing herself 'to find the group' (left) as demonstrated by the screenshot seconds later with the output of both partners (right)	256
13.5	Example of multiple instances of overt attention to model structure (left) aligned to a few turns later (right)	257

Tables

2.1	A contingency table showing the four possible combinations of events relating to the presence or absence of a target cue and an outcome	26
4.1	Success rates for each relative clause type	73
5.1	Italian conjugations	94
5.2	Examples of experimental sentences	97
5.3	Descriptive statistics	100
5.4	Results of mixed model analysis of participants' early and late processing of verb interest areas	101
6.1	Skipping rate in percentage for both the low- and high-salient morphemes in the explicit and implicit condition, and in total	119
6.2	Mean fixation times, standard deviations, and grammatical sensitivity index values for the ungrammatical and grammatical trials of both the low- and high-salient morphemes in the explicit and implicit condition	120
7.1	GJT accuracy for salience level by age of onset (marginal means for age at testing as covariate)	138
7.2	Salience and its components for the structures on the grammaticality judgment test	143

8.1	OVS learning by input distribution	154
8.2	OVS scores by L1 background	155
8.3	OVS learning by instructions provided	156
8.4	Salience as exploitation of the learning environment	157
9.1	A summary of Non-Conflated Input Enhancement (NCIE) studies	172
9.2	A summary of online studies	179
10.1	Biodata for participants by group	191
10.2	Sample sentences from the training phase	192
10.3	Descriptive results for the recognition memory task	194
10.4	Regression model results for accuracy for hits in the recognition test	195
12.1	Noun patterns	228
12.2	Adjective patterns	229
12.3	Item analysis, forced choice adjective completion task	233
13.1	Participant characteristics	251
13.2	Example chatlog of participants 2 and 5 interacting on the beginning of an abstract in the experimental session 1	254
13.3	Use of 'Vocab' by both participants 2 and 5	256
13.4	Descriptive baseline and *PSLA*	257
13.5	Higher values than baseline plus 1 (bold) or 2 (bold italics) SD for participant 1	258
13.6	Identified Source of Lexical Alignment (ISLA) based on baseline comparison for all participants	259
13.7	Relationship between fixation count and alignment (U.S. group)	260
13.8	Identified Source of Lexical Alignment (ISLA) based on statistical analysis (U.S. group)	260
14.1	Descriptive statistics for noticing, mode, and recasts	281
14.2	Descriptive statistics for noticing and contingency	281
14.3	Learner noticing in relation to modified output and mode	282
A.1	Data used in the empirical studies in this volume	295

CONTRIBUTORS

Iris Alfi-Shabtay is Senior Lecturer at Levinsky College of Education, Tel Aviv, Israel. Her main research fields are: first and second language acquisition, bilingualism, second language learning, assessment, and intervention in the L2 classroom.

Jennifer Behney is Assistant Professor of Italian, applied linguistics, and foreign language education at Youngstown State University, USA. Her research interests include grammatical gender acquisition, facilitation in spoken word recognition, eye-tracking, and foreign language teacher training. Her work appears in *Studies in Second Language Acquisition* and *Foreign Language Annals*.

Ludovic De Cuypere is Professor of English Linguistics and Research Methodology at the Vrije Universiteit Brussel and teaching assistant in the Linguistics Department of Ghent University, Belgium, where he provides statistical consultancy and teaches quantitative research methods for linguists. His research focuses on linguistic variation, which he has studied from a synchronic, diachronic, and language acquisition perspective, using quantitative methods. He has published on a variety of topics such as iconicity, alternating syntactic constructions, lexical semantics, language change, and language acquisition, and on a wide range of languages, including English, Old English, German, Swedish, Portuguese, and Hindi.

Robert DeKeyser is Professor of Second Language Acquisition at the University of Maryland, USA. His research is mainly on second language acquisition, with emphasis on cognitive-psychological aspects such as implicit versus explicit learning, automatization of rule knowledge, and individual differences and their interaction with instructional treatments. He has been published in a variety of journals. He has also contributed chapters to several highly regarded handbooks, and published an edited volume entitled *Practice in a Second Language: Perspectives from Applied Linguistics and Cognitive Psychology*.

Nick Ellis is Professor of Psychology and Linguistics at the University of Michigan, USA. His research interests include language acquisition, cognition, emergentism, corpus linguistics, cognitive linguistics, applied linguistics, and psycholinguistics. Recent books include: *Usage-based Approaches to Language Acquisition and Processing: Cognitive and Corpus Investigations of Construction Grammar* (2016, with Römer and O'Donnell), *Language as a Complex Adaptive System* (2009, with Larsen-Freeman), and *Handbook of Cognitive Linguistics and Second Language Acquisition* (2008, with Robinson). He serves as General Editor of *Language Learning*.

Susan M. Gass is University Distinguished Professor at Michigan State University, USA. She has published widely in the field of Second Language Acquisition and is the winner of numerous local, national, and international awards for her research and contributions to the field. She is recent co-author of *Second Language Research* and *Stimulated Recall Methodology in Applied Linguistics and L2 Research*, both co-authored with Alison Mackey and published by Routledge. She is also author, with Jennifer Behney and Luke Plonsky, of *Second Language Acquisition: An Introductory Course* (2013, fourth edition, published by Routledge).

Phillip Hamrick is Assistant Professor of Second Language Acquisition and Psycholinguistics and Principal Investigator of the Language and Cognition Research Laboratory in the TESL Program in the Department of English at Kent State University, USA. His research focuses on the roles of general cognitive mechanisms in second language acquisition and processing, particularly declarative/procedural memory, implicit/explicit learning, and statistical learning.

Debra M. Hardison is Associate Professor in the TESOL and Second Language Studies programs at Michigan State University, USA. Her research focuses on auditory-visual integration in spoken language processing, the role of learner variables in the development of oral skills, co-speech gesture, and the applications of technology in perception and production training of the segmental and suprasegmental aspects of language.

Alex Housen is Professor of Linguistics and Applied Linguistics in the Department of Linguistics and Literary Studies at the Vrije Universiteit Brussel, Belgium. His research focuses on linguistic, cognitive, and social factors in second language acquisition, bilingualism, and bilingual and second language education. His recent publications deal with receptive L2 grammar development, L2 complexity-accuracy-fluency (CAF), and cognitive mechanisms in SLA.

Chae-Eun Kim received her PhD degree from the Department of Linguistics at the University of Hawaii at Manoa, USA. She is Assistant Professor in the Department of English at Chosun University. Her main research interests are first and second language acquisition, and sentence processing in first and second languages.

Kitaek Kim is Assistant Professor in the Department of English Language Education at Gyeongin National University of Education, South Korea, where he has taught since receiving his PhD from the University of Hawaii at Manoa in 2014. His research interests include second language acquisition and heritage language acquisition.

Donna Lardiere is Professor of Linguistics at Georgetown University, USA. She specializes in formal linguistic approaches to language acquisition, particularly adult second language acquisition. Her research interests include examining the relationship between language acquisition and linguistic theory, the extent to which it is possible for adult language learners to attain nativelike knowledge of morphosyntactic properties of second languages, and the effects of one's native or prior language knowledge on acquiring another language as an adult.

Ronald P. Leow is Professor of Applied Linguistics and Director of Spanish Language Instruction at Georgetown University, USA. His areas of expertise include language curriculum development, teacher education, Instructed Language Learning, psycholinguistics, cognitive processes in language learning, research methodology, and Computer Assisted Language Learning (CALL). Professor Leow has published extensively in prestigious journals and has co-edited several books including *A psycholinguistic approach to technology and language learning* (2016). His single-authored book titled *Explicit learning in the L2 Classroom: A student-centered approach* (Routledge) appeared in 2015.

Alexandra Martin is a PhD student in Spanish Applied Linguistics at Georgetown University, USA. Her main research interests include heritage and second language learning in computerized environments, especially synchronous computer-mediated communication (SCMC). She is also interested in task-based language learning and teaching (TBLT), and curriculum design.

Kim McDonough is Professor and Canada Research Chair in Applied Linguistics at Concordia University, Montreal, Canada. Her current research interests include structural priming, joint attention, task-based interaction, and collaborative writing.

Marije Michel is Lecturer for Second Language Learning and Teaching at Lancaster University, UK. Her research interests include cognitive and interactive aspects of second language acquisition, task-based language teaching (TBLT), digitally mediated language learning, and teacher education in light of multilingual and intercultural diversity in the classroom. Marije has published in leading international peer-reviewed journals. In her recent work, she uses eye-tracking methodology to investigate attentional processes during computer-mediated communication and L2 writing.

Ryan T. Miller is Assistant Professor in the English Department at Kent State University, USA. His research focuses on second language reading and writing. He investigates cross-linguistic transfer and support of L2 reading comprehension and reading sub-skills, and development of academic and discipline-specific writing skills and genre knowledge.

William O'Grady is Professor of Linguistics at the University of Hawaii at Manoa, USA. He has worked extensively on emergentist approaches to syntax and language acquisition, as well as on issues in Korean, typology, language revitalization, and heritage languages. He is the co-editor, with Brian MacWhinney, of the *Handbook of Language Emergence* (2015).

Dorit Ravid is Professor at the School of Education (Humanities) and the Department of Communications Disorders (Medicine), Tel Aviv University, Israel. She has published three books and numerous articles on language acquisition and the development of linguistic literacy in Hebrew (and Arabic). She is deeply committed to studying the causes and effects of low socio-economic background on the development of language and literacy skills.

Kelli Ryan is a PhD candidate in Evaluation and Measurement at Kent State University, USA, with a focus on assessment and applied statistics. She has an MA in Teaching English as a Second Language and has worked as an English as a Second Language instructor for 6 years.

John Sarkissian is Professor of Latin and Greek and Chair of the Department of Foreign Languages at Youngstown State University, USA. He has served in the past as Chief Faculty Consultant for AP Latin and as Chair of the SAT II: Latin committee and as a program reviewer for the Council for the Accreditation of Educator Preparation (CAEP). His previous scholarship has been in the area of Latin poetry, and this article represents his first foray into second language acquisition research.

Meng Shi received his PhD in statistics from the University of Pittsburgh and worked as a biostatistician at Walter Reed Army Medical Center.

Hannelore Simoens is a PhD student of Applied Linguistics in the Department of Linguistics and Literary Studies at the Vrije Universiteit Brussel, Belgium. Her research focuses on linguistic and cognitive factors in second language acquisition. She co-guest edited, with Alex Housen, the 2016 special issue of *Studies in Second Language Acquisition on Cognitive Perspectives on Difficulty and Complexity in L2*.

Bryan Smith is Associate Professor of Applied Linguistics at Arizona State University, USA, where he conducts research and teaches courses on Computer-Assisted Language Learning and instructed SLA. He is also the co-editor of the *CALICO Journal*.

Patti Spinner is Associate Professor at Michigan State University, USA. Her research interests are in the second language acquisition of morphosyntax, particularly the acquisition of features such as grammatical gender, case, number, and tense. Recent work includes work on Chinese classifiers and noun class in Swahili.

Pavel Trofimovich is Professor of Applied Linguistics at Concordia University, Montreal, Canada. His research focuses on cognitive aspects of second language processing, second language speech learning, sociolinguistic aspects of second language acquisition, and the teaching of second language pronunciation.

Lorena Valmori graduated from the Second Language Studies doctoral program at Michigan State University, USA. Her teaching experience has informed her research interests in motivational dynamics, identify, and emotions in second language learning. She is currently "cultore della materia" at the Università di Modena e Reggio Emilia, Italy. She recently published in *Language Teaching*.

Christopher A. Was is Associate Professor in the Department of Psychological Sciences at Kent State University, USA. His research interests are in the areas of models of working memory, complex cognitive processes, and metacognition. More recently his research has focused on implicit learning processes and their relationship to intelligence. He has published over 50 peer-reviewed papers, chapters, and refereed conference proceedings in the areas of learning, educational psychology, and cognitive psychology.

Nicole Ziegler (PhD, Georgetown University) is Assistant Professor of Second Language Studies at the University of Hawaii at Manoa, USA. Her research program focuses on adult and child instructed second language acquisition, including mixed method and interdisciplinary research in L2 conversational interaction, task-based language teaching, and computer-assisted language learning.

1
SALIENCE IN SECOND LANGUAGE ACQUISITION AND RELATED FIELDS

Susan M. Gass, Patti Spinner, and Jennifer Behney

Preliminaries

When considering how salience is used within the context of second language acquisition (SLA), there are at least two angles from which to consider the construct. On the one hand, we need to understand what is salient. Are there linguistic features that themselves are salient and/or can features be made salient (perceptual and constructed salience, respectively)? In both cases, the assumption is that salience is a factor that makes something easier to perceive. On the other hand, we need to understand how salience is used by language learners. This book is an attempt to understand both dimensions.

The word *salient* is frequently used in everyday speech, but it often lacks precision in that the determination of what is and what is not salient is often left to an individual to figure out. The *American Heritage Dictionary* defines salient as "projecting or jutting beyond a line or surface; protruding up or out." *Merriam-Webster*[1] has as its first listing "moving by leaps or springs." According to the online Oxford Dictionaries, the more common current usage listed as its first meaning is "most noticeable or important; prominent; conspicuous"[2].

The origins of the term go back to 16th century heraldry from the Latin '*salire*' meaning 'to leap' with the idea of an animal on its hind legs ready to leap, as in *a lion salient*. Its first use in modern English came in 1836, again referring to an animal, but with a slightly different meaning: "What fresh, clean, and youthful salience in the lynx" (Hunt, 1836, p. 479[3]). However, it was not until 1938 that the word *salience* began to be used in academia, particularly in the area of personality studies.

> The different proportions of salience and embedding give the process and content of every experience its special character.
>
> *(Stern, 1938)*

and

> At other times . . . consciousness is embedded . . . more deeply; there is less clearness, less salience. Salience represents an act of pointing, a directedness of the person toward something that at the moment has special significance for him.
>
> *(Allport, 1938)*

Salience has been and is currently relevant to numerous areas of language-related research. In fact, in recent years there have been in depth treatments of salience (e.g., Chiarcos, Claus, & Grabski, 2011; Giora, 2003) and even a workshop held in Freiburg, Germany (2014) with the title of *Perceptual Linguistic Salience*. In describing their workshop, the organizers refer to significant work on semantic-pragmatic salience that can account, *inter alia* for the "interpretation of figurative utterances, . . . implicatures, and discursive links"[4] and note that perceptual salience is only beginning to receive significant attention. They distinguish between bottom-up and top-down perceptual salience. Top-down salience refers to a stimulus that is 'cognitively preactivated.' An example of this type of salience occurs when "a stimulus is expected because it is part of a cognitive routine, if it has recently been mentioned, or due to current intentions of the perceiver." The attention driven to this stimulus comes from the individual. In bottom-up salience, it is the stimulus itself which attracts attention. A particular stimulus may stand out (be salient) because of physical properties, but also because of a surprise factor when expectations are violated. Gass (1988, p. 202), in her discussion of stages of acquisition alludes to this when she notes that "at more advanced stages of learning, stages at which expectations of language data are well established, something which is unusual because of its infrequency may stand out for a learner." Different types of salience are elaborated on in Chapter 2 of this volume, as well as in other chapters.

This volume deals specifically with second language research. However, before discussing our particular context, we frame the discussion more broadly and refer to research in other related contexts. We select four contexts for brief mention: child language acquisition, sign language, sociolinguistics/dialect contact, and language change.

Child Language

The construct of salience has played a role in the understanding of how children learn language. What emerges is a picture of the relevance of salience, typically in combination with other factors. Literature exists to show how salience is significant in areas of phonology (Dietrich, Swingley, & Werker, 2007; Peters, 1985), lexis (Bortfeld, Shaw, & Depowski, 2013; Hollich, Hirsh-Pasek, & Golinkoff, 2000; Pruden, Hirsh-Pasek, Golinkoff, & Hennon, 2006), morphology (Cameron-Faulkner, Lieven, & Theakston, 2007), and syntax (auxiliaries) (Theakston, Lieven, Pine, & Rowland, 2005). We provide brief examples of how salience plays a role in each of these areas.

In morphology, Cameron-Faulkner et al. (2007) investigate English multi-word negation over a period of approximately one year (2;3–3;4), finding that the child's development followed the order of *no* → *not* → *'nt*. When considering the speed with which the child traversed these negators, the authors concluded that their results supported an input-driven model. Important for our purposes is their claim that *no* is more salient in the input primarily because it occurs frequently in the input as a single-word utterance. In other words, it is salience that contributes to its early adoption.

Dietrich et al. (2007) investigated the acquisition of phonological distinctions by young children (18 months) from two native language backgrounds: Dutch and English. Their interest was: 1) the loss of ability to utilize speech sounds that are not relevant to their language, and 2) which phonetic cues are relevant for lexical distinctions. They invoke salience as a key construct and argue that 'salient phonetic variation' (e.g., vowel duration) is used in language-specific ways. In other words, "children's phonological knowledge already guides their interpretation of salient phonetic variation" (p. 16027). We return to a similar concept later in this chapter ("Second Language Acquisition") in a discussion of work by Carroll (2012) in which certain prerequisite knowledge is necessary before salience becomes relevant.

Theakston et al. (2005), taking into account generativist and usage-based accounts, consider the acquisition of English auxiliaries, specifically focusing on auxiliary omission in early speech. They analyzed longitudinal data from children who at the beginning ranged from 1;8–2;0 years. On the basis of their data, they eliminated a number of explanations including a lack of lexical knowledge, performance limitations, input patterns, and innate maturational constraints. This led them to conclude that 'single-factor models' (p. 268) are inappropriate to account for the omission of auxiliaries. Rather, there are many factors that serve to influence the acquisition of auxiliary syntax, phonological salience being one. However, it is not yet clear what the precise relative contribution of each of these (and possibly other) factors is to acquisition.

Significant attention has been paid to the acquisition of lexis as a function of salience (e.g., Bortfeld et al., 2013; Hollich et al., 2000; Pruden et al., 2006). Hollich et al. (2000) summarize a sequence of experimental studies of young children (12 months) and point to salience as one—but certainly not the only—contributing factor to word learning. They make the argument that children as young as 12 months are able to detect a variety of cues (e.g., perceptual salience, eye-gaze), but what they lack is the ability to coordinate various cues in word learning. Once cues are able to be coordinated, word learning moves apace. They conclude by saying:

> children are sensitive to many different sources of information and will change their weightings of these sources at different times in development and in different contexts. Children need attentional and social cues as well as conceptual constraints to overcome the word learning problem.
>
> *(p. 114)*

In other words, salience has been and still is important throughout the area of research into child language acquisition as it is in bilingual and subsequent language learning. In fact, the 2017 issue of the *Annual Review of Applied Linguistics* (Mackey, 2017) contains 18 articles focusing on children's language learning, with the topic of salience being mentioned multiple times.

Sign Language

Research on signed languages as first and second languages has also contributed to the discussion of this construct. In this section, we refer to a few ways that salience has been dealt with in that acquisition context—in particular phonology, visual context, and hand movement.

Phonology (e.g., handshapes in signed languages) is one aspect that has received treatment. We point to an early study (Brentari, 1993) which attempts to establish a sonority hierarchy (visual salience) for American sign language (ASL). The features that the author deals with are path (direction), handshape change, orientation change, and secondary movements. Her basic premise suggests a significant role for perceptual salience. In her words, perceptual salience "underlies the notion of sonority for both signed and spoken languages" (p. 302). Unlike studies in other acquisition contexts, she considers dynamic aspects of perceptual salience given that ASL relies on movement and proposes a scale of perceptual salience to determine the sonority of elements when comparing orientation change versus handshape change.

Another study involving salience in sign languages comes from work by Harris (2001), who compares input (signed and spoken) to children (18 months) with "profound prelingual deafness" (p. 177). The input comes from mothers who are deaf and fluent signers of British Sign Language and mothers who are hearing and enrolled at the time in a signing program. The author's concern was the identification of the type of input that the children received. Among other criteria, one important one was whether the utterance had a salient context that was visible to the child. In her study (as in other studies dealing with visual context), a context is salient if it refers "to an object or action to which the child was attending at the time of the utterance" (p. 178). In other words, the 'here and now' becomes important in signed language learning as it is in spoken language learning as it draws children's attention to the sign. Those who were fluent signers were more successful in providing the salient context, resulting in a "more secure context for early language development" (p. 177).

A more recent study (Thompson, 2006) uses perceptual salience to differentiate ultimate attainment between manual versus non-manual agreement, the latter being eye-gaze. Salience in this work is identified though hand movements (large articulators) which are more perceptually salient than smaller articulators (the eyes). She considers salience to be 'attentionally-based' with the most salient information coming from the focus of attention. In a later paper, Thompson, Vinson, Fox, and Vigliocco (2013), using a visual-world paradigm to investigate lexical access, find that gaze time increased with features that shared visually salient phonological properties such as location and movement, leading them to conclude that lexical processing "is likely driven by perceptual salience" (p. 1450).

Sociolinguistics/Dialect Contact

The most comprehensive treatment of salience in sociolinguistics comes from Rácz (2013), who makes a distinction between cognitive and social salience.

Cognitive salience is "the objective property of linguistic variation that makes it noticeable to the speaker" (p. 1). Social salience, not surprisingly, emphasizes context. Interestingly, while salience is often associated with high frequency in some approaches (see discussion of usage-based accounts in Ellis, Chapter 2), Rácz argues for a seemingly contradictory viewpoint. That is, features are salient when they have a "low probability of occurrence" (p. 9). In particular, salience "is a bottom-up notion, connected to a principal part of human perception, surprise. An entity is surprising if its presence has a high information value compared to its surroundings—that is, when its presence is not probable, but unexpected" (p. 9) (see Ellis, Chapter 2) for his discussion of this aspect of salience). In sum, Rácz defines cognitive salience as mainly surprisal: "A segment is cognitively salient if it has a large surprisal value when compared to an array of language input" (p. 37). Interestingly, he argues that socially salient variables, which are often taken as indices of social identity, are necessarily cognitively salient, which is how they attracted attention in the first place. For this reason, the concepts can be blended to a certain extent:

> Cognitive salience is an attribute of variation that allows language users to pick up on it, whereas social salience means that variation is already used to carry social indexation. Socially salient variables . . . are always cognitively salient (one way or another), which means that the term *salience* can be used without risk of confusion.
>
> (p. 37)

Related to issues discussed previously are those related to dialect contact. MacLeod (2015) presents different ways of determining phonetic accommodation. One is what she refers to as the *criteria-list* approach and the other is the *experimental* approach. In the former, scholars (e.g., Trudgill, 1986) list criteria that are responsible for dialect accommodation, of which salience is an important one. Salience is what makes speakers aware of certain linguistic features. On the other hand, in the experimental approach, experimental techniques are used to determine what is or is not salient; for instance, MacLeod (2012) uses a perception task. Interesting is MacLeod's discussion of gradient salience (see discussion in the following section of work by Giora, 2003; and Kecskes, 2006) in which the argument is that through experimental work, one can quantify scales of salience (as opposed to a dichotomous categorization) and can perform statistical analyses on the outcome.

Language Change

Salience has often been invoked as an explanation of language change (cf. Trudgill, 1986). In an article specifically aimed at making more precise the role of salience in language change, Kerswill and Williams (2002) identify six studies dealing with salience and point out that circularity is often involved in definitions of salience. They advocate, similar to the work by Rácz (2013) discussed previously, for a definition that relies on language-external factors (e.g., cognitive, social psychological, pragmatic, interactional) and argue that there are three components to any understanding of salience (p. 105):

(1) The presence of a linguistic phenomenon whose explanation we suspect may be due to the salience of the linguistic feature or features involved.
(2) Language-internal explanations, such as the presence of phonological contrast, great phonetic distance, internally-defined naturalness, semantic transparency, or a particular syntactic or prosodic environment.
(3) Extra-linguistic cognitive, pragmatic, interactional, social psychological, and sociodemographic factors.

In their model, to be salient, there has to be at least one element from (2). In addition:

> [C]omponent (3) is essential if we are to avoid circularity, and is ultimately the cause of salience. . . . [I]t is the extra-linguistic factors of component (3) that in the end directly motivate speakers to behave in a certain way, and are therefore central to the salience notion.
>
> *(p. 105)*

The effects of these extra-linguistic factors are what lead to a perhaps counterintuitive point: that salience may not be what leads to change; rather, change itself is what makes features salient.

In a similar vein, Rácz (2013) recognizes the importance of:

> social language use in sound change . . . the *social salience* of a variant plays an important role in the patterns of its propagation. The dynamics of language change are better understood when we rely on the concept of social salience, the same way the latter is better understood if we build upon cognitive salience.
>
> *(p. 148)*

Thus, social salience, embedded in cognitive salience, is significant in understanding language change.

Second Language Acquisition

As noted previously, there have been extensive treatments of salience in related areas, but we have not seen a similar detailed treatment to date in the second language literature despite the fact that the construct of salience has played an important role in SLA discussions for at least 50 years and continues to be relevant to discussions in the literature of today.[5] It is likely that part of the reason for the lack of a thorough treatment is that the construct remains elusive. For example, VanPatten and Benati (2010, p. 143) note that "[s]alience is one of those concepts that escapes easy description or definition." Perhaps for this reason, salience is often invoked post-hoc as an explanation for developmental sequences, as Carroll (2012) points out.

Despite the lack of a clear definition, the role of salience has been related to many different aspects of second language acquisition. For example, studies related to vocabulary acquisition appear in the recent literature (e.g., Bruton, Garcia López, & Esquiliche Mesa, 2011; Elgort & Warren, 2014; Ko, 2012; Smith, 2003; Xia & Wolff, 2010). Salience has also played a role in the study of syntax, morphosyntax, pronunciation/phonology, and even pragmatics (e.g., Ayoun, 2004; Bayley & Langman, 2004; Collins et al., 2009; Geyer, 2007; Nakahama, 2009; Saito & Lyster, 2012).

This volume is organized in part around the terms *perceptual* and *constructed salience*, the latter being of particular relevance to SLA. As discussions in the preceding sections suggest, in the former category, one can think about intrinsic salience, which refers to some part of the linguistic form (e.g., stress, syllabicity). This is perhaps the most basic or intuitive definition of salience, and this fact is reflected in many researchers' definitions of salience. Loewen and Reinder (2011) define salience as "how noticeable or explicit a linguistic structure is in the *input*" (p. 152, emphasis in original). VanPatten and Benati (2010, p. 143) say that "salience refers to the degree to which something stands out in the crowd or catches a person's attention." Ravid (1995) defines salience as "the property of a structure that is perceptually distinct from its environment" (p. 117). For example, Italian past tense formation, which consists of an auxiliary and a past participle (e.g., *cucinare*, 'to cook,' *ha cucinato* 'He cooked'), is more salient than Spanish past tense formation which consists of an accented final vowel (e.g., *cocinar*, 'to cook,' *cocinó*, 'He cooked'). Thus, the form itself attracts attention (see Behney et al., Chapter 5).

One can also think of 'grounded' salience, which consists of something being prominent because it is unexpected, or deviates from what typically occurs. This is the surprisal element which serves as the basis for Rácz's (2013) sociolinguistic salience. With regard to second language acquisition, the basis for unexpectedness can come from the L2 itself or from the L1 (or other languages known). An example of surprisal salience emanating from the L2 is infrequency. Gass (1988), in her discussion of what is noticed, made the following claim:

> Something which is very frequent in the ambient speech is likely to be noticed. On the other hand, particularly at more advanced stages of learning, stages at which expectations of language data are well established, something which is unusual because of its infrequency may stand out for a learner.
>
> *(p. 202)*

The L1 also provides a platform for expectations and, hence, salience. For example, a learner who does not expect articles by virtue of not having them in their L1 will not expect them in the L2. When the learner encounters them in the L2, the unexpectedness of the articles creates a space for their salience. This relates to the position taken by Rácz (2013) in sociololinguistic research, although the construct in SLA research goes beyond the unexpected or surprisal factor, as we will see in the chapters of this volume.

Constructed salience occurs when some outside source creates a context for some feature to become prominent. This often occurs in the context of instructed learning, either through the numerous ways that interaction can take place or through what has become known as textual enhancement. With regard to the former, there is a long history in L2 research about the positive benefits of interaction (e.g., Gass, 1997; Gass & Mackey, 2006, 2015; Long, 1996; Mackey, 2007, 2012). It is argued that interaction promotes learning (see also Gascoigne, 2003) because it highlights some part of language by making it salient, a precursor to noticing that feature. In the written mode, salience often comes about through textual enhancement, which occurs through the use of various techniques (e.g., coloring, bolding, the use of capital letters) with the idea that these techniques will create salience and, hence, focus learners' attention on whatever feature is being emphasized. Thus, constructed salience will lead a learner to notice the feature and potentially subsequently process that feature. For instance, Doughty (1991) conducted a study on the acquisition of relative clauses by instructed and non-instructed learners. She argued that drawing learners' attention to the target structure by creating visual salience with highlighting, capitalization, and so on was crucial to improving performance. Although Doughty referred to these attention-drawing techniques as perceptual salience, we refer to them in this volume as constructed salience.

The idea of constructed salience can be traced back to Sharwood Smith's (1991) call for teachers to engage in "input-salience-creation" (p. 120), which he also refers to as *consciousness-raising*. This "denotes a deliberate focus on the formal properties of language with a view to facilitating the development of L2 knowledge" (p. 119) *or input enhancement*, "[t]he process by which language input becomes salient to the learner" (p. 118)—although, as Sharwood Smith points out, what is made salient by the teacher may not necessarily become salient in the learner's system (see also Leow, 1998, 2001, 2009; Sharwood Smith, 1981). Sharwood Smith also distinguishes between externally created salience (e.g., by the teacher) and naturally occurring salience due to the learner's developmental level.

A recent study on constructed salience is Whittle and Lyster (2016), which investigated the acquisition of Italian subject–verb agreement by Chinese-speaking children. The authors proposed that verbal marking would not initially be salient for Chinese speakers, whose L1 lacks similar marking. Learners were exposed to 10 hours of instructional treatment that emphasized communication but also drew attention to the target forms. Accuracy on the target forms improved by the end of the instructional period with comparison to a control group. The authors argue that "salient input" (p. 50) was a crucial part of the success of the treatment.

The Whittle and Lyster (2016) study focuses on morphology. Indeed, the research area in which salience seems to feature the most prominently is the acquisition of grammatical morphemes. Larsen-Freeman (1975) suggested at the end of her article on the acquisition of morphemes that "perceptual salience in language such as stress, segmentation, vowel reduction and position might also be contributing factors in the production of a difficulty ordering" (p. 419). Similarly, in their research on child second language acquisition, Dulay and Burt (1978) recognized the role of perceptual salience, such as the amount of phonetic substance, stress level, and position, stating that it is "an input factor that has not as yet been precisely defined" (p. 78). These issues were also being discussed in child L1 acquisition research at the time (see Brown, 1973, p. 409), and many of these same issues continue to be an object of discussion even in recent literature in child language acquisition (e.g., the role of positional salience in L1 learning of Italian: Longobardi et al., 2015).

Interestingly, Dulay and Burt (1978) also pointed out that definitions of salience can include not only linguistic features such as stress and position but also "internal processing factors which cause certain features in the learner's input to *become* salient" (p. 73, emphasis in original). The latter possibility is not elaborated on in their article; however, it is useful to note that they recognized that salience can occur not only because of some property of the linguistic form but also due to learner-internal and, in the case of constructed salience, learner-external non-linguistic factors.

More recently, various approaches to salience have appeared. One important work in this area is Goldschneider and DeKeyser (2001), a meta-analysis of previous morpheme order studies that explores the acquisition of grammatical functors. The authors investigate five potential contributing factors, each of which can be considered an aspect of salience: perceptual salience, syntactic category, morphophonological regularity, frequency, and semantic complexity. Each of these factors is carefully detailed and explained. For instance, perceptual salience consists of the number of phones in a functor, its syllabicity, and its sonority.

Some of the characterizations of salience in Goldschneider and DeKeyser's study also appear in various ways in a special issue of *The Modern Language Journal*, edited by Ellis and Collins (2006). Their focus is on input and *inter alia* the role of frequency. In describing the papers in their special issue, the editors note that authors deal with how "learning is driven by the frequency and frequency distribution of exemplars within construction, the salience of their form, the significance of their functional interpretation, the match of their meaning to the construction prototype, and the reliability of their mappings" (p. 329).

However, researchers have considered other aspects of salience that go beyond these. For instance, Kecskes (2006) discusses salience in relation to the activation of lexical items and lexical units. Specifically, Kecskes discusses the application of the *graded salience hypothesis* proposed by Giora (2003) to second language acquisition. This hypothesis deals with situations in which words or phrases have multiple meanings. Consider for example the word "mouse," which has at least two meanings: the computer type or the animal type. Giora proposes that salience, which is based on experience, familiarity, and frequency, drives the interpretation that language users make when hearing the word. Kecskes (2006) argues that salience for second language users will probably never match that of native speakers because their experiences are different, and shared by their first language. Thus, salience is not only a linguistic phenomenon, but also a sociocultural phenomenon.

Taking a different approach, Bardovi-Harlig (1987) specifically addresses the relationship between markedness and salience in her work on preposition stranding. She considers the prediction that marked forms are learned after unmarked ones. In her study, learners acquired preposition stranding ('Who did Philip throw the ball to?'), a marked structure, before the unmarked pied-piping structures ('To whom did John give the book?'). To account for this unpredicted order of acquisition, she brings in the factor of salience. She justifies this by pointing out the unequal distribution of the two structures, noting that the marked structure is more common (that is, more data are available) and hence more salient. Bardovi-Harlig refers to work by Gass (1979, 1980), whose study on the acquisition of relative clauses also found an order of acquisition that was not predicted by universals and suggested salience as an explanatory factor.

Kerswill and Williams (2002) suggest a different explanation in their discussion of dative alternation (e.g., *I gave her the ticket/I gave the ticket to her*). They propose that salience occurs not only because of the frequency of the structures in the target language, but also because of the absence of a particular structure in the L1. That is, the L2 structure is new and thus can create a surprisal factor.

Carroll (2012) investigates claims about word length and position in a sentence or utterance in regards to salience. Specifically, she investigates whether words in the middle of sentences are harder to process than words at the ends of sentences (as suggested by Barcroft & VanPatten, 1997), and whether length of words make them more or less salient. She did not find evidence that either sentence position or word length made a difference in how well learners processed words. She questions whether there are any features in the input that are inherently perceptually prominent and calls for further research in this area. Interestingly, she notes that when researchers assume that salience leads to acquisition, they may have it backwards; salience may only occur "after they [L2 learners] have acquired the relevant knowledge of the target language intonation and its role in information structure" (p. 63). It is only after learners are more aware of language structures that they know what to focus on. In other words, salience is an *outcome* of learning and only becomes relevant once prior input sets the stage for recognition.

An important topic that is inextricably intertwined with salience is awareness and noticing. In the area of visual and hearing cognition, salience is considered a property of an object that one sees or hears. Consider, for example, hearing one's own name in a crowded room with multiple speakers—the so-called 'cocktail party effect' whereby one is able to focus one's attention on an auditory stimulus (one's name) against the backdrop of multiple voices and other noise. This example shows that salience is crucial in what one might think of as attention deployment. The Noticing Hypothesis (Schmidt, 1990) states that L2 learning is driven largely by what learners notice in the input (that is, what they are aware of); the input that they notice can then become intake (that is, it is available for storage and/or processing). However, Carroll (2006) points out that many researchers, including those investigating the Noticing Hypothesis, invoke salience as an explanation for acquisition under the assumption that learners have already segmented the speech stream into words. She argues against the Noticing Hypothesis by claiming that the L2 learner must first be able to segment the speech stream into words before noticing can take place and that this type of acquisition occurs below the threshold of awareness.

With this as a brief introduction, we turn to the specifics of the chapters. This volume is divided into four sections, titled Theoretical Approaches, Perceptual Salience, Constructed Salience, and Context and Salience. In some sense, these divisions are artificial and somewhat arbitrary; some chapters could have been placed in more than one of these sections. In the end, we opted for the current division based on the primary focus of each chapter.

In the first section of the volume, the concept of salience is explored in the context of several different theories of language and acquisition. This section thus lays the groundwork for the empirical studies that are to follow. The three articles present three different perspectives. Ellis discusses the role of salience in usage-based approaches to language learning; Lardiere takes a generative approach and discusses the role of salience in the acquisition of features such as grammatical gender; and O'Grady, Kim, and Kim discuss salience in regard to processing determinism.

Not surprisingly, the authors take different stances on the role of salience. Ellis emphasizes the importance of salience in language learning and states that "[S]alience pervades SLA, and L, and A, in no particular order of priority" (p. 34). He explores three different aspects of salience, as defined in psychological research: (1) psychophysical salience, in which the world and our physical and sensory systems cause some stimuli to be more intensely experienced than others; (2) the weighting that we give various environmental cues based on our experience of what is important or useful to us; and (3) the salience that occurs when our expectations are violated (surprisal). Ellis focuses on how these various aspects of salience affect language acquisition and language change.

On the other hand, while Lardiere concedes that salience may play some role in acquisition, she points out that predictions based solely on salience often turn out to be inaccurate. She explores the acquisition of features, focusing on the issue of interpretability. In generative theory, features that are interpretable bear meaning, such as animacy on nouns; features that are uninterpretable are purely grammatical, such as agreement. The goal in her chapter is to examine claims that uninterpretable features may be undetectable to learners and possibly unacquirable after a critical period. Lardiere examines previous work on subject–verb agreement, gender agreement, case marking, and wh-movement and concludes that the detectability of features is not straightforwardly a function of uninterpretability, perceptual salience, or frequency; rather, detectability depends on whether a learner is at a developmental stage at which the input can be analyzed and integrated with the internal grammar. This is not unlike previous research by Carroll (2012), who argued that there needs to be a certain degree of L2 knowledge before salience becomes relevant.

Finally, O'Grady et al. examine how perceptual prominence and semantic prominence have been employed to explain learner behavior with regard to various linguistic phenomena. They examine data on the acquisition of subject–verb agreement, case marking, reflexive pronouns, and relative clauses, and concludes that acquisition data can be accounted for without relying on the notion of salience. A better explanation, they argue, can be found by focusing on processing cost. Processing cost involves at least two elements: first, the burden on computational resources such as working memory; and second, the ways in which input allows for processing routines to be strengthened and entrenched.

The second section is devoted to empirical studies investigating the role of perceptual salience. As we noted previously, the concept of perceptual salience has had an important role in many areas of language study, including first and second language acquisition (both spoken and sign languages), sociolinguistics, and language change; however, its definition varies greatly between frameworks and individual researchers. Some focus on the linguistic property of an element, while others focus on the perception of the individual. For example, Ellis (Chapter 2) refers to Brown's (1973) work, which focuses on linguistic properties, such as the "clarity of acoustical marking" (p. 343), and goes on to say that part of perceptual salience includes the "amount of phonetic substance, stress level, usual serial position in a sentence, and so on." On the other hand, Hickey (2000) states that "salience is a reference to the degree to which speakers are aware of some linguistic feature" (p. 57). So, in this view, salience is not inherent in a linguistic property; something is salient only if it is recognized.

The first three papers in this section (Behney, Spinner, Gass, & Valmori; Simoens, Housen, & De Cuypere; and DeKeyser, Alfi-Shabtay, & Ravid) take the perspective that salience is a linguistic property which, when encountered by an L2 learner, aids in recognition of the form, a precursor to learning. All three of these papers focus on morphology. Behney et al. consider the salience of verbal past tense in Italian; Simoens et al. look at inflectional morphology in an artificially-created language and DeKeyser et al. investigate Hebrew morphology. Behney et al. and Simoens et al. use eye-tracking to examine these issues, while DeKeyser et al. use a judgment task.

Behney et al. build on previous research that has found that learners of morphologically rich languages with morphologically poor L1s (e.g., English-speaking learners of Spanish) do not respond to incongruencies in verbal inflection in the same way as native speakers or learners with morphologically rich L1s. Their eye-tracking study considers whether this apparent lack of sensitivity to verbal incongruencies by speakers of morphologically poor languages holds in cases in which the verbal morphology is more salient, as is the case in the Italian compound past tense consisting of an auxiliary and past participle (e.g., *ha mangiato*, 'has eaten'). Their data come from English-speaking learners of Italian with a focus on congruent and incongruent verb-adverb combinations (*ieri ha mangiato* 'yesterday he ate' and **ieri mangia* 'yesterday he eats'). They find that learners spent more time on past verbs than present verbs in early processing and that learners fixated more on verbs in incongruent than in congruent sentences in late processing. Regression data suggest that learners are sensitive to incongruencies and that salience plays a role in that sensitivity.

Simoens et al., also using eye-tracking methodology, investigate salience in the context of implicit learning. Their participants are native speakers of Dutch learning a semi-artificial language (Englishti). They investigate a lower salience suffix—*u* and a higher salience suffix—*olp*. They propose that learners are more likely to skip the lower salience suffix and to spend more time attending to the higher salience suffix; additionally, they propose that learners will be more sensitive to the higher salience suffix and more aware of it. However, they note that these differences may only occur with implicit tasks, because explicit tasks may encourage top-down processing mechanisms that override bottom-up processing. Their results support these predictions to a large extent.

In the chapter by DeKeyser et al., data are presented documenting the role salience plays in the acquisition of Hebrew as a second language, both as a main effect and in interaction with age of acquisition. The data come from Russian-speaking immigrants in Israel. Data from 22 aspects of Hebrew morphology were divided into three categories (based on definitions from Goldschneider & DeKeyser, 2001): high, mid, and low salience. Particularly interesting is that the role of salience is not static across ages and is not static when all aspects of Hebrew morphology are considered. They find that as age of acquisition increases, so does the influence of the level of salience. Because DeKeyser et al. believe that salience is more of a factor for explicit learning, they conclude that the importance of explicit learning conditions increases with age. Additionally, their results show that not all aspects of salience contribute equally to the role of salience. The most important contributors are stress on morphemes and distance in agreement patterns.

The third section focuses on constructed salience. If we think of salience as something that is prominent or striking, we can think of it as organically prominent or striking or artificially prominent or striking. While the previous section dealt with salience that emanated from the linguistic form itself or referred to something that stemmed from an individual's perception of language, this section deals with pedagogically manipulating second language forms in order to make them more prominent.

One important type of constructed salience has been more commonly referred to as *input enhancement* or *textual enhancement*. Leow and Martin provide a critical overview of textual enhancement as it relates to the classroom. They extend the typical approach to include a review of concurrent data-elicitation procedures, namely, eye-tracking and think-alouds. They include these measures because, as they argue, both can provide more complete information as to the locus of attention during reading. Does enhancement facilitate learning by drawing attention to particular forms of interest? A review of the literature leads them to suggest that salience via enhancement does not result in deeper processing when the goal of reading is to extract meaning. Their review further suggests that salience of form does not constitute a major rule in learning. What is more important is what happens after that first initial recognition and how learners further process these forms (see Gass, 1988).

The chapter by Ryan, Hamrick, Miller, and Was also deals with textual enhancement. To understand the role of salience, they use a methodological tool novel to SLA research, pupillometry. Their goal is to investigate whether deeper processing, or what they call cognitive effort, moderated the effects of textual enhancement. The measure that they use to determine cognitive effort—namely, changes in pupil diameter—shows that cognitive effort differentially predicts accuracy in word form learning. For those with textual enhancement (during a learning phase), cognitive effort predicts performance, but cognitive effort does not predict performance for those without textual enhancement. This leaves us with the conclusion that there is an interaction between textual enhancement and cognitive effort, but just precisely what that interaction is remains to be determined and awaits further investigation.

In the final chapter in this section, Hardison experimentally manipulates the effects of contextual and visual cues on spoken word identification. Data from a large database of Korean and Japanese learners of English and native speakers of English focuses on the increased salience of visual cues following perception training. Hardison finds that there is significant improvement in word identification occurring following training. She concludes that sentence context and the temporal precedence of articulatory gestures are important in word identification. With regard to salience, she argues that visual cues are salient and these cues are enhanced through focused training.

The final section, Salience in Context, looks at how salience plays a role in SLA through particular tasks or contexts. Here salience is not referring to how noticeable particular L2 forms are per se as investigated in the section on perceptual salience, nor on how the salience of L2 forms can be increased as in the section on constructed salience, but rather on how the particular task or modality that the L2 learner is working through may enhance the salience of L2 forms. This section considers how the salience of forms in the L2 is influenced by the specific task learners are asked to complete (Sarkissian & Behney); by the input's appearance on the computer screen in text-chat interactions (Michel & Smith); by effectiveness of experimental manipulations involving input distribution, learner characteristics, and aspects of the learning context (McDonough & Trofimovich); and by the modality and contingency of recasts in interaction (Ziegler).

Sarkissian and Behney conduct an eye-tracking study in which they compare two different tasks designed to enhance the salience of Latin case endings on nouns to a different degree. They examine performance on a sentence translation task (low-salience task) that does not oblige low-level Latin learners to process case endings on nouns in the same way as a forced choice adjective completion task (high-salience task). In the case of the latter, the learners had to choose the correct form of the adjective to complete the sentence, thereby drawing their attention to the corresponding noun's case ending. Sarkissian and Behney consider the learners' dwell times on the nouns in each task, learner accuracy in each task, differences between higher and lower performing learners, and awareness of the need to mark agreement through stimulated recall protocols. The authors suggest that L2 tasks can enhance the salience of language features to learners.

In another eye-tracking study, Michel and Smith examine the lexical alignment of L2 English learners as they engage in synchronous computer-mediated communication (SCMC, i.e., text-chat) as they interacted weekly in dyads. Michel and Smith argue that the permanence on the computer screen of SCMC increases the salience of the L2 input as learners have more time to process the language, to monitor their own production, and to notice or attend to new forms. Michel and Smith look at the amount of lexical alignment in terms of three or more consecutive word patterns (n-grams) that are repeated across the partners by comparing measures of eye-gaze on these n-grams with baseline eye-gaze measures. Their findings suggest that the alignment taking place in L2 chat may be due to unconscious implicit processes rather than conscious explicit strategies, similar to L1 alignment. Further, their study provides a methodological contribution to the field by showing how eye-tracking can be used during SCMC along with corpus-based chatlog analyses to investigate the role that salience of words in the chat may influence L2 use by the chat partner.

McDonough and Trofimovich take a usage-based perspective on learning that assumes that learning takes place from exposure to low-variability input, coupled with learner-internal cognitive mechanisms. Their chapter utilizes data from previous studies (including eye-tracking) on the learning of Esperanto transitive constructions in an attempt to understand the experimental conditions that lead to learning. A complex picture emerges. In general, there were three factors that facilitated learning: exposure through the L1 to case markings based on noun definiteness; instructions that emphasized two Esperanto features—namely, accusative marking and variable word order; and the opportunity to produce certain structures.

Ziegler considers the issue of the salience of recasts in L2 interaction as determined by the modality in which the interaction takes place (face-to-face, video-chat, and written text-chat). Her intermediate-advanced level learners of English received corrective feedback as they completed info gap activities, and then they completed stimulated recall protocols. The findings of the study suggest that the face-to-face and video-chat modalities increase the salience of the L2 forms for the learners more than the text-chat. Learners also noticed recasts that were contingent in the interaction—in other words, appearing immediately following the nontarget-like form, more than they noticed non-contingent recasts.

Finally, the volume concludes with an afterword, as we attempt to pull together common themes from the chapters and look forward to future research.

Notes

1 See www.merriam-webster.com/dictionary/salient.
2 See https://en.oxforddictionaries.com/definition/salient.
3 See www.oed.com.proxy2.cl.msu.edu/view/Entry/170000?redirectedFrom=salience#eid.
4 See www.frias.uni-freiburg.de/downloads/veranstaltungen/abstracts-salience.
5 A search of the Linguistics and Language Behavior Abstracts (LLBA) using the terms salient and language acquisition/learning yields nearly 300 references since the turn of the century.

References

Allport, G. W. (1938). *Personality: A psychological interpretation*. New York: H. Holt and Company.
Ayoun, D. (2004). The effectiveness of written recasts in the second language acquisition of aspectual distinctions in French: A follow-up study. *The Modern Language Journal, 88*, 31–55.
Barcroft, J., & VanPatten, B. (1997). Acoustic salience of grammatical forms: The effect of location, stress, and boundedness on Spanish L2 input processing. In W. Glass & A. Teresa Pérez-Leroux (Eds.), *Contemporary perspectives on the acquisition of Spanish, Vol. 2: Production, processing and comprehension* (pp. 109–121). Somerville, MA: Cascadilla Press.
Bardovi-Harlig, K. (1987). Markedness and salience in second language acquisition. *Language Learning, 37*, 385–407.
Bayley, R., & Langman, J. (2004). Variation in the group and the individual: Evidence from second language acquisition. *IRAL—International Review of Applied Linguistics in Language Teaching, 42*, 303–318.
Bortfeld, H., Shaw, K., & Depowski, N. (2013). Disentangling the influence of salience and familiarity in infant word learning: Methodological advances. *Frontiers in Language Sciences, 4*, 1–10.

Brentari, D. (1993). Establishing a sonority hierarchy in American Sign Language: The use of simultaneous structure in phonology. *Phonology, 10*, 281–306.

Brown, R. (1973). *A first language*. Cambridge, MA: Harvard University Press.

Bruton, A., Garcia López, M., & Esquiliche Mesa, R. (2011). Incidental L2 vocabulary learning: An impracticable term? *TESOL Quarterly, 45*, 759–768.

Cameron-Faulkner, T., Lieven, E., & Theakston, A. (2007). What part of no do children not understand? A usage-based account of multiword negation. *Journal of Child Language, 34*, 251–282.

Carroll, S. E. (2006). Salience, awareness and SLA. In M. O'Brien, C. Shea & J. Archibald. (Eds.), *Proceedings of the 8th Generative Approaches to Second Language Acquisition Conference* (pp. 17–24). Sommerville, MA: Cascadilla.

Carroll, S. E. (2012). When is input salient? An exploratory study of sentence location and word length effects on input processing. *IRAL—International Review of Applied Linguistics in Language Teaching, 50*, 39–67.

Chiarcos, C., Claus, B., & Grabski, M. (2011). *Salience: Multidisciplinary perspectives on its function in discourse*. Berlin: Walter de Gruyter.

Collins, L. Trofimovich, P., White, J., Cardoso, W., & Horst, M. (2009). Some input on the easy/difficult grammar question: An empirical study. *The Modern Language Journal, 93*, 336–353.

Dietrich, C., Swingley, D., & Werker, J. (2007). Native language governs interpretation of salient speech sound differences at 18 months. *Proceedings of the National Academy of Sciences, 104*, 16027–16031.

Doughty, C. (1991). Second language instruction does make a difference. *Studies in Second Language Acquisition, 13*, 431–469.

Dulay, H., & Burt, M. (1978). Some remarks on creativity in language acquisition. In W. Ritchie (Ed.), *Second language acquisition research: Issues and implications* (pp. 65–89). New York: Academic Press.

Elgort, I., & Warren, P. (2014). L2 vocabulary learning from reading: Explicit and tacit lexical knowledge and the role of learner and item variables. *Language Learning, 64*, 365–414.

Ellis, N., & Collins, L. (2006). Input and second language acquisition: The roles of frequency, form, and function introduction to the special issue. *The Modern Language Journal, 93*, 329–336.

Gascoigne, C. (2003). A catalogue of corrective moves in French conversation. *The French Review, 77*, 72–83.

Gass, S. (1979). Language transfer and universal grammatical relations. *Language Learning, 29*, 327–344.

Gass, S. (1980). An investigation of syntactic transfer in adult L2 learners. In R. Scarcella & S. Krashen (Eds.), *Research in second language acquisition* (pp. 132–141). Rowley, MA: Newbury House.

Gass, S. (1988). Integrating research areas: A framework for second language studies. *Applied Linguistics, 9*, 198–217.

Gass, S. (1997). *Input, interaction and the second language learner*. Mahwah, NJ: Lawrence Erlbaum Associates.

Gass, S., & Mackey, A. (2006). Input, interaction and output: An overview. In K. Bardovi-Harlig and Z. Dörnyei (Eds.), *AILA review* (pp. 3–17). Amsterdam: John Benjamins.

Gass, S., & Mackey, A. (2015). Input, interaction and output in second language acquisition. In B. VanPatten & J. Williams (Eds.), *Theories in second language acquisition* (2nd ed.) (pp. 180–206). New York: Routledge.

Geyer, N. (2007). The grammar-pragmatics interface in L2 Japanese: The case of contrastive expressions. *Japanese Language and Literature, 41*, 93–117.

Giora, R. (2003). *On our mind: Salience, context, and figurative language.* Oxford: Oxford University Press.

Goldschneider, J., & DeKeyser, R. (2001). Explaining the "natural order of L2 morpheme acquisition" in English: A meta-analysis of multiple determinants. *Language Learning, 55*, 27–77.

Harris, M. (2001). It's all a matter of timing: Sign visibility and sign reference in deaf and hearing mothers of 18-month-old children. *Journal of Deaf Studies and Deaf Education, 6*, 177–185.

Hickey, R. (2000). Salience, stigma and standard. In L. Wright (Ed.), *The development of Standard English, 1300–1800* (pp. 57–72). Cambridge: Cambridge University Press.

Hollich, G., Hirsh-Pasek, K., & Golinkoff, R. (2000). Are children sensitive to multiple cues for word learning? *Monographs of the Society for Research in Child Development, 65*, 1–14.

Hunt, L. (1836). A visit to the zoological gardens. *New Monthly Magazine, 47*, 479.

Kecskes, I. (2006). On my mind: Thoughts about salience, context and figurative language from a second language perspective. *Second Language Research, 22*, 219–237.

Kerswill, P., & Williams, A. (2002). 'Salience' as an explanatory factor in language change: Evidence from dialect levelling in urban England. In M. C. Jones & E. Esch (Eds.), *Language change: The interplay of internal, external and extra-linguistic factors* (pp. 81–110). Berlin: Mouton de Gruyter.

Ko, M.-H. (2012). Glossing and second language vocabulary learning. *TESOL Quarterly, 46*, 56–79.

Larsen-Freeman, D. (1975). The acquisition of grammatical morphemes by adult ESL students. *TESOL Quarterly, 9*, 409–419.

Leow, R. (1998). The effects of amount and type of exposure on adult learners' L2 development in SLA. *The Modern Language Journal, 82*, 49–68.

Leow, R. (2001). Do learners notice enhanced forms while interacting with the L2 input? An online and offline study of the role of written input enhancement in L2 reading. *Hispania, 84*, 496–509.

Leow, R. (2009). Input enhancement and L2 grammatical development: What the research reveals. In J. Watzinger-Tharp & S. L. Katz, (Eds.), *Conceptions of L2 grammar: Theoretical approaches and their application in the L2 classroom* (pp. 16–34). Boston, MA: Heinle Publishers.

Loewen, S., & Reinder, H. (2011). *Key concepts in second language acquisition.* Hampshire, UK: Palgrave MacMillan.

Long, M. H. (1996). The role of the linguistic environment in second language acquisition. In W. Ritchie & T. Bhatia (Eds.), *Handbook of second language acquisition* (pp. 413–468). San Diego, CA: Academic Press.

Longobardi, E., Rossi-Arnaud, C., Spataro, P., Putnick, D., & Bornstein, M. (2015). Children's acquisition of nouns and verbs in Italian: Contrasting the roles of frequency and positional salience in maternal language. *Journal of Child Language, 42*, 95–121.

Mackey, A. (Ed.). (2007). *Conversational interaction in second language acquisition: A collection of empirical studies.* Oxford: Oxford University Press.

Mackey, A. (2012). *Input, interaction, and corrective feedback in L2 learning.* Oxford: Oxford University Press.

Mackey, A. (Ed.) (2017). *Annual review of applied linguistics.* Cambridge: Cambridge University Press.

MacLeod, B. (2012). *The effect of perceptual salience on cross-dialectal phonetic convergence in Spanish* (Unpublished doctoral dissertation). University of Toronto, Toronto, Canada.

MacLeod, B. (2015). A critical evaluation of two approaches to defining perceptual salience. *Ampersand*, *2*, 83–92.

Nakahama, Y. (2009). Cross-linguistic influence on referent introduction and tracking in Japanese as a second language. *The Modern Language Journal*, *93*, 241–260.

Peters, A. (1985). Language segmentation: Operating principles for the perception and analysis of language. In D. Slobin (Ed.), *The crosslinguistic study of language acquisition, Vol. 2: Theoretical issues* (pp. 1029–1067). Mahwah, NJ: Lawrence Erlbaum Associates.

Pruden, S., Hirsh-Pasek, K., Golinkoff, R., & Hennon, E. (2006). The birth of words: Ten-month-olds learn words through perceptual salience. *Child Development*, *77*, 266–280.

Rácz, P. (2013). *Salience in sociolinguistics: A quantitative approach*. Berlin: Mouton de Gruyter.

Ravid, D. (1995). *Language change in child and adult Hebrew*. New York: Oxford University Press.

Saito, K., & Lyster, R. (2012). Investigating the pedagogical potential of recasts for L2 vowel acquisition. *TESOL Quarterly*, *46*, 387–398.

Schmidt, R. (1990). The role of consciousness in second language learning. *Applied Linguistics*, *11*, 129–158.

Sharwood Smith, M. (1981). Consciousness-raising and the second language learner. *Applied Linguistics*, *11*, 159–168.

Sharwood Smith, M. (1991). Speaking to many minds: On the relevance of different types of language information for the L2 learner. *Second Language Research*, *7*, 118–132.

Smith, B. (2003). Computer-mediated negotiated interaction: An expanded model. *The Modern Language Journal*, *87*, 38–57.

Stern, L. (1938). *General psychology: From the personalistic standpoint* (H. Spoerl, Trans.). New York: MacMillan.

Theakston, A., Lieven, E., Pine, J., & Rowland, C. (2005). The acquisition of auxiliary syntax: BE and HAVE. *Cognitive Linguistics*, *16*, 247–277.

Thompson, R. (2006). *Eye gaze in American Sign Language: Linguistic functions for verbs and pronouns* (Unpublished doctoral dissertation). University of California, San Diego.

Thompson, R., Vinson, D., Fox, N., & Vigliocco, G. (2013). Is lexical access driven by temporal order or perceptual salience? Evidence from British Sign Language. *Proceedings of the Annual Conference of the Cognitive Science Society* (pp. 1450–1455). Austin, TX: Cognitive Science Society.

Trudgill, P. (1986). *Dialects in contact*. Oxford: Blackwell.

VanPatten, B., & Benati, A. (2010). *Key terms in second language acquisition*. London: Continuum Press.

Whittle, A., & Lyster, R. (2016). Focus on Italian verbal morphology in multilingual classes. *Language Learning*, *66*, 31–59.

Xia, X., & Wolff, H.-G. (2010). Basic-level salience in second language vocabulary acquisition. In S. Knop, F. Boers, & A. De Rycker (Eds.), *Fostering language teaching efficiency through cognitive linguistics* (pp. 79–97). Berlin, Germany: de Gruyter Mouton.

PART I
Salience in SLA theory

2
SALIENCE IN USAGE-BASED SLA

Nick Ellis

Salience in Psychology, Learning Theory, and Psycholinguistics

Psychological research uses the term salience to refer to the property of a stimulus to stand out from the rest. Salient items or features are attended, are more likely to be perceived, and are more likely to enter into subsequent cognitive processing and learning. Salience can be independently determined by physics and the environment, and by our knowledge of the world. It is useful to think of three aspects of salience, one relating to psychophysics, the other two to what we have learned:

1. The physical world, our embodiment, and our sensory systems come together to cause certain sensations to be more intense (louder, brighter, heavier, etc.) than others. These phenomena are the subject of research in psychophysics (Gescheider, 2013).
2. As we experience the world, we learn from it, and our resultant knowledge values some associations more heavily than others. We know that some stimulus cues are associated with outcomes or possibilities that are important to us, while others are negligible (Gibson, 1977; James, 1890b).
3. We also have expectations about what is going to happen next in known contexts, we are surprised when our expectations are violated, and we pay more attention as a result. These phenomena are the subject of research in associative learning and cognition (Anderson, 2009; Shanks, 1995).

Psychophysical Salience

Loud noises, bright lights, and moving stimuli capture our attention. Salience arises in sensory data from contrasts between items and their context. These stimuli deliver intense signals in the psychophysics of our data-driven perception. Stimuli with unique features compared to their neighbors (Os in a field of Ts, a red poppy in a field of yellow) "pop out" from the scene, but in a shared feature context will not (Os among Qs) (Treisman & Gelade, 1980). These are aspects of bottom-up processing (Shiffrin & Schneider, 1977).

Salient Associations

Attention can also be driven by top-down, memory-dependent, expectation-driven processing. Emotional, cognitive, and motivational factors affect the salience of stimuli. These associations make a stimulus cue "dear." A loved one stands out from the crowd, as does a stimulus with weighty associations ($500,000.0 versus $0.000005, however similar the amount of pixels, characters, or ink in their sensation), or one which matches a motivational state (a meal when hungry but not when full). The units of perception are influenced by prior association: "The chief cerebral conditions of perception are the paths of association irradiating from the sense-impression, which may have been already formed" (James, 1890a, p. 82). Psychological salience is experience-dependent: *hot dog*, *sushi*, and 寿司 mean different things to people of different cultural and linguistic experience. This is why, *contra* sensation, the units of perception cannot be measured in physical terms. They are subjective. Hence George Miller's definition of the units of short-term memory as "chunks": "We are dealing here with a process of organizing or grouping the input into familiar units or chunks, and a great deal of learning has gone into the formation of these familiar units" (Miller, 1956, p. 91).

Context and Surprisal

The evolutionary role of cognition is to predict what is going to happen next. Anticipation affords survival value. The Rational Analysis of Cognition (Anderson, 1990, 1991) is guided by the principle that human psychology can be understood in terms of the operation of a mechanism that is "optimally adapted" to its environment in the sense that the behavior of the mechanism is as efficient as it conceivably could be given the structure of the problem space and the input-outputs mapping it must solve. We find structure in time (Elman, 1990). The brain is a prediction machine (Clark, 2013). One consequence is that it is surprisal, when prediction goes wrong, that maximally drives learning from a single trial. Otherwise, the regularities of the usual course of our experiences sum little by little, trial after trial, to drive our expectations. Cognition is probabilistic, its expectations a conspiracy tuned from statistical learning over our experiences.

Salience and Learning

Rescorla and Wagner (1972) presented a formal model of conditioning which expresses the capacity of any cue (Conditioned Stimulus [CS]; for example, a bell in Pavlovian conditioning) to become associated with an outcome (Unconditioned

Stimulus [US]; for example, food in Pavlovian conditioning) on any given experience of their pairing. This formula summarized more than 80 years of research in associative learning, and it elegantly encapsulates the three factors of psychophysical salience, psychological importance, and surprisal. The role of US surprise and of CS and US salience in the process of conditioning can be summarized as follows:

$$dv = ab(L - V)$$

The associative strength of the US to the CS is referred to by the letter V and the change in this strength which occurs on each trial of conditioning is called dV. On the right side of the equation, a is the salience of the US, b is the salience of the CS, and L is the amount of processing given to a completely unpredicted US. So the salience of the cue (a) and the psychological importance of the outcome (b) are essential factors in any associative learning. As for (L − V), the more a CS is associated with a US, the less additional association the US can induce: "But habit is a great deadener" (Beckett, 1954). Alternatively, with novel associations where V is close to zero, there is much surprisal, and consequently much learning: first impressions, first kiss, first love, first time, etc.

This is arguably the most influential formula in the history of learning theory. Physical salience, psychological salience, and expectation/surprisal all affect what we learn from our experiences of the world.

Cognitive Linguistics and Construction Grammar

Language is intrinsically symbolic. Linguistic forms (cues) are associated with particular meanings or interpretations (outcomes). Cognitive Linguistics calls the units of language 'constructions.' These are form-meaning mappings, conventionalized in the speech community, and entrenched as language knowledge in the learner's mind. Constructions relate the defining properties of their morphological, lexical, and syntactic form with particular semantic, pragmatic, and discourse functions (Goldberg, 1995, 2006). Construction Grammar (Goldberg, 2006; Trousdale & Hoffmann, 2013) argues that all grammatical phenomena can be understood as learned pairings of form (from morphemes, words, and idioms, to partially lexically filled and fully general phrasal patterns) and their associated semantic or discourse functions: "[T]he network of constructions captures our grammatical knowledge in toto, i.e. it's constructions all the way down" (Goldberg, 2006, p. 18). Such beliefs, increasingly influential in the study of child language acquisition, emphasize data-driven, emergent accounts of linguistic systematicities (e.g., Ambridge & Lieven, 2011; Tomasello, 2003).

An adult speaker's knowledge of their language(s), therefore, can be equated to a huge warehouse of constructions that vary in their degree of complexity and abstraction. Constructions can comprise concrete and particular items (as in words and idioms), more abstract classes of items (as in word classes and abstract constructions), or complex combinations of concrete and abstract pieces of language (as mixed constructions). Constructions may be simultaneously represented and stored in multiple forms, at various levels of abstraction (e.g., concrete item: *table* + *s* = *tables* and [Noun] + (morpheme + *s*) = plural things). Constructions can thus be meaningful linguistic symbols in their own right, existing independently of particular lexical items. Nevertheless, constructions and the particular lexical tokens that occupy them attract each other, and grammar, morphology, and lexis are inseparable.

Usage-Based Approaches to First and Second Language Acquisition

Usage-based approaches to language learning hold that we learn linguistic constructions throughout our experience of using language to communicate. Psycholinguistic research provides the evidence of usage-based acquisition in its demonstrations that language processing is exquisitely sensitive to usage frequency at all levels of language representation from phonology, through lexis and syntax, to sentence processing (Ellis, 2002). That language users are sensitive to the input frequencies of these patterns entails that they must have registered their occurrence in processing. These frequency effects are thus compelling evidence for usage-based models of language acquisition which emphasize the role of input. Constructionist accounts of language learning involve the distributional analysis of the language stream and the parallel analysis of contingent perceptuo-motor activity, with abstract constructions being learned as categories from the conspiracy of concrete exemplars of usage following statistical learning mechanisms (Bybee & Hopper, 2001; Christiansen & Chater, 2001; Ellis, 2002; Jurafsky & Martin, 2009) relating input and learner cognition. Language knowledge involves statistical knowledge, so humans learn more easily and process more fluently high frequency forms and 'regular' patterns which are exemplified by many types and which have few competitors (e.g., MacWhinney, 2001). The language system emerges from the conspiracy of these associations. Ellis, Römer, and O'Donnell (2016) and Robinson and Ellis (2008) give more detail of usage-based approaches to SLA.

Lexical and Grammatical Constructions in SLA

Not all constructions are equally learnable by all learners. Even after years of naturalistic exposure, adult second language (L2) learners tend to focus more in their language processing upon open-class words (nouns, verbs, adjectives, and adverbs) than on grammatical cues. Their language attainment has been described as stabilizing at a "Basic Variety" of interlanguage that is less grammatically sophisticated than that of nativelike L1 ability (Bardovi-Harlig, 1992; Klein & Perdue, 1992). This phenomenon, if evident over many years, has been termed "fossilization" (Han & Odlin, 2006). Although naturalistic second language learners are surrounded by language input, the available target language, not all of it becomes intake, that subset of input that actually gets in and which the learner utilizes in some way (Corder, 1967). A classic case study is that of the naturalistic language learner, Wes, who was described as being very fluent, with high levels of strategic competence, but low levels of grammatical accuracy: "using 90% correct in obligatory contexts as the criterion for acquisition, none of the grammatical morphemes counted has changed from unacquired to acquired status over a five year period" (Schmidt, 1984, p. 5).

Although the Basic Variety is sufficient for everyday communicative purposes, grammatical morphemes and closed-class words tend not to be put to full use (e.g., Bardovi-Harlig, 1992; Clahsen & Felser, 2006; Schmidt, 1984; VanPatten, 1996, 2006). So, for example, L2 learners initially make temporal references mostly by use of temporal adverbs, prepositional phrases, serialization, and calendric reference, with the grammatical expression of tense and aspect emerging only slowly thereafter, if at all (Bardovi-Harlig, 1992, 2000; Klein, 1998; Lee, 2002; Meisel, 1987; Noyau, Klein, & Dietrich, 1995). L2 learners have been found to prefer adverbial over inflectional cues to tense in naturalistic SLA (e.g., Bardovi-Harlig, 2000; Noyau et al., 1995), training experiments (e.g., Cintrón-Valentín & Ellis, 2015; Ellis et al., 2014), and studies of L2 language processing alike (e.g., Sagarra & Ellis, 2013; Van-Patten, 2007).

A key challenge for second language acquisition research is therefore to explain why grammatical morphemes and closed-class constructions are more difficult to learn than open-class constructions. Usage-based theories attribute this to three standard learning phenomena relating to salience: The learnability of a construction is affected by: (1) psychophysical salience, (2) contingency of form-function association, and (3) learned attention.

The Psychophysical Salience of Linguistic Constructions

One factor determining the learning of construction form is psychophysical salience. In his landmark study of first language acquisition, Brown breaks down the measurement of perceptual salience, or "clarity of acoustic marking" (1973, p. 343), into "such variables as amount of phonetic substance, stress level, usual serial position in a sentence, and so on" (1973, p. 463). Prepositional phrases, temporal adverbs, and lexical linguistic cues are salient and stressed in the speech stream. Verb inflections are usually not.

Many grammatical form-function relationships in English, like grammatical particles and inflections such as the third-person singular -s, are of low salience in the language stream. This is a result of the well-documented effect of frequency and automatization in the evolution of language. The basic principles of automatization that apply to all kinds of motor activities and skills (like playing a sport or a musical instrument) are that through repetition, sequences of units that were previously independent come to be processed as a single unit or chunk (Ellis, 1996). The more frequently they use a form, the more speakers abbreviate it: this is a law-like relationship across languages. Zipf (1949) summarized this in the principle of least effort—speakers want to minimize articulatory effort and this leads to brevity and phonological reduction. They tend to choose the most frequent words, and the more they use them, automatization of production causes their shortening. Frequently used words become shorter with use. Grammatical functors are the most frequent words of a language, thus they lose their emphasis and tend to become abbreviated and phonologically fused with surrounding material (Bybee, 2003; Jurafsky,

Bell, Gregory, & Raymond, 2001; Zuraw, 2003). In a corpus study by Cutler and Carter (1987), 86% of strong syllables occurred in open-class words and only 14% in closed-class words; for weak syllables, 72% occurred in closed-class words and 28% in open-class words.

Because grammatical function words and bound inflections are short and unstressed, they are difficult to perceive from the input. When grammatical function words (*by, for, no, you*, etc.) are clipped out of connected speech and presented in isolation at levels where their open-class equivalents (*buy, four, know, ewe*, etc.) are perceived 90–100% correctly, adult native speakers can recognize them only 40–50% of the time (Herron & Bates, 1997). Clitics—accent-less words or particles that depend accentually on an adjacent accented word and form a prosodic unit together with it—are the extreme examples of this: the /s/ of 'he's,' /l/ of 'I'll,' and /v/ of 'I've' can never be pronounced in isolation.

In sum, grammatical functors are extremely difficult to perceive from bottom-up auditory evidence alone. Fluent language processors can perceive these elements in continuous speech because their language knowledge provides top-down support. But this is exactly the knowledge that learners lack. Thus the low psychophysical salience of grammatical functors contributes to L2 learners' difficulty in learning them (Ellis, 2006b; Goldschneider & DeKeyser, 2001).

Contingency and Learning

The degree to which animals learn associations between cues and outcomes depends upon the contingency of the relationship. In classical conditioning, it is the reliability of the bell as a predictor of food that determines the ease of acquisition of this association (Rescorla, 1968). In language learning, it is the reliability of the form as a predictor of an interpretation that determines its acquisition and processing (Ellis, 2006a; Gries & Ellis, 2015; Gries & Stefanowitsch, 2004; MacWhinney, 1987). The last 30 years of psychological investigation into human sensitivity to the contingency between cues and outcomes (Shanks, 1995) demonstrates that when given sufficient exposure to a relationship, people's judgments match the contingency specified by ΔP (the one-way dependency statistic, Allan, 1980) which measures the directional association between a cue and an outcome, as illustrated in Table 2.1.

a, b, c, d represent frequencies, so, for example, *a* is the frequency of conjunctions of the cue and the outcome, and c is the number of times the outcome occurred without the cue.

TABLE 2.1 A contingency table showing the four possible combinations of events relating to the presence or absence of a target cue and an outcome

	Outcome	*No Outcome*
Cue	a	b
No cue	c	d

ΔP is the probability of the outcome given the cue $P(O|C)$ minus the probability of the outcome in the absence of the cue $P(O|\neg C)$, calculated using the formula:

$$\Delta P = P(O|C) - P(O|\neg C) = \frac{a}{a+b} - \frac{c}{c+d}$$

When these are the same, when the outcome is just as likely when the cue is present as when it is not, there is no covariation between the two events and ΔP = 0. ΔP approaches 1.0 as the presence of the cue increases the likelihood of the outcome. A learnable cue is one such that when the cue is there, the outcome is there, and when the cue is not there, neither is the outcome; that is, when *a* and *d* are large and *b* and *c* are small.

Construction Contingency

There are rarely 1:1 mappings between forms and their interpretations. The less reliably a form is associated with a function or interpretation, the more difficult learning becomes (Ellis, 2006a; Shanks, 1995). Cue-outcome reliability can be reduced in two directions: forms can have multiple interpretations (polysemy and homophony) and interpretations can be realized by more than once form (synonymy). The same usage-phenomenon whereby frequently used words become shorter drives grammatical functors towards homophony since different functions associated with forms that were originally distinct eventually merge into the same shortened form. An example is the -s suffix in English: in modern English, it has come to encode a plural form (*toys*), it indicates possession (*Mary's toy*), and it marks third-person singular present (*Mary sleeps*). The -s form is abundantly frequent in learners' input, but not reliably associated with any/just one of these meanings/functions (increasing *b* in Table 2.1). Conversely, the plural, possessive, and third-person singular constructions are all realized by more than one form: they are all variably expressed by the allomorphs [s], [z], and [ɨz]. Thus, if we evaluate just one of these, say [ɨz], as a cue for one particular outcome, say plurality, then it is clear that there are many instances of that outcome in the absence of the cue (*c* in Table 2.1). In other words, the low cue-interpretation contingency makes plurals difficult to learn.

This fact that many high frequency grammatical constructions are highly ambiguous in their interpretations poses a challenge to language learners (DeKeyser, 2005; Ellis, 2008; Goldschneider & DeKeyser, 2001).

Psychophysical Salience in Second Language Acquisition and Processing

Goldschneider and DeKeyser (2001) performed a detailed meta-analysis of the "morpheme order studies" that, in the 25 years following Brown's (1973) descriptions of first language acquisition, investigated the order of second language (L2) acquisition of the grammatical functors, progressive *-ing*, plural *-s*, possessive *-s*, articles *a, an, the*, third-person singular present *-s*, and regular past *-ed*. These studies show remarkable commonality in the orders of acquisition of these functors across a wide range of learners of English as a second language (ESL). The meta-analysis investigated whether a combination of five determinants (perceptual salience, semantic complexity, morphophonological regularity, syntactic category, and frequency) could account for the acquisition order. Scores for perceptual salience were composed of three subfactors: the number of phones in the functor (phonetic substance), the presence/absence of a vowel in the surface form (syllabicity), and the total relative sonority of the functor. The major determinants that significantly correlated with acquisition order were: perceptual salience $r = 0.63$, frequency $r = 0.44$, morphophonological regularity $r = 0.41$. When these three factors were combined with semantic complexity and syntactic category in a multiple regression analysis, this combination of five predictors jointly explained 71% of the variance in acquisition order, with salience having the highest predictive power.

To illustrate this, Field (2008) had second language learners of English listen to authentic stretches of spoken English and, when pauses occurred at random intervals, they had to transcribe the last few words. The recognition of grammatical functors fell significantly behind that of lexical words, a finding that was robust across first languages and across levels of proficiency.

It is clear, therefore, that linguistic forms of low psychophysical salience are more difficult to perceive—and, as a consequence, to learn.

Learned Attention

There are other attentional factors which also affect the salience of grammatical functors. The first relates to their redundancy. Grammatical morphemes often appear in redundant contexts in which their interpretation is not essential for correct interpretation of the sentence (Schmidt, 2001; Terrell, 1991; VanPatten, 1996). Tense markers often appear in contexts where other cues have already established the temporal reference (e.g., "*yesterday* he walk*ed*"), plural markers are accompanied by quantifiers or numerals ("*10 toys*"), etc. Hence, their neglect does not result in communicative breakdown, they carry little psychological importance of the outcome (term *b* in the Rescorla-Wagner equation in 2), and the Basic Variety satisfices for everyday communicative purposes (Simon, 1957).

Still again, more importantly so, there are attentional biases that particularly affect L2A. These result from L2 learners' history of learning—from their knowledge of a prior language. Ellis (2006b) attributes L2 difficulties in acquiring inflectional morphology to an effect of learned attention known as "blocking" (Kamin, 1969; Kruschke, 2006; Kruschke & Blair, 2000; Mackintosh, 1975). Blocking is an associative learning phenomenon, occurring in animals and humans alike, that shifts learners' attention to input as a result of prior experience (Rescorla & Wagner, 1972; Shanks, 1995; Wills, 2005). Knowing that a particular stimulus is associated with a particular outcome makes it harder to learn that another cue, subsequently paired with that same outcome, is also a good predictor of it. The prior association "blocks" further associations.

ALL languages have lexical and phrasal means of expressing temporality. So ANYONE with knowledge of ANY first language is aware that that there are reliable and frequently used lexical cues to temporal reference (words like German *gestern*, French *hier*, Spanish *ayer*, English *yesterday*). Such are cues to look out for in an L2 because of their frequency, their reliability of interpretation, and their salience. Learned attention theory holds that, once known, such cues block the acquisition of less salient and less reliable verb tense morphology from analysis of redundant utterances such as *Yesterday I walked*.

A number of theories of SLA incorporate related notions of transfer and learned attention. The Competition Model (MacWhinney, 2001; MacWhinney & Bates, 1989) was explicitly formulated to deal with competition between multiple linguistic cues to interpretation. Input Processing (IP) theory (VanPatten, 1996) includes a *Lexical Preference Principle*: "Learners will process lexical items for meaning before grammatical forms when both encode the same semantic information" (VanPatten, 2006, p. 118), and a *Preference for Nonredundancy Principle*: "Learners are more likely to process nonredundant meaningful grammatical markers before they process redundant meaningful markers" (VanPatten, 2006, p. 119).

Learned Attention and Blocking in SLA

A series of experimental investigations involving the learning of a small number of Latin expressions and their English translations have explored the basic mechanisms of learned attention in SLA. Ellis and Sagarra (2011) illustrates the core design. There were three groups: Adverb Pretraining, Verb Pretraining, and Control. In Phase 1, Adverb Pretraining participants learned two adverbs and their temporal reference—*hodie* today and *heri* yesterday; Verb Pretraining participants learned verbs (shown in either first, second, or third person) and their temporal reference—e.g., *cogito* present or *cogitavisti* past; the Control group had no such pretraining. In Phase 2, all participants were shown sentences which appropriately combined an adverb and a verb (e.g., *heri cogitavi, hodie cogitas, cras cogitabis*) and learned whether these sentences referred to the past, the present, or the future. In Phase 3, the Reception test, all combinations of adverb and verb tense marking were presented individually and participants were asked to judge whether each sentence referred to the past, present, or future. The logic of the design was that in Phase 2 every utterance contained two temporal references—an adverb and a verb inflection. If participants paid equal attention to these two cues, then in Phase 3 their judgments should be equally affected by them. If, however, they paid more attention to adverb (/verb) cues, then their judgments would be swayed towards them in Phase 3.

The Control group illustrate the normal state of affairs when learners are exposed to utterance with both cues and learn from their combination. Multiple regression analysis, when the dependent variable was the mean temporal interpretation for each of the Phase 3 strings and the independent variables were the information conveyed by the adverbial and verbal inflection cues showed in standardized ß coefficients,

Control Group Time = 0.93Adverb + 0.17Verb. The adverb cues far outweighed the verbal inflections in terms of learnability. We believe this is a result of two factors: 1) the greater salience of the adverbial cues, and 2) learned attention to adverbial cues, which blocks the acquisition of verbal morphology.

The two other groups reacted to the cues in quite different ways—the Adverb pretraining group followed the adverb cue, the Verb pretraining group tended to follow the verb cue: Adverb Group Time = 0.99Adverb −0.01Verb; Verb Group Time = 0.76Adverb + 0.60Verb. Pretraining on the verb in non-redundant contexts did allow acquisition of this cue when its processing was task-essential, but still, the adverb predominated.

Ellis and Sagarra (2010) Experiment 2 and Ellis and Sagarra (2011) Experiments 2 and 3 also illustrated long-term language transfer effects whereby the nature of learners' first language (+/− verb tense morphology) biased the acquisition of morphological versus lexical cues to temporal reference in the same subset of Latin. First language speakers of Chinese (no tense morphology) were less able than first language speakers of Spanish or Russian (rich morphology) to acquire inflectional cues from the same language experience under the Control conditions when adverbial and verbal cues were equally available, with learned attention to tense morphology being in standardized ß coefficients: Chinese (−0.02) < English (0.17) < Russian (0.22) < Spanish (0.41) (Ellis & Sagarra, 2011, Table 4). These findings demonstrate long-term attention to language, a processing bias affecting subsequent cue learning that comes from a lifetime of prior L1 usage.

Ellis et al. (2014) replicated Ellis and Sagarra (2010) in demonstrating short-term learned attention in the acquisition of temporal reference in L2 Latin in EFL learners, extending the investigation using eye-tracking indicators to determine the extent to which these biases are overt or covert. Eye-tracking measures showed that early experience of particular cue dimensions affected what participants overtly focused upon during subsequent language processing, and how, in turn, this overt study resulted in covert attentional biases in comprehension and in productive knowledge.

While these learned attention demonstrations concern the first hour of learning Latin, Sagarra and Ellis (2013) show the results of blocking over years of learning in intermediate and advanced learners of Spanish. A total of 120 English (poor morphology) and Romanian (rich morphology) learners of Spanish (rich morphology) and 98 English, Romanian, and Spanish monolinguals read sentences in L2 Spanish (or their L1 for the monolinguals) containing adverb-verb or verb-adverb congruencies/incongruencies. Eye-tracking data revealed significant effects for sensitivity (all participants were sensitive to tense incongruencies), cue location in the sentence (participants spent more time at their preferred cue), L1 experience (morphologically rich L1 learners and monolinguals looked longer at verbs than morphologically poor L1 learners and monolinguals), and L2 experience (intermediate learners read more slowly and regressed longer than advanced learners).

Such experiments demonstrate both short-term and long-term effects when sensitivity to lexical cues blocks subsequent acquisition of inflectional morphology. These learned attention effects have elements of both positive and negative transfer.

Prior use of adverbial cues causes participants to pay more attention to adverbs—positive effects of entrenchment of the practiced cue. Additionally, increased sensitivity to adverb cues is accompanied by a reduced sensitivity to morphological cues—blocking. A meta-analysis of the combined results of Ellis and Sagarra (2010, 2011) demonstrated that the average effect size of entrenchment was large (+1.23) and that of blocking was moderate (-0.52).

Experience with the second language is shaded by attentional biases and other types of interference from the first language. Transfer phenomena pervade SLA (Flege, 2002; Jarvis & Pavlenko, 2008; Lado, 1957; MacWhinney, 1997; Odlin, 1989). As a result of this interference, second language learning is typically limited in success, even if the learner is surrounded by ambient input. Since everything is filtered through the lens of the L1, not all of the relevant input is in fact taken advantage of (hence Corder's distinction between input and intake; Corder, 1967). This is not to say that L2 learning is qualitatively different than L1 learning—second language learners employ the same statistical learning mechanisms that they employed when they acquired their first language. Rather, first language learning is (nearly always) so marvelously successful that it—paradoxically perhaps—hampers second language learning. First language learners have learned to attend to their language environment in one particular way. L2 learners are tasked with reconfiguring the attentional biases of having acquired their first language.

Four Reasons Why L2 Morphology is Difficult to Acquire From Usage-Based Learning

Summing up, grammatical functors abound in the input, but, as a result of: 1) their low salience, 2) their redundancy, 3) the low contingency of their form-function mappings, and 4) adult acquirers' learned attentional biases and L1-tuned automatized processing of language, they are simply not implicitly learned by many naturalistic learners whose attentional focus is on communication.

Implications for Language Teaching

The fact that L2 learners have to learn to adjust their attention biases shaped by their L1 has consequences for L2 instruction. Children acquire their first language primarily in an implicit manner. *Implicit learning* is the learning of complex information without selective attention to what is being learned. L2A, in contrast, is characterized in large parts by *explicit learning*. For reviews on implicit and explicit language learning see Ellis (1994) and Rebuschat (2015).

Schmidt's (2001) Noticing Hypothesis holds that conscious attention to linguistic forms in the input is an important precondition to learning: "[P]eople learn about the things they attend to and do not learn much about the things they do not attend to" (p. 30). In order to successfully acquire specific aspects of their L2, learners must pay conscious and selective (i.e., focused) attention to the target structures. With restricted input, too, compared to L1A, explicit learning and teaching gain even more relevance for the second language learner.

This holds in particular for aspects of form in the L2 that are redundant and/ or lack perceptual salience (like the previously mentioned examples of inflectional morphemes in English). Form-Focused Instruction (FFI) attempts to encourage noticing, drawing learners' attention to linguistic forms that might otherwise be ignored (Ellis, 2012). Variants of FFI vary in the degree and manner in which they recruit learner consciousness and in the role of the learner's metalinguistic awareness of the target forms. Long (1991) and Doughty and Long (2003) describe how a focus on meaning can be improved upon by periodic attention to language as object: during otherwise meaning-focused lessons, learners' attention is briefly shifted to linguistic code features, in context, to induce noticing. This is known as *focus on form*. Doughty and Williams (1998) give the following examples of focus-on-form techniques, ranging from less to more explicit: input flood, when texts are saturated with L2 models; input elaboration; input enhancement, when learner attention is drawn to the target through visual highlighting or auditory stress; corrective feedback on error, such as recasting; and input processing, when learners are given practice in using L2 rather than L1 cues.

Norris and Ortega's (2000) meta-analysis comparing the outcomes from studies that employed differing levels of explicitness of L2 input demonstrated that FFI instruction results in substantial target-oriented L2 gains, that explicit types of instruction are more effective than implicit types, and that the effectiveness of L2 instruction is durable. More recent meta-analyses of effects of type of instruction by Spada and Tomita (2010) and Goo, Granena, Yilmaz, and Novella (2015) likewise report large advantages of explicit instruction in L2 acquisition. However, the studies gathered in these meta-analyses used a wide variety of types of instruction, learner, targeted feature, and method of assessment. There is need to compare FFI methods upon learning of the same target feature in similar populations of learners.

Cintrón-Valentín and Ellis (2015) and Cintrón-Valentín and Ellis (2016) used eye-tracking to investigate the attentional processes whereby different types of FFI overcome learned attention and blocking in learners' online processing of L2 input. English and Chinese native speakers viewed Latin utterances combining lexical and morphological cues to temporality under control conditions (CC) and three types of FFI: verb grammar instruction (VG), verb salience with textual enhancement (VS), and verb pretraining (VP). All groups participated in three phases: exposure, comprehension test, and production test. VG participants viewed a short lesson on Latin tense morphology prior to exposure. VS participants saw the verb inflections highlighted in bold and red during exposure. VP participants had an additional introductory phase when they were presented with solitary verb forms and trained on their English translations. CC participants were significantly more sensitive to the adverbs than verb morphology. Instructed participants showed greater sensitivity to morphological cues in comprehension and production. Eye-tracking revealed how FFI affects learners' attention during online processing and thus modulates long-term blocking of verb morphology.

Such results demonstrate how salience in physical form, learner attention, and instructional focus all variously affect the success of L2 acquisition. Form-focused instruction recruits learners' explicit, conscious processing capacities and allows them to consolidate unitized form-function bindings of novel L2 constructions (Ellis, 2005). Once a construction has been represented in this way, its use in subsequent implicit processing can update the statistical tallying of its frequency of usage and probabilities of form-function mapping.

Language Change: The Linguistic Cycle and Grammaticalization

We have been focusing upon language acquisition in particular speakers. Let us now integrate over the community of speakers. From patterns of language usage, processing, and acquisition, dynamic processes over diachronic timescales and synchronic states, there emerge what de Saussure (1916, p. 135) termed *Panchronic* principles, generalizations of language that exist independently of time, of a given language, or of any concrete linguistic facts. One of these is the "Linguistic Cycle" (Givón, 1971; Hodge, 1970; Van Gelderen, 2011) which describes paths of grammaticalization from lexical to functional category followed by renewal. Givón (1979, p. 209) schematized the process as:

"Discourse > syntax > morphology > morphophonemics > zero" and, more memorably, as "Yesterday's syntax is today's morphology." Hopper and Traugott (2003) focus upon morphologicalization as "Lexical item in specific syntactic context > clitic > affix" which leads in turn to "the end of grammaticalization: loss" (p. 140). Sometimes the form alone is lost; more usually, a dying form is replaced by a newer, usually periphrastic form with a similar meaning (p. 172). The periphrastic replacement is salient both psychophysically (it is several lexical items long), and, as an innovation, it is surprising.

Salience in Language Change

Linguistic evolution proceeds by natural selection from among the competing alternatives made available from the idiolects of individual speakers which vary among them (Croft, 2000; Mufwene, 2001, 2008). Since adults are typically less successful than children at language learning, language use by a high proportion of adult language learners typically means simplification, most obviously manifested in a loss of redundancy and irregularity and an increase in transparency (Trudgill, 2002a, 2002b). The 'Basic Variety' of interlanguage (Klein, 1998; Perdue, 1993) shows similarities with pidgins (Schumann, 1978) because pidgins are the languages that result from maximal contact and adult language learning (McWhorter, 2001). Veronique (1999, 2001) and Becker and Veenstra (2003) detail many parallels between the grammatical structures of French-based Creoles and the Basic Variety of interlanguage of learners of French as a second language, particularly in the 1:1 iconicity of their mapping of function and form (Andersen, 1984), their controller-first, focus-last constituent ordering principles, their lack of verbal morphology, and the order of development of their means of temporal reference.

McWhorter argues that the older a language, the more complexity it has—that is, the more it overtly signals distinctions beyond strict communicative necessity.

The most elaborate languages in these respects are those older, more isolated languages that are spoken by groups of people whose interactions are primarily with other speakers of the language and which thus are learned as native languages by children. But their linguistic complexities pose great difficulties to second language learners, prejudiced by L1 transfer, blocking and entrenchment. So some languages are easier for adults to learn, in an absolute sense, than others: "If one were given a month to learn a language of one's choice, I think one would select Norwegian rather than Faroese, Spanish rather than Latin, and Sranan rather than English" (Trudgill, 1983, p. 106). It is no accident that Faroese, as a low-contact language not subject to adult language learning, has maintained a degree of inflectional complexity which Norwegian has lost. Stasis allows a language, left to its own devices, to develop historical baggage—linguistic overgrowths that, however interesting, are strictly incidental to the needs of human exchange and expression (McWhorter, 2001, 2002, 2004).

Consider again English third-person present -s. English is no longer a language spoken primarily as an L1. The 375 million L1 speakers are in a very definite minority compared to the 750 million EFL and 375 million ESL speakers (Graddol, 2000). This preponderance of adult language learning of English is changing its nature. Seidlhofer (2004, p. 236) describes these changes as English is used across the world as a Lingua Franca. First and foremost on her list of observables is "'dropping' the third-person present tense -s (as in 'She look very sad')."

"Languages are 'streamlined' when history leads them to be learned more as second languages than as first ones, which abbreviates some of the more difficult parts of their grammars" (McWhorter, 2004, p. 51). As complex, adaptive systems, languages emerge, evolve, and change over time (Beckner et al., 2009; Croft, 2000; Ellis, 1998; Ellis & Larsen-Freeman, 2006; Ellis et al., 2016; Larsen-Freeman, 1997; MacWhinney & O'Grady, 2015). Just as they are socially constructed, so too they are honed by social usage (Cadierno & Eskildsen, 2015; Douglas Fir Group, 2016; Hulstijn et al., 2014). They adapt to their speakers. Because children are better language learners than adults (at least, as explained in this chapter's section "Learned Attention and Blocking in SLA," as a result of blocking and learned attention), languages that adults can learn are simpler than languages that only children can learn. Second language acquisition by adults changes the very nature of language itself, in ways that are understandable in terms of the psycholinguistics of salience and general principles of associative learning.

So salience pervades SLA, and L, and A, in no particular order of priority.

References

Allan, L. G. (1980). A note on measurement of contingency between two binary variables in judgment tasks. *Bulletin of the Psychonomic Society, 15*, 147–149.

Ambridge, B., & Lieven, E. (2011). *Child language acquisition: Contrasting theoretical approaches.* Cambridge: Cambridge University Press.

Andersen, R. W. (1984). The one to one principle of interlanguage construction. *Language Learning, 34*, 77–95.

Anderson, J. R. (1990). *The adaptive character of thought*. Hillsdale, NJ: Lawrence Erlbaum Associates.

Anderson, J. R. (1991). Is human cognition adaptive? *Behavioral & Brain Sciences, 14*(3), 471–517.

Anderson, J. R. (2009). *Cognitive psychology and its implications* (7th ed.). New York: Worth Publishers.

Bardovi-Harlig, K. (1992). The use of adverbials and natural order in the development of temporal expression. *IRAL—International Review of Applied Linguistics, 30*, 299–320.

Bardovi-Harlig, K. (2000). *Tense and aspect in second language acquisition: Form, meaning, and use*. Oxford: Blackwell.

Becker, A., & Veenstra, T. (2003). Creole prototypes as basic varieties and inflectional morphology. In C. Dimroth & M. Starren (Eds.), *Information structure and the dynamics of language acquisition* (pp. 235–264). Amsterdam: John Benjamins.

Beckett, S. (1954). *Waiting for godot*. New York: Grove Press.

Beckner, C., Blythe, R. A., Bybee, J., Christiansen, M. H., Croft, W., Ellis, N. C., Holland, J., Ke, J., Larsen-Freeman, D., & Schoenemann, T. (2009). Language is a complex adaptive system: Position paper. *Language Learning, 59*, Supplement 1, 1–26.

Brown, R. (1973). *A first language: The early stages*. Cambridge, MA: Harvard University Press.

Bybee, J. (2003). Mechanisms of change in grammaticalization: The role of frequency. In B. D. Joseph and J. Janda (Eds.) *The handbook of historical linguistics* (pp. 602–623). Oxford: Blackwell.

Bybee, J., & Hopper, P. (Eds.). (2001). *Frequency and the emergence of linguistic structure*. Amsterdam: John Benjamins.

Cadierno, T., & Eskildsen, S. W. (Eds.). (2015). *Usage-based perspectives on second language learning*. Berlin: De Gruyter Mouton.

Christiansen, M. H., & Chater, N. (Eds.). (2001). *Connectionist psycholinguistics*. Westport, CO: Ablex.

Cintrón-Valentín, M., & Ellis, N. C. (2015). Exploring the interface: Explicit focus-on-form instruction and learned attentional biases in L2 Latin. *Studies in Second Language Acquisition, 37*, 197–235.

Cintrón-Valentín, M., & Ellis, N. C. (2016). Salience in second language acquistion: Physical form, learner attention, and instructional focus. *Frontiers in Psychology, Section Language Sciences, 7*, 1284.

Clahsen, H., & Felser, C. (2006). Grammatical processing in language learners. *Applied Psycholinguistics, 27*(1), 3–42.

Clark, A. (2013). Whatever next? Predictive brains, situated agents, and the future of cognitive science. *Behavioral and Brain Sciences, 36*, 181–204.

Corder, S. P. (1967). The significance of learners' errors. *IRAL—International Review of Applied Linguistics, 5*, 161–169.

Croft, W. (2000). *Explaining language change: An evolutionary approach*. London: Longman.

Cutler, A., & Carter, D. M. (1987). The predominance of strong initial syllables in the English vocabulary. *Computer Speech & Language, 2*(3), 133–142.

DeKeyser, R. (2005). What makes learning second-language grammar difficult? A review of issues. *Language Learning, 55*(S1), 1–25.

de Saussure, F. (1916). *Cours de linguistique générale* (Roy Harris, Trans.). London: Duckworth.

Doughty, C., & Long, M. (2003). Optimal psycholinguistic environments for distance foreign language learning. *Language Learning and Technology, 7*, 50–80.

Doughty, C., & Williams, J. (Eds.). (1998). *Focus on form in classroom second language acquisition*. New York: Cambridge University Press.

Douglas Fir Group (Atkinson, D., Byrnes, H., Doran, M., Duff, P., Ellis, N., Hall, J. K., Johnson, K., Lantolf, J., Larsen-Freeman, D., Negueruela, E., Norton, B., Ortega, L., Schumann, J., Swain, M., & Tarone, E.). (2016). A transdisciplinary framework for SLA in a multilingual world. *Modern Language Journal*, *100*, 19–47.

Ellis, N. C. (Ed.). (1994). *Implicit and explicit learning of languages*. San Diego, CA: Academic Press.

Ellis, N. C. (1996). Sequencing in SLA: Phonological memory, chunking, and points of order. *Studies in Second Language Acquisition*, *18*(1), 91–126.

Ellis, N. C. (1998). Emergentism, connectionism and language learning. *Language Learning*, *48*(4), 631–664.

Ellis, N. C. (2002). Frequency effects in language processing: A review with implications for theories of implicit and explicit language acquisition. *Studies in Second Language Acquisition*, *24*(2), 143–188.

Ellis, N. C. (2005). At the interface: Dynamic interactions of explicit and implicit language knowledge. *Studies in Second Language Acquisition*, *27*, 305–352.

Ellis, N. C. (2006a). Language acquisition as rational contingency learning. *Applied Linguistics*, *27*(1), 1–24.

Ellis, N. C. (2006b). Selective attention and transfer phenomena in SLA: Contingency, cue competition, salience, interference, overshadowing, blocking, and perceptual learning. *Applied Linguistics*, *27*(2), 1–31.

Ellis, N. C. (2008). The dynamics of second language emergence: Cycles of language use, language change, and language acquisition. *Modern Language Journal*, *41*(3), 232–249.

Ellis, N. C., Hafeez, K., Martin, K. I., Chen, L., Boland, J., & Sagarra, N. (2014). An eye-tracking study of learned attention in second language acquisition. *Applied Psycholinguistics*, *35*, 547–579.

Ellis, N. C., & Larsen-Freeman, D. (2006). Language emergence: Implications for applied linguistics. *Applied Linguistics*, *27*(4).

Ellis, N. C., Römer, U., & O'Donnell, M. B. (2016). *Language usage, acquisition, and processing: Cognitive and corpus investigations of construction grammar*. Malden, MA: Wiley-Blackwell.

Ellis, N. C., & Sagarra, N. (2010). The bounds of adult language acquisition: Blocking and learned attention *Studies in Second Language Acquisition*, *32*(4), 553–580.

Ellis, N. C., & Sagarra, N. (2011). Learned attention in adult language acquisition: A replication and generalization study and meta-analysis. *Studies in Second Language Acquisition*, *33*(4), 589–624.

Ellis, R. (2012). *Language teaching research and pedagogy*. Hoboken, NJ: Wiley-Blackwell.

Elman, J. L. (1990). Finding structure in time. *Cognitive Science*, *14*, 179–211.

Field, J. (2008). Bricks or mortar: Which parts of the input does a second language listener rely on? *TESOL Quarterly*, *42*(3), 411–432.

Flege, J. (2002). Interactions between the native and second-language phonetic systems. In P. Burmeister, T. Piske, & A. Rohde (Eds.), *An integrated view of language development: Papers in honor of Henning Wode* (pp. 217–244). Trier, Germany: Wissenschaftlicher Verlag Trier.

Gescheider, G. A. (2013). *Psychophysics: The fundamentals*. Hove, UK: Psychology Press.

Gibson, J. J. (1977). The theory of affordances. In R. Shaw & J. Bransford (Eds.), *Perceiving, acting, and knowing* (pp. 67–82). Hillsdale, NJ: Lawrence Erlbaum Associates.

Givón, T. (1971). Historical syntax and synchronic morphology: An archeologist's field trip. *Chicago Linguistic Society*, *7*, 394–415.

Givón, T. (1979). *On understanding grammar*. New York: Academic Press.

Goldberg, A. E. (1995). *Constructions: A construction grammar approach to argument structure.* Chicago: University of Chicago Press.

Goldberg, A. E. (2006). *Constructions at work: The nature of generalization in language.* Oxford: Oxford University Press.

Goldschneider, J. M., & DeKeyser, R. (2001). Explaining the "natural order of L2 morpheme acquisition" in English: A meta-analysis of multiple determinants. *Language Learning, 51*(1), 1–50.

Goo, J., Granena, G., Yilmaz, Y., & Novella, M. (2015). Implicit and explicit instruction in L2 learning. In P. Rebuschat (Ed.), *Implicit and explicit learning of languages* (pp. 443–482). Amsterdam: Benjamins.

Graddol, D. (2000). *The future of English.* London: The British Council.

Gries, S. Th., & Ellis, N. C. (2015). Statistical measures for usage-based linguistics. *Currents in Language Learning, 2,* 228–255.

Gries, S. Th., & Stefanowitsch, A. (2004). Extending collostructional analysis: A corpus-based perspective on alternations. *International Journal of Corpus Linguistics, 9,* 97–129.

Han, Z.-H., & Odlin, T. (Eds.). (2006). *Studies of fossilization in second language acquisition.* Clevedon: Multilingual Matters.

Herron, D., & Bates, E. (1997). Sentential and acoustic factors in the recognition of open- and closed-class words. *Journal of Memory and Language, 37,* 217–239.

Hodge, C. (1970). The linguistic cycle. *Linguistic Sciences, 13,* 1–7.

Hopper, P. J., & Traugott, E. C. (2003). *Grammaticalization* (2nd ed.). Cambridge: Cambridge University Press.

Hulstijn, J. H., Young, R. F., Ortega, L., Bigelow, M. H., DeKeyser, R., Ellis, N. C., Lantolf, J., Alison, M., & Talmy, S. (2014). Bridging the gap: Cognitive and social approaches to research in second language learning and teaching. *Studies in Second Language Acquisition, 33*(3), 361–421.

James, W. (1890a). *The principles of psychology* (Vol. 2). New York: Holt.

James, W. (1890b). *The principles of psychology* (Vol. 1). New York: Dover.

Jarvis, S., & Pavlenko, A. (2008). *Crosslinguistic influence in language and cognition.* New York: Routledge.

Jurafsky, D., Bell, A., Gregory, M., & Raymond, W. D. (2001). Probabilistic relations between words: Evidence from reduction in lexical production. In J. Bybee & P. Hopper (Eds.), *Frequency and the emergence of linguistic structure* (pp. 229–254). Amsterdam: John Benjamins.

Jurafsky, D., & Martin, J. H. (2009). *Speech and language processing: An introduction to natural language processing, computational linguistics, and speech recognition* (2nd ed.). Englewood Cliffs, NJ: Prentice-Hall.

Kamin, L. J. (1969). Predictability, surprise, attention, and conditioning. In B. A. Campbell & R. M. Church (Eds.), *Punishment and aversive behavior* (pp. 276–296). New York: Appleton-Century-Crofts.

Klein, W. (1998). The contribution of second language acquisition research. *Language Learning, 48,* 527–550.

Klein, W., & Perdue, C. (1992). *Utterance structure: Developing grammars again.* Amsterdam: John Benjamins.

Kruschke, J. K. (2006, June). *Learned attention.* Paper presented at the Fifth International Conference on Development and Learning, Bloomington, Indiana, Indiana University.

Kruschke, J. K., & Blair, N. J. (2000). Blocking and backward blocking involve learned inattention. *Psychonomic Bulletin & Review, 7,* 636–645.

Lado, R. (1957). *Linguistics across cultures: Applied linguistics for language teachers.* Ann Arbor: University of Michigan Press.

Larsen-Freeman, D. (1997). Chaos/complexity science and second language acquisition. *Applied Linguistics*, *18*, 141–165.
Lee, J. F. (2002). The incidental acquisition of Spanish future morphology through reading in a second language. *Studies in Second Language Acquisition*, *24*, 55–80.
Long, M. H. (1991). Focus on form: A design feature in language teaching methodology. In K. d. Bot, R. Ginsberg, & C. Kramsch (Eds.), *Foreign language research in cross-cultural perspective* (pp. 39–52). Amsterdam: Benjamins.
Mackintosh, N. J. (1975). A theory of attention: Variations in the associability of stimuli with reinforcement. *Psychological Review*, *82*, 276–298.
MacWhinney, B. (1987). The competition model. In B. MacWhinney (Ed.), *Mechanisms of language acquisition* (pp. 249–308). Hillsdale, NJ: Lawrence Erlbaum Associates.
MacWhinney, B. (1997). Second language acquisition and the Competition Model. In A. M. B. De Groot & J. F. Kroll (Eds.), *Tutorials in bilingualism: Psycholinguistic perspectives* (pp. 113–142). Mahwah, NJ: Lawrence Erlbaum Associates.
MacWhinney, B. (2001). The competition model: The input, the context, and the brain. In P. Robinson (Ed.), *Cognition and second language instruction* (pp. 69–90). New York: Cambridge University Press.
MacWhinney, B., & Bates, E. (1989). *The crosslinguistic study of sentence processing*. Cambridge: Cambridge University Press.
MacWhinney, B., & O'Grady, W. (Eds.). (2015). *The handbook of language emergence*. Oxford: Wiley-Blackwell.
McWhorter, J. (2001). The world's simplest grammars are creole grammars. *Language Typology*, *5*, 125–166.
McWhorter, J. (2002). *The power of Babel: A natural history of language*. San Franciso, CA: W. H. Freeman & Co.
McWhorter, J. (2004). The story of human language lecture 24: Language interrupted. *The Great Courses*. The Teaching Company Limited Partnership. Retrieved May 12, 2017 from http://www.thegreatcourses.com/
Meisel, J. (1987). Reference to past events and actions in the development of natural second language acquisition. In C. Pfaff (Ed.), *First and second language acquisition* (pp. 206–224). New York, NY: Newbury House.
Miller, G. A. (1956). The magical number seven, plus or minus two: Some limits on our capacity for processing information. *Psychological Review*, *63*, 81–97.
Mufwene, S. S. (2001). *The ecology of language evolution*. Cambridge: Cambridge University Press.
Mufwene, S. S. (2008). *Language evolution: Contact, competition and change*. London: Continuum International Publishing Group.
Norris, J., & Ortega, L. (2000). Effectiveness of L2 instruction: A research synthesis and quantitative meta-analysis. *Language Learning*, *50*, 417–528.
Noyau, C., Klein, W., & Dietrich, R. (1995). *Acquisition of temporality in a second language*. Amsterdam: John Benjamins.
Odlin, T. (1989). *Language transfer*. New York: Cambridge University Press.
Perdue, C. (Ed.). (1993). *Adult language acquisition: Crosslinguistic perspectives*. Cambridge: Cambridge University Press.
Rebuschat, P. (Ed.). (2015). *Implicit and explicit learning of language*. Amsterdam: John Benjamins.
Rescorla, R. A. (1968). Probability of shock in the presence and absence of CS in fear conditioning. *Journal of Comparative and Physiological Psychology*, *66*, 1–5.
Rescorla, R. A., & Wagner, A. R. (1972). A theory of Pavlovian conditioning: Variations in the effectiveness of reinforcement and nonreinforcement. In A. H. Black & W. F.

Prokasy (Eds.), *Classical conditioning II: Current theory and research* (pp. 64–99). New York: Appleton-Century-Crofts.

Robinson, P., & Ellis, N. C. (Eds.). (2008). *Handbook of cognitive linguistics and second language acquisition.* London: Routledge.

Sagarra, N., & Ellis, N. C. (2013). From seeing adverbs to seeing morphology: Language experience and adult acquisition of L2 tense. *Studies in Second Language Acquisition, 35*, 261–290.

Schmidt, R. (1984). The strengths and limitations of acquisition: A case study of an untutored language learner. *Language, Learning, and Communication, 3*, 1–16.

Schmidt, R. (2001). Attention. In P. Robinson (Ed.), *Cognition and second language instruction* (pp. 3–32). Cambridge: Cambridge University Press.

Schumann, J. H. (1978). *The pidginisation process: A model for second language acquisition.* Rowley, MA: Newbury House.

Seidlhofer, B. (2004). Research perspectives on teaching English as a Lingua Franca. *Annual Review of Applied Linguistics, 24*, 209–239.

Shanks, D. R. (1995). *The psychology of associative learning.* New York: Cambridge University Press.

Shiffrin, R. M., & Schneider, W. (1977). Controlled and automatic human information processing II: Perceptual learning, automatic attending and a general theory. *Psychological Review, 84*(2), 127.

Simon, H. A. (1957). *Models of man: Social and rational.* New York: Wiley and Sons.

Spada, N., & Tomita, Y. (2010). Interactions between type of instruction and type of language feature: A meta-analysis. *Language Learning, 60*, 263–308.

Terrell, T. (1991). The role of grammar instruction in a communicative approach. *The Modern Language Journal, 75*, 52–63.

Tomasello, M. (2003). *Constructing a language: A usage-based theory of language acquisition.* Boston, MA: Harvard University Press.

Treisman, A. M., & Gelade, G. (1980). A feature-integration theory of attention. *Cognitive Psychology, 12*(1), 97–136.

Trousdale, G., & Hoffmann, T. (Eds.). (2013). *Oxford handbook of construction grammar.* Oxford: Oxford University Press.

Trudgill, P. (1983). *On dialect: Social and geographical perspectives.* Oxford: Basil Blackwell.

Trudgill, P. (2002a). Linguistic and social typology. In J. K. Chambers, P. Trudgill, & N. Schilling-Estes (Eds.), *The handbook of language variation and change* (pp. 707–728). Oxford: Blackwell.

Trudgill, P. (2002b). *Sociolinguistic variation and change.* Edinburgh, United Kingdom: Edinburgh University Press.

Van Gelderen, E. (2011). *The linguistic cycle: Language change and the language faculty.* Oxford: Oxford University Press.

VanPatten, B. (1996). *Input processing and grammar instruction in second language acquisition.* New York: Ablex.

VanPatten, B. (2006). Input processing. In B. VanPatten & J. Williams (Eds.), *Theories in second language acquisition: An introduction* (pp. 115–136). Mahwah, NJ: Lawrence Erlbaum Associates.

VanPatten, B. (2007). Input processing in adult second language acquisition. In B. VanPatten & J. Williams (Ed.), *Theories in second language acquisition* (pp. 115–135). Mahwah, NJ: Lawrence Erlbaum Associates.

Veronique, D. (1999). L'émergence de catégories grammaticales dans les langues créoles: grammaticalisation et réanalyse. In J. Lang & Neumann-Holzschuh (Eds.), *Reanaylse und Grammatikaliesierung in den romanischen Sprachen* (pp. 187–209). Tübingen: Max Niemeyer Verlag.

Veronique, D. (2001). Genèse(s) et changement(s) grammaticaux: quelques modestes leçons tirés de l'émergence des créoles et de l'acquisition des langues étrangères. In M. Matthey (Ed.), *Le changement linguistique: Évolution, variation, hétérogénéité: Travaux neufchâtelois de linguistique 34/35* (pp. 273–303). Neuchâtel, Switzerland.

Wills, A. J. (2005). *New directions in human associative learning*. Mahwah, NJ: Lawrence Erlbaum Associates.

Zipf, G. K. (1949). *Human behaviour and the principle of least effort: An introduction to human ecology*. Cambridge, MA: Addison-Wesley.

Zuraw, K. (2003). Probability in language change. In R. Bod, J. Hay, & S. Jannedy (Eds.), *Probabilistic linguistics* (pp. 139–176). Cambridge, MA: MIT Press.

3

DETECTABILITY IN FEATURE REASSEMBLY

Donna Lardiere

Introduction

The acquisition of the grammatical properties of any language requires detecting language-specific feature contrasts and associating those features with particular (morpho)lexical items of the target language. For example, in English the feature [+definite] is associated (in combination with other features) with lexical items including the definite article *the*, demonstratives *this, that, these,* and *those,* and personal pronominal forms such as *him, her, my, they,* etc. The feature [+plural] is associated with some of the same lexical items, such as *these, those, they, we,* and *our,* as well as with the nominal suffix *-s* (and its related allomorphs) and lexical items such as *oxen, feet,* and *mice*. The realization or expression of such features in a particular context is subject to conditioning factors of various types—phonological, morphosyntactic, lexical, semantic, and/or discursive—or interactions among these which may be quite complex. The pairing of formal features with particular lexical items (including functor items) for individual languages has been described by Chomsky (1998, p. 13, 2001, p. 4) as a process of *feature assembly,* in which each language makes a one-time selection of a subset of features from a presumed universal set of available features, and "a one-time assembly" of the selected subset of features as its lexicon. Chomsky, however, was noncommittal about the actual process by which languages (or more precisely, acquirers of a particular language) do this:

> The properties of features and assembly form a large part of the subject matter of traditional and modern linguistics; I will put these topics aside here, including questions about organization of assembled features within a lexical item.
> *(Chomsky, 1998, p. 13)*

Adopting the metaphor of feature assembly, and always keeping in mind that second language (L2) learners bring to the acquisition task prior knowledge of already fully-assembled lexical items of their native language(s) (L1), let us consider some of the properties of the input that might obscure or complicate the task of learning how to build correct lexical entries and appropriately express the grammatical features of the target language. In particular, I focus on two issues: First, in the following section "The L2 Acquisition of Uninterpretable Features," on the interpretability of features and whether this has any bearing on the accessibility of a particular grammatical contrast; second, in the subsequent section "The Detectability of Co-Occurrence Conditions," on the various conditioning factors that may conspire in determining whether a given grammatical contrast should be expressed or not, especially in cases where the appearance of a functor item in the input is variable and probabilistic, thus presenting the learner with a less-than-straightforward correlation between that form and its grammatical function(s).

The L2 Acquisition of Uninterpretable Features

Within generative (and especially, Chomskian minimalist) syntactic theory of the past couple decades, a distinction is made between features that are inherent properties of lexical items or functional categories (such as gender or animacy on nouns or mood contrasts of clauses) and purely syntax-internal features such as those that motivate movement (such as *wh*-movement or subject-auxiliary inversion) or enter into feature-matching with a controller (such as subject–verb agreement in clauses or gender concord on determiners or adjectives in noun phrases). The former, inherent type of features are considered *interpretable* and interface with the semantic system; the latter type are *uninterpretable* and do not interface with the semantic component although they may still be phonologically expressed.

Essentially, the property of uninterpretability creates some sort of syntactic dependency that triggers a search for feature-matching (Adger & Svenonius, 2011). A useful illustrative example comes from Hawkins and Hattori (2006, p. 270): Finite T[ense] in English is considered to bear uninterpretable person and number agreement features, such that the present-tense forms of *be* vary according to the person and number features of the subject (e.g., *I am, you are, she is*). Although the person and number features of the pronouns *I, you,* and *she* do indeed reflect semantic differences and are thus interpretable, there is no difference in meaning between the different forms of *am, are,* and *is*, so these person/number features are uninterpretable.

The uninterpretability of features has played a significant role in theorizing about the nature of ultimate attainment in SLA, particularly in *representational deficit*-type accounts of non-nativelike attainment (e.g., Franceschina, 2001; Hawkins, 2003, 2005; Hawkins & Chan, 1997; Hawkins & Hattori, 2006; Hawkins & Liszka, 2003; Tsimpli, 2003; Tsimpli & Dimitrakopoulou, 2007; Tsimpli & Mastropavlou, 2008; see also Snape, Leung, & Sharwood Smith, 2009 for a volume of collected papers on this topic). According to this view, the failure of L2 learners to acquire nativelike grammatical representations of the target language is due to the unavailability of formal features in the L2 that are not present in the learner's L1. In a later version of the theory, known as the Interpretability Hypothesis, it is specifically uninterpretable features that are considered inaccessible to adult learners, due to hypothesized critical period effects. In this case, the features that underlie contrasts in agreement, case, and feature-triggered movement—all considered uninterpretable—are not only not salient, but imperceptible and unacquirable despite their phonological presence in the input, similar to the hypothesized imperceptibility of phonemic contrasts not included in the L1 (Brown, 2000; Hawkins & Hattori, 2006; Larson-Hall, 2004).

In contrast to this view, Lardiere (2009, pp. 214–215) argued that any formal grammatical contrast that is detectable in the input should be ultimately acquirable in principle regardless of its (un)interpretability; that is, the learner can associate a difference in minimally contrasting forms with some difference in grammatical function and construct a representation for it. The contrast might not, in fact, be ultimately acquired for independent reasons (including difficulty in detecting it, to be discussed below) but not due to uninterpretability *per se*. Rather, the greater difficulty for the learner who detects a formal contrast lies in feature reassembly—assembling the right combination of features into the right lexical items in the L2 and determining the appropriate conditioning environments for expressing them, especially if the features are configured differently or expressed under different conditions in the L1.

For example, Korean plural marking on a noun implies that the noun is also [+specific], unlike English, whose plural marker is neutral with respect to specificity. Hwang and Lardiere's (2013) study on the L2 acquisition of Korean plural marking by native English speakers found that an uninterpretable [*u*-specific] feature on the Korean plural suffix -*tul* that has no counterpart on English plural marking was successfully acquired by intermediate to advanced proficiency levels, whereas an interpretable [distributive] feature on the same suffix was acquired by only a few learners at the highest proficiency level. These relative levels of difficulty were predicted at least in part on the basis of detectability: the co-occurrence of the Korean plural marker with demonstrative determiners and/or previous mention in the discourse (for specificity) was easier for learners to detect than the semantic distribution of plurality over events, which is marked rather infrequently and completely optionally in Korean, on elements such as adverbs and postpositions where English speakers would not expect it, and is realized in English by a completely different lexical construction (*each of the . . .*). And in fact, the distributive plural in Korean is more likely to be construed as (uninterpretable) agreement with typically null plural subjects even by native-speaking Korean children at least up to the age of 8 years old (Kim, O'Grady, & Deen, 2014) despite the fact that Korean doesn't have number agreement with subjects. The point is that, contra the Interpretability Hypothesis, uninterpretable features are not necessarily harder to acquire than interpretable ones, and just the opposite may at times be the case depending on contextual factors and the requirement to associate formal features with the appropriate lexical items in the L2 in ways that may considerably differ from those of the L1.

In response to Lardiere's claim that the uninterpretability of features is largely irrelevant to ultimate attainment, Birdsong (2009) considered the possibility (or likelihood) that uninterpretable feature contrasts were more prone to phonological reduction, elision or some other weakening of the signal in the input, and thus less detectable, than interpretable feature contrasts. As Birdsong notes, this is an empirical question. I agree it is likely to be the case for much agreement inflectional morphology, which typically correlates with a cluster of properties such as prosodic lightness, morphological integration with a stem, or with tense morphology, locality requirements on antecedents, and absence of discourse-informational restrictions (Svenonius, 2007). But this relative weakness in detectability, I would like to argue, is not likely to reside in the property of uninterpretability itself. In the following subsections, let us consider a few prototypical uninterpretable features for which there is a fair amount of acquisition literature: features responsible for subject–verb agreement, gender agreement, case marking, and wh-movement. Our conclusion will be that uninterpretability as a property of features is fundamentally irrelevant to ultimate attainment, contra the Interpretability Hypothesis.

Subject–Verb Agreement

As mentioned above, the various agreeing forms of present-tense *be* in English reflect uninterpretable number and person features; they are also suppletive and, in some syntactic contexts, non-contractible and therefore not particularly non-salient.

There is abundant evidence not only from English but also from other languages in both first and second language studies that correct agreement in suppletive forms such as copulas, auxiliaries, and modals is acquired substantially earlier and more accurately than agreement spelled out as inflectional affixation (e.g., Clahsen, Penke, & Parodi, 1993/94; Eubank, 1993/94; Haznedar, 2001; Lardiere, 2007; Vainikka & Young-Scholten, 1996; Verrips & Weissenborn, 1992; Zobl & Liceras, 1994). Although Goldschneider and DeKeyser's (2001) meta-analysis of L2 English morpheme orders omitted copular and auxiliary forms from consideration, one of their predictive factors for earlier acquisition was perceptual salience, with the number of phones, syllabicity, and sonority included in the subfactors that rendered a functor more salient, which would obviously apply to agreement forms involving suppletive stem changes. Parodi (2000), in a study of the acquisition of finiteness in L2 German by native speakers of Italian or Spanish, found a striking asymmetry in the accuracy of agreement marking between thematic (lexical) and nonthematic (auxiliary, modal, and copular) verbs from the earliest stages of acquisition, observing that: "While a development towards targetlike agreement can be observed with thematic verbs, nonthematic verbs seem to show targetlike agreement as soon as they occur" (p. 370).

However, in considering the roles of input frequency and perceptual (suppletive) salience in accounting for this asymmetry, Parodi found that they could not wholly account for the discrepancy. Rather, she argued, learners establish a distinct class of nonthematic verbs as the carriers of syntactic person and number agreement features that spell out the Agr[eement] component of the functional category I[nfl]P. Lardiere (2007), in her longitudinal case study of Patty, a native speaker of two Chinese languages (Mandarin and Hokkien) who acquired L2 English in adulthood, found a similar discrepancy in Patty's agreement marking favoring accuracy in nonthematic versus thematic verbs and similarly proposed that IP is the initially-preferred locus for expressing subject–verb agreement in languages that have it (neither Mandarin nor Hokkien has subject–verb agreement marking). That is, Patty was inclined to tie morphological agreement directly to its associated functional position in the clause if possible, rather than onto a lexical thematic verb, going so far as to occasionally overgenerate an auxiliary *be* to indicate finiteness (pp. 90–92):

(1) I *was* suddenly have to write # try English
 this *is* all depends on the doctor's recommendation
 they *are* help people when people in trouble
 he also # *he's* also speak in tongue that day

These data suggest that, while high frequency and increased perceptual salience in the form of greater sonority of suppletive stem changes might enhance the detectability and formal accuracy of agreement in copular and auxiliary morphemes, learners possess (or transfer) a purely syntactic representation for an abstract finiteness feature from the earliest stages of acquisition, regardless of whether uninterpretable agreement is spelled out in the L1 and contra representational deficit proposals.

Gender Agreement

Gender agreement on determiners and adjectives in noun phrases is also considered an uninterpretable feature. Whereas gender on nouns is considered lexically inherent (and therefore entirely acquirable, according to the Interpretability Hypothesis), gender agreement on determiners and adjectives must be computed in the course of the syntactic derivation and is considered uninterpretable. Representational deficit approaches predict that an uninterpretable gender agreement feature in a gendered L2 cannot in principle be acquired by an adult native speaker of a language that has no grammatical gender. A feature reassembly approach would predict that such agreement is in principle acquirable, since gender distinctions are detectable in the input—in many cases, almost solely by observing contrasts on agreeing elements, including pronominal forms.

A study by Franceschina (2001) of Martin, a native speaker of English who was highly proficient in L2 Spanish, found that although Martin's gender and number marking on nouns was perfect, his gender and number agreement on adjectives, determiners, and pronouns was not, leading Franceschina to claim that an uninterpretable gender feature was "altogether absent" from Martin's L2 syntactic representations (p. 243), thus lending support to the Interpretability Hypothesis. However, a closer look at Martin's suppliance of gender and number agreement in obligatory contexts suggests a more complicated picture—he supplied correct agreement for 85.16% of demonstratives, 90.49% of pronouns, 91.07% of articles, and 92.2% of adjectives (from Franceschina's Table 4, p. 236). These percentages, while not perfect, are certainly too high for us to conclude that the uninterpretable agreement features in question are absent. One might in fact be tempted to suggest that the reason Martin's stored knowledge of the lexical gender of nouns was so perfect was due to his ability to detect gender agreement with those nouns from multiple sources—articles, demonstratives, and pronouns—in the first place.

In contrast to Franceschina's view that interpretable (lexical) features are acquirable whereas uninterpretable (agreeing) ones are not, Hopp (2013) reports from a broad review of the literature that errors with gender at advanced L2 proficiency levels are "predominantly restricted to *lexical gender assignment* and constrained by task demands" (p. 35, emphasis added). He also notes that processing constraints such as working memory capacity appear to affect the ability of even very advanced proficiency L2 learners to detect non-adjacent determiner-noun gender agreement violations, whereas even lower-proficiency learners are sensitive to local determiner-noun agreement violations, regardless of L1.

Grüter, Lew-Williams, and Fernald (2012, pp. 208–209) (cited by Hopp) concluded that lexical, rather than syntactic, properties of gender were the primary source of difficulty for very advanced native English learners of L2 Spanish, noting that gender assignment errors in their study were more than 10 times as frequent as agreement errors, mirroring previous findings by Alarcón (2011).

Hopp's (2013) experiment testing the production of gender assignment by 20 native English-speaking advanced to near-native L2 German learners found that, whereas native German controls scored at ceiling, the L2ers' accuracy ranged from 53–100%, with only one L2 learner scoring perfectly correctly. On a subsequent online comprehension task assessing the learners' ability to make predictive use of gender marking on determiners, only those learners who had scored in the 95–100% accuracy range on lexical gender assignment in the production task (9 out of 20) showed targetlike gender agreement in the comprehension task. Hopp concluded that "Mastery of predictive gender agreement in the L2 appears to hinge on overall mastery of lexical gender in the L2" (p. 53). From these findings we may conclude that uninterpretable gender agreement is indeed acquirable by adult L1 speakers of languages without grammatical gender, contra the Interpretability Hypothesis, but targetlike performance relies on the correct assignment of lexical gender to nouns in the first place.

Returning to the issue of detectability, we might ask what enables only some but not all learners to acquire correct lexical gender assignment in the first place. Grüter et al. (2012) surmise that, depending on the learning context, L2 learners are less likely than L1-learning infants to rely on the very tight aural co-occurrence of determiners and nouns in the input that establishes the strength of lexical gender classes. Instead, adult L2ers are more likely to make use of L1 knowledge, metalinguistic information, and written material that presents orthographic gaps between determiners and nouns.

For native speakers of languages lacking in grammatical gender who are learning languages that have it, a parsing-to-learn account is proposed by Dekydtspotter and Renaud (2014). Assuming, perhaps on the basis of frequency, that a native English speaker acquiring French has already established that the (masculine) definite determiner *le* is the closest counterpart to English *the*, the parser upon encountering (feminine) *la* seeks to characterize its value in contrast to *le*; Dekydtspotter and Renaud write: "The existence of the form *le* in the incipient interlanguage lexicon brings the existence of an alternation between *le* 'the-MASC' and *la* 'the-FEM' in the L2 input into the focus of attention" (p. 137). Then, assuming the existence of a universal feature hierarchy in which a nominal Class node is further specified for Animacy and/or Gender (Harley & Ritter, 2002), the parser would reject the possibility of gender assignment based solely on Animacy because, they write, even for a small vocabulary, [±Fem] is a necessary feature of inanimate French nouns such as *la table*, forcing the decoupling of Animacy from Gender such that the learner must realize that the scope of French gender "goes beyond natural gender to grammatical gender" (p. 137). Once the parser registers the new gender-based feature matrix for the definite determiner category, the correct gender exponents will become increasingly activated as more input is encountered.

Case

Along with the features that agree with nouns, structural case is another feature that is considered a "core example" of an uninterpretable formal property (Corver, 2003, p. 62) and "a formal feature par excellence" (Chomsky, 1995, p. 278). Svenonius (2007, p. 19) observes that structural case is not interpretable on the constituent bearing it, which might be definite or indefinite or bear any thematic role; for example, even agents may bear accusative case in ECM constructions or genitive in nominalizations (example [23] from Svenonius, p. 19):

(2) I heard *him* perform a sonata.
     Their destruction of the city was unnecessary.

Similar to agreement, I will argue that the acquisition (or not) of L2 case marking by speakers of a language with little or no case marking arguably has nothing to do with case being an uninterpretable feature. Lardiere (1998) found that Patty, whose native languages also do not include case marking, acquired L2 English pronominal case marking perfectly as a function of clausal finiteness despite frequently omitting from her spoken production other markers of finiteness such as tense inflection on verbs. The examples in (3) demonstrate that subject and object pronouns were distributed correctly in both finite and, especially, nonfinite contexts; those in (4) show correct genitive case marking in nominalization:

(3) that doesn't have anything to do with me leaving home
     maybe they don't want us to use it after office hour
     so for them to learn English, you know . . .
     why do you want me to go?
(4) . . . with the issue my getting pregnant
     how is your hunting for condo?
     the doctor's recommendation

A study by Hopp (2010) investigated L2 knowledge of German case (on definite articles) and subject–verb agreement by native speakers of Dutch, English, or Russian who had either advanced or near-native proficiency in German. For case, the performance of all three L1 near-native groups converged with that of the native controls on offline grammaticality judgment and self-paced reading tasks, leading Hopp to conclude that these learners had attained targetlike knowledge of case (and agreement), even though the L2ers' online reading times were overall slower than those for native speakers.[1]

Note that, like case on English pronouns, case on German determiners is also suppletive; one might therefore expect, as with the copular and auxiliary forms discussed above, it is likely to be more salient than case marking in other languages which is realized as inflectional morphology. And in fact, studies of the acquisition of case marking in L2 Turkish by native English or Greek speakers suggest that at least intermediate-level proficiency learners struggle with inflectional case marking (Gürel, 2000; Haznedar, 2006; Papadopoulou et al., 2011). However, as we will discuss in greater depth shortly, this cannot be the entire story, since the same learners who struggle with inflectional case marking on nouns are far more accurate with tense and agreement inflectional morphology on verbs in L2 Turkish (e.g., Haznedar, 2006; Papadopoulou et al., 2011). For Turkish in particular, accusative case marking is inextricably linked to the specificity of an object; that is, it is omitted if the object is nonspecific, thus presenting a learner with variable input involving another feature that is not tied to accusative case in the same way as in learners' native languages.

Another question that arises with respect to the Interpretability Hypothesis (or any study that considers L1 transfer within a formal grammatical framework) is how one might accurately characterize whether a particular L1 "has" a certain feature such as case or not. For example, English has case marking on pronouns but not on lexical nouns or determiners; does English thus "count" as having case, in the sense that an uninterpretable case feature *anywhere* in a language might be recruited to acquire case distinctions on lexical nouns and/or determiners in an L2 with more robust case marking? English also syncretically conflates pronominal case on direct and indirect objects (typically marked by distinct accusative and dative cases, respectively, in many languages); does this mean that we should expect a distinct feature value for dative to be unavailable to L1 English speakers acquiring languages that mark dative distinctly? Similarly, Turkish has more case distinctions (i.e., feature values) than Greek, so does Greek count as having the "same" uninterpretable case feature? That which makes a feature the "same" cross-linguistically is often tacitly assumed rather than explicitly spelled out in studies that consider the availability of features in the L1 versus the L2, in ways that might make the Interpretability Hypothesis actually somewhat difficult to test.

Wh-Movement

Finally, let us consider the uninterpretable feature(s) considered necessary within this theoretical framework for deriving movement such as *wh*-movement. Departures from canonical word order in a language are clearly among the most detectable phenomena available to learners, although the motivation for such displacement may be harder to discern. Within a minimalist syntactic approach, for languages like English that have obligatory wh-movement, a so-called 'strong' [wh] uninterpretable feature in sentence-initial (C[omplementizer]P[hrase]) position creates a dependency that must be checked or matched by the interpretable [wh] feature of a wh-phrase—thus forcing movement as in (5a), (where the strikethrough indicates the position the wh-constituent has moved from). In contrast, the uninterpretable [wh] feature in wh-in-situ languages such as Korean and Japanese is considered 'weak' and wh-phrases therefore do not move from where they are interpreted (e.g., Adger, 2003; Adger & Svenonius, 2011; Chomsky, 1995, 2001), as shown in (5b) for Korean:[2]

(5) a. What did Mary buy ~~what~~ ?
　　b. Mary-ka　　　mwues-ul　　sa-ss-ni ?
　　　 Mary-NOM　　 what-ACC　　buy-PAST-Q
　　　 'What did Mary buy?'

For L1 speakers of wh-in-situ languages acquiring a wh-movement L2, the placement of the wh-phrase in sentence-initial position would seem especially salient and indeed, Hawkins and Hattori (2006) find "impressively targetlike performance" (p. 280) on various properties associated with wh-movement and constraints on such movement in a range of studies they surveyed by native Japanese speakers acquiring L2 English at advanced proficiency levels (e.g., Miyamoto & Ijima, 2003; Ojima, 2005; Yusa, 1999).

　　The issue here, though, is not whether native speakers of wh-in-situ languages can detect the displacement of wh-phrases in wh-movement L2s—clearly, they can—but whether or not their correct placement of the wh-phrase stems from knowledge of movement that is triggered by the hypothesized uninterpretable wh-feature just described. If so, then learners should also observe the constraints on such movement (traditionally referred to as subjacency-type constraints). These underlying structural constraints are presumably not directly detectable and form the basis for poverty of the stimulus arguments dating back to at least the 1980s (e.g., Chomsky, 1980; Crain, 1991; Crain & Nakayama, 1987; Lightfoot, 1982).

　　For SLA, the results are conflicting and highly theory-internally dependent (that is, depending on which version of generative syntactic theory has been assumed; see Schwartz & Sprouse, 2000 for a discussion of this issue). Earlier studies show both divergence from (Johnson & Newport, 1991; Schachter, 1989,[3] 1990) and convergence with (Li, 1998; Martohardjono, 1993; White & Genesee, 1996; White & Juffs, 1998) native speaker behavior. Lardiere (2007) observed that Patty produced wh-relative clauses with stranded prepositions such as those in (6), where preposition stranding is considered indicative of movement (Baker, 2003) and is not allowed in her (wh-in-situ) L1 Chinese (cf. Hawkins & Chan, 1997).

(6)　you don't know who you should associate with
　　 I didn't understand what he's talking about in the class

　　Hawkins and Hattori (2006) tested advanced native Japanese learners of L2 English on a number of linguistic measures related to interpretive constraints on long-distance wh-movement in English and found they converged with native speaker controls' performance on all but one—failing to reliably differentiate between grammatical and ungrammatical multiple wh-questions such as *"Who did John say bought what?"* versus *"*What did John say who bought?"*[4] Hawkins and Hattori argued that native Japanese speakers rely on obligatory wh-word scrambling to a focal (sentence-initial) position—an option available in Japanese—rather than 'true' wh-movement triggered by an uninterpretable strong [wh] feature to account for why native Japanese speakers are "nevertheless so successful in producing and interpreting English *wh*-interrogatives in many other respects," as reported in several other previous studies (p. 295). That is, they caution that the appearance of nativelike L2 performance that hinges on the acquisition of an uninterpretable feature not present in the native language may nonetheless not accurately reflect the acquisition of the underlying structural properties and constraints assumed to be present in the grammars of native speakers (p. 298).

However, as often occurs in studies that are so heavily reliant on technical details of particular versions of particular theories, there is little agreement and much lively discussion on whether scrambling in Japanese is similar to wh-movement in English, and especially whether long-distance scrambling—like long-distance wh-movement—is subject to similar subjacency-type constraints; several researchers argue that it is (e.g., Kawamura, 2004; Saito, 1992, 2003; Takahashi, 1993; Watanabe, 1992, 2003). Moreover, recent language acquisition research shows that Japanese preschool children are actually sensitive to these constraints (Sugisaki & Murasugi, 2015).

Thus, the question of whether adult L1 speakers of wh-in-situ languages can ultimately acquire nativelike knowledge of the uninterpretable [wh] feature that triggers wh-movement in wh-movement L2s has not been definitively resolved, and we will not try to resolve it here. Note that, although the displacement of wh-phrases is obviously detectable (and detected) in SLA, the underlying uninterpretable feature hypothesized to be responsible for deriving wh-movement is not. This is indeed a case where a particular feature contrast appears to be undetectable. Since the correct placement of wh-phrases might result from one theoretically distinct kind of movement versus another or even from simple base-generation in clause-initial position, it is not easy to state claims about nativelike attainment as clearly as for, say, observations about whether L2ers correctly realize morphological subject–verb agreement, gender, or case in the target language. Nonetheless, as an anonymous reviewer pointed out, there are other grammatical constraints that can indirectly be used by the learner to distinguish between a movement versus a non-movement analysis, such as the presence of reflexive pronouns in sentences like *"Which ballerina did you say you thought injured herself?"* in which the reflexive must be construed with an antecedent within its own clause, or the presence of third singular (3SG) agreement in sentences like *"Which boy did you say likes Mary?"* Such properties may thus serve as cues by which the learner is able to infer wh-movement.

Inflectional Morphology and Uninterpretability

As mentioned previous, certain aspects of inflectional morphology might cause it to be less acoustically salient than suppletive free morphemes, such as prosodic lightness and morphological integration with a stem. This explanation, though, will clearly not suffice in accounting for why the same inflectional suffix—such as English

-*s* and its phonetically-conditioned allomorphs—are acquired at different developmental points for different grammatical functions, as noted by Brown (1973) for L1 acquisition and Zobl and Liceras (1994) and Goldschneider and DeKeyser (2001), among others, for L2 acquisition. Nor is it the case that the suffix -*s* and its allomorphs are particularly unsalient, since strident segments are noisy and considered highly perceptually salient (e.g., Wright, 2004).

In their meta-analysis of the order of acquisition of English functors, Goldschneider and DeKeyser provided accuracy percentages across 12 studies, for which regular plural marking (ranging from 54.31–93.33% accurate) ranked higher than possessive (ranging from 23.08–75%), which in turn was higher than 3SG present agreement (ranging from 7.67–66.61%). Perceptual salience was one of the factors they investigated, and was characterized by them as "how easy it is to hear or perceive a given structure" (solely) given the characteristics of the input (p. 22), their prediction being that the more perceptually salient a functor is, the earlier it will be acquired (p. 23). Since the three -*s* functors they investigated (for plural, possessive and 3SG agreement) are identical in terms of their acoustic properties and allomorphy, we would not expect phonological salience to determine why they are acquired differently.

What about featural complexity? As Goldschneider and DeKeyser point out, plural -*s* expresses a single feature—plural number[5]—whereas 3SG -*s* fuses the features of person, number and tense, thus making it semantically more complex. Do these differences correlate with (un)interpretability and therefore account for the order of acquisition? I think the story is not quite so simple. Whereas tense is considered an interpretable feature, person and number agreement, as previously discussed, are considered uninterpretable. However, note that third person, singular number, and present tense are typically unmarked or default agreement feature values across most of the world's languages that inflect for subject–verb agreement (Bejar, 2003, p. 16; Harley & Ritter, 2002 [who cite many additional older references]). English is unusual in inflecting *only* for 3SG nonpast agreement and thus reflects a highly marked option even for native speakers of languages with much more extensive subject–verb agreement paradigms, for whom the Interpretability Hypothesis would presumably predict little difficulty.

Plural is typically considered an interpretable feature and its morpheme would be expected to be produced earlier and more frequently and accurately than English 3SG agreement—which, in fact, it is, according to the morpheme order studies surveyed by Goldschneider and DeKeyser. But let us look more closely at the contexts in which plural marking is required. The semantic distinction in English between *book* and *book-s* is clearly discernible, at least in most referential contexts; however, the semantic distinction between *three books* and *three book is not. In such contexts where a quantifier denotes more than one, plural marking on the noun, though required in English, is redundant and contributes no additional semantic meaning—it is simply required to match, in an underspecified way, the more highly specified, inherently (interpretable) plural number feature of the quantifier. This "agreeing" instantiation of plural marking on the noun is arguably uninterpretable (see Corver, 2003, pp. 62–64 for some discussion). In many languages with plural morphology, such as Turkish, Korean, Mandarin, Persian, and Indonesian, plural marking is disallowed or otherwise highly restricted on quantified nouns (we return to a discussion of quantified plural marking in Korean in the following section). We might expect, then, that the Interpretability Hypothesis would predict that native speakers of languages with such restrictions on plural marking in quantified contexts would be less likely to mark plurality on nouns in these contexts but have no difficulty in producing plural marking in non-quantified, referentially plural contexts, given that the plural feature in the latter context is interpretable.

The meta-analysis by Goldschneider and DeKeyser did not have access to such information and thus could not speak to this issue, but Lardiere (2007) did distinguish between these contexts in analyzing plural marking in her case study of Patty, whose native/early-acquired languages of Hokkien, Mandarin, and Indonesian all include restrictions on plural marking on quantified noun phrases (NPs). As we might expect, Patty's incidence of plural marking in obligatory contexts by the time of her last spoken recording, at 57.58%, was much higher than her rate of 3SG agreement marking (if we are only considering inflectional affixation on lexical verbs and excluding agreement on auxiliaries and copulas), at a quite dismal 4.54%. As mentioned above, the Interpretability Hypothesis would presumably predict that semantically interpretable plural marking in unquantified, referentially plural contexts should occur at a higher rate than semantically redundant, uninterpretable plurals in quantified contexts, especially since the latter are disallowed in her L1s, but this was not the case. In Patty's spoken production data, plural marking in unquantified contexts reached 55.56%, whereas her plural marking in quantified contexts was a very similar 58.33%. There is virtually no difference between interpretable and uninterpretable plural contexts. In Patty's written data, the occurrence of plural marking in both contexts was much higher, but with no advantage for interpretable pluralization: 70% in unquantified and 84.38% in quantified contexts.

Finally, even though the Interpretability Hypothesis would clearly predict that plural marking should be more accurate than agreement marking, as was observed in the comparison presented above, note that Patty's agreement marking on copular and auxiliary *be* in nonpast obligatory contexts in her spoken production data reached 93.65% accuracy (including contracted forms), compared to 4.54% for 3SG agreement -*s* affixation on lexical verbs.[6] Whatever else this difference might be attributable to (e.g., markedness of the construction, pressure toward paradigm uniformity, difficulty with building a prosodic representation, etc.), it is not a difference in interpretability.

To summarize so far, neither acoustic salience nor semantic interpretability seem able to account for the acquisition data observed. I take it that the Interpretability Hypothesis and Birdsong's (2009) conjecture about the signal weakness of uninterpretable feature spell-outs do not make the right predictions and appear to be largely irrelevant to detectability.

The Detectability of Co-Occurrence Conditions

As discussed by Archibald (2009) for phonology, the input cues to the implementation of a particular feature vary cross-linguistically and the degree of learning

Detectability in Feature Reassembly

difficulty may be influenced by the robustness of the cue to the feature. Archibald observes that if the phonetic cues are robust enough, or if L1 structures and features can be redeployed (or reassembled) in the L2, the L1 "filter" can be overridden (p. 232). But what makes a cue robust? For a phonetic cue to be robust, the learner must have already acquired "a considerable amount" of language-specific knowledge about the L2 phonology and prosodic boundary segmentation for morphemes, words and phrases (Carroll, 2006, p. 18). Indeed, an extensive set of studies by Goad and White (e.g., 2004, 2006, 2008, 2009) has argued that if a prosodic representation specific to the L2 cannot be built by recruiting prosodic features from the learner's L1, the ability to acquire L2 morphology will be negatively affected. The following subsections illustrate the difficulties learners face in acquiring (or reassembling) features when the cues—in some cases cues in multiple domains—for realizing a particular morphosyntactic feature or cluster of features in the target language are quite different from those in the L1.

(Somewhat) Different Features on Different Lexical Items

Recall from this chapter's subsection "Case" that studies of the acquisition of case marking in L2 Turkish found that native speakers of English or Greek experienced difficulty learning the conditions associated with accusative case marking in Turkish (Gürel, 2000; Haznedar, 2006; Papadopoulou et al., 2011), a subject–object–verb (SOV) language which also allows a "scrambled" object–subject–verb (OSV) word order. Note that the accusative case-marking suffix in Turkish appears with specific objects only; if the object lacks an accusative suffix, it is obligatorily interpreted as nonspecific (Gürel, 2000, p. 381, citing Enç, 1991). Moreover, nonspecific objects must remain adjacent to the verb; they are not allowed to scramble. The case suffix itself is perceptually salient in that it is stressed. Oversimplifying, the input thus presents canonical SOV sentences in which the object may be either case-marked or not, depending on whether it is specific or not, as well as OSV sentences in which the object must be case-marked and must be interpreted as specific.

In both English and Greek, indefinite objects (which bear accusative case marking in Greek but, of course, do not in English) may be ambiguous as to whether they are specific or not (example from Papadopoulou et al., p. 181):

(7) o   janis   aγorase   enan   pinaka
     the-NOM   John-NOM   buy-PAST.3SG   a-ACC   painting-ACC
     'John bought a painting.'
     (= 'John bought some painting' or 'John bought a certain painting.')

In Turkish, this ambiguity is resolved by the obligatory use of the accusative marker in case the object is specific (examples from Papadopoulou et al., p. 179):

(8) a. Ali   bir   kitab-ı   al-dı.   (specific)
        Ali   a   book-ACC   buy-PAST
        'A book is such that Ali bought it.'

b. Ali   bir   kitab   al-dı.   (nonspecific)
    Ali   a   book   buy-PAST
    'Ali bought some book or other.'

Both Greek and English mark definiteness rather than specificity. The interaction of accusative case marking in Turkish with specificity and scrambled word order suggests that accurate accusative marking will be difficult to acquire for native English or Greek speakers, for a few reasons having to do with detectability. First, the input appears variable, both in terms of word order and case marking and the relation between them. Second, variability in Turkish word order is generally controlled by discourse-pragmatic factors that would not be initially obvious to native speakers of English, which has more rigid word order and different (mainly prosodic) means for indicating sentential focus. Third, both native English and Greek speaking learners of Turkish will need to de-link specificity from definiteness within discourse contexts that, from the perspective of their L1s, don't saliently distinguish these—a classic feature reassembly problem. That these particular properties of the input would pose difficulties for learners was confirmed in studies comparing the L2 acquisition of case inflection on nouns with tense and agreement inflection on verbs in Turkish, in which verbs are typically (though not always) placed in sentence-final position and consistently obligatorily marked.

For native English speakers, Haznedar (2006) found that her longitudinal case study participant John exhibited a nativelike level of accuracy in the suppliance of tense and agreement inflectional morphology on Turkish verbs throughout the entire five-month recording period, whereas his inflectional case marking on nouns was highly inaccurate. His accurate suppliance of accusative case marking in obligatory contexts in particular was only 8.45%, with accusative case inflection mainly omitted where required. Haznedar provides a sample error from the production data which suggests that the learner fails to recognize that specific objects must be case-marked regardless of their sentential position; the learner perhaps has internalized a purely positional (and inaccurate) rule for which there is variable positive evidence—namely, that objects adjacent to the verb need not be marked (p. 193):

(9) Benim   ailem-X   çok   özlü-yor-um
    my   family-MISSING ACC   very   miss-PRES-1SG
    'I miss my family very much.'

Similarly, Gürel (2000) reported that native English speakers at varying proficiency levels were as accurate as Turkish native speaker controls in detecting grammatical and ungrammatical verb agreement morphology, but differed significantly from native controls on detecting and correcting faulty or missing case inflection on a grammaticality judgment task. In an elicited production task, correct suppliance of accusative case marking in obligatory contexts reached only 53% for the most advanced L2 group tested (compared to 100% for the native controls).

Whereas poor results from L1 speakers of a language that marks case only on pronouns might be expected, the findings from a study of native Greek speakers—whose

L1 does include case marking on full noun phrases—suggest that the difficulty of acquiring Turkish case inflection goes well beyond whether the L1 has such case marking or not. In their study of native Greek speakers acquiring verbal tense and agreement and nominal case marking in L2 Turkish, Papadopoulou et al. (2011) observed the same sort of asymmetry as with the studies involving L1 English speakers previously mentioned: Their most advanced L2 Turkish group (which they characterized as high intermediate proficiency) exhibited a 95% accuracy rate in subject–verb agreement and 92% accuracy with tense inflection on a cloze task, but only 49% accuracy in the suppliance of accusative case. Although most of the errors involved the omission of accusative case suffixes where required, the more advanced learners also incorrectly oversupplied accusative case marking on nonspecific objects, which should be unmarked for accusative case. In an online grammaticality judgment task, all three L2 groups failed to reject ungrammatical OSV sentences in which the scrambled object was unmarked for accusative case (only 38% accuracy across the three groups).

Papadopoulou et al. (2011) point out that the discrepancy in accuracy between verbal tense/agreement and case marking cannot be easily accounted for within the Interpretability Hypothesis, since all these features are grammaticalized in both the L1 and the L2. Moreover, the data suggest that the L2 learners do not seem to be fully aware of the interaction between case morphology and word order. More specifically, whereas the accusative suffix in Turkish also denotes specificity/referentiality, the corresponding morpheme in Greek only bears accusative case (p. 196).

We surmise from these studies that native speakers of languages that rely on indicating definiteness via the use of definite articles have difficulty detecting the redistribution of an overlapping semantic piece of this feature—specificity—onto inflectional elements that have yet another overlapping function—that of case marking, in an L2 that has no definite articles. In this instance, as Papadopoulou et al. point out, the obscuring factor is the way in which these features are grammaticalized in the L1; they write that features "that are differently encoded in the morphosyntax of the L1 are more difficult to be acquired" (p. 197). In terms of detectability, the fact that learners are exposed to L2 input that is (apparently) variable from the perspective of the L1—that is, direct objects are sometimes accusative-marked and sometimes not—is likely to further confound the picture unless and until the learner begins to search for the source of such variability and recognizes that it is discourse-linked (for specificity) and focus-linked (for OSV word order more generally), and that focus which (for native English speakers, anyway) is mainly accomplished via prosodic stress in the L1 is reflected in word order choice in the L2. This is a considerable feature-reassembly challenge. It is worth noting that Goldschneider and DeKeyser (2001) in their meta-analysis of the determinants of (English) morpheme order acquisition—and more specifically of the role of perceptual salience as a potential determinant in that order—were unable to take L1 transfer into consideration. However, it is clear that L2 learners "expecting" to find grammatical features distributed on morpholexical items in the L2 in the same way these are distributed in the L1 are going to have trouble finding them if that distribution is substantially different. In other words, as discussed by Birdsong (2009), learner expectation based on L1 knowledge is a significant contributor to detectability.

Feature Co-Occurrence Hierarchies

In this section I explore the idea that the more deeply embedded a feature is within some sort of feature co-occurrence hierarchy, the less detectable it is. Lardiere (2000) wondered why many L2 learners of English, including Patty, often confused the masculine and feminine forms of 3SG pronouns, since the assignment of either is nearly always based on the semantic (and conceptually familiar) distinction of male or female sex of the discourse referent. In Patty's case, one might consider that her (spoken) L1 Chinese fails to distinguish pronominal gender and therefore this would be a simple issue of L1 transfer; however, neither does her L1 distinguish pronominal case marking, which in her L2 English was perfect. In other words, while Patty often confused *him* or *his* with *her*, or *she* for *he*, she never confused *he* for *him* or *his*, or *she* for *her*. Lardiere, following Beard (1995), suggested a kind of algorithmic procedure that first determined case on the basis of syntactic properties (such as categorial domain and finiteness), but then had to get from particular cases to particular gender spell-outs. For possessive pronouns, for example, once the syntax licenses case assignment within the domain of a noun phrase (i.e., a determiner phrase, or DP) and maps the output to 'Genitive' in the morphological component, yet another mapping to person/number distinctions is required which in turn map onto gender distinctions that are ultimately spelled out as *his*, *her*, or *its* for 3SG forms. Patty was able to perfectly execute the mapping to pronominal case and person/number distinctions, but sometimes faltered by the "time" she got to gender spell-out.

In an analysis somewhat similar in flavor, Hawkins and Casillas (2008) proposed that L2 learners' difficulty with English 3SG nonpast *-s* agreement on verbs was a consequence of the complexity of featural contexts required to realize it. They suggested the following lexical (or Vocabulary) entry: "insert /s/ in the context of a verb which is in the context of a nonpast T, itself in the context of a third person, singular N" (p. 602). More generally, they formulated a Contextual Complexity Hypothesis according to which the more nodes that were required to specify a context for context-sensitive items (such as tense and agreement affixes), the greater the probability that the item would not be retrieved (p. 603).

More recently, Hwang and Lardiere (2013) examined the acquisition of plural marking in L2 Korean by native English speakers, and Lee and Lardiere (2016) the acquisition of plural marking in L2 Korean by native Indonesian speakers and the acquisition of plural marking in L2 Indonesian by native Korean speakers. Both studies relied on a feature-geometry model similar to that proposed by Harley and Ritter (2002) and Gebhardt (2009), finding that the co-occurrence of conditioning features associated with plural marking in Korean (which consists of the suffixation of the syllabic, phonetically salient particle *-tul*) that were more deeply embedded in a feature hierarchy were more difficult for both native English- and Indonesian-speaking learners to acquire. More specifically, Korean distinguishes between numeric quantifiers (such as *sey* 'three') and non-numeric quantifiers (such as *manhun* 'many') such that the non-numerically quantified nouns do not take classifiers and may optionally be plural-marked. However, among numerically quantified nouns, which do require classifiers, a further distinction must be made between human and nonhuman nouns, such that human ones can be optionally pluralized whereas nonhuman ones cannot. This co-occurrence hierarchy is roughly illustrated in (10):

(10)

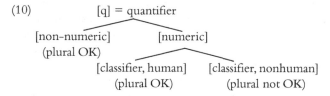

Both the Hwang and Lardiere and the Lee and Lardiere studies found that advanced learners of L2 Korean were able to acquire the distinction between numeric and non-numerically quantified nouns (neither of which are distinguished in either English or Indonesian for purposes of pluralization), but had much greater difficulty acquiring the more deeply embedded human versus nonhuman distinction on numerically quantified nouns.

Interestingly, Harley and Ritter (2002) discuss the L1 acquisition of hierarchically structured features, hypothesizing that a given node must be acquired before its dependents. In their meta-analysis of 10 studies of the L1 acquisition of pronominal person, number and gender features across six genetically distinct languages, their prediction was borne out, supporting their particular proposed hierarchy in which first person would be acquired before second person, singular would be acquired before plural, and neuter/inanimate noun class would be acquired before animate. Returning to the findings of Hwang and Lardiere for L2 Korean plural marking, the data showed that even advanced learners who had acquired the distinction between numeric and non-numeric quantifiers nonetheless overgeneralized Korean's numeric-dependent inanimate/nonhuman *prohibition* on plural marking to human nouns for which it's allowed (even though in English plural marking is allowed, regardless of whether a noun is human or not). Detectability in this case appears to reflect something like default or (un)markedness conditions for grammaticalized feature contrasts, which Harley and Ritter claim are universally hierarchically organized and constrained by fundamental conceptual categories, such as reference, plurality, and taxonomy (pp. 482, 518). At the very least, the data presented in this section show that the detectability of features requiring extra computational "steps"—however this is theoretically framed—appears to be more difficult the more steps that are required.

Conclusion

A theme that emerges from the preceding sections is that the detectability of grammatical feature contrasts is not limited to—and is likely only peripherally related to—the notion of perceptual salience if, by "perceptual," we mean "how easy it is to hear or perceive a given structure" and more specifically, as referring "solely to the characteristics of the input itself" as employed by Goldschneider and DeKeyser (2001, p. 22). We have seen that the interpretability versus uninterpretability of grammatical features is largely unconnected to their ability to be detected and acquired, whereas how features are distributed on morpholexical items in the L2 in comparison to the L1 seems to matter quite a lot. The complexity of computational steps required to retrieve a morpholexical item and the presence of conditioning factors—such as the co-occurrence of other morphosyntactic features and the particular discourse and pragmatic contexts (which themselves may be grammaticalized differently than in the L1) in which these features are expressed—also appear to have a substantial impact on detectability.

The point is that these properties require the learner to construct a mental representation for the L2 grammar that, rather than faithfully reflecting some objective properties such as acoustic noisiness and frequency of objects "out there" in the input, instead reflect how input is *analyzed*—that is, computed in a parse (Dekydtspotter & Renaud, 2014)—and integrated with existing grammatical knowledge. Such mental representations are undoubtedly at least initially informed (in some cases, possibly thwarted) by the learner's representation of the L1 or other prior language knowledge (Schwartz & Sprouse, 1996). Carroll (2006) and Carroll and Shea (2007) argue for a similar view with respect to the notion of salience in regard to phonology and the perception of prosodic focus. Carroll (2006) points out that the perception of prosodic prominence must be mediated by phonetic and phonological representations and is an *effect* of speech and information structure processing rather than a universal input to such processing (p. 19). Carroll and Shea (2007, p. 99) write:

> . . . perceptual salience is not an objective, acoustic property of the speech signal. Instead, salience is a perceptual effect resulting from speech perception and language processing. There are many phenomena which can lead to perceptions of prosodic prominence, most of which can only be explained in terms of abstract mental representations, i.e., phenomena which are not in the signal.

Along the same lines, the apparent *optionality* or variability in the realization of some kinds of features in the input such as plural marking in Korean or accusative case marking in Turkish—objectively a matter of input (in)frequency—makes the acquisition problem considerably harder only to the extent that learners are attempting to construct a mental representation that could account for such optionality. The detectability of features, in short, is neither a function of particular acoustic properties nor input frequency in the environment, but rather a function of the extent to which the expression of those features in particular contexts might be predicted or expected within the learner's internally-generated grammatical representation of the target language at a particular developmental stage.

Notes

1 In an online speeded grammaticality judgment task, only the near-native L1 Russian group performed like the native German controls in detecting case violations—a finding Hopp

attributes to the fact that Russian, but not Dutch or English, has case distinctions on "full noun phrases" (as mentioned previously, English has only pronominal case distinctions, while Dutch has no case). However, Hopp argues that the discrepancy between the Russian near-native group and the English and Dutch groups reflects language processing (in)efficiency rather than knowledge of case itself (which is intact across all three near-native L2 groups). From a morphological standpoint, this result is interesting, given that nominative versus accusative case marking in his experimental German sentences was realized exclusively on definite articles, which don't exist in Russian, but do exist in English and Dutch.

2 Although the previously-used terminology of 'strong' and 'weak' has changed in the theory (e.g., to the presence or absence of a so-called 'EPP feature' requiring movement into a specifier position), the idea is essentially similar—for a purely formal (i.e., uninterpretable) feature to be valued by a semantically interpretable feature requires that the matching features be within the same relevant domain (however this is defined), triggering movement if needed.

3 As pointed out by Hawkins (2001, p. 296), an analysis of individual results showed that some of the Korean participants in Schachter's (1989) study did perform like English native speakers, indicating that some late learners could achieve nativelike intuitions.

4 It might be noted, though, that one native Japanese speaker did perform within English native-speaker range, though the authors suspected a possible response bias therefore rendering a conclusion for this particular speaker "undecidable" (p. 293), and that approximately 37% of the native English-speaking controls failed the syntax qualifying test involving various long-distance wh-movement interpretation types and were excluded from the experimental analysis.

5 Note this is not strictly true—the plural morpheme in English is also used to encode genericity, the expression of which has a more complex semantics and varies cross-linguistically. However, there was no information available in the studies surveyed by Goldschneider and DeKeyser which would have distinguished between referential plural and generic plural usage. Lardiere's (2007) detailed case study of Patty included differentiation of quantified versus non-quantified plural marking contexts (to be discussed ahead), but did not separately consider generic plural marking.

6 This percentage for copular/auxiliary *be* nonpast agreement includes all person/number distinctions, whereas affixation for lexical verbs is obviously limited to 3SG agreement.

References

Adger, D. (2003). *Core syntax: A minimalist approach*. Oxford: Oxford University Press.

Adger, D., & Svenonius, P. (2011). Features in minimalist syntax. In C. Boeckx (Ed.), *The Oxford handbook of linguistic minimalism* (pp. 27–51). Oxford: Oxford University Press.

Alarcón, I. V. (2011). Spanish gender agreement under complete and incomplete acquisition: Early and late bilinguals' linguistic behavior within the noun phrase. *Bilingualism: Language and Cognition, 14*, 332–350.

Archibald, J. (2009). Phonological feature re-assembly and the importance of phonetic cues. *Second Language Research, 25*, 231–233.

Baker, M. (2003). *Lexical categories: Verbs, nouns and adjectives*. Cambridge: Cambridge University Press.

Beard, R. (1995). *Lexeme-morpheme base morphology*. Albany, NY: SUNY Press.

Bejar, S. (2003). *Phi-syntax: A theory of agreement* (Unpublished doctoral dissertation). University of Toronto, Toronto.

Brown, C. (2000). The interrelation between speech perception and phonological acquisition from infant to adult. In J. Archibald (Ed.), *Second language acquisition and linguistic theory* (pp. 4–63). Malden, MA: Blackwell.

Brown, R. (1973). *A first language*. Cambridge, MA: Harvard University Press.
Birdsong, D. (2009). Uninterpretable features: Psychology and plasticity in second language learnability. *Second Language Research, 25*, 235–243.
Carroll, S. E. (2006). Salience, awareness and SLA. In M. G. O'Brien, C. Shea, & J. Archibald (Eds.), *Proceedings of the 8th Generative Approaches to Second Language Acquisition Conference (GASLA 2006)* (pp. 17–24). Somerville, MA: Cascadilla Press.
Carroll, S. E., & Shea, C. (2007). Salience, focus and second language acquisition. *Nouveaux cahiers de linguistique française, 28*, 99–106.
Chomsky, N. (1980). *Rules and representations*. New York: Columbia University Press.
Chomsky, N. (1995). *The minimalist program*. Cambridge, MA: MIT Press.
Chomsky, N. (1998). Minimalist inquiries: The framework. *MIT Working Papers in Linguistics, 15*, 1–56.
Chomsky, N. (2001). Derivation by phase. In M. Kenstowicz (Ed.), *Ken Hale: A life in language* (pp. 1–52). Cambridge, MA: MIT Press.
Clahsen, H., Penke, M., & Parodi, T. (1993/94). Functional categories in early child German. *Language Acquisition, 3*, 395–429.
Corver, N. (2003). Perfect projections. In R. van Hout, A. Hulk, F. Kuiken, & R. Towell (Eds.), *The Lexicon-syntax-interface in second language acquisition* (pp. 45–69). Amsterdam: John Benjamins.
Crain, S. (1991). Language acquisition in the absence of experience. *Behavioral and Brain Sciences, 14*, 596–612.
Crain, S., & Nakayama, M. (1987). Structure dependence in grammar formation. *Language, 63*, 522–543.
Dekydtspotter, L., & Renaud, C. (2014). On second language parsing and grammatical development: The parser in second language acquisition. *Linguistic Approaches to Bilingualism, 4*, 131–165.
Enç, M. (1991). The semantics of specificity. *Linguistic Inquiry, 22*, 1–25.
Eubank, L. (1993/94). On the transfer of parametric values in L2 development. *Language Acquisition, 3*, 183–208.
Franceschina, F. (2001). Morphological or syntactic deficits in near-native speakers? An assessment of some current proposals. *Second Language Research, 17*, 213–247.
Gebhardt, L. (2009). *Numeral classifiers and the structure of DP* (Unpublished doctoral dissertation). Northwestern University, Evanston, IL, USA.
Goad, H., & White, L. (2004). Ultimate attainment of L2 inflection: Effects of L1 prosodic structure. In S. Foster-Cohen, M. Sharwood Smith, A. Sorace, & M. Ota (Eds.), *EUROSLA Yearbook 4* (pp. 119–145). Amsterdam: John Benjamins.
Goad, H., & White, L. (2006). Ultimate attainment in interlanguage grammars: A prosodic approach. *Second Language Research, 22*, 243–268.
Goad, H., & White, L. (2008). Prosodic structure and the representation of L2 functional morphology: A nativist approach. *Lingua, 118*, 577–594.
Goad, H., & White, L. (2009). Prosodic transfer and the representation of determiners in Turkish-English interlanguage. In N. Snape, Y.-k. I. Leung, & M. Sharwood Smith (Eds.), *Representational deficits in SLA: Studies in honor of Roger Hawkins* (pp. 1–26). Amsterdam: John Benjamins.
Goldschneider, J. M., & DeKeyser, R. M. (2001). Explaining the "natural order of L2 morpheme acquisition" in English: A meta-analysis of multiple determinants. *Language Learning, 51*, 1–50.
Grüter, T., Lew-Williams, C., & Fernald, A. (2012). Grammatical gender in L2: A production or a real-time processing problem? *Second Language Research, 28*, 191–215.

Gürel, A. (2000). Missing case inflection: Implications for second language acquisition. In C. Howell, S. A. Fish, & T. Keith-Lucas (Eds.), *Proceedings of the 24th Boston University Conference on Language Development (BUCLD 24)* (pp. 379–390). Somerville, MA: Cascadilla Press.

Harley, H., & Ritter, E. (2002). Person and number in pronouns: A feature-geometric analysis. *Language, 78*, 482–526.

Hawkins, R. (2001). *Second language syntax.* Malden, MA: Blackwell.

Hawkins, R. (2003). *Representational deficit' theories of SLA: Evidence, counterevidence and implications.* Plenary paper presented at EUROSLA, Edinburgh, United Kingdom.

Hawkins, R. (2005). Revisiting wh-movement: The availability of an uninterpretable [wh] feature in interlanguage grammars. In L. Dekydtspotter, R. A. Sprouse, & A. Liljestrand (Eds.), *Proceedings of the 7th Generative Approaches to Second Language Acquisition Conference (GASLA 2004)* (pp. 124–137). Somerville, MA: Cascadilla Press.

Hawkins, R., & Casillas, G. (2008). Explaining frequency of verb morphology in early L2 speech. *Lingua, 118*, 595–612.

Hawkins, R., & Chan, C. (1997). The partial availability of universal grammar in second language acquisition: The 'failed functional features hypothesis'. *Second Language Research, 13*, 187–226.

Hawkins, R., & Hattori, H. (2006). Interpretation of English multiple wh-questions by Japanese speakers: A missing uninterpretable feature account. *Second Language Research, 22*, 269–301.

Hawkins, R., & Liszka, S. (2003). Locating the source of defective past tense marking in advanced L2 English speakers. In R. van Hout, A. Hulk, F. Kuiken, & R. Towell (Eds.), *The Lexicon-syntax-interface in second language acquisition* (pp. 21–44). Amsterdam: John Benjamins.

Haznedar, B. (2001). The acquisition of the IP system in child L2 acquisition. *Studies in Second Language Acquisition, 23*, 1–39.

Haznedar, B. (2006). Persistent problems with case morphology in L2 acquisition. In L. Conxita (Ed.), *Interfaces in multilingualism: Acquisition and representation* (pp. 179–206). Amsterdam: John Benjamins.

Hopp, H. (2010). Ultimate attainment in L2 inflectional morphology: Performance similarities between non-native and native speakers. *Lingua, 120*, 901–931.

Hopp, H. (2013). Grammatical gender in adult L2 acquisition: Relations between lexical and syntactic variability. *Second Language Research, 29*, 33–56.

Hwang, S. H., & Lardiere, D. (2013). Plural-marking in L2 Korean: A feature-based approach. *Second Language Research, 29*, 57–86.

Johnson, J., & Newport, E. (1991). Critical period effects on universal properties of language: The status of subjacency in the acquisition of a second language. *Cognition, 39*, 215–258.

Kawamura, T. (2004). A feature-checking analysis of Japanese scrambling. *Journal of Linguistics, 40*, 45–68.

Kim, C.-E., O'Grady, W., & Deen, K. (2014). The extrinsic plural marker in Korean: Five studies. *Korean Linguistics, 16*, 1–17.

Lardiere, D. (1998). Case and tense in the 'fossilized' steady state. *Second Language Research, 14*, 1–26.

Lardiere, D. (2000). Mapping features to forms in second language acquisition. In J. Archibald (Ed.), *Second language acquisition and linguistic theory* (pp. 102–129). Malden, MA: Blackwell.

Lardiere, D. (2007). *Ultimate attainment in second language acquisition: A case study.* Mahwah, NJ: Lawrence Erlbaum Associates.

Lardiere, D. (2009). Some thoughts on a contrastive analysis of features in second language acquisition. *Second Language Research*, 25, 173–227.

Larson-Hall, J. (2004). Predicting perceptual success with segments: A test of Japanese speakers of Russian. *Second Language Research*, 20, 32–76.

Lee, E., & Lardiere, D. (2016). L2 acquisition of number marking in Korean and Indonesian: A feature-based approach. In D. Stringer, J. Garrett, B. Halloran, & S. Mossman (Eds.), *Proceedings of the 13th Generative Approaches to Second Language Acquisition Conference (GASLA 2015)* (pp. 113–123). Somerville, MA: Cascadilla Press.

Li, X. (1998). Adult accessibility to UG: An issue revisited. In S. Flynn, G. Martohardjono, & W. O'Neil (Eds.), *The generative study of second language acquisition* (pp. 89–110). Mahwah, NJ: Lawrence Erlbaum Associates.

Lightfoot, D. (1982). *The language lottery: Toward a biology of grammars*. Cambridge, MA: MIT Press.

Martohardjono, G. (1993). *Wh-movement in the acquisition of a second language: A crosslinguistic study of three languages with and without overt movement* (Unpublished doctoral dissertation). Cornell University, Ithaca, New York.

Miyamoto, Y., & Ijima, Y. (2003). On the existence of scrambling in the grammar of elementary EFL learners. In S. Foster-Cohen & S. Pekarek Doehler (Eds.), *EUROSLA Yearbook 3* (pp. 7–27). Amsterdam: John Benjamins.

Ojima, S. (2005). *Theory and evidence in second language research: The acquisition of English by native speakers of Japanese* (Unpublished doctoral dissertation). University of Essex, Colchester, UK.

Papadopoulou, D., Varlokosta, S., Kaili, H., Prokou, S., & Revithiadou, A. (2011). Case morphology and word order in second language Turkish: Evidence from Greek learners. *Second Language Research*, 27, 173–205.

Parodi, T. (2000). Finiteness and verb placement in second language acquisition. *Second Language Research*, 16, 355–381.

Saito, M. (1992). Long-distance scrambling in Japanese. *Journal of East Asian Linguistics*, 1, 69–118.

Saito, M. (2003). A derivational approach to the interpretation of scrambling chains. *Lingua*, 113, 481–518.

Schachter, J. (1989). Testing a proposed universal. In S. Gass & J. Schachter (Eds.), *Linguistic perspectives on second language acquisition* (pp. 73–88). Cambridge: Cambridge University Press.

Schachter, J. (1990). On the issue of completeness in second language acquisition. *Second Language Research*, 6, 93–124.

Schwartz, B. D., & Sprouse, R. A. (1996). L2 cognitive states and the full transfer/full access model. *Second Language Research*, 12, 40–72.

Schwartz, B. D., & Sprouse, R. A. (2000). When syntactic theories evolve: Consequences for L2 acquisition research. In J. Archibald (Ed.), *Second language acquisition and linguistic theory* (pp. 156–186). Malden, MA: Blackwell.

Snape, N., Leung, Y.-k. I., & Sharwood Smith, M. (Eds.). (2009). *Representational deficits in SLA: Studies in honor or Roger Hawkins*. Amsterdam: John Benjamins.

Sugisaki, K., & Murasugi, K. (2015). The acquisition of wh-islands in Japanese: A preliminary study. *Nanzan Linguistics*, 10, 43–53.

Svenonius, P. (2007). Interpreting uninterpretable features. *Linguistic Analysis*, 33, 375–413.

Takahashi, D. (1993). Movement of wh-phrases in Japanese. *Natural Language and Linguistic Theory*, 11, 655–678.

Tsimpli, I.-M. (2003). *Features in language development*. Paper presented at EUROSLA, University of Edinburgh, Edinburgh, United Kingdom.

Tsimpli, I.-M., & Dimitrakopoulou, M. (2007). The interpretability hypothesis: Evidence from wh-interrogatives in second language acquisition. *Second Language Research, 23,* 215–242.

Tsimpli, I.-M., & Mastropavlou, M. (2008). Feature interpretability in L2 acquisition and SLI: Greek clitics and determiners. In J. M. Liceras, H. Zobl, & H. Goodluck (Eds.), *The role of formal features in second language acquisition* (pp. 142–183). New York: Lawrence Erlbaum Associates.

Vainikka, A., & Young-Scholten, M. (1996). Gradual development of L2 phrase structure. *Second Language Research, 12,* 7–39.

Verrips, M., & Weissenborn, J. (1992). Verb placement in early German and French: The independence of finiteness and agreement. In J. M. Meisel (Ed.), *The acquisition of verb placement: Functional categories and V2 phenomena in language acquisition* (pp. 283–331). Dordrecht: Kluwer.

Watanabe, A. (1992). Subjacency and S-structure movement of wh-in-situ. *Journal of East Asian Linguistics, 1,* 255–291.

Watanabe, A. (2003). Wh-in-situ languages. In M. Baltin & C. Collins (Eds.), *Handbook of contemporary syntactic theory* (pp. 203–225). Oxford, UK: Blackwell Publishers.

White, L., & Genesee, F. (1996). How native is near-native? The issue of ultimate attainment in adult second language acquisition. *Second Language Research, 11,* 233–265.

White, L., & Juffs, A. (1998). Constraints on wh-movement in two different contexts of non-native language acquisition: Competence and processing. In S. Flynn, G. Martohardjono, & W. O'Neil (Eds.), *The generative study of second language acquisition* (pp. 111–130). Mahwah, NJ: Lawrence Erlbaum Associates.

Wright, R. (2004). A review of perceptual cues and cue robustness. In B. Hayes, D. Steriade, & R. Kirchner (Eds.), *Phonetically based phonology* (pp. 34–57). Cambridge: Cambridge University Press.

Yusa, N. (1999). Multiple specifiers and wh-island effects. In E. Klein & G. Martohardjono (Eds.), *The development of second language grammars: A generative approach* (pp. 289–317). Amsterdam: John Benjamins.

Zobl, H., & Liceras, J. (1994). Functional categories and acquisition orders. *Language Learning, 44,* 159–180.

4

THE ROLE OF SALIENCE IN LINGUISTIC DEVELOPMENT

A Contrarian View

William O'Grady, Kitaek Kim, and Chae-Eun Kim

Introduction

Two fundamental questions lie at the heart of linguistic inquiry: why do languages have the particular properties that they do, and how are those properties acquired in the course of first and second language learning? Ideally, an explanatory theory of language should provide a unified answer to both questions. Indeed, that is precisely the goal of traditional work on Universal Grammar, which proposes a theory that accounts both for the properties of language and for how those properties emerge so consistently in the course of development. Recent emergentist work has a similar goal, which it pursues by seeking to explain linguistic properties and their acquisition in terms of more fundamental forces and factors (e.g., O'Grady, 2005, 2015a, 2015b).

The viability of emergentist approaches to language depends on their ability to identify the particular mechanisms that shape development. One idea, dubbed 'processing determinism' by O'Grady (2015b), focuses on the role of processing cost, as determined by two complementary factors. On the one hand, there are internal pressures that stem from the burden that particular operations place on working memory, leading languages (and learners) to favor certain types of morphosyntactic options over others. On the other hand, there are external factors such as frequency of occurrence, which creates opportunities for routines to be strengthened and entrenched through repeated activation (e.g., Paradis, 2004, p. 28).

The question that we wish to address here has to do with whether the factors that help shape development might include some form of salience, as frequently suggested in the acquisition literature. In early work, salience was treated largely as an acoustic/perceptual phenomenon. Brown (1973, p. 409) suggested that the concept be broken down into variables such as phonetic substance, stress level, and serial position in the sentence. A very similar approach was initially adopted by Goldschneider and DeKeyser (2001) as part of their meta-analysis of developmental order in second language acquisition, and views along these lines have been expressed by many others as well, including O'Grady, Kwak, Lee, and Lee (2011).

More recently, the notion of salience has been expanded in work on language acquisition to encompass features and items that "stand out from the rest" in various senses (Carroll, 2006; Carroll & Shea, 2007; Ellis, 2016, p. 342). For example, Goldschneider and DeKeyser (2001, p. 35) suggest that low semantic complexity, morphophonological regularity, and membership in an open syntactic category such as noun or verb all count as instances of salience. Other proposed extensions include certain associations between linguistic elements, the frequency or infrequency of particular patterns in the input, and surprisal effects that arise in response to failed expectations about what is to come next in the course of processing (e.g., Ellis, 2016).

We question the value of salience as an explanatory notion for two reasons. First, we believe that the developmental facts that traditionally are explained with reference to acoustic prominence (the prototypical example of a salience effect) are better explained in other ways, as we will show. Second, we believe that the expansion of the notion of salience to encompass a broad range of non-acoustic effects, sometimes without convincing independent evidence, is in fact unnecessary, given the availability of alternative processing-based explanations.

We will explore these matters by examining three developmental phenomena for which salience-based explanations have been proposed: early success in the interpretation of reflexive pronouns, the role of 'hierarchy effects' in shaping the emergence of relative clauses, and difficulties in the mastery of inflectional morphology, ranging from the verbal suffix -s in English to case marking in Korean. We propose an alternative account for each of these phenomena that features processing cost as the key explanatory concept. We conclude by urging a reassessment of apparent salience effects, with a view to their integration into a larger processing-based account of language and learning.

Reflexive Pronouns

It has long been understood that prototypical reflexive pronouns in English and many other languages seek out a "co-argument antecedent" (Jespersen, 1933, p. 111). Thus, the reflexive pronoun in (1), the direct object of *cut*, can only refer to Richard, the subject of the same verb. It cannot refer to David, let alone to some unnamed party.

(1) David just found out what happened. [**Richard** cut **himself** while playing with scissors.]

Interestingly, this fact seems to be mastered very quickly in the course of both first and second language acquisition; see O'Grady (2015a) for discussion of various details.

O'Grady (2015a) proposes that the procedure responsible for the interpretation of reflexive pronouns is the product of internal processing pressure. The key idea is that the burden on working memory is minimized if the reflexive pronoun is interpreted immediately and locally, without the need to access less available options, such as an NP in another clause or even in another sentence. (In the example below, PRED = predicate; r = Richard.)

(2) How sentence-level processing might map the sentence *Richard cut himself* onto a semantic representation in real time:
   a. The nominal *Richard* is encountered and is assigned a referent (represented here as the index r).
   Richard
   　r
   b. The transitive verb *cut* is encountered and its two-place predicate-argument structure is projected, with Richard as the first argument.
   Richard cut
   　CUT
   　$<r\_>$
   c. The reflexive pronoun is encountered and identified as the verb's second argument (represented by the symbol x), thereby triggering the search for an antecedent.
   Richard cut himself.
   　CUT
   　$<r\ x>$
   d. The processor interprets the reflexive pronoun immediately and locally with the help of the previously identified referent of the verb's first argument, Richard.
   Richard cut himself.
   　CUT
   　$<r\ x>$
   　　↳r

This proposal contrasts with the idea, quite commonly proposed (e.g., Huang, 2005; Mitkov, 2002, p. 50), that reflexive pronouns take as their antecedent the most salient NP in the sentence. But what makes an NP salient enough to serve as the antecedent of a reflexive pronoun? It can't be because it is sentence-initial—*Richard* is the sentence-initial NP in (3), but it can't be the antecedent for the reflexive pronoun.

(3) *****Richard's** sister cut himself while playing with scissors.

Salience also cannot be equated with an NP's proximity to the reflexive pronoun—Richard is the closest NP in (4), but it can't serve as antecedent for *himself*.

(4) *Some friends of **Richard** cut himself while playing with scissors.

Salience also can't be defined in terms of a grammatical relation such as 'subject.' There are two subjects in the next sentence, but only the second one can be the antecedent for the reflexive pronoun, even though the first one could well be foremost in the speaker's mind as well as discoursally and acoustically prominent.

(5) Well, **JERRY** thinks that Richard cut himself while playing with scissors.

Moreover, there are patterns such as (6) in which the antecedent for the reflexive pronoun is not even a subject.

(6) I described **Richard** to himself (so that he'd know how funny the costume looked).

Crucially, though, all of these examples fit easily into the processing-based analysis, since in each case the reflexive pronoun must be associated with a co-argument, consistent with the idea that the search for an antecedent must minimize processing cost.

The interpretation of plain pronouns (*him, her,* etc.) works very differently. As the following example shows, plain pronouns do not permit a co-argument antecedent: unlike *himself, him* cannot refer to Richard; instead, it must refer to an individual named elsewhere in the sentence (e.g., David) or even to someone not mentioned in the sentence.

(7) Plain pronoun (distant antecedent):
 [$_S$ David said [$_S$ Richard cut ***him*** while playing with scissors]].

For this reason, there is no single processing routine that can pick out an antecedent for a plain pronoun. Instead, listeners have to rely on pragmatic factors, including clues from the context and the extra-linguistic situation, to identify the pronoun's referent. This in turn has developmental consequences, as we would expect if considerations of processing cost shape the courses of acquisition.

Experimental work by Clackson, Felser, and Clahsen (2011) is suggestive in this regard, as can be seen by considering the following illustrative example from an eye-tracking study that they conducted.

(8) *Peter* was waiting outside the corner shop. He watched as *Mr. Jones* bought a huge box of popcorn for ***him/himself*** over the counter.

Here, *Peter* is discoursally prominent (i.e., salient, based on its position and topicality), but *Mr. Jones* is the pronoun's co-argument and should therefore be the preferred antecedent on processing grounds. Based on eye-tracking data involving pictures such as the one in Figure 4.1, Clackson et al. found that children aged 6–9 treat *both* Peter and Mr. Jones as potential referents regardless of the type of pronoun. Crucially, though, they always end up making the right choice for reflexive pronouns, selecting Mr. Jones as the antecedent and thereby minimizing processing cost.

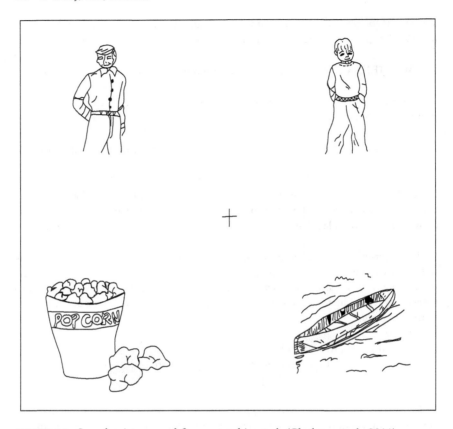

FIGURE 4.1 Sample picture used for eye-tracking task (Clackson et al., 2011)

Interestingly, they do not fare so well with plain pronouns, which they sometimes wrongly associate with the nearer antecedent (*Mr. Jones* rather than *Peter*), essentially treating them as if they were reflexive pronouns; see Conroy, Takahashi, Lidz, and Phillips (2009) for extensive discussion of this phenomenon. We interpret this as further evidence in support of processing determinism: the single low-cost processing routine associated with reflexive pronouns is preferred to the open-ended pragmatic reasoning that is required to interpret plain pronouns, even when the antecedent is discoursally prominent.

Relative Clauses

Studies of the acquisition of relative clauses have yielded many important findings in the literature on sentence processing and language learning. One such finding, well documented for both first and second language learners, involves a strong preference for subject relative clauses over other relative clause types in both comprehension and production (O'Grady, 2011, and the references cited there), consistent with the 'accessibility hierarchy' first proposed by Keenan and Comrie (1977) and subsequently amended by Hawkins (2004, p. 117), as follows.

(9) Subject > Direct Object > Indirect Object/Oblique

Because the subject advantage appears to hold cross-linguistically, attempts to explain it must accommodate very different types of languages. Kim and O'Grady (2016) explored alternative explanations for hierarchy effects by considering the production of relative clauses by 5- and 6-year-old monolingual children learning English and Korean as a first language. The contrast between the two languages is particularly sharp and therefore highly relevant to the challenge of offering a unified explanation for the subject advantage: English is an SVO language, with no case marking and post-nominal relative clauses; in contrast, Korean is an SOV language, with case marking and pre-nominal relative clauses.

(10) a. Typical English relative clause (post-nominal, SVO order, no case marking)
the boy [that _ lost the bag]
b. Typical Korean relative clause (pre-nominal, SOV order, case marking)
[_kapang-ul   ilh-un]   sonyen
  bag-Acc   lose-Pst.RC   boy
'the boy that lost the bag'

In Kim and O'Grady's experiment, the job of the child was simply to describe the person over whom an arrow appeared in pictures such as those in Figures 4.2 through 4.5 below. An accompanying prompt provided a context that encouraged the use of a relative clause (RC). The experiments focused on two contrasts, the first of which was between subject relative clauses and indirect object relative clauses, so chosen because

Step 1 Prompt: "In the first picture, a boy is giving a bag to a girl. In the second picture, a girl is giving a bag to a boy."

FIGURE 4.2   Sample protocol used to elicit a subject RC

Step 2: An arrow appears over the boy in the picture on the left. Targeted response: "the boy [that _ is giving a bag to the girl]."

FIGURE 4.2 (Continued)

each involves a head that is prototypically animate. Figures 4.2 and 4.3 illustrate the materials used to elicit relative clauses of these types.

The second contrast involved direct object and oblique relative clauses, each of which typically modify an inanimate head. Figures 4.4 and 4.5 illustrate the materials used to elicit these two patterns.

Step 1 Prompt: "In the first picture, a boy is giving a bag to a girl. In the second picture, a girl is giving a bag to a boy."

FIGURE 4.3 Sample protocol used to elicit an indirect object RC

Step 2: An arrow appears over the boy in the picture on the right. Targeted response: "the boy [that the girl is giving a bag to _]."

FIGURE 4.3 (Continued)

Step 1 Prompt: "In the first picture, a boy is putting a book on a box. In the second picture, a girl is putting a book on a box."

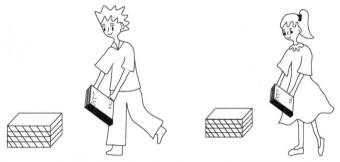

Step 2: An arrow indicates the book in the picture on the left. Targeted response: "the book [that the boy is putting _ on a box]."

FIGURE 4.4 Sample protocol used to elicit a direct object RC

Step 1: Prompt: "In the first picture, a boy is putting a book on a box. In the second picture, a girl is putting a book on a box."

Step 2: An arrow indicates the box in the picture on the left. Targeted response: "the box [that the boy is putting the book on _]."

FIGURE 4.5 Sample protocol used to elicit an oblique RC

Table 4.1 (next page) reports the production rates for the four types of relative clauses under consideration here.

Consistent with the amended version of the Keenan-Comrie hierarchy, both groups of learners were significantly more successful at producing subject relative clauses than the other three types of relative clauses; moreover, also as predicted, the success rate for direct object relative clauses was significantly higher than those for indirect object and

TABLE 4.1 Success rates for each relative clause type

RC type	Learners of English	Learners of Korean
Subject	94.3%	80.8%
Indirect Object	2.9%	8.0%
Direct Object	47.6%	74.4%
Oblique	26.7%	14.4%

oblique relative clause patterns (similar results were found in a parallel study of Korean-speaking adult learners of English as a second language). But why?

One possibility, put forward by Diessel and Tomasello (2005), is that subject relative clauses have the advantage of manifesting the same salient SVO word order widely found elsewhere in English. (On the salience of the dominant word order, see Comrie, 1997.)

(11) a. Subject relative clause:
     the boy   [that _ lost   the bag]
     SUBJ   VERB   DIR OBJ

   b. Direct object relative clause:
     the bag   [that the boy lost _]
     DIR OBJ   SUBJ   VERB

Crucially, however, this idea fails to generalize to Korean, in which there is also a preference for subject relative clauses in Kim and O'Grady's child participants, in the adult native speakers who they also studied (see also Kwon et al., 2010), in adult second language learners (O'Grady, Lee, & Choo, 2003), and in adult heritage learners (O'Grady et al., 2011). Yet, as the following examples help illustrate, *neither* subject relative clauses *nor* direct object relative clauses manifest the canonical SOV order of Korean.

(12) a. subject RC
     [_ kapang-ul   ilh-un]   sonyen
       bag-Acc   lose-Pst.RC   boy
       DIR OBJ   VERB   SUBJ
     'the boy that lost the bag'
   b. direct object RC
     [sonyen-i   _ ilh-un]   kapang
       boy-Nom   lose-Pst.RC bag
       SUBJ   VERB   DIR OBJ
     'the bag that the boy lost'

Still another idea relies on a different notion of salience: there is a preference for relativizing NPs that occur in more prominent earlier positions of a sentence (e.g., Ferreira & Dell, 2000; Montag & MacDonald, 2009, p. 2594). A salience account based on linear prominence is compatible with the asymmetries in English, since the subject precedes the direct object, which in turn precedes indirect objects and obliques.

(13) a. Subject—direct object—indirect object:
'Mary gave a bag to the boy.'
SUBJ   DIR OBJ   IND OBJ
b. Subject—direct object—oblique:
'Mary placed the book on the floor.'
SUBJ   DIR OBJ   OBL

However, it fails for Korean, in which indirect objects and obliques typically *precede* the direct object.

(14) a. Subject—indirect object—direct object:
Mary-ka   sonyen-eykey   kapang-ul   cwu-ess-eyo.
Mary-Nom   boy-to   bag-Acc   give-Pst-Sent.Ender
SUBJ   IND OBJ   DIR OBJ
'Mary gave a bag to the boy.'
b. Subject—oblique—direct object:
Mary-ka   patak-ey   chayk-ul   noh-ess-eyo
Mary-Nom   floor-on   book-Acc   put-Pst-Sent.Ender
SUBJ   OBL   DIR OBJ
'Mary placed the book on the floor.'

Kim and O'Grady propose a processing explanation for hierarchy effects that posits the interaction of two general propensities:

- Relative clauses must be about the referent of the noun they modify (Kuno, 1976; MacWhinney, 2005).
- Topicality ('aboutness') is strongly associated with the subject, less strongly with the direct object, and barely at all with obliques (Aissen, 1999; Givón, 1984, pp. 138, 170–171; Lambrecht, 1994, p. 136).

From a processing perspective then, subject relative clauses are preferred as the default pattern, since the two general requirements align perfectly—the relative clause is about the referent of the subject, which in turn is the default topic to begin with. In contrast, direct object, indirect object, and oblique relative clauses require that the relative clause be construed in a less canonical way, presumably at additional processing cost, so that it is about something other than the referent of its subject.[1]

Of course, one could propose that topicality creates salience (e.g., Chiriacescu, 2011), but this idea would have to somehow be reconciled with the contrary claim that focal (i.e., non-topical) information—typically expressed by *non*-subjects—is salient (e.g., Gee, 1999, p. 121). Alternatively, one could assume that both topics and non-topics are salient, or that they are salient in different ways, but this would just mean that virtually everything is salient, robbing the notion of any explanatory value. In contrast, topicality is a well-grounded and widely accepted feature in its own right, as is the aboutness requirement on relative clauses. Explanations for hierarchy effects in the acquisition of relative clauses are not enhanced by invoking salience in any of its many senses.

Inflection

It has long been a point of consensus that inflectional markers are acquired with delay and difficulty compared to lexical morphemes, in both first and second language acquisition (Brown, 1973; Dulay & Burt, 1973; Goldschneider & DeKeyser, 2001). This state of affairs is typically attributed, at least in part, to the low phonetic salience of grammatical morphemes. We believe that this idea is on the wrong track, for reasons that we will outline, and that processing-based considerations offer a more promising account of the facts. The English third-person singular suffix -s (*He works hard*; *She likes math*) is a case in point.

Agreement in English

It is well known that verbal -s is mastered late in the course of both first language acquisition and second language learning. The delay has long been attributed, at least in part, to the low acoustic salience of -s (DeKeyser, 2016, p. 354). A problematic feature of this account is that there is no reason to think that learners have trouble hearing word-final s in general: as far as we know, normal 3- and 4-year olds can easily distinguish *no* from *nose*, and *sick* from *six*.[2] Indeed, there is quite direct evidence that much younger children are sensitive to the presence or absence of the -s suffix.

Soderstrom, Wexler, and Jusczyk (2002) conducted a preferential listening task with 28 English-speaking infants aged 18.4–19.6 months that focused on the agreement contrast in pairs of sentences such as the following:

(15) a. At the bakery, a team bakes the bread.
     b. At the bakery, a team bake the bread.

The infants listened longer (9.8 versus 8.2 seconds) to sets of sentences that manifested verbal agreement than to those that didn't, indicating an awareness of the agreement suffix and of its appropriateness in at least certain contexts; see also Shi (2014). Brown (1973, p. 410) once observed that "the child will not learn what [s/he] cannot hear;" see also Cazden and Brown (1975, p. 303). This is obviously true, but it appears that children can hear more than we once thought.

Why then do learners appear to have difficulty acquiring verbal -s? We believe that the answer lies in two simple facts, one relating to linguistic typology and the other to language learning. First, as Schachter (1985, p. 71) notes, languages employ different 'coding strategies' to distinguish a subject from other arguments in the sentence; word order, verbal inflection and case marking—alone or in combination—are all commonly used for this purpose, depending on the language. Second, as outlined by Bates and MacWhinney (1987), the processing operations (or 'routines') needed to implement these strategies vary in strength depending on the availability and reliability of the corresponding cues—the key insight of what has come to be called the Competition Model. English offers an illustrative example.

English employs (at least) two separate morphosyntactic strategies for encoding and decoding non-pronominal subjects: word order (the subject tends to precede the verb) and verbal inflection (present tense verbs agree with a third-person singular subject).

(16) Marvin works hard.
     ↑   ↑
    pre-verbal inflection
    position

For the sake of exposition, we can formulate the relevant processing routines very schematically, focusing just on the particular morphosyntactic cue to which they are sensitive, in the spirit of the Competition Model.

(17) The word order routine:
    NP V . . .
    ↕
    Subject
(18) The inflection-based routine:
    V-s
    ↕
    3.Sg Subject

A key feature of processing-based approaches to language is that processing routines are strengthened to varying degrees in the course of use (e.g., Bates & MacWhinney, 1987; Herschensohn, 2009; Langacker, 1987, p. 59; O'Grady, 2015a, 2015b; Paradis, 2004). Assuming that (all other things being equal), frequency of activation is the major determinant of a routine's strength, the word order routine should be more deeply entrenched than the agreement routine. Roland, Dick, and Elman (2007) report that about 95% of all sentences in the Switchboard corpus have the subject in pre-verbal position—a rate of occurrence that is far higher than that of verbal -s, which is found only when the subject is third-person singular and the verb is in the present tense.

Let us assume a 'stronger first' approach to the activation of competing processing routines: all other things being equal, the stronger routine will be more easily accessible. We will further assume that activation of the second, weaker routine is commonly pre-empted, as a way to reduce processing cost. Let us call this Activation Avoidance.[3]

(19) Activation Avoidance
    Under conditions of stress on the processor's resources, language users tend to rely on stronger processing routines and to avoid activation of weaker ones.

This idea is compatible with two striking developmental facts involving agreement in English.

First, there is evidence that the -s suffix is underused rather than overused by learners. Two- and 3-year-olds often fail to employ the -s suffix (Activation Avoidance), but they rarely produce it where it is not called for (Keeney & Wolfe, 1972; Lukyanenko & Fisher, 2014; Wexler, 2011). The situation for second language learners appears to be similar: agreement errors tend strongly to consist of omissions rather than the overuse of -s (Haznedar & Schwartz, 1997, for child L2 learners; and Prévost & White, 2000, for adult learners).[4] These facts align well with the idea that inflectional errors reflect a reluctance to activate a weak routine rather than the absence of the routine or a mistake in how it is formulated.

Second, there are indications of greater attention to the agreement routine in production than in comprehension. Whereas success in the use of the third-person singular suffix reaches the 90% criterion on elicited production tasks around age 4;0 or earlier (Johnson, de Villiers, & Seymour, 2005, p. 326; Rice & Wexler, 2002), the ability to exploit this suffix for the purposes of comprehension appears to emerge more slowly. In a study of 62 children aged 3–6, Johnson et al. report that it was not until age 5 or later that their participants were able to use the agreement marker at even above-chance accuracy to interpret sentences such as *The cat sleeps on the bed* versus *The cats sleep on the bed*; see also Legendre et al. (2014). This too makes sense. Success in production requires the activation and use of even weak routines. An English sentence that is produced without attention to agreement is noticeably unacceptable (**He go there every day*); in contrast, failure to activate the agreement routine in comprehension is essentially without consequences, since the stronger word-order-based routine gives the right interpretive result in the vast majority of sentences.

In sum, while it is true that various inflectional suffixes in English, including verbal -s, are low in acoustic salience, this may not be responsible for their late mastery. As we have argued, there is reason to think that delays in the use of verbal -s reflect a reluctance to activate weak routines when processing resources come under stress. As we will see next, the study of case in Korean provides support for this account.

Case in Korean

Korean makes use of two morphosyntactic coding strategies to distinguish subjects from direct objects. On the one hand, the subject usually precedes the direct object (Korean is an SOV language); on the other hand, the subject is typically marked by the nominative case suffix (-*ka*) and the direct object by the accusative suffix (-*lul*).

(20) Thokki-**ka**   oli-**lul**   anacwu-eyo.
     rabbit-Nom duck-Acc hug-SE
     'The rabbit is hugging the duck.'

As we will see shortly, when there is a conflict between the two strategies, priority goes to case marking.

We can represent the processing routines for Korean case and word order in schematic form as follows.

(21) The word order routine:
NP   NP   V
↕   ↕
Subj *Dir Obj*
(agent) *(patient)*
[except where overruled by the case-marking routine]

(22) The case-marking routine:
NP-NOM ⟷ *subject (agent)*
NP-ACC ⟷ *direct object (patient)*

Salience is not in play here in the way that it might potentially be in the case of the verbal suffix *-s* in English. This is because case markers in Korean are no less perceptible than other morphemes with the same phonological composition: *hwa-ka* 'anger + nominative case' has exactly the same pronunciation as the compound *hwa-ka* 'picture-person' ('artist'), in which *ka* is a lexical morpheme (with the meaning 'person') rather than a case marker. Similarly, *han-ul* 'grudge + accusative case' is pronounced just like *hanul* 'sky' (a single bi-syllablic morpheme, with no case marker).

From a processing perspective, though, there is good reason to think, based on frequency of activation, that the case-based routine is substantially weaker than the routine based on word order. That is because case is commonly dropped in Korean, especially in casual speech: based on longitudinal data from three mother-child dyads, Cho (1981, pp. 45–46) reports that mothers use the accusative case only about 3% of the time and the nominative slightly more than half the time (54.1%) in SOV and OSV patterns. In contrast, word order is highly reliable in these constructions, with SOV patterns occurring about ten times more frequently than their OSV counterparts (Cho, p. 35).

Let us now turn to two concrete examples. In SOV sentences, where the first NP carries the nominative case and the second NP is marked by the accusative, the two routines yield the same result.

(23)   Thokki-**ka**   oli-**lul**   anacwu-eyo.
                   rabbit-NOM duck-ACC hug-SE
Case: *Subject*   *Dir Obj*
Word order: *Subject*   *Dir Obj*
                   'The rabbit is hugging the duck.'

In an OSV sentence, in contrast, the two routines diverge: the weakly entrenched case-sensitive routine treats the first NP as the direct object by virtue of the accusative case marker, while the word-order routine treats it as the subject by virtue of its position.

(24)   Oli-**lul**   thokki-**ka**   anacwu-eyo.
         duck-Acc   rabbit-Nom   hug-SE
Case: *Dir Obj*   *Subject*
Word order: *Subject*   *Dir Obj*
         'The rabbit is hugging the duck.'

In such situations, the language learner faces a challenge, as the stronger word-order routine must yield to the weaker case-based routine when the two conflict; see the formulation of (21). But, crucially, the conflict can arise only if the case routine is activated in the first place. We predict that it often will not be, because of learners' propensity to avoid recourse to weakly entrenched procedures. Korean thus offers a crucial test for our hypothesis.

A key piece of evidence comes from studies in which participants indicate their understanding of sentences such as (24) by matching them with one of two pictures, as illustrated in Figure 4.6.

Children learning Korean as a first language typically do poorly on such tasks, misinterpreting OSV patterns as if they were SOV sentences, but not vice versa (Cho, 1981; Chung, 1994; Jin, Kim, & Song, 2015). Similar problems have been documented for child heritage learners (Kim, O'Grady, & Schwartz, in press; Song et al., 1997) as well as for beginning adult learners of Korean as a second language (Ha, 2012; Ha & Choi, 2012). There is thus good reason to believe that the case routine is ineffectual in the early stages of development, as we predict.

Avoidance of weakly entrenched case routines appears to underlie two further developmental phenomena in Korean. First, Kim (2014, p. 68) reports evidence that case is underused rather than overused in children's speech. When 21 child learners of Korean as a first language aged 3;6–6;0 were asked to describe pictures of transitive events in which one entity acted on another, they spontaneously produced the nominative case 77.78% of the time and the optional accusative 42.86% of the time on average. Crucially, they never replaced either case by the other. A comparable trend was observed for 31 heritage learners, aged 8–14, who Kim also studied. This propensity for omission rather than misuse parallels the pattern observed for verbal

FIGURE 4.6 A sample picture, adapted from Song, O'Grady, Cho, and Lee (1997)

agreement in English, and is compatible with the idea that weak routines are often not activated.

Second, we find a difference between production and comprehension parallel to the one documented for the English verbal suffix. Success in production calls for activation of the case routine—especially for subjects of transitive verbs, for which case marking is typically required. In contrast, attention to case in the course of comprehension has a much lower priority since word order typically suffices to identify the subject and direct object, as we have seen. This contrast is clearly reflected in the performance of nine 'mid-proficiency' learners of Korean as a first language (mean age 4;9) in Kim's study. Although the children performed at chance (46%) on OSV patterns in a comprehension task based on picture selection (p. 57), they *produced* the nominative case on the subject over 80% of the time when describing pictures of transitive events (p. 68). Large asymmetries of the same type were also noted for the 31 heritage language learners who Kim studied.

Summary and Further Challenges

In sum, there is good reason to question salience-based accounts for developmental delays in the use of inflection. Although many inflectional markers are acoustically weak (verbal -*s* in English is a prototypical example), their emergence follows a path that is identical in key respects to that of far more salient grammatical morphemes, such as the case markers of Korean. All have essentially the same signature profile: 1) competition of the inflectional routine with a stronger routine, 2) underuse (but never overuse) of the inflectional routine, and 3) a greater incentive to activate the routine in production than in comprehension. These facts jointly point toward the reality of Activation Avoidance: under conditions of processing stress (the normal state of affairs for learners), weak routines are less likely to be activated, especially when a stronger routine can be invoked. Acoustic prominence is essentially irrelevant; the explanatory burden falls largely on the operation of the processor and the degree to which its routines are entrenched at different points in development.

Still, many challenges remain. One involves the question of whether inflection-based routines always lag behind a routine that exploits word order—a potential salience effect, since word order is arguably more noticeable than a suffix. Turkish is highly relevant in this regard.

Word order seems to be less fixed in Turkish than in Korean. According to a corpus study conducted by Slobin and Bever (1982), more than 50% of the sentences with an overt subject and direct object occur in a word order other than the 'canonical' SOV pattern (see also Özge, Marinis, & Zeyrek, 2013, p. 272)—in contrast, SOV patterns outnumber OSV patterns by a factor of 10:1 in Korean maternal speech. In addition, case in Turkish is simpler than in Korean: there is an accusative suffix, but no nominative.

(25) Goril aslan-**i** bul-du. (Özge et al., 2013, p. 272)
 gorilla lion-Acc find-Pst
 'The gorilla found the lion.'

Under these circumstances, it seems reasonable to suppose that the accusative case routine takes on a greater importance and that its frequent activation could contribute to its early entrenchment, making it less likely to be pre-empted by routines based on word order.

Interestingly, the developmental facts for Turkish point in precisely that direction, as shown by the results of an act-out comprehension task conducted by Slobin and Bever (1982) with 48 monolingual children aged 2;0–4;4. The authors report a success rate greater than 75% on OSV patterns, even among 2-year-old participants. This finding appears to confirm the possibility of the early entrenchment of inflectional routines under the right circumstances, as our approach predicts.

A second issue stems from the large number of studies in the literature that purport to show the effect of acoustic salience on inflectional development. The problem here is that apparent salience effects are often confounded with processing effects, as in the case of verbal -*s* in English, making it difficult to determine exactly what is going on. Brown, Pfeiler, de León, and Pye's (2013) study of the development of agreement in four Mayan languages offers an additional example in this regard. The authors report a robust effect of affix position and prosodic prominence: suffixes, which are stressed in Mayan, are acquired earlier than prefixes, which are unstressed. However, the authors themselves acknowledge the possibility of an alternative processing-based account: Cutler, Hawkins, and Gilligan (1985) draw on a broad range of typological facts to argue that stems are best processed before affixes, thereby conferring an advantage on suffixes over prefixes.

Yet another issue involves the large number of inflectional contrasts for which there are no competing word order routines—gender, number (plurality), tense, and definiteness all come to mind in this regard. Developmental delays have been reported for these phenomena at least from the time of Berko's (1958) pioneering work, but it is not clear why this should be so on our account, since there is apparently no competing routine.

A possible answer can be derived from a telling typological fact: in many languages, basic semantic contrasts are not encoded morphologically. For example, the following sentence from Thai provides no marking for case, agreement, number, gender, tense, or definiteness. The context determines whether the verb should be given a past or a present interpretation, and whether *khon* should be interpreted as singular or plural, as definite or indefinite, and so on.

(26) chạn hěn khon
    I   see person
    'I see/saw a/the person/people.'

We see a similar situation in Indonesian and Malay, which together have more than 200 million speakers. As the following sentence (identical in the two closely related languages) helps illustrate, there is no inflectional marking of any sort.

(27) aku mem-baca buku
    I   active-read book
    'I am reading/did read a book/books.'

In languages of this type, pragmatic reasoning is paramount: listeners draw on information from the context and the situation to locate an event in time, to ascertain whether a noun has more than one referent, to infer whether it is definite, and so on. In principle, exactly the same option is available to learners and speakers of any language, including English. Herein may lie the 'competition' that initially impedes attention to morphosyntactic cues such as definite articles, tense suffixes, and the like. We leave this possibility for future research.

Conclusion

We do not deny that some things can 'stand out' from others because of their acoustic, visual, or conceptual features. Nor do we deny the plausibility of Brown's (1973, p. 409) surmise that salience will turn out to be a 'minor determinant' of developmental order. But that is not the question; the question is whether salience plays a crucial role in shaping naturalistic development. Obviously, nothing can be ruled out at this point. The literature abounds with examples of apparent salience effects, a number of which receive attention in the other chapters of this volume. It remains to be seen to what extent these effects might lend themselves to reanalysis in terms of processing-related factors.

Of necessity we have had to focus here on three case studies, each involving a major milestone in the acquisition of language: learners' early mastery of reflexive pronouns, preferences in the production and comprehension of relative clauses, and the emergence of verbal and nominal inflection. As we have noted, the developmental trajectory for these phenomena appears to be shaped by a calculus of processing cost that is sensitive to two factors. On the one hand, there is the burden that particular operations place on internal computational resources such as working memory—a key factor in understanding why reflexive pronouns and relative clauses have the particular properties that they do and why those properties emerge in the way that they do. On the other hand, there are external factors relating to the opportunities that input provides for particular processing routines to be strengthened and ultimately entrenched—a factor of potential relevance to phenomena of all types, including the inflectional contrasts on which we have focused here.

Despite several decades of intense study, most aspects of language acquisition remain mysterious, and even modest attempts at explanation typically fail to muster a consensus. Indeed, progress in the field is arguably more often marked by figuring out what doesn't have explanatory import than what does. We have followed this path here by calling into question the role of salience in shaping development. Our conclusion, put simply, is that it has little impact, if any. Hopefully, time and further research will clarify this matter.

Acknowledgements

The authors express their gratitude to the following individuals for their comments, queries, and advice: the editors of this volume, two anonymous referees, Kevin Gregg, Amy Schafer, Peter Chong, Yuphaphann Hoonchamlong, Hyunah Ahn,

Kamil Deen, Bonnie Schwartz, and other members of the Language Acquisition Research Group at the University of Hawai'i at Mānoa.

Notes

1 McDaniel, McKee, Cowart, and Garrett (2015) offer a somewhat different processing-based account based on sentence planning. Although they use the term 'salience' in stating their hypothesis (see their 'property 2'), that notion is implemented in structural and computational terms that are fully compatible with the sort of processing-based approach that we advocate.
2 Intriguingly, the same is true in the case of individuals whose inflectional difficulties stem from specific language impairment (e.g., Pinker, 1994, p. 325).
3 There is no reason to think that the conditions that discourage activation of weak routines are limited to the early stages of first and second language acquisition. They could very well also be associated with specific language impairment and neurological disorders such as agrammatic aphasia.
4 Indeed, underuse of inflectional marking seems to be the default state of affairs across many languages (see, e.g., Hyams, 1999). It is important not to confuse the suppression of a morpheme with the overgeneralization of an allomorph of that morpheme. There is no incompatibility between the fact that the past-tense suffix is often dropped by children learning English and the fact that, *when the suffix is used*, there is a tendency to overgeneralize its most basic allomorph (*-ed*, as in *runned, goed, eated*, and so on).

References

Aissen, J. (1999). Markedness and subject choice in optimality theory. *Natural Language and Linguistic Theory, 17,* 672–711.
Bates, E., & MacWhinney, B. (1987). Competition, variation and language learning. In B. MacWhinney (Ed.), *Mechanisms of language acquisition* (pp. 157–193). Mahwah, NJ: Lawrence Erlbaum Associates.
Berko, J. (1958). The child's learning of English morphology. *Word, 14,* 150–177.
Brown, P., Pfeiler, B., de León, L., & Pye, C. (2013). The acquisition of agreement in four Mayan languages. In E. Bavin & S. Stoll (Eds.), *The acquisition of ergativity* (pp. 271–306). Amsterdam: John Benjamins.
Brown, R. (1973). *A first language: The early stages.* Cambridge, MA: Harvard University Press.
Carroll, S. (2006). Salience, awareness and SLA. In M. O'Brien, C. Shea & J. Archibald (Eds.), *Proceedings of the 8th Generative Approaches to Second Language Acquisition Conference* (pp. 17–24). Somerville, MA: Cascadilla Press.
Carroll, S., & Shea, C. (2007). Salience, focus and second language acquisition. *Nouveaux cahiers de linguistique française, 28,* 99–106.
Cazden, C., & Brown, R. (1975). The early development of the mother tongue. In E. Lenneberg & E. Lenneberg (Eds.), *Foundations of language development* (Vol. 1, pp. 299–310). New York: Academic Press.
Chiriacescu, I. S. (2011). *Factors contributing to the salience of referents.* Retrieve from www.uni-stuttgart.de/linguistik/sfb732/files/chiriacescu2011-salience-referents.pdf
Cho, S. W. (1981). *The acquisition of word order in Korean* (Unpublished master's thesis). University of Calgary, Alberta, Canada.
Chung, G. N. (1994). *Case and its acquisition in Korean* (Unpublished doctoral dissertation). University of Texas at Austin, Austin, TX.

Clackson, K., Felser, C., & Clahsen, H. (2011). Children's processing of reflexives and pronouns in English: Evidence from eye-movements during listening. *Journal of Memory and Language, 65,* 128–144.

Comrie. B. (1997). On the origin of the basic variety. *Second Language Research, 13,* 367–373.

Conroy, A., Takahashi, E., Lidz, J., & Phillips, C. (2009). Equal treatment for all antecedents: How children succeed with principle B. *Linguistic Inquiry, 40,* 446–486.

Cutler, A., Hawkins, J., & Gilligan, G. (1985). The suffixing preference: A processing explanation. *Linguistics, 23,* 723–758.

DeKeyser, R. (2016). Of moving targets and chameleons: Why the concept of difficulty is so hard to pin down. *Studies in Second Language Acquisition, 38,* 353–363.

Diessel, H., & Tomasello, M. (2005). A new look at the acquisition of relative clauses. *Language, 81,* 1–25.

Dulay, H. C., & Burt, M. K. (1973). Should we teach children syntax? *Language Learning, 23,* 245–258.

Ellis, N. (2016). Salience, cognition, language complexity, and complex adaptive systems. *Studies in Second Language Acquisition, 38,* 341–351.

Ferreira, V., & Dell, G. (2000). Effect of ambiguity and lexical availability on syntactic and lexical production. *Cognitive Psychology, 40,* 296–340.

Gee, J. (1999). *An introduction to discourse analysis: Theory and method* (2nd ed.). New York: Routledge.

Givón, T. (1984). *Syntax: A functional-typological introduction, Vol. 1*. Amsterdam: John Benjamins.

Goldschneider, J., & DeKeyser, R. (2001). Explaining the "natural order of L2 morpheme acquisition" in English: A meta-analysis of multiple determinants. *Language Learning, 51,* 1–50.

Ha, K. M. (2012). Adult second language learners' acquisition in OSV word order with case markers in Korea (Unpublished master's thesis). California State University at San Diego, San Diego, CA.

Ha, K. M., & Choi, S. (2012). Adult second language learners' acquisition of word order and case markers in Korean. *The Korean Language in America, 17,* 1–23.

Hawkins, J. (2004). *Efficiency and complexity in grammars*. Oxford: Oxford University Press.

Haznedar, B., & Schwartz, B. (1997). Are there optional infinitives in child L2 acquisition? In E. Hughes, M. Hughes, & A. Greenhill (Eds.), *Proceedings of the 21st Annual Boston University Conference on Language Development* (pp. 257–268). Somerville, MA: Cascadilla Press.

Herschensohn, J. (2009). Fundamental and gradient differences in language development. *Studies in Second Language Acquisition, 31,* 259–289.

Huang, Y. (2005). Anaphora and the pragmatics-syntax interface. In L. Horn & G. Ward (Eds.), *The handbook of pragmatics* (pp. 288–314). Boston: Blackwell.

Hyams, N. (1999). Underspecification and modality in early syntax: A formalist perspective on language acquisition. In M. Darnell, E. Moravcsik, M. Noonan, & K. Wheatley (Eds.). *Functionalism and formalism in linguistics* (Vol. 1, pp. 387–416). Amsterdam: John Benjamins.

Jespersen, O. (1933). *Essentials of English grammar*. London: Unwin & Allen.

Jin, K.-S., Kim, M. J., & Song H.-J. (2015). The development of Korean preschoolers' ability to understand transitive sentences using case-markers. *The Korean Journal of Developmental Psychology, 28,* 75–90.

Johnson, V., de Villiers, J., & Seymour, H. (2005). Agreement without understanding? The case of third person singular /s/. *First Language, 25,* 317–330.

Keenan, E., & Comrie, B. (1977). Noun phrase accessibility and universal grammar. *Linguistic Inquiry, 8*, 63–100.

Keeney, T., & Wolfe, J. (1972). The acquisition of agreement in English. *Journal of Verbal Learning and Verbal Behavior, 11*, 698–705.

Kim, C.-E., & O'Grady, W. (2016). Asymmetries in children's production of relative clauses: Data from English and Korean. *Journal of Child Language, 43*, 1038–1071.

Kim, K. (2014). Unveiling linguistic competence by facilitating performance (Unpublished doctoral dissertation). University of Hawaii at Manoa, Honolulu, HI.

Kim, K., O'Grady, W., & Schwartz, B. (in press). Case in heritage Korean. *Linguistic Approaches to Bilingualism*.

Kuno, S. (1976). Subject, theme, and the speaker's empathy a reexamination of relativization phenomena. In C. Li (Ed.), *Subject and topic* (pp. 417–444). San Diego: Academic Press.

Kwon, N., Gordon, P., Lee, Y., Kluender, R., & Polinsky, M. (2010). Cognitive and linguistic factors affecting subject/object asymmetries: An eye-tracking study of prenominal relative clauses in Korean. *Language, 86*, 546–582.

Lambrecht, K. (1994). *Information structure and syntactic form: Topic, focus and the representation of discourse referents*. Cambridge, UK: Cambridge University Press.

Langacker, R. (1987). *Foundations of cognitive grammar, Vol. 1: Theoretical prerequisites*. Stanford, CA: Stanford University Press.

Legendre, G., Culbertson, J., Zaroukian, E., Hsin, L., Barrière, I., & Nazzi, T. (2014). Is children's comprehension of subject–verb agreement universally late? Comparative evidence from French, English, and Spanish. *Lingua, 144*, 21–39.

Lukyanenko, C., & Fisher, C. (2014). 30-month-olds use verb agreement features in online sentence processing. In W. Orman & M. Valleau (Eds.), *Proceedings of the 38th Annual Boston University Conference on Language Development* (Vol. 2, pp. 292–305). Somerville, MA: Cascadilla Press.

MacWhinney, B. (2005). The emergence of grammar from perspective taking. In D. Pecher & R. Zwann (Eds.), *Grounding cognition* (pp. 198–223). Cambridge, UK: Cambridge University Press.

McDaniel, D., McKee, C., Cowart, W., & Garrett, M. (2015). The role of the language production system in shaping grammars. *Language, 91*, 415–441.

Mitkov, R. (2002). *Anaphora resolution*. New York: Longman.

Montag, J., & MacDonald, M. (2009). Word order doesn't matter: Relative clause production in English and Japanese. In N. Taatgen & H. van Rijn (Eds.), *Proceedings of the Thirty-First Annual Conference of the Cognitive Science Society* (pp. 2594–2599). Austin, TX: Cognitive Science Society.

O'Grady, W. (2005). *Syntactic carpentry: An emergentist approach to syntax*. Mahwah, NJ: Lawrence Erlbaum Associates.

O'Grady, W. (2011). Relative clauses: Processing and acquisition. In E. Kidd (Ed.), *The acquisition of relative clauses: Processing, typology and function* (pp. 13–38). Amsterdam: John Benjamins.

O'Grady, W. (2015a). Anaphora and the case for emergentism. In B. MacWhinney & W. O'Grady (Eds.), *The Handbook of language emergence* (pp. 100–122). Boston: Wiley-Blackwell.

O'Grady, W. (2015b). Processing determinism. *Language Learning, 65*, 6–32.

O'Grady, W., Kwak, H.-Y., Lee, M., & Lee, O.-S. (2011). An emergentist perspective on partial language acquisition. *Studies in Second Language Acquisition, 33*, 223–245.

O'Grady, W., Lee, M., & Choo, M. (2003). A subject object asymmetry in the acquisition of relative clauses in Korean as a second language. *Studies in Second Language Acquisition, 25*, 433–448.

Özge D., Marinis, T., & Zeyrek, D. (2013). Object-first orders in Turkish do not pose a challenge during processing. In U. Özge (Ed.), *Proceedings of the 8th Workshop on Altaic Formal Linguistics: MIT Working Papers in Linguistics* (pp. 269–280). Cambridge, MA: MIT, Department of Linguistics.

Paradis, M. (2004). *A neurolinguistic theory of bilingualism*. Amsterdam: John Benjamins.

Pinker, S. (1994). *The language instinct: How the mind creates language*. New York: Morrow.

Prévost, P., & White, L. (2000). Missing surface inflection or impairment in second language acquisition? Evidence from tense and agreement. *Second Language Research, 16*, 103–133.

Rice, M., & Wexler, K. (2002). *Test of early grammatical impairment*. San Antonio: Psychological Corporation.

Roland, D., Dick, F., & Elman, J. (2007). Frequency of basic English grammatical structures: A corpus analysis. *Journal of Memory and Language, 57*, 348–379.

Schachter, P. (1985). Parts-of-speech systems. In T. Shopen (Ed.), *Language typology and syntactic description, Vol. 1: Clause structure* (pp. 3–61). New York: Cambridge University Press.

Shi, R. (2014). Functional morphemes and early language acquisition. *Child Development Perspectives, 8*, 6–11.

Slobin, D., & Bever, T. (1982). Children used canonical sentence schemas: A crosslinguistic study of word order and inflections. *Cognition, 12*, 229–265.

Soderstrom, M., Wexler, K., & Jusczyk, P. (2002). English-learning toddlers' sensitivity to agreement morphology in receptive grammar. In B. Skarabela, S. Fish, & A. Do (Eds.) *Proceedings of the 26th Annual Boston University Conference on Language Development* (Vol. 2, pp. 643–652). Somerville, MA: Cascadilla Press.

Song, M., O'Grady, W., Cho, S., & Lee, M. (1997). The learning and teaching of Korean in community schools. In Y. H. Kim (Ed.), *Korean language in America 2* (pp. 111–127). Los Angeles, CA: American Association of Teachers of Korean.

Wexler, K. (2011). Grammatical computation in the optional infinitive stage. In J. de Villiers & T. Roeper (Eds.), *Handbook of generative approaches to language acquisition* (pp. 53–118). Netherlands: Springer.

PART II
Perceptual Salience in SLA

5

THE L2 ACQUISITION OF ITALIAN TENSE

The Role of Salience

*Jennifer Behney, Patti Spinner,
Susan M. Gass, and Lorena Valmori*

Introduction

It is well established that morphological marking is frequently difficult for second language learners to acquire, especially when learners whose L1 is morphologically poor are learning a morphologically rich language (e.g., Sagarra & Ellis, 2013). Various explanations have been put forward for this phenomenon, two of which we mention here. The first considers the relationship between the L1 and the L2, and the second takes into account specific characteristics of the L2. In the first instance, the issue centers on differences in feature representation between the L1 and the L2, under the assumption that features that are not present in the L1 may not be available to the L2 learner (e.g., Franceschina, 2005; Hawkins & Liszka, 2003), or that L1-based processing strategies block subsequent attention to appropriate cues in the L2 (e.g., Sagarra & Ellis, 2013). In the second explanation, scholars have proposed that the source of difficulty is not the contrast between language-specific features in the L1 and target language, but rather certain characteristics of L2 representation or processing that are common to all second language learners. Because learners cannot process language fully (at least at early stages of development), they are forced to rely on other information for interpretation, such as lexical or real-world knowledge (e.g., Clahsen & Felser, 2006a, 2006b; VanPatten, 2007; VanPatten & Keating, 2007). The question we raise in this chapter is the extent to which salience of morphological form in combination with lexical information influences the detection of linguistic features in the L2, and the extent to which this information is used in interpretation (cf. Tomlin & Villa, 1994 where detection is a result of alertness and orientation and is defined as the "cognitive registration of some stimuli," p. 190). Tomlin and Villa further state that "[O]nce a token or instance of a grammatical alternation is detected, it is then available for further processing" (p. 198).

Ellis (Chapter 2) refers to salience in the following manner: the term salience is used "to refer to the property of a stimulus to stand out from the rest. Salient items or features are attended, are more likely to be perceived, and are more likely to enter into subsequent cognitive processing and learning." In his synthesis of the literature, he notes that salience can be: 1) psychophysical (he provides the example of red poppies in a field of yellow, where the red poppy "pops out"), 2) associational (he provides the example of a loved one standing out in a crowd of others), or 3) surprisal given a particular context. With regard to surprisal, context influences our predictions about the world and when that prediction is unmet or something out of the ordinary happens, it becomes salient and our attention is drawn to it (see also Gass, 1988). An example of salience in the sense of surprise evoking a reaction can be seen in the case of humor where something is often humorous because of its incongruity or because of its unexpectedness. Closer to home, Ellis (2016, p. 347) cites work by Cerezo, Caras, and Leow (2016) to exemplify surprisal. The participants in the Cerezo et al. study were involved in a gaming task, and it was the surprise factor (Ohhh!) that resulted in learning. As one participant said:

> Ohhh! It is an object! Because, that's why *gustan* agrees with the subject. The class is pleasing to her, making her the object and the class the subject. That's why it doesn't follow a literal English translation! There we go. I just had a breakthrough. Thank God. And that's why I'm also doing the Spanish lab now while we're learning all about this.
>
> *(Cerezo et al., 2016, Online Appendix A)*

In the context of the present chapter, the first type of salience—psychophysical salience—is the most relevant. Specifically, we examine the issue of how morphological marking can be more or less salient across languages, or even between various forms in a single language. Consider Spanish, for example, the language that is the subject of investigation in a number of studies investigating English speakers' ability to acquire morphology. The difference between various tense, aspect, and person markers in Spanish is marked with suffixes of varying length. The contrast between first and third person in the present tense often differs by a single letter and a single phoneme: that is, -*o* versus -*a*. This contrast may be somewhat challenging to perceive, both in writing and in speech. On the other hand, the contrast between present and imperfect forms could be presumed to be easier to detect. In Spanish, the simple present suffix for third person is a single letter/phoneme *(-a)*, but the imperfect form is three letters/phonemes, and two syllables *(-aba)*.

We assume that morphological markers are more salient when they stand out from their surroundings. This salience leads to easier detection. Any number of factors could be influential here, but we make the relatively straightforward assumption that greater length (in letters, phonemes, and/or syllables) makes a morphological marker more salient. In other words, contrasts between markers are more salient and, hence, more easily detectible when their length and/or syllabicity differs (e.g., -*a* versus—*aba*). This view is compatible with Gass's (1988) framework, in which input is converted into output through five processing stages, the first one being apperception. Gass argued that "the apperceived input is that bit of language which is noticed by the learner because of some particular features" (p. 202). As a consequence, when a language feature is more salient because of its length in written input or because it is more acoustically obvious, it stands out and is more likely be detected (apperceived). This is not unlike Tomlin and Villa's (1994) construct of detection.

An additional issue regarding salience is whether features in the first language could influence the degree to which learners are "tuned into" the morphology of the L2. That is, it is possible that having particular types of morphological marking in the native language could make similar types of marking salient in the L2. If this is the case, the question is to what extent the marking needs to be similar between the two languages for learners to detect it easily.

To investigate this issue, we focus on two areas of Ellis' framework: psychophysical salience, what we here refer to as perceptual salience; and, to a lesser extent, surprisal. With regard to the former, we examined a language in which past tense morphology consists of two words and differs significantly in length from present tense morphology (see discussion of bound/free morphemes in Goldschneider & DeKeyser, 2001). With regard to the latter, our methodology pairs present tense morphology with past tense lexical phrases/items and vice versa. This contradictory information leads to a surprise factor that we predict will result in greater focus on the morphosyntax of the L2.

The L2 Acquisition of Morphology

As noted earlier, morphology is known to be problematic for second language learners (see Slabakova, 2013 for various explanations of issues related to morphology). Some researchers have suggested that the problem is especially pronounced with speakers of morphologically poor languages, such as English or Chinese, who learn a morphologically rich L2, such as Spanish or Italian.

For example, it may be that English learners of Spanish do not attend to morphological markings as much as native speakers given the relative absence of morphological marking in their L1 English. This issue was investigated by Sagarra and Ellis (2013), who measured the eye movements of 120 low- and high-level learners of Spanish as they read sentences containing adverb-verb and verb-adverb tense congruencies or incongruencies, as can be seen in Examples 1 and 2.

(1) Congruent: *Creen que el chico **cocinó** algo **ayer** para la fiesta.*
 they believe that the boy cooked something yesterday for the party
 'They believe that the boy **cooked** something **yesterday** for the party.'
(2) Incongruent: *Creen que el chico **cocina** algo **ayer** para la fiesta.*
 they believe that the boy cooks something yesterday for the party
 'They believe that the boy **cooks** something **yesterday** for the party.'

The authors focused on the time spent reading verbs—the locus of the morphological marking of tense—and adverbs, which provide lexical information regarding tense. There were two groups of learners. One group consisted of native speakers of English, a morphologically poor language relative to Spanish. The second group consisted of speakers of Romanian, which has an inflectional system that is rich in a similar way to that of Spanish. Both the English-speaking group and the Romanian-speaking group were sensitive to tense morphology in that they took longer to read the incongruent sentences than the congruent ones. However, the English-speaking learners looked at verbs less than the Romanian speakers, presumably relying more heavily on adverbs rather than morphology for sentence interpretation. Sagarra and Ellis concluded that learners focus more on the cues that are most prevalent in the L1—in this case, adverbs for English speakers and verbs for Romanian speakers. The consequence is that acquisition may be impeded when a different set of cues is prevalent.

In another experiment investigating English speakers' sensitivity to Spanish morphology, VanPatten, Keating, and Leeser (2012) examined non-advanced learners' sensitivity to two syntactic structures (subject–verb inversion and adverb placement) and person/number marking on verbs in a self-paced reading task. In the case of person/number marking, sentences were included where the marking on verbs was either congruent or incongruent with the subject of the verb, as can be seen in Examples 3–6.

(3) Congruent: *Ahora Pedro toma el refresco en el salon*
'Now Pedro $_{3rd\ sing}$ drinks $_{3rd\ sing}$ the soft drink in the living room'
(4) Incongruent: *Ahora Pedro tomo el refresco...*
'Now Pedro$_{3rd\ sing}$ drink $_{1st\ sing}$ the soft drink...'
(5) Congruent: *Ahora tú tocas el piano para muchas personas*
'Now you $_{2nd\ sing}$ play $_{2nd\ sing}$ the piano for several people'
(6) Incongruent: *Ahora tú tocan el piano...*
'Now you $_{2nd\ sing}$ play $_{3rd\ pl}$ the piano...'

Like the native speaker control group, the English-speaking learners of Spanish were sensitive to ungrammaticalities on the two syntactic structures. However, unlike the controls, these relatively early learners failed to show sensitivity to ungrammaticalities on person/number marking. According to VanPatten et al. (2012), part of the reason for the lack of sensitivity is the absence of rich morphology in the L1. As they put it, "English speakers learning Spanish would not begin the acquisition of Spanish with either a parsing system that expects surface agreement or with a hypothesis space in the grammar that expects rich morphology on verbs" (p. 113). The English-speaking learners did not have morphological inflections represented robustly in the L2 grammar, and thus failed to demonstrate sensitivity to incongruencies on the self-paced reading task.

Notably, however, the morphology examined in both of these studies has involved small differences in inflectional endings, such as the first- and third-person singular present tense and preterit morphemes in Spanish (e.g., *el chico cocina* 'the boy cooks' versus *el chico cocinó* 'the boy cooked' (Sagarra & Ellis, 2013) and *Pedro toma* 'Pedro drinks' versus *Pedro tomo* 'Pedro drink $_{1st\ sing}$' (VanPatten et al., 2012)). The differences are not easily noticeable and may take more time and experience to be recognized than more salient contrasts. That is, it is possible that the apparent lack of sensitivity to verbal incongruencies or ungrammaticalities by speakers of morphologically poor languages that has been reported in the literature is partially due to the lack of salience in Spanish verbal marking.

Salience and Verbal Marking

While salience is frequently mentioned as a factor in the findings of L2 research, the role of salience in verbal marking has not often been the object of research. Much research dealing with salience has been concerned with issues of textual enhancement; in other words, externally induced salience. For example, Gass, Svetics, and Lemelin (2003) investigated the role of attention based on different levels of proficiency and different parts of language (syntax, morphosyntax, lexicon). They did this by manipulating instructions and text presentation, making some parts of a text more salient. They found that the greatest improvement from pretest to posttest when items were made salient was in syntax and the least was for the lexicon. With regard to proficiency, there was a diminished effect for the need of items made more salient as a function of proficiency. Winke (2013), in an eye-tracking study, found that textual enhancement (underlining and color) led to what she referred to as noticing, but did not result in greater learning of form. Noticing was important, but was not sufficient for learning (see also Gass, 1997, in the context of interaction-based learning, for an earlier similar statement). In another study, Loewen and Philp (2006) dealt with features that increased salience of recasts. The effectiveness of recasts could be seen in immediate uptake following the recast and in later test scores. Different features of salience (e.g., stress, declarative intonation, interrogative intonation, shortened length) contribute to the differential effectiveness (see review by Sharwood Smith & Truscott, 2014 on externally-manipulated input).

With respect to perceptual salience, Goldschneider and DeKeyser (2001) conducted a meta-analysis of the well-known morpheme order studies of L2 grammatical functors (see also Larsen-Freeman, 1975; Dulay & Burt, 1978) and considered this type of salience (defined as "how easy it is to hear or perceive a given structure," p. 22) as one of five determinants that contribute to a large portion of the variance in the order of acquisition. Their careful consideration of various definitions of perceptual salience provided a platform for further consideration of this construct.

A recent article by Cintrón-Valentín and Ellis (2016) investigates a similar issue by considering psychophysical salience. Specifically, they argue that language learners tend to focus on open-class words such as adjectives, adverbs, and nouns, as opposed to grammatical particles, such as morphological markings. Morphological markings are of "low salience in the language stream" (p. 3), possibly because the more something is used, the more it is abbreviated (cf. Zipf, 1949). The 2016 study, which builds upon earlier work (Cintrón-Valentín & Ellis, 2015), examined to what extent learners attended to verbal morphology and adverbs, and how form-focused instruction could influence the learners' attention. The participants were L1 speakers of Chinese learning Latin morphology. This group of learners

94 Behney, Spinner, Gass, and Valmori

was used because of the lack of verbal morphology in Chinese and the heavy use of verbal morphology in Latin. Participants were placed into one of four groups, a control group and three experimental groups with different types of pretraining: 1) verb grammar explicit instruction, 2) verb salience [textual enhancement], and 3) verb pretraining [which "gives learners opportunity to infer how verb tense morphology works by processing Latin verb forms for temporality and providing feedback on their correctness" (p. 6)]. Pretraining was followed by sentence exposure and then by comprehension tests. Eye-tracking data were also collected. Their results showed that the control group paid greater attention to adverbs (which are presumably more salient) than to verbal endings (see also Ellis & Sagarra, 2010, 2011; and Cintrón-Valentín & Ellis, 2015). However, form-focused instruction was successful at increasing learners' attention to the less salient morphological endings, a process which Cintrón-Valentín and Ellis (2016) refer to as "salience-raising" (p. 7). The study thus demonstrates that while various aspects of language may be naturally more or less salient for some groups of language learners, it may be possible to overcome these patterns.

In a study of Italian morphology in primary school, Whittle and Lyster (2016) investigated the role of form-focused instruction on the acquisition of Italian verb forms (first singular, second singular, and third plural) by L1 Chinese children. They found that form-focused instruction because it provided "salient input" (p. 50) was successful in increasing the accuracy rates of these forms.

Tense in Italian

The study reported in this chapter investigates present and past tense forms in Italian. In Italian, there are three patterns of conjugation of verbs. In the present tense, in the singular, regular verbs add a single vowel to the end of each base form;[1] in the plural, the ending is either bi- or tri-syllabic. Examples are given below (see Table 5.1).

The current focus is on the past tense, which can be expressed in one of two ways in Italian. One is called the *passato remoto* and the other the *passato prossimo*. The former, not often used in everyday speech, more or less parallels the present tense in that it is made up of verb endings added to the base (e.g., *-ai, asti, -ò, -ammo, -aste, -arono*). When used, it refers to something in the distant past. On the other

TABLE 5.1 Italian conjugations

	guardare *(to look at)*	***vedere*** *(to see)*	***dormire*** *(to sleep)*
1st singular	guard*o*	ved*o*	dorm*o*
2nd singular	guard*i*	ved*i*	dorm*i*
3rd singular	guard*a*	ved*e*	dorm*e*
1st plural	guard*iamo*	ved*iamo*	dorm*iamo*
2nd plural	guard*ate*	ved*ete*	dorm*ite*
3rd plural	guard*ano*	ved*ono*	dorm*ono*

hand, the *passato prossimo* is a compound tense that combines the present indicative of the auxiliary verb (*avere* 'have' for transitive and unergative verbs, and *essere* 'be' for unaccusative verbs) with the past participle of the verb (e.g., *ho guardato* 'I looked at,' *ho venduto* 'I sold,' *ho dormito*, 'I slept'). The object of study in this study is the *passato prossimo* for two reasons: 1) it is the commonly used form and the one that students are most exposed to, and 2) it is the more salient of the two and therefore allows us to investigate salience as a contributing factor to the acquisition of morphosyntax. When compared to the Spanish data from Sagarra and Ellis (2013), Italian provides an opportunity to determine the extent to which salience plays a role in recognition of incongruency. The *passato prossimo* stands out *vis-à-vis* the present tense. In particular, the Italian past tense is made up of two words (auxiliary and past participle). The specific comparison between Italian and Spanish is given in examples 7 and 8.[2]

	Language	Present tense	Past tense
(7)	Spanish	*el chico cocina*	*el chico cocinó*
		'the boy cooks'	'the boy cooked'
(8)	Italian	*il ragazzo cucina*	*il ragazzo ha cucinato*
		'the boy cooks'	'the boy cooked' (lit. 'has cooked')

The general question guiding this study is: does the finding of learners' lack of sensitivity to incongruency between verbs and adverbs hold in cases in which the contrast between present and past verbal morphology is more salient, as is the case with the Italian compound past tense? As Ellis (Chapter 2) has noted, "Stimuli with unique features compared to their neighbors (Os in a field of Ts, a red poppy in a field of yellow), "pop out" from the scene but in a shared feature context will not (Os among Qs)" (Treisman & Gelade, 1980). In terms of the linguistic features investigated in the present study, the Spanish difference between *cocina* and *cocinó* (the Os and the Qs) is less salient[3] than the Italian difference between *cucina* and *ha cucinato* (the Os and the Ts).

The research questions are as follows:

RQ1: Are English-speaking learners of Italian sensitive to incongruous adverb meaning/verb tense marking in Italian?
RQ2: Are learners more sensitive to incongruency when the verb is in the past (more salient) than when the verb is in the present?

Method

Participants

The L2 learners in this study were 23 fourth-semester Italian students at a large Midwestern state university. They were all native speakers of English between the ages of 19–24 ($M = 20.74$, $SD = 1.01$). There were 16 females and seven males, and their self-reported proficiency means (on a scale from 1 [very poor] to 5 [excellent]) were:

reading $M = 3.2$, writing $M = 3.0$, listening $M = 2.8$, and speaking $M = 2.1$. The participants had also studied one or two foreign languages other than Italian: Spanish (14), French (five), Latin (four), Mandarin Chinese (two), and German (one).[4] In addition, two participants reported having Italian-speaking grandparents at home and two had visited their family in Italy multiple times. Finally, two participants participated in a 6-week study abroad program in Italy.

Materials

The experimental sentences included 24 nouns (as subjects and direct objects), 31 verbs, and three adverbs of time. They were created by translating the sentences in Sagarra and Ellis (2013) into Italian, adapting them, and creating similar sentences so that they included only Italian transitive regular verbs. Two of the authors in this study, who were experienced teaching instructors at the level of the current participants and who were familiar with the materials used in Italian classes, verified that the words were likely to be known by learners at the level of our participants. This was confirmed through a questionnaire following the experiment in which we asked participants to respond to a 3-point Likert scale as to their knowledge of the word prior to the testing session: 1 ('I do not know this word'), 2 ('I have heard of this word'), or 3 ('I know this word'). The appropriateness of the original selection of words was confirmed with participants responding that they had heard of or had known 94.9% of the words ($M = 56.0$ [out of 59 words], $SD = 3.1$).

There were five practice sentences and 80 experimental sentences. Of the 80 experimental Italian sentences, 32 targeted past and present tense verbs (16 with past adverbs and 16 with present adverbs), and 48 were filler sentences. Both filler and experimental sentences included half congruent and half incongruent sentences. Number and gender incongruencies were used in the filler sentences. Neither the practice sentences nor the fillers included present or past adverbs or the past tense. Experimental sentences contained congruent and incongruent verb-adverb combinations, as in Sagarra and Ellis (2013). There were four versions of each of the 16 sentences with past adverbs and the 16 sentences with present adverbs: (a) adverb—verb congruent; (b) adverb—verb incongruent; (c) verb—adverb congruent; (d) verb—adverb incongruent (See Table 5.2). The sentences were randomized and each participant read only one of the four possible versions. Further, the sentences were controlled for vocabulary and length; all sentences contained regular transitive verbs of three to four syllables and were 10–14 words long.

Procedure

Participants signed a consent form and then completed a background questionnaire, which included information about the foreign languages they had studied (number of years and general proficiency) and their self-rated Italian proficiency in reading, writing, listening, and speaking on a 5-point Likert scale.

TABLE 5.2 Examples of experimental sentences

Condition		Example
Past adverb sentences (*ieri; la settimana scorsa*)	Congruent adverb-verb	*Sappiamo che **ieri** la bambina **ha portato** la torta per il suo compleanno.* 'We know that **yesterday** the girl **brought** the cake for her birthday.'
	Incongruent adverb-verb	**Sappiamo che **ieri** la bambina **porta** la torta per il suo compleanno.* *'We know that **yesterday** the girl **brings** the cake for her birthday.'
	Congruent verb-adverb	*Sappiamo che la bambina **ha portato** la torta **ieri** per il suo compleanno.* 'We know that the girl **brought** the cake **yesterday** for her birthday.'
	Incongruent verb-adverb	**Sappiamo che la bambina **porta** la torta **ieri** per il suo compleanno.* *'We know that the girl **brings** the cake **yesterday** for her birthday.'
Comprehension question		*Era il compleanno della bambina. VERO FALSO* 'It was the girl's birthday.' TRUE FALSE
Present adverb sentences (*adesso*)	Congruent adverb-verb	*Vedo che **adesso** la figlia **studia** francese con un'amica.* 'I see that **now** the daughter **studies** French with a friend.'
	Incongruent adverb-verb	**Vedo che **adesso** la figlia **ha studiato** francese con un'amica.* *'I see that **now** the daughter **studied** French with a friend.'
	Congruent verb-adverb	*Vedo che la figlia **studia** francese **adesso** con un'amica.* 'I see that the daughter **studies** French **now** with a friend.'
	Incongruent verb-adverb	**Vedo che la figlia **ha studiato** francese **adesso** con un'amica.* *'I see that the daughter **studied** French **now** with a friend.'
Comprehension question		*La figlia non ha amiche. VERO FALSO* 'The daughter does not have friends.' TRUE FALSE

Next, participants completed an eye-tracking task. The procedure was carried out on an EyeLink 1000 eye-tracker with a desk-mounted monocular eye-tracking camera, with chin and forehead rest and a 19-inch computer screen. Following a nine-point calibration, participants' eyes were tracked while reading the 85 sentences in Italian. Each sentence was followed by a comprehension question (true-false) in a design partially based on Sagarra and Ellis (2013). The sentences were written in Courier New font size 20 and were double-spaced. To prevent participant fatigue, there was a break after the practice session (five sentences), after every 20 sentences, and upon participants' request. A calibration was carried out after each break.

Sentences stayed on the screen 12 seconds before moving to the comprehension question; comprehension questions timed out after 10 seconds.

There were two interest areas for each sentence, one on the adverbs of time and the other on the verbs. In the case of words with four characters or less (e.g., the adverb *ieri* 'yesterday'), an extra space was added before and after the word as shorter words tend to be skipped.

Analysis

The data were analyzed in two ways: 1) dwell times, and 2) regressions. In the case of dwell times, we considered (a) *early processing*, or the milliseconds it took for the learners' eyes to pass through an interest area before leaving it in either direction, either by moving forward with the reading or by looking back (first run dwell time) (Frenck-Mestre, 2005), and (b) *late processing*, or all fixations occurring in the interest area after the initial pass through. Late processing was calculated by subtracting the first run dwell time from the total dwell time.

Fixation times that were faster than 120 ms were removed from the dataset and those that were two standard deviations above or below the mean were trimmed and replaced with the cutoff value. This is in line with standard procedures in psycholinguistic research (e.g., Rayner & Pollatsek, 1989) to be reasonably confident that participants processed the word. Also removed from the data were those sentences where the comprehension question was incorrectly answered, the assumption being that they had not processed the sentence appropriately.[5] From the initial dataset of 736 sentences, we were left with 582 sentences where the comprehension questions were accurate (79% of the data).

We first conducted a paired samples *t*-test to compare participants' total dwell time on verbs in congruent and incongruent sentences. Then, we conducted two linear mixed models, one on early processing data and one on late processing data, with factors of congruency (congruent versus incongruent), position of the verb in the sentence (adverb-verb versus verb-adverb), and tense of the verb (past versus present).

The last analysis we conducted was a count of regressions out of the point where incongruency became apparent (either verb or adverb). Our assumption relies on the notion of the eye-mind link (Pollatsek, Reichle, & Rayner, 2006; Reichle, Pollatsek, & Rayner 2012; see also Winke, Godfroid, & Gass, 2013). In short, assuming an association between eye movements and the human mind, we can gain insight about difficulties in processing by following the paths of a participant's eyes. When incongruencies are encountered and recognized as such, participants will go back (regress) in an attempt to understand the area of confusion. Regressions, therefore, are a signal that an incongruency has been recognized.

Results

In order to investigate whether the English-speaking learners of Italian were sensitive to incongruous adverb-verb marking in Italian (RQ 1), we compared the average total fixation time on the verb interest area (total dwell time on verbs) for congruous and incongruous target sentences, early and late processing combined. The paired samples t-test showed that participants spent significantly more time on verb interest areas in incongruent sentences (M = 1497, SD = 491.40) than in congruent sentences (M = 1305, SD = 390.26), t (22) = −3.11, p = .005, d = 0.43 regardless of adverb position. Another way to consider the effect of congruency is to consider the number of times participants regressed after having reached the interest area where congruency or incongruency becomes apparent. Taking this analysis into account, we considered all regressions from that point and found approximately an almost equal number of regressions out of incongruent sentences (148) as out of congruent sentences (141). Thus, RQ1 was confirmed with one analysis, but not another.

In order to investigate whether learners are more sensitive to incongruency when the verb is in the past than when it is in the present (RQ 2), we ran two linear mixed model analyses, one on the early processing data and one on the late processing data. These analyses enabled us to take into account the different length of the verbs in the present and past tense. The number of letters of the verbs was thus included in the linear mixed models as a random and a fixed effect. With the mixed model analyses, we tested the possible effects of congruency (congruent/incongruent), verb position (adverb/verb or verb/adverb), and tense of verb (past/present) on early processing (i.e., first run dwell time) and late processing (i.e., total dwell time minus first run dwell time). Table 5.3 shows the descriptive data for early and late processing for the different levels of congruency, verb position, and tense.

Results (see Table 5.4) show that there was a significant difference in learners' early processing of the verbs according to the verb tense, with participants fixating on verbs in the past tense significantly longer than verbs in the present tense regardless of their congruency with the adverbs, even after word length is accounted for. There was no significant main effect of either congruency or verb position in early processing. The participants in this study thus spent more time looking at past tense verbs than present tense verbs upon first encountering them, regardless of congruency.

However, the analysis of participants' late processing of the verbs showed a different pattern; here, participants did not spend more time on verbs in the past tense, as there was no significant main effect of verb tense. The main effects of congruency and verb position, which approach significance (see Table 5.4), show that learners fixated longer on the verb when the verb was in the first position and when the tense of the verb was incongruent with the adverb.

More interesting from our perspective was the number of regressions that occurred after reaching the point where a sentence became congruous or incongruous. Our research question asked whether sentences with past tense incongruencies were more likely to trigger more regressions than sentences with present tense verb incongruencies. We did find this to be the case with 85 regressions out of the incongruent past tense interest areas compared to 63 regressions out of incongruous present tense interest areas. In both instances, there was not a big difference

TABLE 5.3 Descriptive statistics

Measure	Congruency	Tense of verb	Verb position	M	SD	Verb position	Tense of verb	M	SD
Early processing	Congruent	Present	1	517.31	283.66	2	Present	518.95	299.63
		Past	1	850.94	435.69	2	Past	881.79	453.74
	Incongruent	Present	1	553.93	368.24	2	Present	549.88	240.79
		Past	1	922.16	488.43	2	Past	852.41	513.31
Late processing	Congruent	Present	1	805.86	528.80	2	Present	752.54	536.39
		Past	1	1184.95	763.61	2	Past	1002.96	734.83
	Incongruent	Present	1	1047.74	669.81	2	Present	797.02	567.25
		Past	1	1213.52	808.01	2	Past	1214.83	747.45

TABLE 5.4 Results of mixed model analysis of participants' early and late processing of verb interest areas

Measure	Variable	F	df	p
Early processing	Congruency	.513	537	.474
	Verb position	.096	537	.757
	Tense of verb	6.804	537	.009
Late processing	Congruency	3.490	417	.062
	Verb position	3.296	417	.070
	Tense of verb	.001	417	.975

between the triggering element with an approximate equal amount of triggering coming from adverbs as from verbs (42 adverbs versus 43 verbs, in the case of past tense incongruencies; 34 adverbs versus 29 verbs, in the case of present tense incongruencies).

Discussion

Congruency (Research Question 1)

The first research question asked whether English-speaking learners of Italian were sensitive to incongruent adverb meaning/verb tense marking in Italian. The data were analyzed by comparing all congruent with all incongruent sentences, regardless of adverb placement and regardless of tense. The *t*-test showed that the overall total dwell time that learners spent on incongruent sentences was longer than on congruent sentences, indicating that learners were indeed sensitive to tense/adverb incongruency.

This awareness of a mismatch between the verb and adverb did not, however, induce learners to regress out of the second element (i.e., the point—the verb or adverb—at which they became aware of the incongruency) of the incongruent sentences more than they did out of the second element in sentences that did not contain any mismatch—that is, that were congruent. We suggest that although the incongruency or mismatch was prominent enough to slow the learners down as they read the incongruent sentences, the learners were not sophisticated enough in their L2 proficiency to understand the precise locus of the incongruency that would have allowed them to go back into the sentence to search out the source of the mismatch. Similar suggestions were made by Gass (1983) who found that learners were able to identify the general locus of errors in their own sentences before being able to identify and/or correct the particulars of their own errors.

Additionally, the second linear mixed model on late processing found that learners spent more time fixating on verbs in incongruent sentences than in congruent sentences, which is also evidence that these English-speaking learners of Italian are in fact sensitive to mismatches between adverb meaning and verb tense. The fact that learners were sensitive to incongruency only in the late processing (as was seen in Table 5.4) could be explained by the possibility that it takes longer for low proficiency learners to recognize a problem in the sentence. In early processing, the learners do not show sensitivity to incongruency. This may be a reflection of the low proficiency level of these learners resulting in relatively slow processing. In other words, recognition of incongruency may take longer.

Present and Past (Research Question 2)

The second research question asked if learners were more sensitive to incongruency in past verbs than in present verbs. The first linear mixed model analysis showed that in general, learners spent more time looking at verbs that were in the past tense than at verbs that were in the present tense the first time that they passed through the sentence (i.e., first run dwell time), even compensating for the longer length of past tense verbs. Therefore, the salience of a two-word compound verb resulted in greater attention by the learners as they passed through the verb interest areas the first time.

As further evidence of the importance of the salience of the two-word past tense as compared to the single-word present tense, learners showed more regressions out of the verb interest areas in incongruent sentences if the verb was past tense ($N = 85$) than they did if the verb was present tense ($N = 63$). Both types of sentences showed mismatches in tense, but those where the verb was past tense were more salient to the learners and resulted in more regressions out.

The findings of sensitivity to incongruency in our study contrast with those of VanPatten et al. (2012), who found that English-speaking learners at a non-advanced level were not sensitive to ungrammaticalities in Spanish agreement marking. The argument that we put forward for this difference in findings is the fact that the contrast between morphological markers in the VanPatten et al. study was much less salient (one letter change) than the contrast between markers in the current study (one versus two words). That is, the more salient marking of past tense in Italian may have made it easier for learners to attend to it in the input which may, in turn, lead to a more robust representation in the interlanguage grammar. The two-word status of the past tense Italian verb compared to the one-word present tense results in greater apperception by the learner than the much less salient one-letter difference in Spanish (see, e.g., Gass, 1988).

Assuming that this explanation is plausible, we suggest that there are two possibilities to explain the importance of salience in learners' sensitivity to morphological marking. First, it is possible that the salience of morphological marking is crucial for all learners; that is, L2 learners with any L1 background will show greater sensitivity to morphological marking (or at least demonstrate sensitivity to it on an online task such as the one presented in this chapter) if the marking is more salient. The other possibility is that the salience of morphological marking is facilitated for learners who speak languages with little inflectional morphology (e.g., English, Chinese), whereas speakers of languages with rich morphology are not similarly advantaged by salience.

We note too that verbs trigger more regressions than adverbs in general (155 versus 134). It may be that learners are more tuned into the importance of verbal morphology than commonly assumed of English learners (see for example Sagarra & Ellis, 2013) and therefore are more likely to go back into the sentence to resolve mismatches by verbs than by adverbs. This finding too could be related to the salience of the verb as compared to the adverb.

Finally, because of the finding of the differences between how learners process past and present verbs in relation to (in)congruency, we compared regressions out of all present verb sentences with all past verb sentences (regardless of congruency). There was only a small difference with regressions out of present tense verb interest areas being about equal to regressions out of past tense verb interest areas (147 versus 142). This finding suggests that salience alone (past versus present) does not result in a greater number of regressions. Rather when incongruencies are encountered, salience plays an important role when considering whether or not those incongruencies are recognized.

Conclusion

The findings of this study suggest that the salience of tense marking plays a role in L2 learners' sensitivity to incongruencies in online tasks. Fourth-semester learners of Italian completed an eye-tracking task where they read sentences that were congruent and incongruent in terms of tense marking (adverb meaning/verb tense). They showed sensitivity to incongruency in the total dwell time that they spent fixating the verbs overall. They also showed sensitivity to incongruency in late processing. In early processing, they spent more time fixating on past tense verbs. Finally, they showed more regressions out of incongruent verbs when that incongruent verb was in the past tense than in the present tense. We argue that the compound nature of the verb in the Italian past tense (perceptual salience) and its comparison to the one-word present tense make it more salient to L2 learners, like the red poppies on a field of yellow in Ellis' psychophysical explanation of salience. It may be that learners whose L1s are morphologically poor languages are not sensitive to L2 morphological incongruencies when those incongruencies lack salience. Our data suggest, on the other hand, that when the verbal morphology is salient, sensitivity is apparent.

There are, however, further questions that remain. First, is this importance of salience true of all speakers, or just those with morphologically poor L1s like the English learners in our study? Second, is the importance of salience true for tense marking only, or for all kinds of morphological marking? All these questions are crucial as we continue to understand how L2 learners process morphology in the different contexts in which they occur.

Acknowledgements

We are grateful to SeHoon Jung for assistance with data analysis and to Aline Godfroid whose feedback on ways to analyze the data helped us through many aspects of the process of analysis. We further thank those in the audience of SLRF 2015 who provided us with helpful feedback. Despite all this help, all errors are our own.

Notes

1 Irregular verbs often modify the base forms. Base forms ending in vowels (*mangiare*, 'to eat') do not double the *-i* in the second person singular. Thus, 'you eat' is *mangi* and not *mangii*.
2 Spanish has a similar construction (*haber* + past participle) which is used similarly to the present perfect in English. It appears to have the meaning of the English present perfect. Italian past has a true past meaning and does not have the same distribution as Spanish *haber* + participle. Importantly, Sagarra and Ellis (2013) used the one-word past tense and ours was a comparison with their study.
3 The difference is likely to be less obvious in the written form where there is a single letter difference (a versus ó) as opposed to aural input where the accented final syllable may make the difference more obvious. However, even in aural input, the difference may not be easily perceptible. In an experiment reported in Cintrón-Valentín and Ellis (2016), the authors dealt with differences in aural and written modality finding that attention is more effective in the written mode as opposed to the aural mode. As they (2016) point out, "the fleeting nature of spoken language does not afford listeners the control of scrutiny of input as does visual presentation, and these differences could well affect the degree to which forms are salient in the input" (p. 18).
4 Some of the students had studied more than one language. However, none of them had any great familiarity with any of these languages.
5 There is not uniformity of opinion as to the viability of removing sentences when comprehension is not accurate. We took the more conservative approach and removed such sentences, leaving us with a set of sentences about which we felt confident that some processing had occurred.

References

Cerezo, L., Caras, A., & Leow, R. (2016). The effectiveness of guided induction versus deductive instruction on the development of complex Spanish *gustar* structures: An analysis of learning outcomes and processes. *Studies in Second Language Acquisition, 38*, 265–291.

Cintrón-Valentín, M., & Ellis, N. (2015). Exploring the interface: Explicit focus-on-form instruction and learned attentional biases in L2 Latin. *Studies in Second Language Acquisition, 37*, 197–235.

Cintrón-Valentín, M., & Ellis, N. (2016). Salience in second language acquisition: Physical form, learner attention, and instructional focus. *Frontiers in Psychology, 7*, 1–21.

Clahsen, H., & Felser, C. (2006a). Continuity and shallow structures in language processing. *Applied Psycholinguistics, 27*, 107–126.

Clahsen, H., & Felser, C. (2006b). Grammatical processing in language learners. *Applied Psycholinguistics, 27*, 3–42.

Dulay, H., & Burt, M. (1978). Some remarks on creativity in language acquisition. In W. Ritchie (Ed.), *Second language research: Issues and implications* (pp. 65–89). New York: Academic Press.

Ellis, N. C. (2016). Salience, cognition, language complexity, and complex adaptive systems. *Studies in Second Language Acquisition, 38*, 341–351.

Ellis, N. C., & Sagarra, N. (2010). The bounds of adult language acquisition: Blocking and learned attention. *Studies in Second Language Acquisition, 32*, 553–580.

Ellis, N. C., & Sagarra, N. (2011). Learned attention in adult language acquisition: A replication and generalization study and meta-analysis. *Studies in Second Language Acquisition, 33*(4), 589–624.

Franceschina, F. (2005). *Fossilized second language grammars: The acquisition of grammatical gender*. Amsterdam: John Benjamins.

Frenck-Mestre, C. (2005). Eye-movement recording as a tool for studying syntactic processing in a second language: A review of methodologies and experimental findings. *Second Language Research, 21*, 175–198.

Gass, S. (1983). The development of L2 intuitions. *TESOL Quarterly, 17*, 273–291.

Gass, S. (1988). Integrating research areas: A framework for second language studies. *Applied Linguistics, 9*, 198–217.

Gass, S. (1997). *Input, interaction and the second language learner.* Mahwah, NJ: Lawrence Erlbaum Associates.

Gass, S., Svetics, I., & Lemelin, S. (2003). Differential effects of attention. *Language Learning, 53*, 497–545.

Goldschneider, J., & DeKeyser, R. (2001). Explaining the "natural order of L2 morpheme acquisition" in English: A meta-analysis of multiple determinants. *Language Learning, 51*, 1–50.

Hawkins, R., & Liszka, S. (2003). Locating the source of defective past tense marking in advanced L2 English speakers. In R. van Hout, A. Hulk, F. Kuiken, & R. Towell (Eds.), *The interface between syntax and lexicon in second language acquisition* (pp. 21–44). Amsterdam: John Benjamins.

Larsen-Freeman, D. (1975). The acquisition of grammatical morphemes by adult ESL students. *TESOL Quarterly, 9*, 409–419.

Loewen, S., & Philp, J. (2006). Recasts in the adult English L2 classroom: Characteristics, explicitness, and effectiveness. *The Modern Language Journal, 90*, 536–556.

Pollatsek, A., Reichle, E., & Rayner, K. (2006). Tests of the E-Z Reader model: Exploring the interface between cognition and eye-movement control. *Cognitive Psychology, 52*, 1–56.

Rayner, K., & Pollatsek, A. (1989). *The psychology of reading.* Englewood Cliffs, NJ: Prentice Hall.

Reichle, E., Pollatsek, A., & Rayner, K. (2012). Using E-Z Reader to simulate eye movements in nonreading tasks: A unified framework for understanding the eye-mind link. *Psychological Review, 119*, 155–185.

Sagarra, N., & Ellis, N. (2013). From seeing adverbs to seeing verbal morphology: Language experience and adult acquisition of L2 tense. *Studies in Second Language Acquisition, 35*, 261–290.

Sharwood Smith, M., & Truscott, J. (2014). Explaining input enhancement: A MOGUL perspective. *International Review of Applied Linguistics in Language Teaching, 52*, 253–281.

Slabakova, R. (2013). *Second language acquisition.* Oxford: Oxford University Press.

Tomlin, R. S., & Villa, V. (1994). Attention in cognitive science and second language acquisition. *Studies in Second Language Acquisition, 16*, 183–203.

Treisman, A. M., & Gelade, G. (1980). A feature-integration theory of attention. *Cognitive Psychology, 12*, 97–136.

VanPatten, B. (2007). Input processing in adult second language acquisition. In B. VanPatten & J. Williams (Eds.), *Theories in second language acquisition: An introduction* (pp. 115–135). Mahwah, NJ: Lawrence Erlbaum Associates.

VanPatten, B., & Keating, G. D. (2007, April). *Getting tense.* Paper presented at the annual meeting of the American Association of Applied Linguistics, Costa Mesa, CA.

VanPatten, B., Keating, G. D., & Leeser, M. J. (2012). Missing verbal inflections as a representational problem: Evidence from self-paced reading. *Linguistic Approaches to Bilingualism, 2*, 109–140.

Whittle, A., & Lyster, R. (2016). Focus on Italian verbal morphology in multilingual classes. *Langauge Learning, 66*, 31–59.

Winke, P. (2013). The effects of input enhancement on grammar learning and comprehension: A modified replication of Lee (2007) with eye-movement data. *Studies in Second Language Acquisition, 35,* 323–352.

Winke, P., Godfroid, A., & Gass, S. (2013). Introduction to the special issue: Eye-movement recordings in second language research. *Studies in Second Language Acquisition, 35,* 205–212.

Zipf, G. K. (1949). *Human behaviour and the principle of least effort: An introduction to human ecology.* Cambridge, MA: Addison-Wesley.

6

THE EFFECT OF PERCEPTUAL SALIENCE ON PROCESSING L2 INFLECTIONAL MORPHOLOGY

Hannelore Simoens, Alex Housen, and Ludovic De Cuypere

Introduction

Acquiring grammatical morphology is a daunting task for most second language (L2) learners (Collins et al., 2009; DeKeyser, 2005; Williams, 2005). Research investigating the L2 acquisition of inflectional morphology has suggested a lack of sensitivity in processing L2 inflectional morphemes, with the premise that it is processing difficulty that makes its acquisition so difficult (Cintrón-Valentín & N. Ellis, 2015; N. Ellis & Larsen-Freeman, 2006; Godfroid & Uggen, 2013; Hopp, 2010; Leung & Williams, 2011, 2012; Marsden, Williams, & Liu, 2013; Prévost & White, 2000). One of the factors impinging on the early stages of L2 processing is the salience of the morpheme in question. Salience affects—either in a facilitative or constraining way—learners' access to the morpheme in the L2 input by interacting with the cognitive mechanisms of attention and awareness (Collins et al., 2009; Schmidt, 1990, 1993). Without salience, L2 learners easily gloss over the language feature, thereby failing to attend and, consequently, to learn it. This is especially the case in implicit learning contexts, where learners are left to their own devices to pick up regularities from the input. In fact, salience has been shown to be a driving force in many implicit learning contexts (Van Den Bos & Poletiek, 2008), yet SLA research has only just begun to consider its influence (cf. Carroll, 2012; DeKeyser, 2005; Goldschneider & DeKeyser, 2001; Sagarra & N. Ellis, 2013). The study discussed in this chapter uses eye-tracking and verbal reports to explore how salience impacts on the processing[1] of L2 inflectional morphology, with a special focus on how *perceptual* salience interacts with the learner's allocation of attention and awareness to perceive and select target features in the input and turn them into intake—processes which have been claimed to represent the crucial first steps in the chain of cognitive processes that may ultimately lead to learning (i.e., the formation of a mental representation in long-term memory) (Schmidt, 1990, 2001; Tomlin & Villa, 1994; Robinson, 1995; Williams, 2005).

The next section considers the link between salience and the constructs of attention, awareness, and intake, all of which are directly related to input processing (see VanPatten, 2009), or the passage between input and intake. Given that "intake is by definition the information that can subsequently be used for acquisition" (Truscott & Sharwood Smith, 2011, p. 498), the conversion of input to intake is central to an understanding of SLA, as is the study of factors that steer and mediate this process.

Salience and L2 Processing

The human mind can only process a limited part of the input that it receives from perceptual experience (Carrasco, 2011). The selection mechanism that underlies the decision of which elements in the input receive further cognitive processing therefore plays a central role, serving as an information gating system. Attention plays a key role in this process, because it turns looking into seeing, thereby selecting relevant information out of irrelevant noise (for reviews, see Carrasco, 2011; Tatler, Hayhoe, Land, & Ballard, 2011).

Also in cognitive SLA research, the study of attention has occupied a central place (e.g., Alanen, 1995; Gass, Svetics, & Lemelin, 2003; Leow, 1998; Robinson, 1996a, 1996b; Schmidt, 2001; Tomlin & Villa, 1994). Although its precise nature and role in SLA have always been a matter of debate, it is now generally agreed that L2 learners are exposed to more input than they can cope with and that attention is important in accounting for the ways that learners sort through the input. Schmidt (2001), for instance, claims that attention "is necessary in order to understand virtually every aspect of second language acquisition" (p. 1), further suggesting that "SLA is largely driven by what learners pay attention to" (p. 2).

Importantly, the selection of information in the input is driven by two types of attentional mechanisms. Top-down mechanisms allocate attention as determined by the task demands, the learner's intentions, or other explicit user-driven means; in implicit learning contexts, however, attention is mostly captured by bottom-up mechanisms (Navalpakkam, Koch, Rangel, & Perona, 2010; Parkhurst, Law, & Niebur, 2002; Peters, Iyer, Itti, & Koch, 2005; Tatler, Baddeley, & Gilchrist, 2005).

Bottom-up processing occurs when attention is attracted to stimuli in an automatic, unconscious manner. This occurs when the stimulus is sufficiently *salient*—that is, when it is sufficiently *distinct* from the context in which it is embedded. Salience can result from the physical properties of a stimulus, and/or from affective or cognitive factors (N. Ellis, 2016; Sagarra & N. Ellis, 2013). In the present study, salience only refers to the physical characteristics of the stimulus itself, that is, *physical* or *perceptual* salience (for an overview of other determinants and types of salience, such as psychological salience, see Gass et al., Chapter 1; Sagarra & N. Ellis, 2013; N. Ellis, 2016; N. Ellis, Chapter 2). The term *perceptual salience* then, refers to the quality of a stimulus to stand out by virtue of its physical properties such as its size, intensity, clarity, or location (Styles, 2006). Within SLA research, sentence position (Barcroft & VanPatten, 1997; Carroll, 2012; VanPatten, 1996), word length (Carroll, 2012; Streefkerk, 2002), and syllable stress (de Jong, 1995)—amongst other linguistic properties—have been claimed to contribute to the perceptual salience of lexical items. For grammatical morphology, the linguistic phenomenon investigated in the present study, perceptual salience has been associated with the number of phones or (in written input) letters (i.e., phonetic or orthographic substance), the presence of a vowel in the morpheme's surface form (syllabicity), and the total relative sonority of the morpheme (Brown, 1973; Collins et al., 2009; Godfroid, 2016; Godfroid & Uggen, 2013; Goldschneider & DeKeyser, 2001).

The assumption is that salient stimuli are more likely to be perceived and attended to, and hence, are more likely to enter into subsequent processing and, ultimately, learning (N. Ellis, 2016; Schmidt, 1990, 1995, 2001). Conversely, but equally important, stimuli that are not salient may escape attention altogether. Recent research on visual processing has shown that stimuli that are made less salient by their peripheral location in the visual field are never perceived, regardless of their importance (Pringle, Irwin, Kramer, & Atchley, 2001; Rensink, 2002; Stelzer & Wickens, 2006). Also in the SLA literature, it has been argued that non-salient linguistic features, such as unvoiced consonants or sounds at the end of phrases, are often insufficiently perceived, and hence not readily incorporated into the learner's speech system (see Ellis, 2006a, 2006b; Robinson, 1995; Schmidt, 2001; Wickens, 2007). L2 learners may thus fail to detect a number of linguistic features that are present but that are not perceptually salient in the input.

Clearly, bottom-up attention to perceptually salient stimuli is an important part of our language learning abilities. However, the case for a link between perceptual salience and awareness may be less clear, in part because the nature, role, and importance of awareness in SLA is more elusive and contentious.

The specific details of the main theoretical models of awareness in SLA, and its relationship with attention and intake (Gass, 1997; McLaughlin, 1987; Robinson, 1995, 1996a; Schmidt, 1990, 1993, 1995, 2001; Swain, 2005; Tomlin & Villa, 1994; VanPatten, 2007) are less relevant here (see Leow and Bowles [2005] for a review, and Leow [2015] for an ambitious attempt to synthesize and reconcile them). The most widely accepted view (though not held by Tomlin and Villa [1994]), which draws on Schmidt's Noticing Hypothesis, is that "awareness entails attention" (Gass et al., 2003) and that attention controls access to 'awareness as noticing.' Awareness as noticing represents an intermediate form of attention (in between awareness as perception and awareness as understanding), a cognitive state where stimuli are subjectively experienced. Awareness as noticing has been posited as necessary "for converting input to intake" and, hence, as "necessary for language learning" (Schmidt, 1990, p. 129). As Truscott and Sharwood Smith (2011) point out, awareness as "[n]oticing is more than just awareness of input; it involves awareness specifically of forms in the input" (p. 501).

Without some level of awareness, input is processed too shallowly to be cognitively registered, or 'taken in.' Intake is "what is both detected and then further activated following the allocations of attentional resources from a central executive" (Robinson, 1995, p. 297).

In sum, most theoretical models of the cognitive processes in SLA allow for at least a facilitatory if not a necessary role of some form of awareness in the early phases of acquisition—that is, in the conversion of input to intake, especially awareness of linguistic forms. Under this scenario, a role for perceptual salience in capturing learners' awareness of linguistic stimuli in the input and on intake can be hypothesized. However, while there is general agreement on the importance of awareness as noticing for learning single items or simple and reliable rules (e.g., DeKeyser, 2005; Hulstijn, 1995; Leow, 2009), the role of awareness in learning irregular, unreliable, and pattern-based features of language, such as much of grammatical morphology (the linguistic phenomenon investigated in the current study), is more contested (Godfroid & Uggen, 2013; Williams, 2005).

Despite its apparent importance in determining bottom-up attention and possibly also mediating awareness, not many empirical studies have directly investigated the influence of salience on L2 processes. Exceptions are Carroll (2006); Barcroft and B. VanPatten (1997), and the work by DeKeyser and N. Ellis and their respective collaborators. However, even in these studies salience is often invoked post-hoc, rather than being the primary or independent variable of investigation. For instance, Goldschneider and DeKeyser (2001) conducted a meta-analysis that investigated the natural order of morpheme acquisition by looking at five objective properties of grammatical morphemes: perceptual salience, semantic complexity, morphophonological regularity, syntactic category, and frequency. Results showed that a composite salience factor contributed most strongly to the observed order. Perceptual salience has also been called upon to explain that L2 learners produce lexical cues for time before they produce the equivalent inflectional cues (tense markers) (N. Ellis & Sagarra, 2010, 2011; Sagarra & N. Ellis, 2013), one of the reasons being that temporal adverbs are perceptually more salient than verbal inflections (because adverbs are independent items and appear more often at sentence-initial positions). The low salience of verbal inflections is thought to make them less perceptible in the L2 input and hence less susceptible to learning processes (N. Ellis, 2006, 2016; Goldschneider & DeKeyser, 2001).

In conclusion, there are both theoretical arguments and increasing empirical evidence to suggest that salience is a key determinant of L2 learners' processing and learning. To move beyond *post-hoc* accounts, however, we need to empirically investigate how L2 learners actually process L2 features with various degrees of salience (see also Cintrón-Valentín & Ellis, 2015, 2016). The present study set out to do this for inflectional features of language.

The general research questions which the current study sought to answer are the following: what is the effect of the perceptual salience of L2 inflectional morphemes on L2 learners' processing of these morphemes in written input, and how is this effect mediated by the conditions of the task that learners perform?

The study is specifically set in the context of implicit learning during a meaning-focused reading task performed under two different task conditions (created by introducing two different secondary tasks at some point during the reading task). To address the general research questions, we recorded L2 learners' eye movements to high and low-salient inflectional morphemes in written texts with an eye-tracker, which provides measures of readers' cognitive processing, particularly attentional processing (cf. Rayner, 2009; Winke, Godfroid, & Gass, 2013). Eye-tracking is also particularly suited to investigate the perceptual processes that underlie salience (Schütz, Braun, & Gegenfurtner, 2011). In addition, we also elicited immediate retrospective verbal reports to gauge learners' awareness of the target morphemes (Bowles, 2010; Egi, 2004; Leow & Bowles, 2005; Truscott & Sharwood Smith, 2011).

The specific research questions of the study are the following (with operational constructs to be defined in the following sections):

RQ1a: What is the effect of the perceptual salience of L2 inflectional morphemes on L2 learners' attentional *perception* (viewing) of the target morphemes (as operationalized by learners' eye movements; more specifically the *skipping rate* of the target morphemes, reflecting low-level or early-stage attentional processing)?

RQ1b: Is there a difference in the effect of the perceptual salience of L2 inflectional morphemes on L2 learners' *perception* of these morphemes when operating under an *implicit versus explicit processing condition* (as operationalised by a difference in the nature of the secondary task that learners had to perform while reading, viz., answering comprehension questions versus making grammatical judgments)?

RQ2a: What is the effect of the perceptual salience of L2 inflectional morphemes on L2 learners' further attentional processing as reflected in their *grammatical sensitivity* to these morphemes, which in turn can be taken as indicative of *intake* (and as operationalized by learners' eye movements, more specifically the difference in fixation times between grammatical versus ungrammatical uses of the target morphemes, reflecting sensitivity to aspects of the form-meaning properties of these morphemes)?

RQ2b: Is there a difference in the effect of the perceptual salience of L2 inflectional morphemes on L2 learners' grammatical sensitivity to these morphemes when operating under an *implicit* versus *explicit* processing condition?

RQ3a: What is the effect of the perceptual salience of L2 inflectional morphemes on L2 learners' *awareness* of these morphemes (as operationalized by learners' reporting of form and/or meaning-related properties of the target morphemes during retrospective verbal reports)?

RQ3b: Is there a difference in the effect of the perceptual salience of L2 inflectional morphemes on L2 learners' *awareness* of these morphemes when operating under an *implicit* versus *explicit* processing condition?

We hypothesize for research questions (1a), (2a), and (3a) that higher perceptual salience of the target structure leads to: (a) more early attentional processing—that is, more perception of the target morpheme (i.e., less skipping and longer fixation times); (b) higher grammatical sensitivity to ungrammatical instances of the target morphemes, suggesting (more) intake (or low-level implicit learning/knowledge);[2] and (c) a higher rate of reporting and, hence, higher awareness of the target morpheme.

In addition, and in line with Robinson's (1995, 2001) proposal that task conditions may modulate the extent and nature of L2 input processing top-down to the extent that under explicit task conditions bottom-up attentional processing (as engendered by perceptual salience) is overruled by the kind of top-down attentional processing that the explicit task condition engenders, we hypothesize for the (b) research questions that learners in the explicit processing condition will show less skipping, and higher grammatical sensitivity to and higher awareness of both the low- and the high-salient morphemes. That is, we expect to see no (or very little) effect of perceptual salience in skipping rate, grammatical sensitivity, or verbal reporting in the explicit task condition.

Method

Participants

Twenty-eight native speakers of Dutch participated voluntarily in the study.[3] They were either students or staff members at the Vrije University Brussel, Belgium. Their ages ranged from 18–57 years (Mean$_{age}$ = 31; SD$_{age}$ = 11; although this age range appears to be large, there was only one participant older than 50). They all reported proficient knowledge of English, which is important given that the semi-artificial target language is largely based on English. All participants also had at least some knowledge of another L2 (particularly French, Spanish, German, and Italian), but none of these languages contained the target structure. They furthermore had normal or corrected-to-normal vision, and were naïve regarding the purpose of the experiment.

Importantly, while every participant was first exposed to the same training, they were randomly assigned to one of two task conditions, an implicit condition (n = 14; Mean$_{age}$ = 36; SD$_{age}$ = 11) that included a yes/no-comprehension question after each sentence, or an explicit condition (n = 14; Mean$_{age}$ = 26; SD$_{age}$ = 8) that included a yes/no-comprehension question after each sentence. This was done to avoid the possibility that the online L2 processing behavior of the participants would vary according to whether the secondary task was a meaning-based comprehension question or a grammaticality judgment (cf. Leeser, Brandl, & Weissglass, 2011). Given our choice of a semi-artificial language, we could not use native controls.

Materials

Target Language

In the present study, participants' eyes were tracked while they read 240 sentences in a semi-artificial language. The use of a semi-artificial language has been shown to be useful for various reasons. It not only has the advantage of controlling previous knowledge and outside exposure, but perhaps more importantly, it allows the researcher to remove a number of linguistic constraints on an already complex experimental design (DeKeyser, 1995). Compared to coping with a fully artificial—and hence, fully novel—language, a semi-artificial language is also more advantageous because it does not deplete available cognitive resources as it is already partly or even largely acquired (Rogers, Révész, & Rebuschat, 2015). We have combined English, as the participants' well-known L2, with two artificially constructed inflectional morphemes as the target of this study. This led to the creation of a semi-artificial language, which is henceforth referred to as *Englishti*. Englishti is lexically, morphologically, and syntactically entirely built on English, but with additional artificial inflections on the noun.

Target Morphemes

Nouns in Englishti can receive a possessive suffix, either "-olp" or "-u," that agrees in biological gender with accompanying possessive pronominal determinatives "his" and "her," respectively, hence "*his* hotel*olp*" and "*her* hotel*u*." This rule does not apply in any of the participants' known languages (though it applies in other languages such as Turkish, Persian, Arabic, and Finnish). The two suffixes in question differ in perceptual salience, which in this study has been operationalised as the visual length (or orthographic substance) of the morpheme, corresponding to its number of letters. Following this criterion, the artificial inflection "-olp" is, with three letters, considered to be the perceptually high-salient morpheme, whereas the artificial inflection "-u" is with one letter considered to be the perceptually low-salient one. The two morphemes have also been controlled for a range of other potentially intervening variables, including: 1) their presence in the participants' L1 or other languages the participants knew, 2) their phonotactical permissibility in the participants' L1 and in English, 3) their position in a word as suffixes, 4) the first letter being a vowel (to avoid consonant clusters with final stem letters), and 5) low mono- and trigram frequency (to avoid the formation of existing words when suffixes are attached).

The two target suffixes are attached to existing English noun stems that are further controlled for: 1) grammatical category (only nouns), 2) morphological structure (only simple nouns), 3) frequency (only words in high-frequency word band of Zipf scale [Brysbaert & New, 2009]), 4) syllabicity (two syllables), 5) ambiguity (no meaning ambiguity), 6) predictability (not predictable from context; via pretesting), 7) cognate status with Dutch (at least partial overlap with Dutch [Van Assche, Duyck, & Brysbaert, 2013]), 8) neighborhood density (maximum two neighbors; via WordGen [Duyck, Desmet, Verbeke, & Brysbaert, 2004]), 9) concreteness (only concrete nouns; via concreteness ratings [Brysbaert, Warriner, & Kuperman, 2014]), and 10) biological gender (only nouns without clear gender). We also used short (five-letter) and long (seven-letter) word stems to control for potential length effects that would make one critical noun stem + suffix combination more salient than the other (via WordGen [Duyck et al., 2004]). On the basis of these criteria, we selected 40 noun stems in total.

The critical noun stem + suffix combinations were embedded in a sentence context that was as consistent as possible, both within and across sentences. Each critical sentence, also called a critical item, consisted of eight words. The critical noun stem + suffix combinations always appeared as a direct object in the sixth position, with the two preceding and the two following words being tightly controlled. This is to avoid potential influences of sentence context on the processing of the target suffixes, for instance, in parafoveal and spillover regions (Keating & Jegerski, 2015). The critical items also only contained highly frequent vocabulary (according to Zipf scale [Brysbaert & New, 2009]). Finally, the critical items were interspersed with filler items.

Training Phase

Unbeknownst to the participants, the reading task consisted of two phases: a training phase and a testing phase. During the training phase, the participants only had to read the blocks of texts and answer yes/no comprehension questions (see upcoming "Instructions" and "Procedures" sections). The participants were thus flooded with 160 written Englishti sentences, of which 40 contained the critical suffixes. Twenty noun stems therefore appeared twice with critical suffixes, once with "-u" and once with "-olp," totalling 20 sentences with the perceptually low-salient "-u" morpheme and 20 sentences with the perceptually high-salient "-olp" morpheme. For each critical item in the training phase, there were three filler items. In other words, the 40 critical items were matched with 120 fillers, resulting in 40 story blocks of each four sentences with only one critical item per block. The purpose of the fillers was to obscure the critical items and thus the specific research objectives from participants (Keating & Jegerski, 2015). For the same purpose, each story in the training phase contained one distractor, a fully artificial lexical word that was generated with WordGen (Duyck et al., 2004). The sentences within each block had a fixed order, but the blocks were pseudorandomized so that a critical item was always followed by a filler item. The critical items in the training phase always involved grammatical instances of the target morphemes, i.e., *his* with "-olp" and *her* with "-u" (e.g., "*his* hotel*olp*," "*her* hotel*u*").

Testing Phase

The training was followed by a testing phase of 80 written sentences, of which 40 contained the critical suffixes. In this testing phase, 20 noun stem + suffix combinations from the training were repeated once, either with "-u" or "-olp," and completed with 20 novel noun stem + suffix combinations that also appeared only once, either with "-u" or "-olp," to test the participants' ability to generalize. This produced 20 exposures to the perceptually low-salient "-u" morpheme and 20 exposures to the perceptually high-salient "-olp" morpheme. The 40 critical items in the testing phase were interspersed with 40 filler items, resulting in 80 individual sentences. The sentences in the testing phase were pseudorandomised so that no two critical items followed each other. In contrast to the training phase, where all critical items are grammatical, in the testing phase half of the critical items incorporated a mismatch between the cue and the morpheme, hence rendering ungrammatical target morphemes, i.e., *his* with "-u" and *her* with "-olp" (e.g., "*his* *hotel*u*," "*her* *hotel*olp*"). The critical items were therefore counterbalanced across participants to avoid the possibility that factors other than those studied were responsible for the obtained results. Participants who had intake of the critical morphemes were expected to have longer eye-fixation times on the ungrammatical items than on the grammatical control items. In other words, by comparing participants' eye-fixation durations for the matched grammatical and ungrammatical items, one can infer whether participants show online sensitivity towards the critical inflectional morphemes (cf. Godfroid, 2016; Leeser et al., 2011).

Instructions

The participants were told that the study's purpose was to investigate how L2 learners read from a computer screen (Godfroid, Boers, & Housen, 2013). At the start of the training phase, an instruction screen informed them that they would read 40 stories of four sentences each written in Englishti, which was presented as a new language evolved from English. They were furthermore informed that they would receive a yes/no-comprehension question after each story, so as to ensure a focus on meaning during training. Half of the questions required a positive response and half a negative response. Because the participants were oriented to the meaning of the sentences and because the reading requires little, if any, intent to learn the critical morphemes, any learning from the training phase is likely to be a byproduct and, hence, incidental and implicit—that is, without the intention to learn it and without awareness of it.

After the training, the participants received a second instruction screen for the testing phase, which differed depending on the condition to which they were randomly assigned. There were two task conditions. The participants in the implicit condition were told they would receive a second reading assignment of 80 Englishti sentences that was identical to the previous one, except that this time they would receive a yes/no-comprehension question after each sentence; they were thus not aware of any ungrammatical sentences. Again, half of the questions required a positive response and half a negative response. The participants in the explicit condition were also told that they would receive a second reading assignment of 80 Englishti sentences, but, instead of yes/no-comprehension questions, they would be asked whether the sentence was grammatical or ungrammatical in Englishti. Half of the critical items were grammatical and half ungrammatical. This way each participant worked through 240 sentences in total, 160 training and 80 testing, with one sentence per screen. Prior to the training and testing phase, participants' eyes were calibrated. Between the sentences, participants saw a blank screen with a fixation cross to correct for drift. Both the training and testing phase were preceded by practice items.

Measures

Throughout the reading task, the participants' eye movements were recorded with a head-mounted eye-tracker. We also assembled two other measures from the reading task, namely the grammaticality judgment scores and comprehension scores. The grammaticality judgment scores are considered a measure of explicit knowledge, but will not be discussed here due to space limitations. The comprehension scores reflected participants' processing for meaning and served as a check for accurate task completion. Participants with less than 75% on the comprehension questions were excluded (cf. Granena, 2013); no participant obtained such a low score, however. In addition, we included a measure of awareness, namely retrospective interviews. In sum, the reading task produced three types of output: eye movement data, grammaticality judgments scores, and comprehension scores, complemented with awareness data from retrospective interviews.

Grammatical Sensitivity Index

The primary data were the eye movements, which we used to gauge participants' processing of the target inflectional morphemes, also called the participants' sensitivity towards the target inflectional morphemes (alternatively, some researchers—notably

Godfroid, 2016; Granena, 2013; Jiang, 2007; Lim & Christianson, 2015—consider this a measure of implicit knowledge). Sensitivity to grammatical violations has been measured more commonly using self-paced reading (see, for instance, Coughlin & Tremblay, 2013; Jiang, Novokshanova, Masuda, & Wang, 2011; Roberts & Liszka, 2013; Sagarra & Herschensohn, 2010; and VanPatten, Keating, & Leeser, 2012). However, its use in eye-tracking allows for a more fine-grained temporal insight in morphological processing than the segment-by-segment presentation in self-paced reading (Godfroid et al., 2015). In particular, eye movements may be able to separate effects at an early processing stage from effects at a later processing stage (Bertram, 2011). The employment of eye-tracking thus offers a rich temporal analysis of morphological processing, something that cannot be achieved by most of the methods currently employed to study morphological processing (Bertram & Hyönä, 2002). Even so, not many eye-movement studies have used grammatical and ungrammatical sentences to investigate readers' sensitivity towards the violated structures (but see Godfroid, 2016; N. Ellis et al., 2014; Keating, 2009; Lim & Christianson, 2015; Sagarra & Ellis, 2013; Behney et al., Chapter 5).

Essentially, eye-fixation times function as a "processing load measure" (Tanenhaus & Trueswell, 2006, p. 875): longer eye-fixation times to the ungrammatical condition suggest an increased processing load, which is assumed to reflect a reader's sensitivity to the grammatical violation (Godfroid et al., 2015). Evidence for grammatical sensitivity in eye-tracking research thus comes from a significant slowdown in eye-fixation times to ungrammatical morphemes compared to matched grammatical ones (Godfroid, 2016; Granena, 2013). We obtained a Grammatical Sensitivity Index (GSI) by subtracting the eye-fixation times on grammatical morphemes from the eye-fixation times on matched ungrammatical morphemes; that is, GSI = $ms_{ungrammatical} - ms_{grammatical}$. A high GSI score points to a slowdown in the ungrammatical condition, which is assumed to reflect grammatical sensitivity. In contrast, GSIs close to zero and negative GSIs suggest a lack of sensitivity or reverse sensitivity, which indicates a lack of processing (no sensitivity) or an erroneous interlanguage grammar rule (reverse sensitivity) (Godfroid, 2016).

In this study, eye-movement data were collected with a head-mounted EyeLink II (SR Research), while the reading task was presented to the participants in Courier New font size 20 on a 19-inch computer screen. Only eye movements from the testing phase were analyzed, hence the online processing behavior of the participants may differ according to the testing conditions. We specifically focused on first fixation duration, first run dwell time, total time and rereading time. First fixation duration is a measure of the mean time spent reading the first time the eye lands on the target area. First run dwell time is a cumulative measure of the mean time spent reading before the eyes move off of the target, regardless of the number of fixations on the target. Total time, then, is the sum of all fixations on the target area. Rereading time is not provided directly by the EyeLink output; rather, it was computed by subtracting first pass reading time of the target area from the total time spent fixating on the area. Whereas first fixation duration and first run dwell time are considered measures of early processing, total time and rereading time are considered measures of late processing. If there is an effect in first fixation duration, one may conclude that the effect was early and that later processing stages did not contribute to the effect. However, if there is only a solid effect in total time, the effect started to arise at later stages of processing (Bertram, 2011; Clifton, Staub, & Rayner, 2007).

In addition, given the importance of perceptual salience on the decision where the eyes fixate, we include skipping as another eye movement measure. Skipping is the phenomenon where readers do not fixate on each linguistic feature in the text, and has mostly been investigated in relation to words. Whereas most words are fixated at least once, some words—especially shorter (Drieghe, Brysbaert, Desmet, & De Baecke, 2004), functional (Carpenter & Just, 1983), and more frequent (Bertram, 2011; Rayner, Sereno, & Raney, 1996) ones—are skipped altogether. To be precise, about 30% of the words in a text do not receive a direct fixation during reading (Rayner, 1998). It has been said that skipped words are often already processed on the previous word, hence parafoveally. If that is the case, eye-fixation times before word skip are assumed to be inflated to allow for the completion of processing of the word to be skipped (Rayner & Pollatsek, 1987). However, as Bertram (2011) notes, there is little evidence that morphological information of a given word is preprocessed on the preceding word in alphabetic languages. Skipping of morphemes thus probably results in a lack of attending, processing, and hence learning of the morphemes. However, if the L2 learner fixates on the morpheme at least once, we can assert that the learner has at least attended to its form.

Grammaticality Judgments

From the reading task, we obtained another type of output, namely the grammaticality judgments from the participants in the explicit condition. Since there was no time limit, this is considered a measure of explicit knowledge. It was a computer-delivered test consisting of 80 sentences, of which 40 addressed the critical sentences; thus there were 20 sentences to be judged for each of the two target inflectional suffixes. Half of the critical sentences were grammatical, half ungrammatical. Participants were asked to indicate whether each sentence was grammatical or ungrammatical by pressing the left or right mouse button, corresponding respectively to the grammatical or ungrammatical response. No feedback was provided. A percentage accuracy score was calculated. Due to space limitations, however, these results will not be discussed here.

One concern with the use of grammaticality judgments during an experiment that also measures L2 learners' sensitivity to ungrammaticalities is that it may increase the application of explicit knowledge during the primary task of reading for meaning, and hence influence the L2 learners' online processing behavior that is simultaneously measured. Indeed, it has been shown empirically with self-paced reading that the online processing behavior of L2 learners can vary according to whether the secondary task is an acceptability judgment or a meaning-based comprehension question (Leeser, Brandl, & Weissglass, 2011).

Retrospective Interviews

After the reading task, the participants were interviewed in Dutch about their awareness of the target morphemes. This interview was audio-recorded. Participants were first asked what they thought the experiment was about. They were then asked what struck them during the experiment, or whether they noticed anything odd during the experiment and, if so, what the oddity was. If they mentioned both "-olp" and "-u," they were asked whether they felt that these were governed by a certain system, grammar, or rule, and, if so, what this was. For those who did mention "-olp" and "-u," they were asked when during the experiment they became aware of these suffixes. The researcher then asked whether they thought some items were ungrammatical and in what way, especially to participants in the implicit condition. We believed that if the participants were aware of the meaning of the morphemes, they were likely to report their observations at this point.

If the participants did not mention "-olp" and/or "-u," the researcher asked whether they felt there was something special about some nouns they read. If they still did not report the morphemes in question, the researcher would point out "-olp" and "-u" and ask whether they could recall these. This was followed by the same questions asked of the participants who did mention the morphemes. All participants were asked about the frequency of the morphemes, that is, whether they felt that "-olp" and "-u" occurred equally frequent or whether one occurred more frequently than the other. This question has been included following Kahneman's (2011) statement that "a salient event that attracts your attention will be easily retrieved from memory (. . .) You are therefore likely to exaggerate the frequency of it" (p. 130). Finally, the researcher revealed the true rules behind the morphemes, if necessary, and asked the participants whether they had thought about these rules at any point during the experiment. Based on participants' retrospective verbal reports, we distinguished, first, between the participants who became aware of the formal occurrence of the morphemes—that is, who could recall these morphemes, and those who did not—and secondly, between the participants who also became aware of the meaning of the morphemes—that is, who deduced the rules governing the morphemes, and those who did not. This way we are able to triangulate eye movement and grammaticality judgment data with verbal reports.

Procedure

Each participant was tested individually in a quiet room. After filling out the consent form and background questionnaire, the participants were seated on an adjustable chair at a viewing distance of 70 cm from the computer screen and rested on a chinrest. The eye-tracker was then placed on participants' head and adjusted where needed. After participants read the instructions on the computer screen, a nine-point eye-tracker calibration was performed before the training phase, and then again before the testing phase. Calibrations were performed binocularly but only the best calibrated eye was recorded. Prior to each sentence, the calibration was checked by presenting a fixation point on the center-left of the screen. Settings for participants who showed a discrepancy between where their eye fixated and the location of the calibration points were immediately recalibrated. Following an accurate calibration, the experimental items were presented one at a time. In the training phase, each story block of four sentences was followed by a yes/no-comprehension question. In the testing phase, the participants were asked for each sentence to either respond to a yes/no-comprehension question again (in implicit testing condition) or to judge the grammaticality of each sentence (in explicit testing condition). The experiment was self-paced and participants could stretch before any nine-point calibration. The eye-tracked reading task was immediately followed by the retrospective interview. The whole experiment lasted one session of approximately 1 hour, 15 minutes.

Results

First, we present the results on the L2 learner's early attention to form—that is, whether or not they perceived the target morphemes in the input. This is measured by learners' eye movements; more specifically, the rate with which they skipped the morphemes. Then we analyze another eye movement measure, namely the durations of their fixations. We specifically analyze the difference in fixation duration between the grammatical and ungrammatical structure of a morpheme, viz., the Grammatical Sensitivity Index. This should reflect sensitivity to aspects of the form–meaning properties of these morphemes, and hence, a higher level of processing. Finally, we consider the retrospective verbal data that gives us insight into the learners' awareness of the morphemes.

Skipping

As shown in Table 6.1, the eye-tracking data revealed that 49%, or almost half of the occurrences, of the perceptually low-salient u-morpheme did not receive a fixation, compared to 18% of the perceptually high-salient olp-morpheme, with $X^2(1, N = 28) = 111.08, p < .0001$. In the implicit condition, the percentage of skipping of the perceptually low- and high-salient morphemes increased up to 60% and 24%, respectively, with $X^2(1, N = 28) = 71.434, p < .0001$. In contrast, in the explicit condition, the percentage of skipping of the perceptually low- and high-salient morphemes dropped down to 36% and 11%, respectively, with $X^2(1, N = 28) = 41.267, p < .0001$.

The effect of grammaticality did not show in the skipping rate, as no significant differences were observed between the grammatical and ungrammatical morphemes, neither for the perceptually low-salient nor for the perceptually high-salient morpheme, and neither in the implicit nor in the explicit condition. Still, there was a tendency towards lower skipping rates for the ungrammatical morphemes than for the grammatical morphemes in all cases except the low-salient morpheme in the implicit condition.

Stimuli that are skipped are often already processed parafoveally—that is, on the previous word—and this should show in inflated durations on this previous word (see supra; Rayner & Pollatsek, 1987). We therefore evaluated the first run dwell times for

TABLE 6.1 Skipping rate in percentage for both the low- and high-salient morphemes in the explicit and implicit condition, and in total

	Explicit Condition		Implicit Condition		Total	
	High-Salient	Low-Salient	High-Salient	Low-Salient	High-Salient	Low-Salient
% Skipped	36%	11%	24%	60%	18%	49%

the word prior to the u-morpheme and the word prior to the olp-morpheme, using nonparametric Wilcoxon rank-sum tests. These analyses showed no significant differences, however, $W = 128320, p = .24$, with median first run dwell times of 284 ms ($M = 349$, $SD = 227$) and 276 ms ($M = 341$, $SD = 208$) for the word prior to the high and the word prior to the low-salient morpheme, respectively.

Grammatical Sensitivity Index

In what follows, we present the results of the eye-tracking analyses for the different eye-fixation duration measures—that is first fixation duration, first run dwell time, total time, and rereading time. Any fixation durations falling outside of a subject's mean ± 2.5 SD were removed. Fixations slower than 80 ms were either integrated with a neighboring fixation, or eliminated because such short fixations do not seem to reflect cognitive processing of the target word (Rayner, 1998; Rayner & Pollatsek, 1987). The descriptive statistics for the trimmed fixation durations are presented in Table 6.2, according to the implicit and explicit condition.

The first analyses compared the first fixation (FFD) and first run dwell (FRDT) times on grammatical and ungrammatical trials of high and low-salient morphemes in the implicit and explicit condition. A [2 (Grammaticality) × 2 (Salience) × 2 (Condition)] mixed-design analysis of variance (ANOVA) of the first fixation durations

TABLE 6.2 Mean fixation times, standard deviations, and grammatical sensitivity index values for the ungrammatical and grammatical trials of both the low- and high-salient morphemes in the explicit and implicit condition

	Explicit Condition					
	Low-Salient			*High-Salient*		
	Grammatical	*Ungrammatical*	*GSI*	*Grammatical*	*Ungrammatical*	*GSI*
FFD	237 (97)	227 (83)	−10	246 (92)	240 (81)	6
FRDT	251 (116)	244 (113)	−7	283 (135)	295 (142)	12
TT	420 (304)	360 (260)	−60	511 (334)	623 (386)	112
RRT	153 (257)	108 (218)	−45	192 (275)	303 (322)	111
	Implicit Condition					
	Low-Salient			*High-Salient*		
	Grammatical	*Ungrammatical*	*GSI*	*Grammatical*	*Ungrammatical*	*GSI*
FFD	224 (77)	242 (81)	18	232 (84)	232 (73)	0
FRDT	237 (105)	249 (98)	12	254 (126)	284 (143)	30
TT	268 (141)	309 (156)	41	406 (301)	389 (272)	17
RRT	31 (85)	59 (142)	28	125 (222)	99 (188)	26

Notes: GSI—Grammatical Sensitivity Index. FFD—First Fixation Duration. FRDT—First Run Dwell Time. TT—Total Time. RRT—Rereading Time.

indicated that none of the effects were significant, meaning that no differences were found in first fixation durations between the grammatical versus ungrammatical, high- versus low-salient, and explicit versus implicit condition morphemes. The analysis of the first run dwell times yielded similar results, but here the main effect of Salience was significant, $F(1,673) = 11.678, p < .001$, implying that all participants looked significantly longer at high-salient morphemes ($M = 279, SD = 137$) than at low-salient morphemes ($M = 245, SD = 109$) in the first run. However, the non-significant main and interaction effects of Grammaticality suggested an overall lack of sensitivity towards the morphemes on these measures.

Analyses of the total dwell time and rereading time measures yielded altogether different results. A [2 (Grammaticality) × 2 (Salience) × 2 (Condition)] ANOVA of the (log-transformed) total times (TT) showed a three-way interaction among Condition, Salience, and Grammaticality [$F(1,678) = 5.6, p = .02$] and two significant main effects for Salience [$F(1,678) = 15, p < .0001$] and Condition [$F(1,678) = 14, p < .0001$]. Figure 6.1 visualizes the interaction effect.

To follow up on these interactions, participants' total dwell times and rereading times on grammatical and ungrammatical morphemes were evaluated for each salience

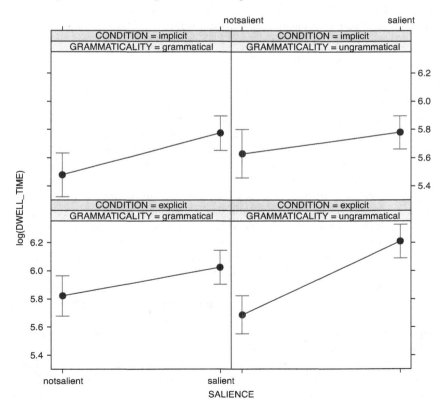

FIGURE 6.1 Salience by conditions of grammaticality and explicitness

type and for each condition separately, using nonparametric Wilcoxon rank-sum tests. The analysis of the total time evidenced a significant effect of Grammaticality for the high-salient morphemes in the explicit condition, $W = 4763, p < .05$, but no effect of Grammaticality for all other morphemes. In particular, participants in the explicit condition fixated in total significantly longer on the ungrammatical high-salient morphemes ($M = 623, SD = 386$) than on the grammatical high-salient morphemes ($M = 511, SD = 334$). In the implicit condition, however, the difference between the ungrammatical high-salient ($M = 389, SD = 272$) and the grammatical high-salient ($M = 406, SD = 301$) morphemes was nowhere near significant, $W = 5350.5, p = .9$. Similarly, there were no significant differences between the ungrammatical and grammatical low-salient morphemes in neither the implicit, $W = 1259.5, p = .06$, nor the explicit, $W = 3230.5, p = .19$, condition.

The analysis of the rereading times (RRT) yielded results similar to those of the total time analysis, with a significant effect for the three-way interaction among Salience, Grammaticality and Condition ($F (1,237) = 10, p = .001$). The Wilcoxon rank-sum tests pointed out that participants in the explicit condition reread the ungrammatical high-salient morpheme ($M = 303, SD = 322$) significantly longer than its grammatical match ($M = 192, SD = 275$), $W = 4727, p = .02$, while none of the other comparisons between grammatical and ungrammatical morphemes proved significant.

Retrospective Verbal Reports

We also analyzed the retrospective verbal reports to identify the participants who became aware of the target morphemes in the reading task. To examine the verbal report data more closely, we distinguished between meaning and form awareness, with the former being awareness of the underlying rules—that is, being able to report the meaning of the morphemes—and the latter being awareness of the occurrence of these morphemes—that is, being able to report their formal presence in the reading task. Only one participant correctly deduced the rules governing the target morphemes. Accordingly, this is the only participant who became aware of the grammatical violations in the reading task. Since none of the other participants reported ungrammatical morphemes or morpheme rules, it was assumed that they had no conscious knowledge of the target morphemes' function during reading.

Not only did the participants fail to provide the correct rules, many could not recall the formal occurrence of the target morphemes. When asked whether they could remember the words or word endings that were new to them, only 14 participants (50%) reported the formal presence of the perceptually low-salient u-morpheme, while 17 participants (61%) reported the perceptually high-salient olp-morpheme. Based on a test for equality of proportions, there is no difference between these proportions ($p = .59$).

The awareness of the participants differed, however, according to the condition to which they had been assigned. In the explicit condition, 10 of the 14 participants (71%) reported awareness of the presence of "-u" and 12 of the 14 (86%) reported the presence of "-olp." In the implicit condition, in contrast, only four participants (29%) were aware of the presence of "-u" and five (36%) of the presence of "-olp." The low number of participants becoming aware of the morphemes' presence is surprising, given the high frequency with which the morphemes occurred in the experiment, and all the more so given the combination of an existing, well-known language with artificial target morphemes that one would expect to naturally stand out.

Participants were also asked whether they felt both morphemes occurred with equal frequency, or one morpheme occurred more frequently than the other, and, if so, which. Seven of the 28 participants (25%) correctly indicated that both morphemes were equally frequent. Only three participants (11%) believed that the perceptually low-salient morpheme "-u" appeared more frequently, while 18 (64%) responded that the perceptually high-salient morpheme "-olp" occurred more often, which is significantly higher than expected (test for equality of proportions: $p < .0001$). This suggests that high-salient morphemes are thus taken to be more frequent than low-salient ones.

Discussion

We hypothesized that higher perceptual salience of the target structure leads to: 1) more early attentional processing—that is, more viewing of the target morpheme (i.e., less skipping); 2) higher grammatical sensitivity to the target morphemes, suggesting more intake; and 3) a higher rate of reporting of and, hence, higher awareness of the target morpheme. However, we also hypothesized that the effect of salience would be overruled by the kind of top-down attentional processing that the explicit task condition engenders. That is, we expected to see no (or very little) effect of perceptual salience in skipping rate, grammatical sensitivity, or verbal reporting in the explicit task condition.

These predictions are partly borne out by the results. For the skipping rate measure, the high-salient morpheme was consistently fixated on more often, regardless of the task condition. L2 morphemes of higher salience thus attracted more fixations than those of lower salience. This indicates that salience exerts control over the visual selection system, and, hence, early attention allocation. Without salience, L2 learners easily gloss over the morphemes, thereby failing to perceive them in the input. In other words, salience facilitated our learners' early attention allocation to the form of the target morphemes in the L2 input. The next question then, is whether salience also facilitated further processing mechanisms.

To address this question, we discuss the data on eye-fixation durations. We specifically take the grammatical sensitivity data as evidence of sensitivity not just to the form, but also to the meaning of the morpheme. For first fixation duration and first run dwell time, neither the high- nor low-salient L2 morpheme showed significant differences between the grammatical and ungrammatical structure, suggesting that the facilitating effect that salience had on the attention to form is not retained when it comes to meaning, at least not during the first fixations on the morpheme. This is true for both the implicit and the explicit task condition.

Another picture emerges from the total and rereading time measures, where later fixations on the morphemes are considered. For both measures, the difference in fixation durations between the grammatical and the ungrammatical structure was significant for the high-salient morpheme, yet only under explicit task conditions. When instructed to focus on grammar, the L2 learners showed sensitivity towards ungrammaticalities of the high-salient L2 morpheme. This points to some evidence of intake of the form-meaning properties of these morphemes. For the low-salient morpheme, no such sensitivity was found in either condition. Hence, a morpheme would have to be both salient and task-relevant to become a candidate for further processing. Participants may thus not process the morphemes if they are not focused on grammar, however salient the morphemes may be. In the explicit condition, the combination of bottom-up salience with top-down grammar support is exactly what facilitated processing of the most salient morpheme. The fact that participants only exhibited sensitivity to the high-salient morphemes when the secondary task was a grammaticality judgment but not when it was a meaning-based comprehension question also indicates that the secondary task indeed impacts the L2 learners' processing behavior, as Leeser et al. (2011) have claimed.

It is also worth emphasizing that the fact that the participants only showed sensitivity towards the high-salient morpheme on the total and rereading time measures, relative to first fixation duration measures, may signal the L2 learners' genuine attempts to access the morpheme's function: they were trying to make sense of it. When participants first looked at the morphemes, the morphemes were not yet embedded in any form-meaning mapping network. That is, the form of the high-salient morphemes already stood out at the first glance, but its mapping to meaning was only achieved at a later stage.

If our account of form-meaning processing is correct (and more research is needed to confirm it), then it must have happened without the participants becoming aware of it. When looking at the retrospective verbal reports, only one participant succeeded in reporting the correct form-meaning mapping rules. Hence, although participants may have shown sensitivity towards ungrammaticalities in their eye movement data, this sensitivity must have been achieved outside their awareness. That is, this sensitivity tapped into their *implicit* learning processes.

Conclusion

The present study explored the effect of perceptual salience on processing aspects of grammatical morphology in a second language. We found that high perceptual salience facilitates learners' processing of L2 morphemes, because it interacts with attentional mechanisms. Especially when it comes to the form, the high-salient morphemes were better attended to than the low-salient ones. Salience was also beneficial for later processing stages, where learners try to make sense of the meaning of the morpheme. However, this was only true when combined with a task that provided a top-down focus on grammar. We therefore infer that an L2 morpheme is preferably both perceptually salient and task-relevant if further processing is to occur. This is not to say that incidental intake of the morphemes is not possible, but they will be picked up more easily when they are both salient in the input and relevant to the task.

As always, the results and findings about the impact of perceptual salience presented here have to be interpreted with the necessary caution and as with all experimental psycholinguistic studies, the usual methodological limitations also apply here (e.g., limited sample size). Probably more relevant, however, are limitations on how we operationalized perceptual salience in this study, namely in terms of orthographic length or substance (e.g., number of letters: one versus three). Perhaps a clearer effect of perceptual salience than in this study can be found by increasing the difference in the substance of the target morphemes (e.g., one versus five letters). Also, perceptual salience is not only a matter of orthographic or phonological substance; other factors, such as syllabicity (cf. English 3SG -s versus Progressive -ing) and sonority (cf. the /t/ and /d/ allomorphs of the English verbal -ed suffix) contribute to the perceptual salience of inflectional morphemes.

Furthermore, despite our efforts to control as many intervening factors as possible, some factors may still have intervened in determining our target morphemes' overall salience and, hence, our learners' processing of the target morphemes. One such factor is markedness. The masculine category is the default (or conceptually most salient) category in most languages of the world, including the ones involved in this study, and is therefore typically formally unmarked (Battistella, 1996). In this study, however, both masculine (-olp) and feminine (-u) received explicit morphological marking, thus possibly giving additional salience to the default masculine category. To gauge the net effect of perceptual salience, future research should control for the effect of markedness by counterbalancing the distribution of the high- and low-salient morpheme over the masculine and feminine category.

This example also stresses the more general point that in addition to perceptual salience (the physical properties of a linguistic feature), many other factors can contribute to a linguistic feature's overall salience or quality to 'stand out', including its frequency, transparency, or morphophonological regularity to name but a few (DeKeyser, 2005; N. Ellis, 2016). Clearly, salience is a composite, multicomponential, and multidimensional concept that emerges from the interactions among the target stimulus, the context in which it occurs and, last but not least, the learner. For salience, including perceptual salience, is ultimately subjective. What is salient for one learner may not be so for another—and hence, what attracts one learner's attention or raises one learner's awareness may not attract or raise another learner's.

A better understanding of the role of salience in relation to the cognitive mechanisms of attention and awareness thus seems crucially important in our ongoing investigations. Indeed, for the constructs of attention and awareness to have any relevance for a theory of SLA, we need to account for *why* learners attend to, or become aware of, what they attend to and become aware of. Salience—and perceptual salience in particular—may be an essential component of such an account.

Notes

1 For the sake of definitional and operational precision, we use the term 'processing' (or 'processing for acquisition,' as opposed to 'processing for comprehension or production') as an umbrella term for the chain of cognitive operations that a linguistic feature

undergoes, from its initial detection in the linguistic environment ('input') and its first (and possibly temporary) registration in short-term memory ('intake'), to its subsequent analysis (e.g., parsing) of form and meaning and, ultimately, to its storage as an internal representation in long-term memory (i.e., a unit of knowledge, evidence of 'learning' in the narrow sense of the term) and its activation for L2 use.

We use the term 'input processing' in a more narrow sense to refer to the cognitive mechanisms that operate in the first phases of the chain of acquisitional process (i.e., from input to intake), in particular the mechanisms of attention and awareness (cf. Godfroid et al., 2013; Leow, 2015; Robinson, 2001; Schmidt, 1990, 2001; Tomlin & Villa, 1994).

2 Grammatical sensitivity (operationalized as increased reaction or fixation times on ungrammatical items) has been taken as evidence for implicit knowledge (Granena, 2013; Jiang, 2007; Lim & Christianson, 2015) or implicit learning (Leung & Williams, 2011, 2012, 2014).

3 Originally, there were 40 participants in the experiment, but we had to exclude 12 due to technical issues, amongst others.

References

Alanen, R. (1995). Input enhancement and rule presentation in second language acquisition. In R. Schmidt (Ed.), *Attention and awareness in foreign language learning* (pp. 1–63). Honolulu, HI: University of Hawaii, Second Language Teaching & Curriculum Center.

Barcroft, J., & VanPatten, B. (1997). Acoustic salience of grammatical forms: The effect of location, stress, and boundedness on Spanish L2 input processing. In T. Pérez-Leroux & W. Glass (Eds.), *Contemporary perspectives on the acquisition of Spanish, Vol. 2: Production, processing, and comprehension* (pp. 109–122). Somerville, MA: Cascadilla Press.

Battistella, E. (1996). *The logic of markedness*. Oxford: Oxford University Press.

Bertram, R. (2011). Eye movements and morphological processing in reading. *The Mental Lexicon, 6*(1), 83–109.

Bertram, R., & Hyönä, J. (2002, October). *Word processing and the optimal viewing position*. Poster presented at the 3rd International Conference on the Mental Lexicon, Banff, Canada.

Bowles, M. (2010). *The think-aloud controversy in language acquisition research*. London: Routledge.

Brown, R. (1973). *A first language*. Cambridge, MA: Harvard University Press.

Brysbaert, M., & New, B. (2009). Moving beyond Kučera and Francis: A critical evaluation of current word frequency norms and the introduction of a new and improved word frequency measure for American English. *Behavior Research Methods, 41*(4), 977–990.

Brysbaert, M., Warriner, A. B., & Kuperman, V. (2014). Concreteness ratings for 40 thousand generally known English word lemmas. *Behavior Research Methods, 46*, 904–911.

Carpenter, P. A., & Just, M. A. (1983). What your eyes do while your mind is reading. In K. Rayner (Ed.), *Eye movements in reading: Perceptual and language processes* (pp. 275–307). New York: Academic Press.

Carrasco, M. (2011). Visual attention: The past 25 years. *Vision Research, 51*(13), 1484–1525.

Carroll, S. (2006). Salience, awareness and SLA. In M. G. O'Brien, C. Shea, & J. Archibald (Eds.), *Proceedings of the 8th Generative Approaches to Second Language Acquisition Conference (GASLA 2006): The Banff Conference* (pp. 17–24). Somerville, MA: Cascadilla Press.

Carroll, S. E. (2012). When is input salient? An exploratory study of sentence location and word length effects on input processing. *International Review of Applied Linguistics in Language Teaching, 50*, 39–67.

Cintrón-Valentín, M., & Ellis, N. (2015). Exploring the interface: Explicit focus-on-form instruction and learned attentional biases in L2 Latin. *Studies in Second Language Acquisition, 37*, 197–235.

Cintrón-Valentín, M., & Ellis, N. (2016). Salience in second language acquisition: Physical form, learner attention, and instructional focus. *Frontiers in Psychology, 7*, 1–21.

Clifton, C., Jr., Staub, A., & Rayner, K. (2007). Eye movements in reading words and sentences. In R. Van Gompel, M. Fisher, W. Murray, & R. L. Hill (Eds.), *Eye movement research: A window on mind and brain* (pp. 341–372). Oxford: Elsevier Ltd.

Collins, L., Trofimovich, P., White, J., Cardoso, W., & Horst, M. (2009). Some input on the easy/difficult grammar question: An empirical study. *The Modern Language Journal, 93*, 336–353.

Coughlin, C. E., & Tremblay, A. T. (2013). Proficiency and working memory based explanations for nonnative speakers' sensitivity to agreement in sentence processing. *Applied Psycholinguistics, 34*(3), 615–646.

de Jong, K. (1995). The supraglottal articulation of prominence in English: Linguistic stress as localized hyperarticulation. *Journal of Acoustical Society of America, 97*(1), 491–504.

DeKeyser, R. (1995). Learning second language grammar rules: An experiment with a miniature linguistic system. *Studies in Second Language Acquisition, 17*, 379–410.

DeKeyser, R. (2005). What makes learning second-language grammar difficult? A review of issues. *Language Learning, 55*, Supplement 1, 1–25.

Drieghe, D., Brysbaert, M., Desmet, T., & De Baecke, C. (2004). Word skipping in reading: On the interplay of linguistic and visual factors. *European Journal of Cognitive Psychology, 16*(1–2), 79–103.

Duyck, W., Desmet, T., Verbeke, L. P., & Brysbaert, M. (2004). WordGen: A tool for word selection and nonword generation in Dutch, English, German, and French. *Behavior Research Methods, Instruments, & Computers, 36*(3), 488–499.

Egi, T. (2004). Verbal reports, noticing, and SLA research. *Language Awareness, 13*, 243–264.

Ellis, N. C. (2006). Selective attention and transfer phenomena in SLA: Contingency, cue competition, salience, interference, overshadowing, blocking, and perceptual learning. *Applied Linguistics, 27*, 1–31.

Ellis, N. C. (2016). Salience, cognition, language complexity, and complex adaptive systems. *Studies in Second Language Acquisition, 38*(2), 341–351.

Ellis, N. C., Hafee, K., Martin, K., Chen, L., & Boland, J. (2014). An eye-tracking study of learned attention in second language acquisition. *Applied Psycholinguistics, 35*(3), 547–579.

Ellis, N. C., & Larsen-Freeman, D. (2006). Language emergence: Implications for applied linguistics: Introduction to the special issue. *Applied Linguistics, 27*(4), 558–589.

Ellis, N. C., & Sagarra, N. (2010). The bounds of adult language acquisition: Blocking and learned attention. *Studies in Second Language Acquisition, 32*, 553–580.

Ellis, N. C., & Sagarra, N. (2011). Blocking and learned attention in language acquisition: A replication and generalization study. *Studies in Second Language Acquisition, 33*, 589–624.

Ellis, R. (2006a). Current issues in the teaching of grammar: An SLA perspective. *TESOL Quarterly, 40*(1), 83–107.

Ellis, R. (2006b). Modelling learning difficulty and second language proficiency: The differential contributions of implicit and explicit knowledge. *Applied Linguistics, 27*(3), 431–463.

Gass, S. (1997). *Input, interaction, and the second language learner*. Mahwah, NJ: Lawrence Erlbaum Associates.

Gass, S., Svetics, I., & Lemelin, S. (2003). Differential effects of attention. *Language Learning, 53*, 497–545.

Godfroid, A. (2016). The effects of implicit instruction on implicit and explicit knowledge development. *Studies in Second Language Acquisition, 38*, 177–215.

Godfroid, A., Boers, F., & Housen, A. (2013). An eye for words: Gauging the role of attention in incidental L2 vocabulary acquisition by means of eye-tracking. *Studies in Second Language Acquisition, 35*(3), 483–517.

Godfroid, A., Loewen, S., Jung, S., Park, J., Gass, S. M., & Ellis, R. (2015). Timed and untimed grammaticality judgments measure distinct types of knowledge. *Studies in Second Language Acquisition, 37*, 269–297.

Godfroid, A., & Uggen, M. S. (2013). Attention to irregular verbs by beginning learners of German. *Studies in Second Language Acquisition, 35*, 291–322.

Goldschneider, J., & DeKeyser, R. (2001). Explaining the "natural order of L2 morpheme acquisition" in English: A meta-analysis of multiple determinants. *Language Learning, 51*(1), 1–50.

Granena, G. (2013). Individual differences in sequence learning ability and second language acquisition in early childhood and adulthood. *Language Learning, 63*(4), 665–703.

Hopp, H. (2010). Ultimate attainment in L2 inflectional morphology: Performance similarities between non-native and native speakers. *Lingua, 120*, 901–931.

Hulstijn, J. (1995). Not all grammar rules are equal: Giving grammar instruction its proper place in foreign language teaching. In R. Schmidt (Ed.), *Attention and awareness in foreign language learning* (pp. 359–386). Honolulu: University of Hawaii.

Jiang, N. (2007). Selective integration of linguistic knowledge in adult second language learning. *Language Learning, 57*, 1–33.

Jiang, N., Novokshanova, E., Masuda, K., & Wang, X. (2011). Morphological congruency and the acquisition of L2 morphemes. *Language Learning, 61*, 940–967.

Kahneman, D. (2011). *Thinking, fast and slow*. New York: Farrar, Straus & Giroux.

Keating, G. D. (2009). Sensitivity to violations of gender agreement in native and nonnative Spanish: An eye-movement investigation. *Language Learning, 59*(3), 503–535.

Keating, G. D., & Jegerski, J. (2015). Experimental designs in sentence processing research. *Studies in Second Language Acquisition, 37*(1), 1–32.

Leeser, M. J., Brandl, A., & Weissglass, C. (2011). Task effects in second language sentence processing research. In P. Trofimovich & K. McDonough (Eds.), *Applying priming methods to L2 learning, teaching and research: Insights from psycholinguistics* (pp. 179–198). Amsterdam: John Benjamins.

Leow, R. (1998). Toward operationalizing the process of attention in second language acquisition: Evidence for Tomlin and Villa's (1994) fine-grained analysis of attention. *Applied Psycholinguistics, 19*, 133–159.

Leow, R. (2009). Input enhancement and L2 grammatical development: What the research reveals. In J. Watzinger-Tharp & S. L. Katz, (Eds.), *Conceptions of L2 grammar: Theoretical approaches and their application in the L2 classroom* (pp. 16–34). Boston, MA: Heinle Publishers.

Leow, R. (2015). *Explicit learning in the L2 classroom: A student-centered approach*. New York: Routledge.

Leow, R., & Bowles, M. (2005). Attention and awareness in SLA. In C. Sanz (Ed.), *Mind and context in adult second language acquisition* (pp. 179–203). Washington, DC: Georgetown University Press.

Leung, J. H. C., & Williams, J. N. (2011). The implicit learning of mappings between forms and contextually derived meanings. *Studies in Second Language Acquisition, 33*(1), 33–55.

Leung, J. H. C., & Williams, J. N. (2012). Constraints on implicit learning of grammatical form-meaning connections. *Language Learning, 62*(2), 634–662.

Leung, J. H. C., & Williams, J. N. (2014). Crosslinguistic differences in implicit language learning. *Studies in Second Language Acquisition, 29*(1), 1–23.

Lim, J. H., & Christianson, K. (2015). Second language sensitivity to agreement errors: Evidence from eye movements during comprehension and translation. *Applied Psycholinguistics, 36*(6), 1283–1315.

Marsden, E., Williams, J., & Liu, X. (2013). Learning novel morphology: The role of meaning and orientation of attention at initial exposure. *Studies in Second Language Acquisition, 35*(4), 619.

McLaughlin, B. (1987). *Theories of second language learning.* London: Edward Arnold.

Navalpakkam, V., Koch, C. Rangel, A., & Perona, P. (2010). Understanding how reward and saliency affect overt attention and decisions. *Journal of Vision, 10*(7), 32.

Parkhurst, D., Law, K., & Niebur, E. (2002). Modeling the role of salience in the allocation of overt visual attention. *Vision Research, 42*(1), 107–123.

Peters, R., Iyer, A., Itti, L., & Koch, C. (2005). Components of bottom-up gaze allocation in natural images. *Vision Research, 45,* 2397–2416.

Prévost, P., & White, L. (2000). Missing surface inflection or impairment in second language acquisition? Evidence from tense and agreement. *Second Language Research, 16,* 103–133.

Pringle, H., Irwin, D., Kramer, A., & Atchley, P. (2001). The role of attentional breadth in perceptual change detection. *Psychonomic Bulletin & Review, 8,* 89–95.

Rayner, K. (1998). Eye movements in reading and information processing: 20 years of research. *Psychological Bulletin, 124*(3), 372–422.

Rayner, K. (2009). Eye movements and attention in reading, scene perception, and visual search. *The Quarterly Journal of Experimental Psychology, 62,* 1457–1506.

Rayner, K., & Pollatsek, A. (1987). Eye movements in reading: A tutorial review. In M. Coltheart (Ed.), *Attention and performance* (Vol. 12, pp. 327–362). Mahwah, NJ: Lawrence Erlbaum Associates.

Rayner, K., Sereno, S., & Raney, G. (1996). Eye movement control in reading: A comparison of two types of models. *Journal of Experimental Psychology: Human Perception and Performance, 22,* 1188–1200.

Rensink, R. A. (2002). Change detection. *Annual Review of Psychology, 53*(1), 245–277.

Roberts, L., & Liszka, S. (2013). Processing tense/aspect agreement violations on-line in the second language: A self-paced reading study with French and German L2 learners of English. *Second Language Research, 29,* 413–439.

Robinson, P. (1995). Attention, memory, and the "noticing" hypothesis. *Language Learning, 45*(2), 283–331.

Robinson, P. (1996a). *Consciousness, rules, and instructed second language acquisition.* New York: Peter Lang.

Robinson, P. (1996b). Learning simple and complex second language rules under implicit, incidental, rule-search, and instructed conditions. *Studies in Second Language Acquisition, 18*(1), 27–67.

Robinson, P. (2001). Individual differences, cognitive abilities, aptitude complexes and learning conditions in second language acquisition. *Second Language Research, 17,* 368–392.

Rogers, J., Révész, A., & Rebuschat, P. (2015). Challenges in implicit learning research: Validating a novel artificial language. In P. Rebuschat (Ed.), *Implicit and explicit learning of languages* (pp. 273–298). Amsterdam: John Benjamins.

Sagarra, N., & Ellis, N. C. (2013). From seeing adverbs to seeing verbal morphology: Language experience and adult acquisition of L2 tense. *Studies in Second Language Acquisition, 35,* 261–290.

Sagarra, N., & Herschensohn, J. (2010). The role of proficiency and working memory in gender and number agreement processing in L1 and L2 Spanish. *Lingua, 120*(8), 2022–2039.

Schmidt, R. (1990). The role of consciousness in second language learning. *Applied Linguistics, 11*(2), 129–158.

Schmidt, R. (1993). Awareness and second language acquisition. *Annual Review of Applied Linguistics, 13*, 206–226.
Schmidt, R. (1995). Consciousness and foreign language learning: A tutorial on the role of attention and awareness in learning. In R. Schmidt (Ed.), *Attention and awareness in foreign language learning* (pp. 1–63). Honolulu: Second Language Teaching and Curriculum Center, University of Hawaii at Manoa.
Schmidt, R. (2001). Attention. In P. Robinson (Ed.), *Cognition and second language instruction* (pp. 3–32). Cambridge: Cambridge University Press.
Schütz, A. C., Braun, D. I., & Gegenfurtner, K. R. (2011). Eye movements and perception: A selective review. *Journal of Vision, 11*(5), 1–30.
Stelzer, E. M., & Wickens, C. D. (2006). Pilots strategically compensate for display enlargements in surveillance and flight control tasks. *Human Factors, 48*(1), 166–181.
Streefkerk, B. M. (2002). *Prominence: Acoustic and lexical/syntactic correlates*. Utrecht: LOT.
Styles, E. (2006). *The psychology of attention* (2nd ed.). Hove: Psychology Press.
Swain, M. (2005). The output hypothesis: Theory and research. In E. Hinkel (Ed.), *Handbook of research in second language teaching and learning* (pp. 471–483). Mahwah, NJ: Lawrence Erlbaum Associates.
Tanenhaus, M. K., & Trueswell, J. C. (2006). Eye movements and spoken language comprehension. In M. Traxler & M. Gernsbacher (Eds.), *Handbook of psycholinguistics* (pp. 863–900). Oxford: Elsevier Press.
Tatler, B., Baddeley, R., & Gilchrist, I. (2005). Visual correlates of fixation selection: Effects of scale and time. *Vision Research, 45*(5), 643–659.
Tatler, B., Hayhoe, M., Land, M., & Ballard, D. (2011). Eye guidance in natural vision: Reinterpreting salience. *Journal of Vision, 11*(5), 1–23.
Tomlin, R. S., & Villa, V. (1994). Attention in cognitive science and second language acquisition. *Studies in Second Language Acquisition, 16*, 183–203.
Truscott, J., & Sharwood Smith, M. (2011). Input, intake, and consciousness: The quest for a theoretical foundation. *Studies in Second Language Acquisition, 33*, 497–528.
Van Assche, E., Duyck, W., & Brysbaert, M. (2013). Verb processing by bilinguals in sentence contexts: The effect of cognate status and verb tense. *Studies in Second Language Acquisition, 35*(2), 237–259.
Van Den Bos, E., & Poletiek, F. H. (2008). Effects of grammar complexity on artificial grammar learning. *Memory & Cognition, 36*(6), 1122–1131.
VanPatten, B. (1996). *Input processing and grammar instruction in second language acquisition*. Westport, CT: Ablex.
VanPatten, B. (2007). Input processing in adult SLA. In B. VanPatten & J. Williams (Eds.), *Theories in second language acquisition* (pp. 115–135). Mahwah, NJ: Lawrence Erlbaum Associates.
VanPatten, B. (2009). Processing matters in input enhancement. In T. Piske & M. Young-Scholten (Eds.), *Input matters in SLA* (pp. 47–61). Clevedon: Multilingual Matters.
VanPatten, B., Keating, G. D., & Leeser, M. J. (2012). Missing verbal inflections as a representational problem: Evidence from self-paced reading. *Linguistic Approaches to Bilingualism, 2*, 109–140.
Wickens, C. (2007). Attention to the second language. *International Review of Applied Linguistics, 45*, 177–191.
Williams, J. N. (2005). Learning without awareness. *Studies in Second Langauge Acquisition, 27*, 269–304.
Winke, P., Godfroid, A., & Gass, S. (2013). Eye-movement recordings in second language research. *Studies in Second Language Acquisition, 35*, 205–212.

7

THE ROLE OF SALIENCE IN THE ACQUISITION OF HEBREW AS A SECOND LANGUAGE

Interaction With Age of Acquisition

Robert DeKeyser, Iris Alfi-Shabtay, Dorit Ravid, and Meng Shi

Age Effects in Second Language Learning

Research on age effects in second language acquisition (SLA) goes back more than half a century and has focused on a decline in ultimate attainment (UA) as a function of age of acquisition (AoA), in particular for acquisition onset ranging from early childhood to late adolescence. Penfield and Roberts (1959) already used the decline in "brain plasticity" with age as an argument for early immersion education, and Lenneberg (1967) assumed that increasing lateralization in particular was to blame for the decline with age. These vague neurological explanations are now out of date, but the concept of a critical period as described by Lenneberg is still the focus of much ongoing research on the acquisition of all domains of language and in a variety of second languages (L2s).

After a first wave of empirical research on the acquisition of phonology (e.g., Asher & García, 1969; Oyama, 1976) and morphosyntax (e.g., Johnson & Newport, 1989; Patkowski, 1980), the first critical voices were raised, at that time trying to show mainly that acquisition in these two domains did not *necessarily* decline with age in childhood or adolescence (e.g., Birdsong, 1992; Birdsong & Molis, 2001; Bongaerts, Planken, & Schils, 1995; White & Genesee, 1996), i.e., that nativelike performance in at least some aspects of language was perfectly possible—perhaps even relatively common—for late acquirers. A number of methodological problems have been pointed out with these studies, however (see, e.g., DeKeyser, 2006; Long, 2007), and even though some more recent research still aims at documenting 'exceptions' to the critical period (e.g., van Boxtel, Bongaerts, & Coppen, 2005), the vast majority of age-effect studies in the last 15 years or so have focused on the exact shape of the AoA-UA function (for more detail, see e.g., DeKeyser et al., 2010; Hakuta, Bialystok, & Wiley, 2003), on what domains of language are most affected (see especially Abrahamsson & Hyltenstam, 2009; Granena & Long, 2013), and on why there is a decline with age. The question of why has received a variety of answers, ranging from confounds of maturation with other variables (especially motivation, quality of input, amount of education in L2, and amount of exposure to L1 versus L2; see e.g., Hakuta et al., 2003; Jia & Aaronson, 2003; Jia, Aaronson, & Wu, 2002; Monner et al., 2013) to truly maturational explanations such as growth in working memory (Monner et al., 2013; Newport, 1990) or a gradual shift from implicit to explicit learning processes (DeKeyser, 2000; DeKeyser et al., 2010).

Finding a convincing explanation for the age effects documented is not only important for a better understanding of the phenomenon, but to some extent also to provide explanatory adequacy for the critical period hypothesis (CPH). It can certainly be argued that thus far we only have descriptive adequacy. Hakuta (2001), in particular, posited that it is hard to take the CPH seriously as long as only quantitative differences in outcome are documented and not qualitative differences in learning processes. Establishing such qualitative differences would be a crucial step in reaching explanatory adequacy, whether the ultimate explanation for the CP is in changes in the learning processes themselves or in neurological changes, especially as it is not obvious which of the two would be cause or effect of the other. Given, however, that the data for critical period studies are typically collected many years after the (first stages of) learning took place, this evidence must necessarily be indirect.

One such form of evidence is documenting how learning at different ages is predicted by different aptitudes. The first study to investigate this was DeKeyser (2000), who found that the ability for explicit language learning measured by tests like the Modern Language Aptitude Test (Carroll & Sapon, 1959) was predictive of success for adults but not for children, and more specifically that among participants with AoA > 16, only those with high aptitude did well on a grammaticality judgment test. Abrahamsson and Hyltenstam (2008) replicated the finding that only high-aptitude adults scored high on ultimate attainment tests, but found that aptitude for explicit learning predicted proficiency for all age groups. DeKeyser et al. (2010) replicated the findings obtained with Hungarian L1/English L2 speakers in the 2000 study, this time with Russian learners of English and Russian learners of Hebrew: explicit aptitude predicted proficiency for adult learners only.

Granena and Long (2013) corroborated the findings from DeKeyser (2000) and DeKeyser et al. (2010), i.e., predictive value of explicit aptitude for adult learners only, but in their case for pronunciation and vocabulary/collocations instead of grammar. Granena (2013), on the other hand, found evidence that ability for implicit learning predicted achievement for all AoAs; and Granena (2014) that explicit aptitude predicted achievement in a study with young learners, but only for an untimed grammaticality judgment test, and only for some structures.

It seems to be the case, then, that on average, explicit aptitude plays a bigger role for adult learners than for children, but the picture is far from clear-cut: the outcomes depend on structure tested and testing format. In particular, the argument for the role of implicit aptitude at all ages is based on an interpretation of untimed grammaticality tests, which certainly are not a pure measure of implicit knowledge (see, e.g., Suzuki, 2015, Suzuki & DeKeyser, 2015, and Suzuki & DeKeyser, in press). On the other hand, the results where explicit aptitude *was* predictive of performance by early acquirers were obtained with difficult grammaticality judgment tests that may induce explicit processes even when implicit knowledge is available. It can certainly be argued, then, that a fair amount of evidence shows a bigger involvement of aptitude for implicit learning in children than in adults, and a bigger involvement of aptitude for explicit learning in adults than in children, suggesting a shift from implicit to explicit processes with age.

Another way of establishing qualitative differences as a function of age, besides the psychological (individual differences) approach is to document how different linguistic structures are differentially affected by age of acquisition. If it is true that explicit learning processes are more involved for adults than for children, then one would expect the salience of the L2 structures involved to play a bigger role for adults than for children, because explicit learning is known to be much more sensitive to salience than implicit processes (see, e.g., Reber, Kassin, Lewis, & Cantor, 1980, experiment 1). In other words, the less salient a structure is, the bigger the decline in ultimate attainment with increasing age of arrival should be, because low salience means extra difficulty for explicit processes. Some preliminary evidence for this pattern was found in DeKeyser (2000), who pointed out that structures differing strongly in salience, but that were otherwise comparable, showed very different AoA effects. Performance on inversion in questions, for instance, strongly declined with age for wh-questions, but not for yes-no questions. DeKeyser argued that this may be because the inversion in yes-no questions is very salient, as there it is the primary way (besides intonation) of signaling a question, and the inverted verb is in initial and therefore salient position; but in wh-questions it is primarily the wh-word that signals a question and that is in salient position, while the inversion is in the middle of the sentence and carries little functional load, as the interrogative is already marked by the wh-word and the intonation. These explanations were post-hoc, however, and therefore it was important to carry out a study specifically designed to test the hypothesis that salience interacts with age, and preferably in a language very different from English and with much richer morphology, as explained in more detail in the next section.

Salience in Second Language Learning

As the chapters in the first part of this book make clear, many definitions of salience exist. From our point of view, they fall into three categories: narrow (meaning is not taken into account; the criteria are only perceptual, i.e., syllabic or not, stressed or not, number of phones, sonority of phones, position in sentence; e.g., Brown, 1973, p. 409); wide (including the salience of the meaning in the physical, psychological, or linguistic context, e.g., Ellis, in press); and medium (nothing extra-linguistic, but everything linguistic, i.e., noticeability of form for auditory, positional, or paradigmatic reasons; clarity of meaning, and transparency of form-meaning mapping). A definition in the third category is the one used in Goldschneider and DeKeyser (2001), who argued that the five predictors of order of acquisition in their meta-analysis of the English L2 "morpheme studies" (perceptual salience, morphophonological regularity, semantic complexity, syntactic category, and frequency) can all be seen as aspects of salience. The predictive power of the individual components of salience could not be determined clearly, however, because of the high degree of collinearity between these variables in the regression.

The operationalization used by Goldschneider and DeKeyser (2001) is the one we used for this study on age and salience as determinants of morpheme acquisition in Hebrew L2 among Russian immigrants in Israel, not only because salience in this sense was highly predictive of the order in which morphemes were acquired in Goldschneider and DeKeyser (2001), but also because we thought it important to use the same definition for a language which is morphologically about as different from English as can be, both in the sense that it is morphologically rich (Berman, 1978, 1981) and in the sense that aspects of salience that overlap in English usually do not overlap in Hebrew.

The Current Study

Given the need to test the hypothesis that salience interacts with age, and the need to test the predictive value of salience and its components in an L2 that fits this purpose better than English L2, a logical next step was to conduct a study on Hebrew L2. An extra advantage of Hebrew was the large number of immigrants in Israel with the same native language, Russian, especially around Tel Aviv.

Methodology

Subjects

The participants in this study were 52 Russian-speaking immigrants in Israel who were between 2–40 years old at the time of immigration (this was part of a larger study including Russian-speaking immigrants in North America also, as well as immigrants who were older than 40 at the time of immigration; the overall patterns in the data were reported in DeKeyser et al. [2010]). The participants had been exposed to Hebrew in Israel for at least 8 years ($max.$ = 20, M = 12, SD = 2.09), and all lived in various communities close to Tel Aviv. At the time of testing, each was at least 18 years old.

Instruments

All participants took a grammaticality judgment test in Hebrew consisting of 204 items representing 22 elements of Hebrew morphology, involving definite articles, numerals, noun plurals, adjective agreement, and verb agreement (see Appendix A for more detail). They were also administered a verbal aptitude test: the verbal sections of the Russian version of the Inter-University Psychometric Entrance Test (National Institute for Testing and Evaluation, 2001; see DeKeyser et al. [2010] for data on reliability and validity). The participants answered an extensive biographical questionnaire about their language background, language preference, use of and proficiency in Hebrew, educational background, social and economic situation, motivation, age at testing, and age of acquisition.

Procedure

The participants were tested individually or in small groups, usually at home. They were given the questionnaire first, then the grammaticality judgment test, and finally the aptitude test.

Results

The Role of Age

The overall patterns for the effect of age of acquisition (AoA) were reported in DeKeyser et al. (2010) and are briefly summarized here. The correlation analyses for all participants tested in Hebrew (n = 75), spanning a range of AoA from 2–68, and showed a large negative correlation between age of acquisition and ultimate attainment as measured by the grammaticality judgment test ($r = -0.79; p < .001$). They also showed a negligible correlation of ultimate attainment with length of residence ($r = 0.19$; ns), and a sizeable correlation with age at testing ($r = -0.77; p < .01$). Therefore, age at testing was used as a covariate in all further analyses.

Given that so much of the debate on age effects in the last few years has focused on discontinuities in the age-proficiency function, we did separate analyses for three different age brackets, i.e., 0–17, 18–40, and 40+ years. The first cutoff was chosen because age 17 has often been mentioned in the literature as a rough end-point for the critical period (e.g., Johnson & Newport, 1989), and the second because age 40 is often considered the beginning of middle age (e.g., Collins English Dictionary, 2014). For arrivals of up to age 17, the raw correlation between AoA and GJT, with age at testing partialed out, was $r = -0.51; p < .05$. For the 18–40 group, the same partial correlation between AoA and GJT was much smaller ($r = -0.12$; ns), and for the group with AoA over 40 it was somewhat higher but still not significant ($r = 0.33$; ns). As we argued in DeKeyser et al. (2010), the impact of age at testing for this group indicates that a very different phenomenon is going on here, which has nothing to do anymore with the critical period (presumably the effect of more advanced age on test performance; recall that, given the minimum length of residence for this study, people in the AoA 40+ group must have been 49 at the very least at the time of testing, and in most cases must have been 60+). Therefore, we decided to limit the present analysis to the 52 participants who were no older than 40 at the time of onset.

The Interaction Between Age and Salience

All 22 structures represented on the test were given a score for eight subcomponents of salience, five taken from Goldschneider and DeKeyser (2001), i.e., syllabicity (+/−), length (in phones), homonymy (+/−), e.g., *'te-saper' (she)-Future-tell/ (you)-Future-tell=she/ you will tell; (you)-tell-Imperative=tell*), allomorphy (number of morphophonological variants, potentially on the stem), e.g. *'bat='girl'; 'bit-i, girl-possessive=my girl'; bnot ha-kfar 'girl=Pl, Fem the-village=the girls of the village*), and semantic complexity (number of meanings expressed by the morpheme in question); and three new ones added for Hebrew, i.e., stress (+/−), distance, and mismatch (*even* 'stone, Sing, Fem; *avan-im* stone, Plm Masc suffix/*evenot* 'stone-Pl Fem=stones'). Distance here refers to the distance expressed in morphemes in agreement patterns between the grammatical morpheme expressing agreement and the lexeme it agrees with. Mismatch is the label we use for gender mismatches in noun plural suffixes, generally dictated by the phonological form and grammatical gender of the singular form of the noun, particularly for plural nouns that undergo stem change.

For each structure, the scores for the eight aspects of salience were summed (scores for stress, syllabicity, and length being positive; and scores for homonymy, allomorphy, semantic complexity, distance, and mismatch being negative). Ideally, of course, one would have a theoretically justified way of weighting the different components, but there are no established criteria to do that, so giving each component equal weight at this stage of the analysis seemed preferable. The 22 structures (see Appendix A) were then divided into three groups (high, mid, low) according to this total score for all aspects of salience. We chose this division into three groups rather than using a continuous scale for a number of reasons: 1) the continuous scale would not be an interval scale, only ordinal, and would hence impute a degree of precision the instruments don't have and/or limit what can be done with the numbers statistically; and 2) the interaction between the two grouping variables (age group and salience level) is more intuitively interpretable than the interaction with a continuous variable (and an ANCOVA for the age groups with salience as a covariate would not be possible, given that the regression lines are not parallel).

Examples of the three salience categories are:

> High salience: *maxshir/maxshirim* ('tool/tools'): regular noun plural; salience aspects: +syllabic, +stress, -mismatch (it is a masculine noun and takes a masculine plural suffix), -distance (suffix attached directly to noun), -homophony (but possible allomorphy with two other plural suffixes), -semantic complexity.
>
> Mid salience: *ha-sdinim (shel Dan) xadashim* ('the sheets (of Dan) are new-PL'): regular plural of predicative adjective, masculine suffix agreeing with masculine plural noun; salience aspects: +syllabic, +stress, -mismatch (takes a masculine plural suffix to agree with a masculine plural noun), but +distance from agreement source (as the adjective is far from the head noun), and possible allomorphy with two other plural suffixes; -length, -homonymy and -semantic complexity. The interface of adjectives with nouns has implications for syntactic complexity and for the information structure of discourse (Englebretson, 1997). Hebrew adjectives have been found to place a cognitive burden on L2 learners whose L1 has a different morphological typology, as is the case for English.
>
> *(Alfi-Shabtay & Ravid, 2012)*
>
> Low salience: *ha-beycim (shel ima) gdolot* ('the eggs (FEM but with MASC. suffix) of the mother are big (PL FEM)'): irregular plural predicative adjective;

salience aspects: +syllabic, +stress, -homonymy, but +distance, allomorphy with two other plural suffixes, -length, and +mismatch (as the feminine noun beycim 'eggs' ends with a masculine suffix -im instead of a feminine plural suffix -ot). This may lead to misinterpretation of the form as a masculine gender in adjective inflection, such as *beycim gdolim 'eggs [FEM] big,' when the feminine suffix -ot is required.

(Ravid, 1995)

In order to investigate the hypothesized interaction between age and salience, we decided to divide the participants into three groups, ages 0–7, 8–17, and 17+ (see Figure 7.1), taking as the two cutoff points ages that are commonly found in the literature as presumed beginning and end points of the period of decline sometimes referred to as the critical period in a narrow sense (the wider sense referring to the whole period from birth to age 17 or so).

A two-way 3x3 ANCOVA was carried out with age group and salience category as independent variables, subjects' age at testing as covariate, and proficiency (GJT score) as the dependent variable. A significant interaction was found between salience levels and age of onset ($F = 3.18$, $p = .033$; Greenhouse-Geisser correction; partial $\eta^2 = 0.12$) in the sense that salience becomes more important with higher age of acquisition. Figure 7.1 shows the sources of this interaction; dotted lines between two means indicate a significant difference at $p < .05$. The differences are minor at mid- and high levels of salience, but when the salience level is low, the GJT scores decrease with increasing age of onset. Marginal means are presented in Table 7.1, adjusted for the covariate effect of age at testing.

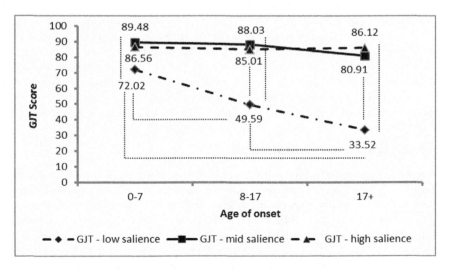

FIGURE 7.1 Interaction between salience level and age of acquisition

TABLE 7.1 GJT accuracy for salience level by age of onset (marginal means for age at testing as covariate)

	Age of Onset			
Salience	0–7	8–17	17–40	Total
Low	72.02	49.59	33.52	51.71
	(13.54)	(15.43)	(15.39)	(20.88)
Mid	89.48	88.03	80.91	86.14
	(7.44)	(16.81)	(19.63)	(18.80)
High	86.56	85.01	86.12	85.90
	(8.77)	(14.21)	(18.65)	(17.15)
Total	82.68	74.21	66.85	74.58
	(8.06)	(14.64)	(14.00)	(15.85)

Further Analysis: What Aspects of Salience Interact With Age?

In order to identify the contribution of various aspects of salience to acquisition, both as a main effect and in interaction with age, two repeated-measures logistic regression models were fitted to the data, one with interaction and one without. The repeated model was used because ordinary logistic regression analysis is not appropriate here, given that every structure (with its eight predictive characteristics) is measured on the same individuals; the analysis must take into account the dependence of the scores within each individual. See Appendix B for further details about the model.

With age and eight aspects of salience entered in the analysis, a borderline interaction effect with age was found for stress ($p = .09$) and distance ($p = .08$), in the sense that these two aspects of salience seem to become increasingly important with increasing age of acquisition. A main effect was found for several other aspects of salience: syllabicity ($p < .0001$), length ($p < .0001$), homonymy ($p < .01$), and mismatch ($p < .0001$). Two other aspects of salience, allomorphy and semantic complexity, did not show a significant effect. It should be taken into account, however, that semantic complexity showed a strong correlation with both stress and length.

Conclusions and Implications

The results of this study show that salience in the broad sense of the word has a large impact on the success rate for the acquisition of specific elements of morphology. Some aspects of salience appear to facilitate acquisition at all ages; others become particularly important for older learners. The growing importance of salience with increasing age is another indicator—along with the growing importance of aptitude for explicit learning documented in DeKeyser (2000) and DeKeyser et al. (2010)—that the age-induced changes in acquisition are of a qualitative and not just quantitative nature. Both the increasing reliance on aptitude for explicit learning and the increasing importance of (aspects of) salience with age suggest that the age differences that have been documented in much of the literature reflect qualitative, not just quantitative, differences, and that these qualitative differences result from a shift from largely implicit to largely explicit learning processes.

Implications for Further Research

This study is the first to look at the interaction between salience and age, and therefore certainly needs replication. It would be very useful to do a similar study with a different morphologically rich L2, such as Arabic or Japanese. At the same time, studying acquisition of the same L2 by populations with different L1s, using the same operational definitions, could also contribute much needed evidence for generalization across language pairs. Ultimately, expanding the scope of this study by including not only morphological but also syntactic patterns may shed further light on the role of age, salience, and their interaction. Understanding the role of salience in L2 acquisition is important because salience—unlike age, aptitude, or motivation—is a factor that can be manipulated in second language instruction (through various forms of input enhancement and explicit focus on form). Knowing what elements of salience, or rather lack of it, are most problematic and for what age groups could therefore constitute important information for evidence-based teaching. At the same time, of course, taking salience into account will be important for further research on age effects and may contribute to a better understanding of the roles of (different kinds of) aptitudes.

References

Abrahamsson, N., & Hyltenstam, K. (2008). The robustness of aptitude effects in near-native second language acquisition. *Studies in Second Language Acquisition, 30*(4), 481–509.

Abrahamsson, N., & Hyltenstam, K. (2009). Age of onset and nativelikeness in a second language: Listener perception versus linguistic scrutiny. *Language Learning, 59*(2), 249–306.

Alfi-Shabtay, I., & Ravid, D. (2012). Adjective inflection in Hebrew: A psycholinguistic study of Russian, English, and Arabic with native Hebrew speakers. In M. Leikin, M. Schwarts, & Y. Tobin (Eds.), *Current issues in bilingualism: Cognitive and socio-linguistic perspectives* (pp. 159–178). New York: Springer.

Asher, J. J., & García, R. (1969). The optimal age to learn a foreign language. *The Modern Language Journal, 53*, 334–341.

Berman, R. (1978). *Modern Hebrew structure*. Tel Aviv: Tel Aviv University Press.

Berman, R. (1981). Regularity vs. anomaly: The acquisition of inflectional morphology. *Journal of Child Language, 8*, 265–282.

Birdsong, D. (1992). Ultimate attainment in second language acquisition. *Language, 68*(4), 706–755.

Birdsong, D., & Molis, M. (2001). On the evidence for maturational constraints in second-language acquisition. *Journal of Memory and Language, 44*, 235–249.

Bongaerts, T., Planken, B., & Schils, E. (1995). Can late learners attain a native accent in a foreign language? A test of the critical period hypothesis. In D. Singleton & Z. Lengyel (Eds.), *The age factor in second language acquisition* (pp. 30–50). Clevedon, UK: Multilingual Matters.

Brown, R. (1973). *A first language: The early stages.* Cambridge, MA: Harvard University Press.

Carroll, J. B., & Sapon, S. (1959). *Modern language aptitude test: Form A.* New York: The Psychological Corporation.

Collins English dictionary (12th ed.). (2014). Glasgow, United Kingdom: Collins.

DeKeyser, R. M. (2000). The robustness of critical period effects in second language acquisition. *Studies in Second Language Acquisition, 22*(4), 499–533.

DeKeyser, R. M. (2006). A critique of recent arguments against the critical period hypothesis. In C. Abello-Contesse, R. Chacón-Beltrán, M. D. López-Jiménez, & M. M. Torreblanca-López (Eds.), *Age in L2 acquisition and teaching* (pp. 49–58). Bern, Switzerland: Peter Lang.

DeKeyser, R. M., Alfi-Shabtay, I., & Ravid, D. (2010). Cross-linguistic evidence for the nature of age effects in second language acquisition. *Applied Psycholinguistics, 31*(3), 413–438.

Ellis, N. C. (in press). Salience in language usage, learning, and change. In M. Hundt, S. Pfenninger, & S. Mollin (Eds.), *The changing English language: Psycholinguistic perspectives.* Cambridge, UK: Cambridge University Press.

Englebretson, R. (1997). Genre and grammar: Predicative and attributive adjectives in spoken English. *Berkeley Linguistics Society, 23,* 411–421.

Goldschneider, J. M., & DeKeyser, R. M. (2001). Explaining the "natural order of L2 morpheme acquisition" in English: A meta-analysis of multiple determinants. *Language Learning, 51*(1), 1–50.

Granena, G. (2013). Individual differences in sequence learning ability and second language acquisition in early childhood and adulthood. *Language Learning, 63*(4), 665–703.

Granena, G. (2014). Language aptitude and long-term achievement in early childhood L2 learners. *Applied Linguistics, 35*(4), 483–503.

Granena, G., & Long, M. (2013). Age of onset, length of residence, language aptitude, and ultimate L2 attainment in three linguistic domains. *Second Language Research, 29*(3), 311–343.

Hakuta, K. (2001). A critical period for second language acquisition? In D. Bailey, J. Bruer, F. Symons, & J. Lichtman (Eds.), *Critical thinking about critical periods* (pp. 193–205). Baltimore, MD: Paul H. Brookes.

Hakuta, K., Bialystok, E., & Wiley, E. (2003). Critical evidence: A test of the critical-period hypothesis for second-language acquisition. *Psychological Science, 14*(1), 31–38.

Jia, G., & Aaronson, D. (2003). A longitudinal study of Chinese children and adolescents learning English in the United States. *Applied Psycholinguistics, 24*(1), 131–161.

Jia, G., Aaronson, D., & Wu, Y. (2002). Long-term language attainment of bilingual immigrants: Predictive variables and language group differences. *Applied Psycholinguistics, 23*(4), 599–621.

Johnson, J. S., & Newport, E. L. (1989). Critical period effects in second language learning: The influence of maturational state on the acquisition of English as a second language. *Cognitive Psychology, 21,* 60–99.

Lenneberg, E. H. (1967). *Biological foundations of language.* New York: Wiley.

Long, M. (2007). *Problems in SLA.* Mahwah, NJ: Lawrence Erlbaum Associates.

Monner, D., Vatz, K., Morini, G., Hwang, S.-O., & DeKeyser, R. (2013). A neural network model of the effects of entrenchment and memory development on grammatical gender learning. *Bilingualism: Language and Cognition, 16*(2), 246–265.

Newport, E. (1990). Maturational constraints on language learning. *Cognitive Science, 14,* 11–28.

Oyama, S. (1976). A sensitive period for the acquisition of a nonnative phonological system. *Journal of Psycholinguistic Research, 5*(3), 261–283.
Patkowski, M. S. (1980). The sensitive period for the acquisition of syntax in a second language. *Language Learning, 30*, 449–472.
Penfield, W., & Roberts, L. (1959). *Speech and brain-mechanisms*. Princeton, NJ: Princeton University Press.
Ravid, D. (1995). *Language change in child and adult Hebrew: A psycholinguistic perspective*. New York: Oxford University Press.
Reber, A., Kassin, S., Lewis, S., & Cantor, G. (1980). On the relationship between implicit and explicit modes in the learning of a complex rule structure. *Journal of Experimental Psychology: Human Learning and Memory, 6*, 492–502.
Suzuki, Y. (2015). *Using new measures of implicit L2 knowledge to study the interface of explicit and implicit knowledge* (Unpublished doctoral dissertation). University of Maryland, College Park, MD.
Suzuki, Y., & DeKeyser, R. (2015). Does elicited imitation measure implicit knowledge? Evidence from the word-monitoring task. *Language Learning, 65*(4), 860–895.
Suzuki, Y., & DeKeyser, R. (in press). The interface of explicit and implicit knowledge in a second language. *Language Learning*.
van Boxtel, S., Bongaerts, T., & Coppen, P.-A. (2005). Native-like attainment of dummy subjects in Dutch and the role of the L1. *IRAL—International Review of Applied Linguistics, 43*, 355–380.
White, L., & Genesee, F. (1996). How native is near-native? The issue of ultimate attainment in adult second language acquisition. *Second Language Research, 12*(3), 233–265.

APPENDIX A

The structures in this table are listed in descending order of salience. For example, 'noun plurals' is categorized as high salience (3) in Hebrew, whereas definite article in complex constructions is categorized as low salience (1). The table provides a key for calculating the scores of the different structures by the various criteria explained in the text. Each of the eight categories of salience has a different scale, e.g., **stress**: 0–1 [e.g., noun plurals, no suffix *maxshir* 'tool' is more stressed (1) than numerals Fm *arba* 'four']; **syllabicity**: 0–1 [e.g., numeral masculine *shalosh* 'three' (1) versus numerals Fm Irreg *tesha* 'nine' (0)]; **length**: 1–2 [e.g, adjective agreement, Sg regular in NP *shaxor* 'black' (2) versus Numerals Fm *arba* 'four' (1)]; **homonomy**: 0–1 [e.g, verb agreement, past tense *hevanta* '(you)-understood' (0) versus verb agreement, future tense *yitxatnu* '(they-will)-get married' (1)]; **allomorphy:** 0–2 [e.g., verb agreement, past tense *hevanta* (you)-understood (0), verb agreement, present tense *medaberet* (you)-are talking (1), adjective agreement, Sg regular in NP *mehira* 'fast' (2)]; **mismatch**: 0–2 [e.g., noun plurals, no suffix *maxshir* 'tool' (0), noun plurals, mismatched suffix *milim* 'words' (1), Numeral Masc Irreg *shiva sulamot* 'seven ledders' (2)]; **semantic complexity**: 1–5 [e.g., plural in NP with mass noun *mayim xamim* 'hot water' (1) versus definite article in complex construction *nehag ha-otobus* 'the-bus driver' (5)], **distance**: 0–2 [e.g., noun plurals no suffix *naxshir* 'tool (0) versus adjective agreement, plural in predicate position with mass noun *ha-kos nekiya* 'the glass is empty' (2)]. Scores for stress, syllabicity, and length are positive as they contribute to salience; scores for homonymy, allomorphy, semantic complexity, distance, and mismatch are negative. Structures with a total score above 0 fall into category 3 (highest salience), those with a score of 0 into category 2 (mid salience) and those with a score below 0 into category 1 (low salience).

TABLE 7.2 Salience and its components for the structures on the grammaticality judgment test

	Category								
	salience category	*stress*	*syllabicity*	*length*	*Homonymy*	*allomorphy*	*mismatch*	*semantic complexity*	*distance*
Noun plurals									
No suffix	3	1	1	2	0	−2	0	−2	0
Mismatched suffix	3	1	1	2	0	−2	−1	−2	0
Adjective agreement									
Sg regular in NP	3	1	1	2	0	−2	0	−2	−1
Sg regular in predicate	2	1	1	2	0	−2	0	−2	−2
Sg irregular in NP	2	1	1	2	0	−2	−1	−2	−1
Sg irregular in predicate	2	1	1	2	0	−2	−1	−2	−2
Pl regular in NP	3	1	1	2	0	−1	0	−2	−1
Pl regular in predicate	3	1	1	2	0	−1	0	−2	−2
Pl irregular in NP	3	1	1	2	0	−1	−1	−2	−1
Pl irregular in predicate	2	1	1	2	0	−1	−1	−2	−2
Pl in NP with mass	3	1	1	2	0	−1	0	−1	−1
Pl in Pred with mass	3	1	1	2	0	−1	0	−1	−2
Category									
Verb agreement									
Past tense	2	0	1	2	0	0	0	−3	−2
Future tense	2	1	1	2	−1	0	0	−3	−2
Present tense	3	1	1	2	0	−1	0	−2	−2
Morpho-phonology	1	1	1	1	−1	−1	−1	−2	−2

(*Continued*)

TABLE 7.2 (Continued)

	Category salience category	stress	syllabicity	length	Homonymy	allomorphy	mismatch	semantic complexity	distance
Definite article									
Definite article in simplex constructions	1	0	1	1	0	−1	0	−5	−1
Definite article in complex constructions	1	0	1	1	0	−1	0	−5	−2
Numerals									
Numerals Masc	1	1	1	1	−1	0	−1	−4	−1
Numerals Fm	1	0	0	1	0	0	−1	−4	−1
Numerals Masc Irreg	1	1	1	1	−1	0	−2	−4	−1
Numerals Fm Irreg	1	0	0	1	0	0	−2	−4	−1

APPENDIX B

Model with interaction:
   Let Y_{ij} be the number of correct ith person scores on jth structure.

$$Y_{ij} \sim \text{Binomial}(N_j, \Pi_{ij})$$

where N_j is the number of question in jth structure
   Π_{ij} is the true percentage correct for the ith person on jth structure

$$\begin{aligned}\text{Logit}(\Pi_{ij}) = {}& \alpha + \beta_1 age_i + \beta_2 X_{j2} + \beta_3 X_{j3} + \beta_4 X_{j4} + \beta_5 X_{j5} + \beta_6 X_{j6} \\ & + \beta_7 X_{j7} + \beta_8 X_{j8} + \beta_9 X_{j9} + \gamma_{12}\, age_i \star X_{j2} + \gamma_{13}\, age_i \star X_{j3} \\ & + \gamma_{14}\, age_i \star X_{j4} + \gamma_{15}\, age_i \star X_{j5} + \gamma_{16}\, age_i \star X_{j6} + \gamma_{17}\, age_i \\ & \star X_{j7} + \gamma_{18}\, age_i \star X_{j8} + \gamma_{19}\, age_i \star X_{j9} + \Gamma_i\end{aligned}$$

where age_i = age of ith person,
   X_{j2} = value of X_2 on jth structure, j = 2, . . . ,9,
and
   Γ_i is the random effect on jth person where the random effects are independently identical distributed as $N(0, \sigma\Gamma)$

From the SAS output, there are no statistically significant interactions between eight grammatical characteristics and age with exception of X_2 and X_9, which shows borderline significances with P-value of 0.0895 and 0.0813, respectively. We then fit another model without interaction to test the main effect of the eight grammatical characteristics on scores of structures.

Model without interaction:

$$\text{Logit}(\Pi_{ij}) = \alpha + \beta_1 \text{age}_i + \beta_2 X_{j2} + \beta_3 X_{j3} + \beta_4 X_{j4} + \beta_5 X_{j5} + \beta_6 X_{j6} + \beta_7 X_{j7} + \beta_8 X_{j8} + \beta_9 X_{j9} + \Gamma_i$$

This model yielded significant outcomes for X_3 (P-value < 0.0001), X_4 (P-value < 0.0001), X_5 (P-value = 0.002), X_7 (P-value < 0.0001), and age (P-value < 0.0001).

Note:
X_2 = stress
X_3 = syllabicity
X_4 = length
X_5 = homonymy
X_6 = allomorphy
X_7 = mismatch
X_8 = semantic complexity
X_9 = distance

8
SALIENCE AND NOVEL L2 PATTERN LEARNING

Kim McDonough and Pavel Trofimovich

Introduction

According to frequency-based approaches to acquisition, exposure to exemplars and the engagement of cognitive mechanisms are believed to facilitate the acquisition of constructions (Bybee, 2008; Ellis, 2012; Goldberg, 2009; Tomasello, 2003). As defined by Goldberg (2006), constructions refer to learned pairings of form and function that include individual words and abstract linguistic patterns (e.g., the verb–object–locative construction [Subj + V + Obj + PP], as in *he put the box in the kitchen*) and that are governed by lexical and semantic rules. At various stages in the acquisition of a construction, different types of input may be particularly useful. In the initial stage when learners are first associating a form with its meaning, providing input which contains sentences constructed from a limited set of lexical items (i.e., low-variability input) may help them recognize the underlying similarity in structural relationships, rather than perceive each exemplar as a unique construction. Furthermore, low-variability input in which a key lexical item in the construction occurs with high token frequency (i.e., skewed distribution) may be particularly helpful as compared to input in which each key lexical item occurs with equal token frequency (i.e., balanced distribution). However, later in the acquisition process when learners are generalizing a construction to new lexical items or consolidating related constructions into a more abstract representation, input that provides greater lexical variety may promote pattern extension.

The Challenge of Novel L2 Pattern Learning

Empirical studies by Goldberg and colleagues with English first language (L1) speakers demonstrated that low-variability input with a skewed distribution promoted fast form-meaning mapping of a novel construction (Casenhiser & Goldberg,

2005; Goldberg & Casenhiser, 2008; Goldberg, Casenhiser, & Sethuraman, 2004; Goldberg, Casenhiser, & White, 2007; McDonough & Trofimovich, 2015). These studies involved the appearance construction, which was created using English nouns (Ns) and nonce verbs (Vs) following the N_1N_2V—*o* word order, with the corresponding meaning of N_1 appears in/on N_2 (e.g., *the spot the king moopoed, the sailor the pond naifoed*). However, although L2 researchers have found positive effects for low-variability input and construction learning, they have not reported advantages for a skewed distribution (Brooks, Kwoka, & Kempe, 2017; McDonough & Nekrasova-Becker, 2014; Nakamura, 2012; Year & Gordon, 2009). Within this line of research, our initial studies tested the effectiveness of low-variability input, with both skewed and balanced distributions, at helping L2 speakers learn the Esperanto transitive construction, while our later studies explored additional factors that might enhance construction learning. Nevertheless, across all studies that tested the Esperanto transitive, the participants' (N = 417) accuracy rate was only 40% for the most difficult sentence type, which is the OVS transitive (Fulga & McDonough, 2016; McDonough & Fulga, 2015; McDonough & Trofimovich, 2013, 2016; McDonough, Trofimovich, Dao, & Dion, 2016).

When faced with learners' relatively poor performance in our initial study, we searched for reasons why accuracy rates were so low and examined several factors that might positively affect pattern learning. A key learning challenge is the nature of the Esperanto transitive construction, which consists of both morphological and syntactic features. In terms of morphology, the suffix *-n* is added to mark all nouns as objects, regardless of their other features, such as animacy or definiteness. For example, the word apple (*pomo*) appears without an affix when it functions as the subject, but receives the *-n* suffix when it functions as the object (*pomon*). Nouns occur without indefinite articles, and subjects do not have agreement features with verbs, such as for person or number. In terms of syntax, word order in Esperanto transitive constructions is variable, as the accusative suffix differentiates subjects from objects. Although many word orders are possible, the most commonly used are SVO and OVS (Cox, 2011; Harlow, 1995), as in *knabo mordas pomon* and *pomon mordas knabo* (boy bites apple). As an example, both *filino mordas pomon* [SVO] and *pomon mordas filino* [OVS] express the meaning of 'girl bites apple.'

Unlike the appearance construction tested by Goldberg and colleagues, whose meaning could be understood by relying on word order, Esperanto transitives require reliance on morphology. For learners who are accustomed to using word order as a dominant cue for sentence interpretation, their initial tendency would be to interpret the first noun in an Esperanto transitive as the agent regardless of its case marking, which is consistent with predictions of the unified competition model of language acquisition (MacWhinney, 2012). This model holds that learners' L2 comprehension and production are shaped by the competition of all linguistic cues to utterance interpretation, including cues that come from their previously learned languages. Furthermore, even when there are similarities in how a speaker's previously learned languages encode argument roles, L2 learners may rely on word order as a general default strategy when processing morphology (Ferreira, 2003).

Put simply, the need to adopt morphology rather than word order as the most reliable cue for sentence interpretation may have contributed to the low accuracy rates for Esperanto transitives. In fact, previous research has shown how difficult it is for learners to adopt new morphosyntactic cues in L2 development (e.g., Gass, 1987; Jiang, 2007; Kempe & MacWhinney, 1998).

In order to enhance the likelihood that learners would learn that morphology—as opposed to word order—is the most effective strategy for understanding Esperanto transitives, we implemented a variety of experimental manipulations. In the first studies (Fulga & McDonough, 2016; McDonough & Trofimovich, 2013), we examined the effectiveness of low-variability input by manipulating several variables: the input distribution of training sentences (balanced or skewed), the instructions provided to the learners (deductive or inductive), and the nature of the visual images (color or black/white because color visuals have been found to positively influence recall, recognition memory, and semantic processing). Although we found no main effects for input distribution, type of instructions, or visual images, there was a significant interaction between input distribution and instructions. The combination of balanced input and instructions that told participants about the rules governing Esperanto transitives was most effective. The participants' language background was also examined (Fulga & McDonough, 2016; McDonough & Fulga, 2015), with both studies showing that learners whose first languages (L1s) had differential case marking based on definiteness were most successful. In later studies, we explored the potential contribution of learners' working memory and statistical learning abilities to novel pattern learning (McDonough & Trofimovich, 2016), and explored whether one-on-one learning tasks with an interlocutor would facilitate greater learning than listening activities administered to a group of learners (McDonough & Trofimovich, 2016). More details about these studies and their findings are discussed in subsequent sections that focus more narrowly on specific conceptualizations of salience.

Salience and Novel L2 Pattern Learning

In order to provide greater insight into these data, this chapter examines the effectiveness of the various experimental manipulations tested across the five studies. The goal is to consider the broader construct of salience in terms of how the specific characteristics of target materials, learner-internal factors, and learners' use of the learning environment may have affected the likelihood that they would learn the novel pattern. In discussing salience, as it applies to L2 learning and use, we draw on the multifaceted conceptualization of salience proposed by Ellis (2016). According to Ellis, salience can be determined through various aspects of the physical world and a person's experience with it, such that salience can be understood as a "property of the stimulus, and of the learner . . . , and of the context" (p. 344). These three aspects of salience correspond closely to several experimental manipulations employed in our research, which allows us to explore several facets of salience as being more or less relevant to the challenge faced by L2 learners in acquiring novel morphosyntactic patterns.

The first aspect of salience relevant to our research on the learning of Esperanto transitives pertains to salience as understood as the psychophysical characteristics of stimuli or objects in the world (see Ellis, Chapter 2). Applied to language, physical characteristics of salience would correspond to the properties of input that would make some of its aspects—compared to others—more distinct perceptually and hence more memorable to the learner. For example, in a meta-analysis of the research targeting the learning of English morphology, Goldschneider and DeKeyser (2001) showed that learners' accuracy with various morphological markers was associated with the perceptual salience of these markers (e.g., in terms of their status as free or bound morphemes; see also Behney, Gass, Spinner, and Valmori, Chapter 5), their frequency in the language, and the ease with which they can be readily associated with specific meanings (i.e., reliability of form-function mapping).

A focus on various distributions of low-variability input (skewed versus balanced), which represents a common theme in research on L2 morphosyntactic learning, aligns well with the view of salience as the property of the stimulus, in the sense that a particular distribution of input might make the key morphological aspect of Esperanto (accusative case marking) distinct, thus enabling learners to forge an initial link between the marker and its meaning and/or to extend this association beyond a few representative exemplars in the input. In our Esperanto studies, the skewed distribution included Esperanto transitive constructions created from a limited number of lexical nouns, but one noun occurred as an object with high token frequency. Having one noun in accusative case with high token frequency might help learners extract the underlying structure of the exemplars using that noun, such that the structure can then be generalized to other nouns. Although the balanced distribution similarly included Esperanto transitive constructions created from a limited number of nouns, each noun occurred as an object with equally low token frequency. Having the accusative suffix occur consistently across all nouns may help learners identify its relationship to other sentence elements.

The second aspect of salience relevant to the data on the learning of the Esperanto transitives relates to what Ellis (2016) termed the "top-down, memory-dependent, expectation-driven" account of salience (p. 343), which captures how prior knowledge, experience, or expectations can render certain aspects of input more or less salient for learners. Put differently, the cognitive and experiential toolkit that learners bring to the task of language learning might determine which aspects of input will be attended to and which might be processed less deeply or not processed at all. For instance, the specific instructions given to learners in a learning activity might create a set of top-down expectations that would guide them, in their processing of input, to attend to some of its aspects at the expense of others. As an example, learners who are given explicit information about grammatical rules might orient to language in the input differently than learners who are told to pay attention to the meaning of utterances. Similarly, learners whose L1s allow for overt case marking might be particularly sensitive to case marking in Esperanto due to their extensive experience with case marking in previously learned language(s), compared to learners whose

L1s do not mark case or whose L1s mark case based on various semantic-pragmatic properties of nouns, such as animacy or definiteness.

In our studies, learners' L1 backgrounds were classified into categories identified by Sinnemäki (2014) in terms of whether and how the languages marked case on objects. Some languages never use case to indicate which noun functions as the object in a transitive construction, such as Cantonese, Dutch, English, French, Italian, Lao, Mandarin, Portuguese, Tagalog, Thai, and Vietnamese. This contrasts with Esperanto and other languages (e.g., Icelandic and Georgian) where overt case marking occurs regardless of a noun's semantic properties, which is referred to as nonrestrictive case marking. However, some languages have differential object case marking, in which nouns receive overt accusative affixes depending on their semantic-pragmatic properties, which include animacy, definiteness, information structure, and kinship terms. Commonly referenced semantic-pragmatic properties are animacy (Hindi, Telugu, Malayalam) and definiteness (Farsi, Turkish). Differential case marking has a narrower scope than restrictive case marking, where factors other than semantic-pragmatic properties (such as gender, number, word order, and plurality) determine whether accusative affixes are used. Languages with restrictive case marking include German, Japanese, Korean, Polish, and Russian.

Yet another aspect of salience which might be relevant to the learning of novel morphosyntactic structures by L2 learners is what Ellis (2016, p. 344) called a "context and surprisal" account of salience. Assuming that most learning situations are characterized by highly contextualized, embedded interactions between learners and their learning environments, this aspect of salience involves the extent to which the broader learning context might enhance certain aspects of input, creating the element of 'surprisal,' or heightened relevance of input within a contextualized learning situation. In this sense, some learning situations might be richer than others in terms of such situational affordances. For example, unlike non-interactive learning tasks administered in a group setting using timed presentation slides, one-on-one listening and speaking activities with an interlocutor might provide learners with opportunities to produce target utterances and receive feedback from an interlocutor, request repetition of difficult structures, and take the needed time to associate the form of utterances with their meanings depicted in images. Our most recent Esperanto study, which employed eye-tracking measures, explored whether such situational affordances (feedback and interlocutor eye-gaze) might enhance certain aspects of input for learners, making it easier for them to create form-meaning associations for difficult morphosyntactic patterns and extend this initial knowledge beyond a few trained exemplars.

To summarize, the goal of this chapter is to revisit our previous data targeting the learning of the Esperanto transitive construction by L2 learners, analyzing these data through the lens of salience conceptualized as a "stimulus-learner-context complex" (Ellis, 2016, p. 345). The current analysis is guided by the following research question: "Across all studies, what factors associated with various aspects of salience facilitated L2 morphosyntactic pattern learning?" The following section provides an overview of the general research paradigm followed across all studies, but highlights methodological differences that reflect specific dimensions of salience.

Method

Participants

The participants were English L2 speakers ($N = 417$) who were studying degree programs at universities in Thailand and Canada. They were adults, ranging in age from their late teens to late twenties. They were relatively equally divided across gender (52% women), and came from a variety of L1 backgrounds (see "Salience as a Property of the Learner" subsection ahead for details). None of the participants had any prior knowledge of Esperanto.

Materials and Procedure

All experiments implemented learning and test materials. The learning materials were created to provide participants with low-variability input in the form of a small set of lexical items (4–7 nouns, 2–3 verbs) that were used to create equal numbers of SVO and OVS sentences (22–32 items total). The nouns were either used an equal number of times as objects (balanced distribution) or one noun occurred more frequently as the object (skewed distribution). The participants were first trained in the meaning of the lexical items, which involved the presentation of visual images paired with the corresponding orthographic forms, followed by presentation of visual images only. Following a vocabulary test to ensure that the word meanings had been acquired, most of the participants heard sentences and selected which of two visual images corresponded to their meaning, with the exception of the earliest study (McDonough & Trofimovich, 2013), where the participants selected one of two visual images to indicate which noun in each sentence was the object.

The learning phase was followed by a test phase, which included an immediate test using the same lexical items as the learning phase (6–12 items), a generalization test in which new lexical items were targeted (12–30 items), or both tests. When included, the purpose of the generalization test was to determine whether the knowledge participants had acquired was lexically-specific or could be applied to new nouns. The test items could not be correctly identified based on the meaning of lexical items only, because the visual images depicted fully reversible events. In order to understand the sentence correctly and select the corresponding image, participants had to rely on the accusative -*n* suffix rather than word order (either SVO or OVS). For example, participants had to select between an image of a horse chasing a bull or an image of a bull chasing a horse when they heard the test sentence *tauron pelas cevalo* [OVS] "horse chases bull."

For the majority of the studies, timed presentation slides with embedded visual images and audio files were created to control delivery and response times. Participants received answer sheets with sets of images in rows, and their task was to select the correct image for each sentence. The participants completed the experimental materials in groups (6–30), after a researcher explained the tasks, gave instructions, and clarified any questions. For the majority of the studies, there were no opportunities to produce Esperanto transitives during the learning activities. However, for the most recent study that included eye-tracking data, participants had an individual session with a researcher who carried out the materials in a one-on-one setting without the use of prerecorded, timed presentation slides. Non-verbal cues, such as eye-gaze and pointing gestures, were used by the researchers in an attempt to draw participants' attention to the correct visual image, which were displayed on posterboards. Furthermore, participants were asked to produce Esperanto transitive sentences as part of the learning phase, and the researcher provided feedback in the form of recasts in response to their grammatical errors.

Analysis

Learning of the Esperanto transitive construction was operationalized in three studies through d' values, which are a measure of sensitivity (corrected for response bias) at discriminating between two response alternatives. In the remaining two studies (McDonough & Trofimovich, 2016; McDonough et al., 2016), simple accuracy rates (number correct) was summed for all test items or only the OVS items. In order to compare across all studies, the current analysis operationalized learning in terms of OVS accuracy rates only, which reflect the participants' ability to understand the more difficult Esperanto transitive that requires understanding of case marking. Participants can interpret SVO transitives correctly by relying on SVO word order by using knowledge from previously known languages, including their knowledge of English as an L2, or by applying a general processing strategy to interpret the first noun as agent. Due to variation in the number of tests and test items, the raw scores for OVS items were converted to proportions (OVS items correct over total OVS items). Either independent-samples t-tests or one-way ANOVAs were used to compare participants' performance based on the aspect of salience being investigated.

Results

The research question asked what factors associated with salience facilitated L2 morphosyntactic pattern learning. To address this question, data across all our Esperanto studies were compared to test the effectiveness of three possible conceptualizations of salience at facilitating L2 speakers' ability to learn a novel morphosyntactic pattern: external manipulations to the learning materials, learner-internal variables (L1 background and expectations created through task instructions), and learners' use of the learning environment.

Salience as a Property of the Stimulus

To explore whether the researchers' efforts to enhance the salience of the key morphological and syntactic features of the Esperanto transitive construction affected pattern learning, we examined the impact of manipulating the input distribution of the target construction. The majority of the studies provided balanced input, which was low-variability input where the transitive construction appeared with a small

TABLE 8.1 OVS learning by input distribution

Distribution	n	M	SD	95% CI
Skewed	93	0.38	0.30	[0.32, 0.44]
Balanced	324	0.41	0.38	[0.37, 0.45]

Note: CI = confidence interval.

set of lexical items, with each target noun used an equal number of times. However, in light of claims about the benefits of low-variability input in which one exemplar occurs with high token frequency (i.e., skewed input), two of the initial studies compared learning materials with either a balanced or skewed input distribution (Fulga & McDonough, 2016; McDonough & Trofimovich, 2013).

As shown in Table 8.1, there was little difference in the OVS scores based on input distribution, and an independent-samples *t*-test confirmed that there was no statistically significant difference in the proportion scores: $t(415) = 0.76$, $p = .450$, $d = 0.09$. Thus, the findings for OVS proportion scores from the entire dataset confirm the results of both prior Esperanto studies that measured performance based on d' prime sensitivity values (Fulga & McDonough, 2016; McDonough & Trofimovich, 2013). In addition, the absence of any advantage for skewed input with Esperanto transitives confirms the findings of previous studies that targeted a wider range of structures, including Samoan ergatives (Nakamura, 2012), English datives (Year & Gordon, 2009), and Russian case inflections (Brooks et al., 2017).

Salience as a Property of the Learner

The second conceptualization of salience we investigated involved: 1) learners' individual differences, particularly in terms of their prior experience with case marking in previously learned languages; and 2) the amount and type of explicit information about Esperanto provided to the participants. These two manipulated variables dealt with learner-internal aspects of salience—namely, effects of prior knowledge and of expectations created through task instructions on the learning of the Esperanto transitive construction.

With respect to learners' individual differences, it is possible that linguistic information may be more or less salient to learners based on their own cognitive, psychological, or social characteristics. For example, studies of working memory or statistical learning ability have investigated whether high-scoring learners are more likely to detect linguistic regularities than learners with lower scores. We explored an individual difference (i.e., L1 background) that has been shown to play a role in L2 speakers' orientation to linguistic information. Although this variable was included in the experimental design in only two studies (Fulga & McDonough, 2016; McDonough & Fulga, 2015), we collected information about learners' L1 background in all studies.

Across the dataset, the majority of the participants (56%) spoke L1s that did not use case marking, which included mostly Thai L1 speakers along with L1 speakers of

TABLE 8.2 OVS scores by L1 background

L1 group	N	M	SD	95% CI
No case marking	232	0.34	0.32	[0.30, 0.38]
Definiteness	129	0.56	0.40	[0.48, 0.63]
Animacy	58	0.33	0.34	[0.24, 0.42]

Mandarin, Portuguese, and Vietnamese. The remaining participants spoke languages with differential object marking based on either definiteness (30%), mostly Farsi, but also Arabic and Tamil; or animacy (14%), distributed across French, Gujarati, Hindi, Punjabi, Spanish, and Telugu. Four participants who spoke L1s with restrictive case marking (i.e., limited to a subset of objects regardless of influencing factors, as in Japanese and Russian) were excluded from this analysis. In terms of any additional previously known languages, most participants reported only knowing their L1 and English. Less than one-third of the participants reported knowledge of heritage languages, primarily Mandarin, as well as some proficiency in French or Spanish as an additional L2. As shown in Table 8.2, the participants from definiteness L1s scored higher (0.56) than those with animacy L1s (0.33) or L1s without case marking (0.34).

Because the homogeneity of variance assumption was violated, a one-way ANOVA with the Welch F ratio is reported. The ANOVA indicated that there was a statistically significant difference among the scores, Welch's $F(2, 143.06) = 14.36$, $p = .001$. Games-Howell post-hoc tests indicated that the definiteness L1 group scored significantly higher than animacy L1 group ($p < .001$, $d = 0.62$) and the no case marking group ($p < .001$, $d = 0.61$), but there was no difference between the animacy and no case marking groups ($p = .982$, $d = 0.03$). Thus, the findings confirm the main effect for L1 background (definiteness > animacy) reported previously (Fulga & McDonough, 2016) as well as the superior performance of definiteness groups as compared to no case marking groups (McDonough & Fulga, 2015), both of which reported d' prime sensitivity values.

The second learner-specific manipulation concerned the instructions given to learners about the Esperanto transitive construction prior to carrying out the learning task, although this variable was only directly tested in one study (McDonough & Trofimovich, 2013). Nevertheless, in reviewing the experimental materials used across all five studies, we identified four types of information that participants received. Some participants (11%) were told explicitly the two key rules governing the Esperanto transitive construction, which are flexible word order (specifically SVO or OVS) and the accusative -n affix. Approximately one-third of the participants (32%) were informed that Esperanto had flexible word order, so they needed to pay attention to the noun endings in order to understand the sentences. Almost half of the participants (45%) were told only that they should pay attention to the noun endings while listening to the sentences. Finally, participants in the last condition (12%) were not given any information about Esperanto or suggestions about what to attend to while listening.

TABLE 8.3 OVS learning by instructions provided

Information about Esperanto	n	M	SD	95% CI
Flexible word order + -n suffix	47	0.58	0.19	[0.53, 0.64]
Flexible word order, pay attention to noun endings	135	0.36	0.33	[0.30, 0.41]
Pay attention to noun endings	187	0.40	0.41	[0.34, 0.46]
None	48	0.37	0.34	[0.27, 0.47]

The mean OVS scores are provided in Table 8.3, and there was a statistically significant difference among the scores: Welch's $F(3, 147.91) = 12.67, p = .001$. Games-Howell post-hoc tests indicated that participants who received information about both Esperanto rules scored significantly higher than those who were told only about its flexible word order and encouraged to pay attention to the noun endings ($p < .001, d = 0.82$). They also scored significantly higher than participants who were told to pay attention to noun endings only ($p < .001, d = 0.56$) and those who were given no information at all ($p = .002, d = 0.76$). None of the other comparisons reached statistical significance. Thus, it appears that the most effective experimental manipulation across the studies was to inform the participants explicitly about the two key morphosyntactic rules governing the Esperanto transitive construction. Simply providing information about word order alone or in combination with the suggestion that participants pay attention to noun endings was no more effective than withholding all information.

Salience as a Property of the Learning Environment

Our last analysis examined salience as conceptualized in terms of how learners make use of the learning opportunities available in a given environment. Whereas salience as external manipulation focused on what researchers can do to make an aspect of language more "learnable," here the focus is on whether learners exploit opportunities that are present in the learning context. Specifically, we focus on learning through one-on-one interactions, in which participants had opportunities to produce OVS transitives and receive feedback from an interlocutor, request repetition of OVS sentences, and take as much time as they needed to identify which picture corresponded with a sentence they heard. As described previously, our latest eye-tracking study (McDonough et al., 2016) implemented the learning phase through individual, interactive listening and speaking activities, rather than through a group-administered, timed slideshow presentation. The regression analysis indicated that both production of OVS sentences and eye-gaze length to images while listening to OVS sentences predicted accuracy. Eye-gaze was measured as the total duration of eye-gaze (in seconds) calculated from the time participants looked at the correct picture while or after hearing the sentence until the moment they gave an answer.

In order to shed further light on how these learner behaviors impacted test accuracy, we classified each participant in terms of how they made use of the interactive learning environment. As shown in Table 8.4, approximately one-third of the

TABLE 8.4 Salience as exploitation of the learning environment

Learning behaviors	n	M	SD	95% CI
Produced accurate OVS transitives	14	0.59	0.30	[0.42, 0.77]
Long eye-gaze to OVS visual images	13	0.47	0.32	[0.28, 0.66]
Neither	21	0.16	0.25	[0.05, 0.28]
Non-interactive learning context	369	0.41	0.36	[0.37, 0.44]

participants either produced at least three accurate OVS transitives during the learning tasks ($Mdn = 1$) or spent an average of at least 3.75 seconds looking at the correct images for the interlocutor's OVS transitive sentences ($Mdn = 3.40$) before providing an answer. The other participants (44%) failed to engage in these behaviors with similar frequency, such as never producing any OVS transitives or having only short glances to the OVS images. Learners who produced OVS transitives had the highest test accuracy (0.59), followed by those with long eye-gaze (0.47). In contrast, learners who did not as fully exploit these learning opportunities scored much lower (0.16). For comparison purposes, we also included the data for 369 participants who learned the Esperanto transitives in a group-administered, non-interactive context using timed presentation slides.

A one-way ANOVA indicated that the difference was statistically significant, Welch's $F(3, 26.61) = 8.02$, $p = .001$. Games-Howell post-hoc tests indicated that the production group ($p = .001$, $d = 1.56$) and the eye-gaze group ($p = .034$, $d = 1.08$) outscored participants who engaged in neither behavior, and that there was no significant difference between the production and eye-gaze groups ($p = .731$, $d = 0.39$). Furthermore, learning in a non-interactive context resulted in higher accuracy, compared to learning one-on-one without engaging in production or (extensive) eye-gaze behaviors ($p = .001$, $d = 0.81$). None of the other comparisons reached statistical significance. In sum, learners' interaction with the learning materials and interlocutor, specifically their production of more OVS sentences and greater time spent looking at OVS images, positively affected their learning. However, one-on-one learning was inferior to timed, non-interactive input presentation if learners failed to exploit at least some aspects of the interaction context, such as opportunities to carefully observe depicted relationships or produce target utterances.

Discussion

The goal of this chapter was to revisit our data on the learning of the Esperanto transitive construction by L2 learners, focusing on the impact of several experimental manipulations in relation to salience as involving stimulus, learner, and context characteristics. Only three manipulations resulted in overall accuracy rates that surpassed both the 0.50 chance performance and the 0.40 overall mean learning rate across the entire dataset ($N = 417$). The learning of the Esperanto transitive structure was most optimal when learners: 1) came from L1 backgrounds with case marking languages based on noun definiteness (0.56); 2) were provided with instructions emphasizing both rules governing Esperanto transitives (0.58)—namely, that all objects are marked by the accusative marker -*n* and that Esperanto has a variable word order; and 3) had the opportunity to produce the difficult OVS structure during a one-on-one learning phase (.59). The duration of learners' eye-gaze to images depicting difficult OVS structures during the (interactive) learning phase was also associated with performance (0.47) that surpassed the overall mean of 0.40, yet this rate was nevertheless below the chance threshold. Given that even the most favorable of conditions (at least among those targeted in this analysis) did not yield learning rates in excess of 60% accuracy, these findings confirm our previous conclusions that the learning of Esperanto transitives—a structure requiring learners to adopt a novel way (through the use of morphology) to express a familiar concept (transitivity)—remains a challenging task for L2 learners.

Input Distribution as Salience

In studies focusing on the learning of L2 morphosyntactic patterns from aural input, the frequency composition of learning materials is often used as a means of drawing learners' attention to important relationships between the target morphosyntactic features and their meaning. As discussed previously, two types of low-variability distributions are typically compared—those exemplifying a construction with a key lexical item that is more frequent than other items in the distribution (skewed input) and those exemplifying a construction with several lexical items sharing the same (low) token frequency (balanced input). Contrary to L1 research targeting the appearance construction in English (e.g., Goldberg et al., 2004, 2007), the current analysis showed that, in the case of learning Esperanto transitives, skewed distributions are not superior to balanced distributions, which is in line with previous work demonstrating no advantage for skewed input as a way of focusing of learners' attention on key features of L2 structures (Brooks et al., 2017; McDonough & Nekrasova-Becker, 2014; Nakamura, 2012).

At least one reason for the difference between research targeting the appearance construction and L2 studies focusing on various other structures relates to the morphosyntactic pattern targeted. In Goldberg's studies, the appearance construction (e.g., as in *the sailor the pond naifoed*) involves two (familiar) English nouns and an English-sounding nonce verb, with argument roles interpretable through reliance on word order only (N_1N_2V), a dominant cue for sentence interpretation (e.g., Ferreira, 2003). And in terms of novelty, both the structure (N_1N_2V) and the meaning (N_1 appears in/on N_2) of the construction are novel. In contrast, the learning challenge for Esperanto transitives concerns the form, or how an already familiar concept (transitivity) relates to a novel morphological affix (-*n*) in the presence of a conflicting word order cue. Thus, skewed input might facilitate novel form-meaning mapping in cases where the only relevant cue (word order) is already familiar to learners. However, skewed input might be of less use in situations when learners need to acquire novel forms to describe somewhat familiar meanings (which encapsulates a typical learning scenario for adult L2 learners), especially when one cue, such as word order, competes with a more relevant key cue, such as a case inflection.

However, it may be that the difference between skewed and balanced input distributions in determining the outcomes of novel L2 morphosyntactic learning is not as extensive as once thought, based on the null finding of the current large-scale comparison. In a study focusing on the learning of Russian case marking from balanced and skewed input, Brooks et al. (2017) showed that balanced input was more beneficial than skewed input at facilitating learners' generalization of case markers to new vocabulary, but that this positive effect was weak, dissipating by the last of the three learning sessions. Brooks et al. argued that the benefit of balanced input resided in its ability to promote category-based learning, unlike skewed input which favored item-based processing (Matthews & Bannard, 2010). Nevertheless, because this benefit was short-lived, even learners exposed to skewed input distribution could accrue enough evidence—given sufficient exposure—to detect and extend underlying patterns. The training procedure used by Brooks et al. (three sessions of about 2 hours each) was among the longest exposure manipulations used thus far. It appears, then, that what is important for morphosyntactic learning might be the availability of sufficient exposure to low-variability input, rather than its precise distributional properties. Put simply, as far as salience is concerned, it is likely the overall learning experience with low-variability input—not its distribution—that helps learners detect novel patterns and expand this knowledge beyond a few trained exemplars.

Learner-Internal Factors as Salience

In terms of salience, understood as the knowledge and expectations that language users bring to the learning task, the current analyses targeted learners' knowledge of case marking in previously learned languages and the amount and type of explicit information that learners received at the onset of the learning task. With respect to L1 influences on morphosyntactic learning, the overall finding was that learners' prior experience with case marking in their L1s was facilitative of pattern learning, compared to cases where learners' previously learned languages featured no case morphology. However, the mere presence of accusative morphology in learners' L1 was insufficient to ensure that learners succeed in the learning of Esperanto transitives. Only learners with L1s that mark case morphology based on noun definiteness (e.g., Arabic, Farsi, and Tamil), but not noun animacy (e.g., French, Hindi, and Spanish), performed above chance. In essence, mere presence of the target feature in learners' L1s is insufficient to promote the learning of an L2 morphosyntactic pattern, but a processing bias—for example, one prioritizing definite nouns inflected for case—might provide learners with just the needed attentional focus to more easily decipher the underlying pattern for a structure, compared to learners who lack such a processing bias. While the precise reasons for definiteness as an experience-driven salience cue should be targeted in future research, an interim conclusion is clear: What learners bring to bear to the learning task—in terms of their previous linguistic knowledge and experience—has consequences for their L2 processing and learning (e.g., Ellis et al., 2014; MacWhinney, 2012; VanPatten, 1996).

In terms of the processing orientation imposed on learners through instruction, providing learners with the full rules governing Esperanto transitives (inflectional morphology, coupled with flexible word order) resulted in above-chance performance, compared to cases where no rules were supplied or when learners were instructed to pay attention to noun endings, with or without information about the flexible word order rule. This result points to the conclusion that learners' success in learning novel morphosyntactic patterns might require explicit instructions which may cue learners in on the relevant properties of the input. These instructions might need to be fairly detailed, as simply telling learners to pay attention to noun endings—with no information as to what to expect—produced no appreciable benefit to their learning rates, as compared to situations when such information was withheld or when it was provided along with the flexible word order rule. A strong explicit component to input-driven tasks in L2 morphosyntactic learning has been noted before, for example, in relation to learning activities conducted in language classrooms (e.g., McDonough & Nekrasova-Becker, 2014; McDonough & Trofimovich, 2013; Year & Gordon, 2009), where the "explicitness" of the learning environment might overshadow a data-driven, implicit orientation of learning tasks. Explicit influences on input-driven L2 morphosyntactic learning have also been noted in lab-based research (Nakamura, 2012), where learners' explicit knowledge of target constructions was linked to their performance accuracy, raising the possibility that explicit knowledge facilitated test performance. Thus, as far as salience is concerned, processing expectations orienting learners explicitly to the target pattern might be particularly useful for the learning of difficult L2 morphosyntactic structures (DeKeyser, 2016).

Learning Context as Salience

If one aspect of salience involves being able to use the affordances offered by the learning environment, then various types of learning environments might differ in the extent to which they promote L2 morphosyntactic learning. In the current dataset, which compared several features of the learning environment (e.g., opportunities to produce target structures and observe images depicting target relationships in one-on-one interaction), only production of target structures during learning activities resulted in above-chance performance with the difficult OVS transitive structure. However, the comparison of an interactive learning context (administered by an interlocutor) with a non-interactive learning activity (conducted in a group session through timed, prerecorded presentation slides) revealed that non-interactive learning (0.41) was overall more beneficial than interactive learning (0.16) when learners never engaged in production of the target structure or looked extensively at the target images, although performance in both situations remained below chance. It appears that, unless learners fully exploit the affordances of interactive learning environments, such environments might be distracting if the learning goal is to extract a novel morphosyntactic pattern.

The finding that production opportunities during learning activities were facilitative of L2 morphosyntactic learning aligns well with prior interaction research showing the importance of production practice (Loewen, 2005; Loewen & Philp, 2006; McDonough, 2005; Sato & Lyster, 2007, 2012) and highlights production practice as an important route to test performance accuracy in morphosyntactic pattern learning. This finding is also in line with structural priming research showing that the production component of priming tasks, rather than the comprehension component, may be associated with learners' subsequent production accuracy rates (McDonough & Kim, 2009; McDonough & Chaikitmongkol, 2010). Thus, the production component of learning activities might drive at least some detection of the targeted morphosyntactic features, likely because generation of utterances requires learners to attend more extensively to the relationship between form and meaning. Put differently, a focus on production as part of learning activities might make morphosyntactic patterns salient to learners, enhancing their subsequent performance.

A preliminary finding of this large-scale analysis concerns the role of eye-gaze duration in morphosyntactic learning. As in our original study (McDonough et al., 2016), the current analysis revealed a positive role for learners' self-initiated looking behaviors to images depicting the meanings of difficult OVS structures during interactive learning tasks. Although the learning rate associated with looks to critical images (0.47) was below chance, it surpassed the 0.40 value for the entire dataset and was among the higher learning rates recorded across our studies. This finding invites further research into potential reasons explaining participants' eye-gaze behavior. Following from prior research (e.g., Goodwin, 1981), one potentially relevant factor is the extent of interlocutor-learner shared eye-gaze, on the assumption that mutual eye-gaze acts as an attention cue leading to common understanding (Richardson & Dale, 2005). Mutual eye-gaze was not directly manipulated in our original study, since the interlocutor explicitly engaged the learner's eye-gaze only in cases when errors were made, prior to delivering feedback (McDonough et al., 2016). What this preliminary finding implies, however, is that learners' eye-gaze behavior is an important aspect of an interactive learning environment, with learners' eye-gaze durations reflective of some aspects of L2 morphosyntactic learning. It would be important, in future research, to examine potential mechanisms underlying such learning (e.g., Godfroid, 2016; Yurovsky, Smith, & Yu, 2013).

Conclusion

Using a large-scale analysis of previously collected datasets, the current chapter synthesized our prior research on the learning of the Esperanto transitive construction, using the broader construct of salience to understand the effect of various experimental manipulations. Taken together, the patterns uncovered through the analysis revealed a complex picture of input-specific, learner-internal, and context-driven influences on the learning of novel L2 morphosyntactic structures. While the emerging pattern of findings is a complex one, it only reflects individual influences of several factors. Therefore, it still remains to be seen how various influences on L2 morphosyntactic learning interact as learning unfolds in real time, with learning—and the role of salience in it—conceptualized as a complex, dynamic, and adaptive phenomenon (Ellis, 2016).

References

Brooks, P. J., Kwoka, N., & Kempe, V. (2017). Distributional effects and individual differences in L2 morphology learning. *Language Learning, 67*, 171–207.

Bybee, J. (2008). Usage-based grammar and second language acquisition. In P. Robinson & N. Ellis (Eds.), *Handbook of cognitive linguistics and second language acquisition* (pp. 216–236). New York: Routledge.

Casenhiser, D., & Goldberg, A. (2005). Fast mapping between a phrasal form and meaning. *Developmental Science, 8*, 500–508.

Cox, G. (2011). *The international auxiliary language Esperanto grammar and commentary* (4th ed.). London: British Esperanto Association Incorporated [Project Guttenberg ebook]. Retrieved from www.archive.org/stream/theinternational35815gut/35815-0.txt

DeKeyser, R. (2016). Of moving targets and chameleons: Why the concept of difficult is so hard to pin down. *Studies in Second Language Acquisition, 38*, 353–363.

Ellis, N. C. (2012). Frequency-based accounts of second language acquisition. In S. M. Gass & A. Mackey (Eds.), *The Routledge handbook of second language acquisition* (pp. 193–210). New York: Routledge.

Ellis, N. C. (2016). Salience, cognition, language complexity, and complex adaptive systems. *Studies in Second Language Acquisition, 38*, 341–351.

Ellis, N. C., Hafeez, K., Martin, K. I., Chen, L., Boland, J., & Sagarra, N. (2014). An eye-tracking study of learned attention in second language acquisition. *Applied Psycholinguistics, 35*, 547–579.

Ferreira, F. (2003). The misinterpretation of noncanonical sentences. *Cognitive Psychology, 47*, 164–203.

Fulga, A., & McDonough, K. (2016). The impact of L1 background and visual information on the effectiveness of low variability input. *Applied Psycholinguistics, 37*, 265–283.

Gass, S. (1987). The resolution of conflicts among competing systems: A bidirectional perspective. *Applied Psycholinguistics, 8*, 329–350.

Godfroid, A. (2016). The effects of implicit instruction on implicit and explicit knowledge development. *Studies in Second Language Acquisition, 38*, 177–215.

Goldberg, A. E. (2006). *Constructions at work: The nature of generalization in language*. Oxford: Oxford University Press.

Goldberg, A. E. (2009). The nature of generalization in language. *Cognitive Linguistics, 20*, 93–127.

Goldberg, A. E., & Casenhiser, D. (2008). Construction learning and second language acquisition. In P. Robinson & N. Ellis (Eds.), *Handbook of cognitive linguistics and second language acquisition* (pp. 197–215). New York: Routledge.

Goldberg, A. E., Casenhiser, D., & Sethuraman, N. (2004). Learning argument structure generalizations. *Cognitive Linguistics, 15*, 289–316.

Goldberg, A. E., Casenhiser, D., & White, T. (2007). Constructions as categories of language. *New Ideas in Psychology, 25*, 70–86.

Goldschneider, J. M., & DeKeyser, R. M. (2001). Explaining the "natural order of morpheme acquisition" in English: A meta-analysis of multiple determinants. *Language Learning, 51*, 1–50.

Goodwin, C. (1981). *Conversational organization: Interaction between speakers and hearers*. New York, NY: Academic Press.

Harlow, D. (1995). *The sixteen rules of Esperanto grammar*. Retrieved from http://donh.best.vwh.net/Esperanto/rules.html

Jiang, N. (2007). Selective integration of linguistic knowledge in adult second language learning. *Language Learning, 57*, 1–33.

Kempe, V., & MacWhinney, B. (1998). The acquisition of case marking by adult learners of Russian and German. *Studies in Second Language Acquisition, 20*, 543–587.

Loewen, S. (2005). Incidental focus on form and second language learning. *Studies in Second Language Acquisition, 27*, 361–386.

Loewen, S., & Philp, J. (2006). Recasts in the adult English L2 classroom: Characteristics, explicitness, and effectiveness. *The Modern Language Journal, 90*, 536–556.

MacWhinney, B. (2012). The logic of the unified model. In S. M. Gass & A. Mackey (Eds.), *The Routledge handbook of second language acquisition* (pp. 211–227). New York: Routledge.

McDonough, K. (2005). Identifying the impact of negative feedback and learners' responses on ESL question development. *Studies in Second Language Acquisition, 27*, 79–103.

McDonough, K., & Chaikitmongkol, W. (2010). Collaborative syntactic priming activities and EFL learners' production of wh-questions. *Canadian Modern Language Review, 66*, 817–841.

McDonough, K., & Fulga, A. (2015). The detection and primed production of novel constructions. *Language Learning, 65*, 353–384.

McDonough, K., & Kim, Y. (2009). Syntactic priming, type frequency, and EFL learners' production of wh-questions. *The Modern Language Journal, 93*, 386–398.

McDonough, K., & Nekrasova-Becker, T. (2014). Comparing the effect of skewed and balanced input on EFL learners' comprehension of the double-object dative construction. *Applied Psycholinguistics, 35*, 419–442.

McDonough, K., & Trofimovich, P. (2013). Learning a novel pattern through balanced and skewed input. *Bilingualism: Language and Cognition, 16*, 654–662.

McDonough, K., & Trofimovich, P. (2015). Structural priming and the acquisition of novel form-meaning mappings. In S. Eskildsen & T. Cardierno (Eds.), *Usage-based perspectives on second language learning* (pp. 105–123). Berlin: Mouten De Gruyter.

McDonough, K., & Trofimovich, P. (2016). The role of statistical learning and working memory in L2 speakers' pattern learning. *The Modern Language Journal, 100*, 428–445.

McDonough, K., Trofimovich, P., Dao, P., & Dion, A. (2016). Interaction and L2 English speakers' morphosyntactic pattern learning. *Studies in Second Language Acquisition*, doi: 10.1017/S0272263116000395.

Matthews, D., & Bannard, C. (2010). Children's production of unfamiliar word sequences is predicted by positional variability and latent classes in a large sample of child-directed speech. *Cognitive Science, 34*, 465–488.

Nakamura, D. (2012). Input skewedness, consistency, and order of frequent verbs in frequency-driven second language construction learning: A replication and extension of Casenhiser and Goldberg (2005) to adult second language acquisition. *International Review of Applied Linguistics, 50*, 31–67.

Richardson, D. C., & Dale, R. (2005). Looking to understand: The coupling between speakers' and listeners' eye movements and its relationship to discourse comprehension. *Cognitive Science, 29*, 1045–1060.

Sato, M., & Lyster, R. (2007). Modified output of Japanese EFL learners: Variable effects of interlocutor vs. feedback types. In A. Mackey (Ed.), *Conversational interaction in second language acquisition: A collection of empirical studies* (pp. 123–142). Oxford: Oxford University Press.

Sato, M., & Lyster, R. (2012). Peer interaction and corrective feedback for accuracy and fluency development: Monitoring, practice, and proceduralization. *Studies in Second Language Acquisition, 34*, 591–626.

Sinnemäki, K. (2014). A typological perspective on differential object marking. *Linguistics, 52*, 281–313.

Tomasello, M. (2003). *Constructing a language: A usage-based theory of language acquisition.* Cambridge, MA: Harvard University Press.

VanPatten, B. (1996). *Input processing and grammar instruction in second language acquisition.* Westport, CT: Ablex.

Year, J., & Gordon, P. (2009). Korean speakers' acquisition of the English ditransitive construction: The role of verb prototype, input distribution, and frequency. *The Modern Language Journal, 93*, 399–417.

Yurovsky, D., Smith, L. B., & Yu, C. (2013). Statistical word learning at scale: The baby's view is better. *Developmental Science, 16*, 959–966.

PART III
Constructed Salience in SLA

9
ENHANCING THE INPUT TO PROMOTE SALIENCE OF THE L2

A Critical Overview

Ronald P. Leow and Alexandra Martin

Introduction

One area of salience in the field of second language acquisition (SLA), and more specifically in this chapter in the sub-strand of instructed SLA (ISLA), that has drawn a plethora of empirical investigation into its role in comprehension and L2 development, is Sharwood Smith's (1991, 1993) notion of input enhancement (IE). This notion, as elaborated in this chapter, has undergone some modification in relation to what Sharwood Smith (1981) originally conceptualized as an attempt to raise L2 learners' consciousness of some grammatical information in the L2 input (an internal process focused on a product—explicit knowledge) to the current definition that focuses more on a process: "[t]he process by which language input becomes salient to the learner is termed 'input enhancement'" (Sharwood Smith, 1991, p. 118). This definition views input enhancement from two perspectives: an *internal* input processing perspective associated with some kind of *external* manipulation of L2 data that may make such data salient to and processed by the L2 learner. Interestingly, Sharwood Smith's relatively broad description of what comprises input enhancement, which is dependent upon degrees of elaboration or duration and explicitness or metalinguistic depth of the enhanced input, appears to have led to different methodological approaches to its operationalization and measurement (Leow, 2007). For example, some instructional strands of research (e.g., *focus on form* and *processing instruction*[1]) appeared to have shared Sharwood Smith's broadest description of input enhancement (a permutation of the different exemplars of his two axes of elaboration and explicitness) that conflates the independent variable enhancement with other instructional independent variables (e.g., feedback, explicit instruction, homework, etc.). On the other hand, other sub-strands of IE research (e.g., *textual enhancement* and *input flooding*, premised on the preponderance of target items eventually leading to their salience in the input) have, in several cases, methodologically teased out the variable (e.g., enhancement) and compared the effects of this variable to its absence on typically two dependent variables—namely, comprehension and L2 development. Overall findings in the textual enhancement (TE) strand of research are typically reported as being mixed, with studies reporting positive effects (e.g., Cho, 2010; Doughty, 1991; Jourdenais et al., 1995; Lee, 2007; Shook, 1994), negative effects (especially on comprehension, e.g., Lee, 2007; Overstreet, 1998; Park & Nassif, 2014), and no effects (e.g., Alanen, 1995; Bowles, 2003; Cho, 2010; Della Putta, 2016; Indrarathne & Kormos, 2016; Issa, Morgan-Short, Villegas, & Raney, 2015; Izumi, 2002; Jahan & Kormos, 2015; Leow, 1997, 2001; Leow, Egi, Nuevo, & Tsai, 2003; Loewen & Inceoglu, 2016; Overstreet, 1998; Park & Nassif, 2014; Song, 2007; J. White, 1998; Winke, 2013; Wong, 2003). However, while the premise of textual enhancement lies minimally in learner attention, only a subset of studies has methodologically operationalized the construct of attention or noticing in their research designs and measured them concurrently[2] (e.g., Bowles, 2003; Gurzynski-Weiss, Al Khalil, Baralt, & Leow, 2015; Leow, 2001; Leow et al., 2003; Sachs & Suh, 2007 for think-alouds[3]; Indrarathne & Kormos, 2016; Issa et al., 2015; Loewen & Inceoglu, 2016; Simard & Foucambert, 2013; Winke, 2013 for eye-tracking). In addition, Leow (2009) pointed out that the input enhancement strand of research should be divided into what is termed "non-conflated" (i.e., a pure comparison between an enhanced versus an unenhanced experimental group) as opposed to "conflated" (i.e., input enhancement formed part of a combination of two or more independent variables). Given the superior advantage of the non-conflated approach to address directly the role of the variable enhancement, this chapter extends this methodological perspective by providing an up-to-date critical overview of the role of textual enhancement in the ISLA literature and, more specifically, TE studies that have employed concurrent data-elicitation procedures (think-alouds and eye-tracking). Suggestions for future research and potential pedagogical implications are also provided.

Theoretical Underpinning

Input enhancement was derived from Sharwood Smith's original concept of "language consciousness-raising" (Sharwood Smith, 1981), which was initially framed within a discussion of Krashen's (1979) and Bialystok's (1978) views on the relationship between explicit knowledge (a conscious analytic awareness of the formal properties of the second/foreign language or L2), and implicit knowledge (an intuitive feeling for what is correct and acceptable). According to Sharwood Smith (1981), language consciousness-raising was essentially a teacher's attempt to promote learners' own discovery or conscious awareness of the formal features of the L2, although such consciousness-raising could also be learner-driven. To avoid the perception of consciousness-raising as "a complete and unrelenting focus on the formal structure of the TL" (p. 160), Sharwood Smith proposed that language consciousness-raising be viewed from two axes: degrees of elaboration or duration and explicitness or metalinguistic depth leading to four basic types of manifestation of consciousness-raising based on a permutation of these two axes (see pp. 161–162 for further elaboration). The initial focus of consciousness-raising, then, was more on product (explicit knowledge) than on process (input processing).

Ten years later, Sharwood Smith (1991) replaced his previous concept of consciousness-raising with that of input enhancement to acknowledge the discrepancy in the two concepts' assumptions regarding the input/intake dichotomy in light of an internal processing (consciousness-raising) versus an external manipulation of the L2 input (input enhancement). In other words, while consciousness-raising assumed that learners became conscious of all the grammatical information they were exposed to, leading to some linguistic change in their mental state, input enhancement assumed that manipulated input (by the teacher) might or might not be taken in by the learners. Thus, in his statement "The process by which language input becomes salient to the learner is termed 'input enhancement'" (p. 118), Sharwood Smith appeared to view input enhancement somewhat more from a process perspective than a product perspective as previously posited for his consciousness-raising concept.

Like consciousness-raising, input enhancement was also viewed from two perspectives, internal and external (Sharwood Smith, 1991). An internal perspective views the L2 input as being enhanced by learners' internal mechanism that makes salient specific features in the input—for example, paying attention to words at the beginning of a sentence. An external perspective views input enhancement as any pedagogical attempt (usually by a teacher) to make more salient specific features of L2 input in an effort to draw learners' attention to these enhanced features. Underlying either perspective is the role that attention plays in facilitating the intake of grammatical or lexical information before such information can be processed further into the learners' language system.

One key feature of input enhancement is Sharwood Smith's (1991) caution that "externally induced salience may not necessarily be registered by the learner and even when it is registered, it may not affect the learning mechanisms per se" (p. 118). According to Sharwood Smith, this caution is based on language learnability (e.g., Hornstein & Lightfoot, 1981), which offers one way of further subcategorizing induced input salience. Learnability theory provides information about the nature of input in terms of various kinds of evidence, usually referred to as being either positive or negative. In other words, while enhanced input may be noticed and taken in by the learner, whether such linguistic information is further processed may be due to the kind of evidence to which learners are exposed (see Sharwood Smith, 1991, pp. 122–125 for further elaboration).

Empirical Studies of Textual Enhancement in ISLA

The input enhancement strand of research has been dominated by the TE strand of research that involves types of typographical cues (usually one or two types) employed to enhance the salience of target linguistic items in written L2 input. Many TE studies have visually modified or enhanced written input via the use of bolding, capitalizing, underlining, italicizing, different fonts and sizes, and so on.[4] Less popular is input flooding usually operationalized by an increase, which can be very differential, in the number of target items in the L2 input. This increase is postulated to promote the salience of target forms and, ultimately, more learner attention.

There are minimally two assumptions associated with these types of enhancement to increase the salience of target items in the L2 input: 1) without enhancement, learners may not pay attention to target items in the L2 input; and 2) paying attention may lead to further processing and potential learning.

Quite a large range of linguistic items has been empirically investigated in studies of TE. These include Spanish imperatives (e.g., Leow, 1997; 2001), Spanish imperfect and preterit forms (e.g., Jourdenais, 1998; Loewen & Inceoglu, 2016), Spanish present perfect forms (e.g., Leow et al., 2003), Spanish relative pronouns (e.g., Shook, 1994), Finnish locative suffixes (e.g., Alanen, 1995), English possessive determiners (e.g., J. White, 1998), English relative clauses (e.g., Izumi, 2002), French past participle agreement (e.g., Wong, 2003), English plural markers (e.g., Simard, 2009), Arabic comparative form and dual pronoun (e.g., Park & Nassif, 2014), English causative 'had' (e.g., Indrarathne & Kormos, 2016), Italian pre-possessive determiner article and differential object marking (Della Putta, 2016), and so on. Different levels of language experience have also been explored, ranging from grade six (e.g., J. White, 1998) to college-level students, including learners from beginning level (e.g., Della Putta, 2016) to upper-intermediate level (e.g., Bowles, 2003). There have been different amounts of L2 exposure to linguistic items in these investigations, ranging from less than an hour (the overwhelming number of studies) to over several days for instructional studies (Doughty, 1991) and input flooding (e.g., J. White, 1998). The lowest number of target items reported was five (e.g., Jahan & Kormos, 2015) while the highest number reported was over 100 (e.g., J. White, 1998).

The textual enhancement strand of research has attracted a relatively large number of studies that have attempted to empirically address its effects on two dependent variables—namely, L2 comprehension and L2 development. The typical research design comprised a pretest—exposure—posttest, with very few studies including a delayed posttest in the design. To measure comprehension, comprehension tests (e.g., LaBrozzi, 2016; Leow, 2001), free-recall protocols (e.g., Cho, 2010; Winke, 2013), or a true/false test (e.g., Overstreet, 1998) have been employed. To measure L2 development, posttests typically were designed to measure learners' intake (often operationalized as recognition and error-correction tasks) (e.g., Leow, 1997; Simard, 2009; Wong, 2003), written production (e.g., picture-cued, sentence completion, sentence combination, narration, fill-in-the-blank) (e.g., Jahan & Kormos, 2015; Leow, 2001; Overstreet, 1998; Shook, 1994), and knowledge (via grammaticality judgment tasks) (e.g., Indrarathne & Kormos, 2016; Izumi, 2002). Overall, the results are mixed, which may be due to: 1) a too-broad description of what comprises input enhancement (Leow, 2007), and 2) methodological differences (Han, Park, & Combs, 2008), and (3) research designs (Leow, 2009).

Given the broad description that the term input enhancement represents in the ISLA literature, Leow (2009) categorized into two sub-strands studies that have incorporated in their research designs Sharwood Smith's (1991) description of input enhancement: 1) those that included some kind of input enhancement in their overall research designs, and 2) those that have methodologically teased out the variable enhancement in their designs. Leow called the first substrand "conflated input enhancement (CIE)" (p. 18) and operationalized IE as a conflation of the variable enhancement plus one or more independent variables (some not methodologically controlled—for example, homework, Doughty, 1991; or feedback, White, Spada, Lightbown, & Ranta, 1991). The second sub-strand, called "non-conflated input enhancement" (NCIE), avoided this conflation with the classic comparison of an enhanced group (+enhanced input) with an unenhanced one (-enhanced input). The division revealed that while CIE studies overall reported superior performances for IE (especially due to amount of exposure and potential contributions from other variables), this superiority was not found in the majority of NCIE studies.

Given the importance of addressing the impact of enhancement as an independent variable, this chapter focuses on studies that fall within the NCIE sub-strand of research and, more specifically, on those that have employed concurrent data elicitations to operationalize and measure the construct attention, upon which TE is premised.

Results

As Table 9.1 reveals, the majority of NCIE studies appear to corroborate the finding reported in Leow's (2009) study: Enhancing written input together with no specific instruction to attend to enhanced items in the input did not promote statistically superior performances on target linguistic forms when compared to a control group exposed to unenhanced input.[5] While 8.7% (2/23) reported a significant benefit for enhancement and 13% (3/23) reported mixed results, an overwhelming number of the studies (78.3%, 18/23) failed to do so. This finding does not appear to corroborate with Lee and Huang's (2008) meta-analysis, conducted on combined CIE and NCIE studies up to that year, that reported a "very small-sized effect ($d = .22$)" (pp. 322–323) for enhancement. With regard to comprehension, Table 9.1 also reveals that enhancement of target items in L2 texts did not appear to be detrimental to overall comprehension of text content. 83.3% (10/12) of the studies reported no significant difference in comprehension between the enhanced and unenhanced conditions while only 16.7% (2/12) reported the unenhanced group's superiority. Once again, this finding fails to corroborate Lee and Huang's (2008) combined CIE/NCIE meta-analysis that reported a "small but negative effect size value yielded by the reading comprehension measures ($d = -0.26$)" (p. 323). A summary of these studies is found in Table 9.1.

To explicate this overall non-significant difference in NCIE studies, it is instructive to critically review the TE studies that have employed online data-elicitation procedures to gain a clearer understanding of the processing and processes involved while L2 readers read enhanced and unenhanced L2 texts (Alanen, 1995; Bowles, 2003; Gurzynski-Weiss et al., 2015; Leow, 2001; Leow et al., 2003; Sachs & Suh, 2007 for think-alouds; Indrarathne & Kormos, 2016; Issa et al., 2015; Loewen & Inceoglu, 2016; Simard & Foucambert, 2013; Winke, 2013 for eye-tracking). A summary of these studies is found in Table 9.2.

As can be seen in Table 9.2, six studies have employed concurrent verbal reports (think-alouds) while five have recently employed the eye-tracking procedure. While concurrent data-elicitation procedures such as eye-tracking and think-aloud

TABLE 9.1 A summary of Non-Conflated Input Enhancement (NCIE) studies

Study & Year	Participants/L2	Exposure Time	Input Enhancement	Target Forms/Structures (Number)	Online/Offline Measures	Delayed Effects	Results
			BENEFITS				
Shook (1994)	125 college-level learners of Spanish 1st/4th semester	Under 1 hour	2 passages: 185 words (perfect) & 217 words (relative pronouns) *Uppercase & bold*	~ Present Perfect (6) ~ Relative Pronouns (6)	~ Offline: Multiple-choice recognition test; Fill-in-the blanks production test	Not addressed	L2 development: Significant benefit; Comprehension: No significant difference (Shook, 1998)
Jourdenais et al. (1995)	10 college-level learners of Spanish 2nd semester	Under 1 hour	210-word passage *Underline, bold, shadow, different font*	~ Preterit (18) ~ Imperfect (10)	~ Offline: Production (essay) test	Not addressed	L2 development: Significant benefit; Comprehension: Not addressed
			MIXED BENEFITS				
Simard (2009)	188 secondary level learners of English Grade 8	Under 1 hour	290-word passage *Italicize/underline/ bold/highlight in yellow/capitalize/ enhance with 5 preceding cues/ enhance with 3 cues (bold, capital, underline)*	~ English plural markers (21)	~ Offline: Multiple-choice recognition test	Not addressed	L2 development: The capital and the 3-cues groups obtained the highest scores at the posttest; Significant differences between the capital and the 3-cues group and the control group re: intake; Comprehension: Not addressed

Cho (2010)	87 high school female learners of English *Grade 10*	80 minutes	2 passages: 170 & 185 words **Bold & underline**	~ Present Perfect (7) & (11)	~ Online: Note-taking (as a measure of noticing) ~ Offline: GJT Fill-in-the-blank test & sentence combination test Reconstruction task Comprehension task (multiple-choice)	Not addressed	L2 development: Significant benefit on test of receptive knowledge; No effect of TE on productive knowledge; Comprehension: No significant difference
LaBrozzi (2016)	125 college-level students of Spanish *3rd semester*	Under 1 hour	470-word passage *Only preterit morpheme was enhanced:* **underline/italicize/bold/** **capitalize/increase font/change font** NO BENEFITS	~ Preterit (10)	~ Offline: Translation task of targeted forms Comprehension test	Not addressed	L2 development: Increased font size (from 12 to 16) was the most effective textual enhancement type re: translation of forms; Comprehension: No significant difference
Alanen (1995)	36 college-level learners of Finnish *Beginning*	Under 1 hour	2 passages: 87 & 98 words *Italicize*	~ Type of locative suffixes (12–13) ~ Consonant Change (5–8)	~ Online: TA ~ Offline: Sentence completion test	Not addressed	L2 development: No significant benefit Comprehension: Not addressed
Leow (1997)	84 college-level learners of Spanish *2nd semester*	Under 1 hour	2 passages: 631 *(long)* **Underline, bold**	~ Formal imperatives 15 (short passage) 24 (long passage)	~ Offline: Multiple-choice recognition test	Not addressed	L2 development: No significant benefit; Comprehension: Not addressed

(*Continued*)

TABLE 9.1 (Continued)

Study & Year	Participants/ L2	Exposure Time	Input Enhancement	Target Forms/ Structures (Number)	Online/Offline Measures	Delayed Effects	Results
Jourdenais (1998)	124 college-level learners of Spanish 2nd semester	During a week period	3 chapters of narrative **Bold, shadow, different font**	~ Preterit (36) ~ Imperfect (36)	~ Offline: Production (essay) test	Not addressed	L2 development: No significant benefit; Comprehension: Not addressed
Overstreet (1998)	50 college-level learners of Spanish 3rd semester	Under 1 hour	2 passages: 210 words (familiar) & 210 words (unfamiliar) **Underline, bold, shadow, different font**	~ Preterit (18) ~ Imperfect (10)	~ Offline: Circle the verb Production (picture-cued essay) test	Not addressed	L2 development: No significant benefit; Comprehension: –TE > +TE
J. White (1998)	86 francophone learners of English Grade 6	During a 2-week period	10-hour instructional package: short stories, fables, poems, etc. **Enlargement, different combinations of bold, italicize, underline**	~ Third-person singular ~ Possessive Pronouns	~ Offline: Oral Picture description test	Addressed	L2 development: No significant benefit at either the immediate or delayed posttests; Comprehension: Not addressed

Leow (2001)	21 college-level learners of Spanish *First year*	Under 1 hour	*242-word passage* ***Underline, bold***	~ Spanish formal imperative (17)	~ Online: TA ~ Offline: Multiple-choice fill-in-the-blank production test Comprehension test	Not addressed due to abnormal distribution of data	Amount of attention: +TE = −TE L2; development: No significant benefit; Comprehension: No significant difference
Izumi (2002)	61 college-level ESL learners *Intermediate level*	During a 2-week period	*5 passages: 180 words (approximately)* ***Bold, shadow, different fonts & sizes***	~ English relativization	~ Online: Note-taking ~ Offline: Sentence combination (picture-cued essay) Interpretation GJT Post-exposure questionnaire	Not addressed	L2 development: No significant benefit; Comprehension: Not addressed
Leow et al. (2003)	72 college-level learners of Spanish *First year*	Under 1 hour	*2 magazine passages* ***Underline, bold, larger font***	~ Perfect (10) and Subjunctive (10) forms	~ Online: TA ~ Offline: Multiple-choice test Comprehension test	Not addressed	Amount of attention: +TE = −TE L2 development: No significant benefit; Comprehension: No significant difference
Bowles (2003)	15 college-level learners of Spanish *4th semester*	Under 1 hour	*242-word passage* ***Underline, bold***	~ Spanish formal imperative (17)	~ Online: TA ~ Offline: Multiple-choice, fill-in-the-blank, production tests Comprehension test	Addressed	Amount of attention: +TE = −TE L2 development: No significant benefit at both immediate and delayed posttests; Comprehension: No significant difference

(*Continued*)

TABLE 9.1 (Continued)

Study & Year	Participants/ L2	Exposure Time	Input Enhancement	Target Forms/ Structures (Number)	Online/Offline Measures	Delayed Effects	Results
Wong (2003)	81 college-level learners of French *2nd semester*	Under 1 hour	*3 articles (526, 465, & 517 words)* **Bold, larger font, italicize, underline**	~ French past participle agreement in relative clauses (16)	~ Offline: Error-correction test	Not addressed	L2 development: No significant benefit; Comprehension: No significant difference
Sachs and Suh (2007)	30 college-level EFL Korean learners *Intermediate level*	Under 1 hour	*3 guided story-retelling tasks* **Bold**	~ English backshifting	~Online: TA ~ Offline: Paper-based multiple-choice text completion Interactive computer-mediated test	Not addressed	L2 development: No significant benefit; Comprehension: Not addressed
Winke (2013)	55 college-level learners of English *Intermediate level*	Under 1 hour	*1 modified news report (# of words not reported)* **Underline and in red**	English passive voice (17)	~Online: ET ~ Offline: Passive form correction task Comprehension test (free recall)	Not addressed	Amount of attention: +TE > −TE L2 development: No significant benefit; Comprehension: No significant difference
Simard and Foucambert (2013)	20 college-level learners of English *Intermediate*	Under 1 hour	*Each page with 350 words* **Bold and underline**	Oblique relatives (20)	~Online: ET ~Offline: Verbal report Comprehension test	Not addressed	Amount of attention: +TE > −TE Comprehension: No significant difference

Park and Nassif (2014)	16 college-level learners of Arabic *Intermediate II*	Under 1 hour for each target form	2 passages: (188 & 178 words) **Enlargement of font, bold and underline**	~ the comparative form (9) ~ the dual pronoun (10)	~ Offline: Fill-in-the-blank task Free production task Free recall task Comprehension test	Not addressed	L2 development: No significant benefit; Comprehension: −TE > +TE (recall of dual pronoun text)
Issa et al. (2015)	43 college-level learners of Spanish *First semester*	Under 1 hour	30 trial sentences and a series of corresponding images **Red font color**	~ Spanish direct object pronouns	~ Online: ET ~ Offline: Interpretation task	Addressed	Amount of attention: +TE = −TE L2 development: No significant benefit (although TE significantly improved from pretest—immediate posttest/delayed posttest)
Jahan and Kormos (2015)	97 college-level learners of English *First year*	About 1 hour	Two reading passages (157 & 220 words) **Bold**	~ will (5) ~ be going to (5) (x two days)	~ Offline: 'Noticing question' Metalinguistic task (explain the functions of the target structures) Fill-in-the-blank task Multiple-choice task Comprehension test	Addressed	Amount of attention: +TE > −TE L2 development: No significant benefit Increase in metalinguistic awareness of 'be going to', but this did not translate into an increase in the production tasks; Comprehension: No significant difference

(*Continued*)

TABLE 9.1 (Continued)

Study & Year	Participants/ L2	Exposure Time	Input Enhancement	Target Forms/ Structures (Number)	Online/Offline Measures	Delayed Effects	Results
Loewen and Inceoglu (2016)	30 college-level learners of Spanish *2nd semester*	Under 1 hour	*211-word passage* **Imperfect verbs highlighted in red** **Preterit verbs highlighted in green**	~ Preterit (18) ~ Imperfect (10)	~Online: ET ~ Offline: Form production Oral picture description task Exit questionnaire to measure awareness	Not addressed	Amount of attention: +TE = –TE L2 development: No significant benefit; Comprehension: Not addressed
Indrarathne and Kormos (2016)	100 college-level learners of English *1st year*	Under 1 hour	*3 passages (# of words not reported)* **Bold**	~ Causative had (21)	~Online: ET (45 participants) ~ Offline: Sentence reconstruction task GJT Comprehension test	Not addressed	Amount of attention: +TE = –TE L2 development: No significant benefit; Comprehension: Not reported
Della Putta (2016)	68 college-level learners of Italian (L1 Spanish) *Absolute beginners*	Not reported	*Five texts in five days; mean length of 427 words* **Bold and color (PPDA)** **Red arrow (to enhance absence of PA)**	Pre-possessive Determiner Article (PPDA) Prepositional Accusative (PA) Average number of TEs per text was 10.4 for PA and 10 for PPDA	~ Offline: Timed GJT Reaction Time (RT)	Addressed	L2 development: No significant benefit For RT, TE slowed down RTs; Comprehension: Not addressed

TABLE 9.2 A summary of online studies

Study & Year	Procedure	Amount Of Attention	Level Of Awareness/ Processing	L2 Development
Alanen (1995)	TA*	n/a**	n/a	+TE = –TE
Leow (2001)	TA	+TE = –TE	+TE = –TE (low level)	+TE = –TE
Bowles (2003)	TA	+TE > –TE	+TE = –TE (low level)	+TE = –TE
Leow et al. (2003)	TA	n/a	+TE = –TE (low level)	+TE = –TE
Sachs and Suh (2007)	TA	n/a	+TE = –TE (low level) +TE > –TE (meta-awareness)	+TE = –TE
Gurzynski-Weiss et al. (2015)	TA	n/a	+TE = –TE (low level)	n/a
Winke (2013)	ET***	+TE > –TE	n/a	+TE = –TE
Simard and Foucambert (2013)	ET	+TE > –TE	n/a	n/a
Issa et al. (2015)	ET	+TE = –TE	n/a	+TE = –TE
Indrarathne and Kormos (2016)	ET	+TE = –TE	n/a	+TE > –TE (relationship between attention and gain scores)
Loewen & Inceoglu, 2016	ET	+ET = –ET	n/a	+TE = –TE

*TA = think alouds
**n/a = not addressed
***ET = eye tracking

protocols both provide insights into *what* and *where* learner attention or noticing was allocated, think-aloud protocols also provide data on *how* learners process the target linguistic items in the input. For amount of attention paid during exposure to the L2 data, both procedures reported mixed findings (for think-alouds, Leow, 2001 versus Bowles, 2003; for eye-tracking, Winke, 2013 and Simard & Foucambert, 2013 versus Issa et al., 2015, Loewen & Inceoglu, 2016, and Indrarathne & Kormos, 2016). Interestingly, both Bowles (2003) (think-alouds) and Winke (2013) (eye-tracking) reported substantial attention paid by the enhanced groups yet no apparent benefit for subsequent learning (Simard and Foucambert, 2013 did not address behavioral data). Similarly, Leow (2001), Issa et al. (2015), Loewen and Inceoglu (2016), and Indrarathne and Kormos (2016) all reported similar amounts of attention paid in both enhanced and unenhanced conditions, but while the first three studies reported no apparent benefit for subsequent performance, Indrarathne and Kormos (2016) did report a significant correlation between attention and gain scores only for the enhanced group.

To account for differential performances between more or less salient conditions, researchers have posited several explanations. Explanations range from type of typographical modification or TE format (e.g., Indrarathne & Kormos, 2016; Simard & Foucambert, 2013), external versus internal salience (Indrarathne & Kormos, 2016), developmental readiness (Winke, 2013), level of communicative value in relation to type of linguistic item (Simard & Foucambert, 2013), motivation (Issa et al., 2015; Winke, 2013), sample size (e.g., Loewen & Inceoglu, 2016; Simard & Foucambert, 2013), experimental condition in relation to the classroom setting (Winke, 2013), to substantial amount of attention related to potential depth of processing (Indrarathne & Kormos, 2016; Issa et al., 2015; Winke, 2013).

Researchers employing concurrent think-aloud protocols provided potential evidence that while attention is indeed paid to items made salient in the L2 input, externally induced salience does not logically lead to deeper processing accompanied by robust learning. They reported that when compared to unenhanced items, enhanced items were not processed at a higher or deeper level, which has been reported to correlate with superior performances (see Leow, 2015 for a review). This finding may indicate that, as Leow (2009) suggested: "learners did not necessarily attempt to process enhanced items in the input for grammatical information but simply to extract semantic information from the targeted forms" (pp. 28–29). This kind of performance is not surprising, given that instructions provided to learners in these studies that included an enhanced versus unenhanced condition typically requested that they read for information. Indeed, as noted previously regarding the eye-tracking studies, the (in)direct notion of depth of processing has been postulated to account for findings in several of the TE studies (Indrarathne & Kormos, 2016; Issa et al., 2015; Winke, 2013). However, perhaps more revealing in relation to *how* participants processed the enhanced items are the qualitative think-aloud data provided in Leow's (2001) and Bowles's (2003) studies regarding their outliers' superior performances on the assessment tasks when compared to the rest of the participants' overall low performances on these tasks. Leow's study, which addressed college-level students of beginning Spanish, reported statistically similar amounts of noticing in his two experimental conditions (enhanced and unenhanced), and no significant difference in performance on either the recognition or controlled written production assessment tasks. Bowles's study replicated Leow's at the fourth-semester level and did report a substantially different amount of noticing among her participants exposed to the enhanced input, although—like the original study—no significant differences in performance between type of experimental condition were found. The data for these outliers, found in *both* enhanced and unenhanced conditions, demonstrated a higher level of awareness of the target items together with accompanying higher levels of processing (Leow, 2012). These data appear to indicate not only the potential inefficacy of externally induced salience (Sharwood Smith, 1991), but also that the process of simply paying attention to salient forms in the L2 data may be insufficient to promote robust intake and L2 development. This finding appears to be replicated in the majority of the eye-tracking studies that addressed L2 development (Indrarathne & Kormos, 2016; Issa et al., 2015; Loewen & Inceoglu, 2016; Winke, 2013). In addition, recall Indrarathne and Kormos's report of their enhanced group's attention correlating significantly with their gain scores (unlike their unenhanced group with a similar amount of attention paid) on both assessment tasks (sentence reformulation and grammaticality judgment). This performance may be accounted for, as postulated by the authors, by a potentially higher level of processing in this enhanced group, a depth perhaps undetected by the eye-tracking procedure (see Leow, Grey, Marijuan, & Moorman, 2014 for a critique of concurrent data-elicitation procedures regarding their strengths and limitations).

The findings of the recent increase of TE studies employing concurrent procedures appear to underscore a theoretical issue that needs to be further probed; namely, the role of attention in the input processing stage in relation to subsequent processing and potential learning of salient or enhanced forms in the L2 input. The concurrent data (think-alouds and eye-tracking) appear to indicate that mere attention to target items made more salient via enhancement in written L2 texts does not allow such items to be further processed robustly when the primary purpose of L2 readers is to access information from the L2 texts. These findings appear to provide support for Leow's (2015) model of the L2 learning process in ISLA that proposes a shift from the attentional aspect of the input processing stage (input to intake) to one of depth of processing in the intake processing stage. This stage along the L2 learning process focuses on *how* preliminary intake is processed after attentional resources have been deployed during input processing.

Future Research

One clear conclusion reported in NCIE studies is that the variable of enhancement designed to increase the salience of target forms in L2 data, when provided in a period of less than one hour, does not appear to hold any superior grammatical benefit when compared to the absence of such externally induced salience. While learners may report paying attention to or noticing substantially more enhanced target items in the input (Bowles, 2003; Simard & Foucambert, 2013; Winke, 2013) when compared to an unenhanced condition, the low level of awareness or depth of processing revealed in online think-aloud data may indicate that internalization of grammatical information may require a higher level of awareness or processing (Indrarathne & Kormos, 2016; Leow, 2001, 2009, 2015; Leow et al., 2003; Shook, 1994). To this end, future investigations into the role of externally induced salience via TE may want to probe deeper into learners' processing, perhaps through eye-tracking, and processes, via concurrent think-aloud protocols, beyond the allocation of mere attentional resources deployed during input processing by manipulating the experimental phase to promote deeper processing. Using a control group that does pay attention for comparative purposes, this design may be able to tease out the potential roles of both attention and subsequent processing during the L2 learning process.

While Leow et al. (2003) addressed type of grammatical linguistic items (Spanish perfect and present subjunctive forms), and reported statistically more attention paid to the perfect form,[6] given the focus on grammatical items in the current TE research, future TE research may also need to investigate its effect on lexical development (see Ryan, Miller, Hamrick, & Was, Chapter 10). Gurzynski-Weiss et al. (2015), in their study of the relationship between type of computerized recast (enhanced versus unenhanced), type of linguistic item (lexis, morphology, and syntax), and level of awareness, reported that type of linguistic item was significantly related to participants' reported level of awareness in the following order: "lexis > morphology > syntax" (p. 165). In addition, as clearly observed in Table 9.1, one major limitation of many TE studies may be the lack of delayed effects. At the same time, given the relatively low gain scores or low performances on the immediate posttests of the majority of the TE studies, whether administering a delayed posttest would be instructive or revealing remains doubtful (see Leow, 2001).

Pedagogical Implications

Given the revelations of the TE literature, teachers should be aware that making L2 grammatical data more salient does not necessarily lead to robust learning. Indeed, the potential impact of the variable TE on grammatical learning appears to be dependent upon factors that include the amount of time spent for exposure and the level of awareness or processing of the enhanced grammatical item. As both NCIE and CIE studies clearly indicate, exposing students to enhanced written L2 texts designed to draw readers' attention to and also promote raising learners' awareness or deeper processing of the grammatical features of the enhanced forms should include some instruction to process these target forms carefully (Indrarathne & Kormos, 2016; Leow, 2009; Shook, 1994; Winke, 2013). Given that L2 readers typically process an L2 text for meaning, this deeper processing of enhanced forms should be promoted after the L2 readers have had a chance to perform this content-based task. As suggested in Leow (2009), for a preliminary introduction to the physical feature of the target forms, students may simply be asked to note the forms. To promote a deeper level of processing or awareness of the linguistic feature(s), students may be requested to formulate an underlying rule or pattern regarding the target forms in the text (see Cerezo, Caras, and Leow [2016] for an exemplar of a guided induction task that promotes learners' deeper processing). In this way, the teacher can receive feedback that not only did students indeed pay attention to the enhanced forms in the text but that they further processed them, a prerequisite for any linguistic information to be taken in robustly by the students (Leow, 2015). The CIE studies also suggest strongly that teachers combine any externally induced salience within an instructional period or interactional session that is focused primarily on the target grammatical form(s) in the input. This type of exposure provides an extended length of exposure and promotes a deeper level of processing or awareness of the target grammatical items (Leow, 2009).

Conclusion

Several recent TE studies employing concurrent data-elicitation procedures (think-alouds and eye-tracking) have provided sharper insights into the role of learner attention while processing textually enhanced input designed to promote salience of target forms and its relationship to comprehension and subsequent L2 development in the ISLA strand of research. The findings appear to suggest that, while these studies have methodologically established that attentional resources have been deployed to process the enhanced items in the input, the role of mere attention does not appear to be major in subsequent robust learning. Indeed, what appears to be crucial is whether and *how* learners do process such forms further, as evidenced in think-aloud protocols, suggested by eye-tracking data, and supported by CIE studies that appeared to have promoted deeper processing of the target forms by including specific instructions to do so. To this end, there is need to move beyond the mere allocation of attentional resources in this strand of TE research to address learners' further processing of enhanced items in the input to shed more light on the L2 learning process. A deeper understanding of cognitive processes employed while processing L2 data externally manipulated to promote salience can have more pertinent ramifications for the L2 instructed setting.

Notes

1 From a *focus on form* perspective, Doughty and Williams (1998) situate input enhancement at the implicit end of exposure to the L2, while Wong (2007) views processing instruction and structured input as input enhancement.
2 Izumi (2002) and Cho (2010) measured noticing via note-taking concurrently performed during exposure to the L2 input, a measure that may be critiqued due to its potential qualitatively poor data.
3 Think-Aloud protocols are typically gathered concurrently (online) while learners are performing a task or reading an L2 text. For non-metacognitive think alouds, learners are requested to say aloud whatever they are thinking during performance and not to explain their thought processes.
4 A smaller number of studies has also defined TE as the insertion of a number of adjuncts in a reading passage in an effort to improve the learning process (e.g., Brantmeier, Callender, Yu, & McDaniel, 2012; Callender, Medina, & Brantmeier, 2013).
5 For CIE studies, as reported in Leow (2009), conflating enhancement with other independent variables (for example, instructions to pay careful attention to the enhanced items) continued to demonstrate superior performances for learners exposed to this condition when compared to another condition exposed to no enhancement.
6 See also Gass, Svetics, Lemelin (2003) who reported attention differentially affecting different parts of language; namely, syntax, morphosyntax, and lexicon.

References

Alanen, R. (1995). Input enhancement and rule presentation in second language acquisition. In R. W. Schmidt (Ed.), *Attention and awareness in foreign language learning* (pp. 259–302). Honolulu, HI: University of Hawaii, Second Language Teaching and Curriculum Center.

Bialystok, E. (1978). A theoretical model of second language learning. *Language Learning*, 28, 69–83.

Bowles, M. (2003). The effects of textual enhancement on language learning: An online/offline study of fourth-semester students. In P. Kempchinsky & C. E. Piñeros (Eds.), *Theory, practice, and acquisition: Papers from the 6th Hispanic Linguistics Symposium and the 5th Conference on the Acquisition of Spanish & Portuguese* (pp. 395–411). Summerville, MA: Cascadilla Press.

Brantmeier, C., Callender, A., Yu, X., & McDaniel, M. (2012). Textual enhancements and comprehension with adult readers of English in China. *Reading in a Foreign Language*, *24*(2), 158.

Callender, A., Medina, A., & Brantmeier, C. (2013). Textual enhancements or interference? Inserted adjuncts and L2 reading with intermediate language learners. *System*, *41*(4), 952–964.

Cerezo, L., Caras, A., & Leow, R. P. (2016). Effectiveness of guided induction versus deductive instruction on the development of complex Spanish "gustar" structures: An analysis of learning outcomes and processes. *Studies in Second Language Acquisition*, *38*, 265–291.

Cho, M. Y. (2010). The effects of input enhancement and written recall on noticing and acquisition. *Innovations in Language Learning and Teaching*, *4*, 71–87.

Della Putta, P. (2016). The effects of textual enhancement on the acquisition of two non-parallel grammatical features by Spanish-speaking learners of Italian. *Studies in Second Language Acquisition*, *38*, 217–238.

Doughty, C. (1991). Second language instruction does make a difference. *Studies in Second Language Acquisition*, *13*, 431–469.

Doughty, C., & Williams, J. (1998). Pedagogical choices in focus on form. In C. Doughty & J. Williams (Eds.), *Focus on form in classroom second language acquisition* (pp. 197–261). Cambridge: Cambridge University Press.

Gass, S. M., Svetics, I., & Lemelin, S. (2003). Differential effects of attention. *Language Learning*, *53*, 497–545.

Gurzynski-Weiss, L., Al Khalil, M., Baralt, M., & Leow, R. P. (2015). Levels of awareness in relation to type of recast and type of linguistic item in computer-mediated communication: A concurrent investigation. In R. P. Leow, L. Cerezo, & M. Baralt (Eds.), *A psycholinguistic approach to technology and language learning* (pp. 151–170). Berlin: De Gruyter Mouton.

Han, Z.-H., Park, E. S., & Combs, C. (2008). Textual enhancement of input: Issues and possibilities. *Applied Linguistics*, *29*, 597–618.

Hornstein, N., & Lightfoot, D. (1981). Introduction. In N. Hornstein & D. Lightfoot (Eds.), *Explanation in linguistics: The logical problem of language acquisition (p. 9–31)*. London: Longman.

Indrarathne, B., & Kormos, J. (2016). Attentional processing of input in explicit and implicit conditions. *Studies in Second Language Acquisition*, *39*, doi: 10.1017/S027226311600019X.

Issa, B., Morgan-Short, K., Villegas, B., & Raney, G. (2015). An eye-tracking study on the role of attention and its relationship with motivation. In L. Roberts, K. McManus, N. Vanek, & D. Trenkic (Eds.), *EUROSLA Yearbook 2015* (pp. 114–142). Amsterdam: John Benjamins.

Izumi, S. (2002). Output, input enhancement, and the noticing hypothesis: An experimental study on ESL relativization. *Studies in Second Language Acquisition*, *24*, 541–577.

Jahan, A., & Kormos, J. (2015). The impact of textual enhancement on EFL learners' grammatical awareness of future plans and intentions. *International Journal of Applied Linguistics*, *25*, 46–66.

Jourdenais, R. (1998). *The effects of textual enhancement on the acquisition of the Spanish preterit and imperfect* (Unpublished doctoral dissertation). Georgetown University, Washington, DC.

Jourdenais, R., Ota, M., Stauffer, S., Boyson, B., & Doughty, C. (1995). Does textual enhancement promote noticing? A think aloud protocol analysis. In R. W. Schmidt (Ed.), *Attention and awareness in foreign language learning* (pp. 183–216). Honolulu, HI: University of Hawaii, Second Language Teaching and Curriculum Center.

Krashen, S. (1979). A response to McLaughlin 'the monitor model, some methodological considerations.' *Language Learning, 29*, 151–167.

LaBrozzi, R. (2016). The effects of textual enhancement type on L2 form recognition and reading comprehension in Spanish. *Language Teaching Research, 20*(1), 75–91.

Lee, S.-K. (2007). Effects of textual enhancement and topic familiarity on Korean EFL students' reading comprehension and L2 learning of passive form. *Language Learning, 57*, 87–118.

Lee, S.-K., & Huang, H.-T. (2008). Visual input enhancement and grammar learning: A meta-analytic review. *Studies in Second Language Acquisition, 30*, 307–331.

Leow, R. P. (1997). The effects of input enhancement and text length on adult L2 readers' comprehension and intake in second language acquisition. *Applied Language Learning, 8*, 151–182.

Leow, R. P. (2001). Do learners notice enhanced forms while interacting with the L2 input? An online and offline study of the role of written input enhancement in L2 reading. *Hispania, 84*, 496–509.

Leow, R. P. (2007). Input enhancement in classroom-based SLA research: An attentional perspective. In C. Gascoigne (Ed.), *Assessing the impact of input enhancement in second language education: Evolution in theory, research and practice* (pp. 37–52). Stillwater, OK: New Forums.

Leow, R. P. (2009). Input enhancement and L2 grammatical development: What the research reveals. In J. Watzinger-Tharp & S. L. Katz, (Eds.), *Conceptions of L2 grammar: Theoretical approaches and their application in the L2 classroom* (pp. 16–34). Boston, MA: Heinle Publishers.

Leow, R. P. (2012). Explicit and implicit learning in the L2 classroom: What does the research suggest? *The European Journal of Applied Linguistics and TEFL, 2*, 117–129.

Leow, R. P. (2015). *Explicit learning in the L2 classroom: A student-centered approach*. New York, NY: Routledge.

Leow, R. P., Egi, T., Nuevo, A.-M., & Tsai, Y. (2003). The roles of textual enhancement and type of linguistic item in adult L2 learners' comprehension and intake. *Applied Language Learning, 13*, 93–108.

Leow, R. P., Grey, S., Marijuan, S., & Moorman, C. (2014). Concurrent data elicitation procedures, processes, and the early stages of L2 learning: A critical overview. *Second Language Research, 30*, 111–127.

Loewen, S., & Inceoglu, S. (2016). The effectiveness of visual input enhancement on the noticing and L2 development of the Spanish past tense. *Studies in Second Language Learning and Teaching, 6*(1), 89–110.

Overstreet, M. H. (1998). Text enhancement and content familiarity: The focus of learner attention. *Spanish Applied Linguistics, 2*, 229–258.

Park, E. S., & Nassif, L. (2014). Textual enhancement of two L2 Arabic forms: A classroom-based study. *Language Awareness, 23*(4), 334–352.

Sachs, R., & Suh, B.-R. (2007). Textually enhanced recasts, learner awareness, and L2 outcomes in synchronous computer-mediated interaction. In A. Mackey (Ed.), *Conversational interaction in second language acquisition: A collection of empirical studies* (pp. 197–227). Oxford: Oxford University Press.

Sharwood Smith, M. (1981). Consciousness-raising and the second language learner. *Applied Linguistics, 2*, 159–168.

Sharwood Smith, M. (1991). Speaking to many minds: On the relevance of different types of language information for the L2 learner. *Second Language Research, 17*, 118–136.

Sharwood Smith, M. (1993). Input enhancement in instructed SLA: Theoretical bases. *Studies in Second Language Acquisition, 15*, 165–179.

Shook, D. J. (1994). FL/L2 reading, grammatical information, and the input-to-intake phenomenon. *Applied Language Learning*, *5*, 57–93.

Shook, D. J. (1998). What FL reading recalls reveal about the input-to-intake phenomenon. *Applied Language Learning*, *9*, 1–39.

Simard, D. (2009). Differential effects of textual enhancement formats on intake. *System*, *37*(1), 124–135.

Simard, D., & Foucambert, D. (2013). Observing noticing while reading in L2. In J. M. Bergsleithner, S. N. Frota, & J. K. Yoshioka (Eds.), *Noticing and second language acquisition: Studies in honor of Richard Schmidt* (pp. 207–226). Honolulu: National Foreign Language Resource Center, University of Hawaii at Mānoa.

Song, M. (2007). Getting learners' attention: Typographical input enhancement, output, and their combined effects. *English Teaching*, *62*, 193–215.

White, J. (1998). Getting the learners' attention: A typographical input enhancement study. In C. Doughty & J. Williams (Eds.), *Focus on form in classroom second language acquisition* (pp. 85–113). Cambridge: Cambridge University Press.

White, L., Spada, N., Lightbown, P., & Ranta, L. (1991). Input enhancement and L2 question formation. *Applied Linguistics*, *4*, 416–432.

Winke, P. (2013). The effects of input enhancement on grammar learning and comprehension: A modified replication of Lee (2007) with eye-movement data. *Studies in Second Language Acquisition*, *35*(2), 323–352.

Wong, W. (2003). Textual enhancement and simplified input: Effects on L2 comprehension and acquisition of non-meaningful grammatical form. *Applied Language Learning*, *13*, 109–132.

Wong, W. (2007). Processing instruction and structured input as input enhancement. In C. Gascoigne (Ed.), *Assessing the impact of input enhancement in second language education: Evolution in theory, research and practice* (pp. 89–106). Stillwater, OK: New Forums.

10
SALIENCE, COGNITIVE EFFORT, AND WORD LEARNING

Insights from Pupillometry

Kelli Ryan, Phillip Hamrick, Ryan T. Miller, and Christopher A. Was

Introduction

Understanding the roles of general cognitive processes in language learning is one of the central goals of research in second language acquisition (SLA). Of these cognitive processes, the role of attention in second language (L2) learning are central to numerous theoretical frameworks (e.g., Ellis, 2006; Gass, 1997; Leow, 2015; Schmidt, 1990; Tomlin & Villa, 1994). As attention plays a critical role in these frameworks, factors that constrain and direct learners' attention should, therefore, also play critical roles. One such factor is salience (e.g., Ellis, 2006; Leow, Egi, Nuevo, & Tsai, 2003). In a given learning context, allocation of attention—and therefore the amount of attention-driven learning—should be at least partly determined by the salience of a given form in the input. On this assumption, researchers have employed a variety of methods aimed at promoting attentional processing, most of which involve making linguistic stimuli more salient. Perhaps the most widely employed method of increasing salience involves some kind of input enhancement (for overviews, see Han, Park, & Combs, 2008; Lee & Huang, 2008; Leow & Martin, Chapter 9).

Input enhancement is typically conceived of as a way for researchers or educators to direct learners' attention to specific information in the input. Sharwood Smith (1991, 1993) argued that this input enhancement makes target information more perceptually salient and more likely to be noticed (see also Gass, 1988; Schmidt, 1990). His theory builds on the assumption that noticing is necessary for learning, and that internally- and externally-driven salience govern the learner's ability to notice particular types of information in the input. To promote learners' noticing in visual modalities, which is our present focus, researchers and educators can manipulate the visual perceptual salience of text-based linguistic features by manipulating the text through techniques like color coding, highlighting, and boldfacing, henceforth referred to as textual enhancement (TE).

The efficacy of externally-generated salience-enhancing techniques, such as TE, has long been the subject of empirical investigation. However, research on the effectiveness of TE has yielded largely mixed results. For example, a meta-analysis conducted by Lee and Huang (2008) found that TE may be beneficial for form learning, but not for meaning comprehension. Specifically, Lee and Huang (2008) confirmed a small positive effect for TE on form learning across 16 studies encompassing 20 samples. In these studies, L2 learners who were exposed to various TE manipulations outperformed their unenhanced counterparts learning the same target forms with a small positive effect size ($d = 0.22$), while a small negative effect size was obtained for learners' meaning comprehension ($d = -0.26$).

In an attempt to shed more light on these complex findings, researchers have resorted to using a variety of techniques to look at the interplay among TE, attention, and learning. One such technique is eye-tracking (Godfroid, Boers, & Housen, 2013; Godfroid & Winke, 2015). For example, Winke (2013) conducted a modified replication of Lee (2007) using eye-tracking technology. Lee's (2007) original study reported that while TE supported the learning of target grammatical forms (the passive voice), it did not improve comprehension of meaning. In fact, Lee (2007) reported a negative effect of TE on a comprehension recall task. In Winke's (2013) modified replication, she also investigated learning of the passive voice in university-level ESL students, via training consisting of form and meaning comprehension. These results indicated that TE did not significantly increase form learning, and it had no negative comprehension effects. Additionally, eye-tracking data suggested that participants exposed to input with TE noticed the passive to a greater degree, as measured by gaze time and rereading. However, this did not itself lead to better learning in the absence of explicit instruction. Thus, Winke's (2013) findings are consistent with Sharwood Smith's (1991) proposal that TE may promote noticing; however, in this case, noticing alone did not result in learning.

Even with eye-tracking studies, though, the reported effects of TE on attention, noticing, and learning have been mixed. For example, contrary to Winke (2013), Loewen and Inceoglu's (2016) eye-tracking study of L2 Spanish learners provided no evidence that enhancement changed learners' attentional processing, as measured by fixation time and self-reported awareness. Additionally, while both enhanced and unenhanced groups improved their knowledge of the Spanish past tense, there was no significant difference between groups in overall performance. Thus, there was no clear link between enhancement and attentional processing or learning gains. Similarly, an eye-tracking study by Indrarathne and Kormos (2016) reported that increased attentional processing was not necessarily a function of TE. Indeed, between enhanced (in the form of bold text) and unenhanced groups, there was no significant difference in learning on production and comprehension testing of the target grammatical forms.

Taken together, the available evidence is mixed with respect to whether TE influences subsequent noticing, attentional processing, or learning. It is possible that other processes beyond noticing and attention are responsible for the varied learning outcomes across studies. Certainly, the degree of elaboration (number of instances) or explicitness of metalinguistic information (Sharwood Smith, 1991) may moderate the efficacy of TE. Similarly, one might also expect that cognitive effort, or the related construct of depth of processing (Leow, 2015; Leow & Mercer, 2015), could moderate the effectiveness of TE.

Depth of Processing and Cognitive Effort

Although attention is important to their account, Leow's depth of processing approach (Leow, 2015; Leow & Mercer, 2015) emphasizes stages in information processing beyond detection (Tomlin & Villa, 1994). Indeed, critical for the present study, Leow and Mercer (2015, p. 2) argue that deeper processing is, among other things, employing "greater cognitive effort during processing while using prior knowledge to strengthen the process." In relation to TE, lower depth of processing may explain some results where enhanced groups do not outperform unenhanced (such as Winke, 2013). For example, when L2 learners see novel enhanced input, they may spend more time wondering why the text is boldface than they do learning or comprehending the text or form (e.g., Bowles, 2003; Leow, 2001). Thus, depth of processing may interact with the salience of information in the L2 input, and there is some evidence for this. For example, in a study on the effects of TE, Leow et al. (2003) reported no significant benefit for learning Spanish past tense forms using enhanced text over unenhanced text at posttest. Despite no apparent benefits of TE on the immediate recognition and comprehension posttest, Leow et al. (2003) did find that the salience of forms, regardless of TE, seemed to be related to the amount of deeper processing reported.

Thus, there may be some interaction between depth of processing or amount of cognitive effort and enhancement, and it is possible that these factors play a role in learning. Indeed, several researchers argue that attentional processing needs to be accompanied by some (at a minimum) low-level cognitive effort (e.g., Gass, 1997; Hulstijn & Laufer, 2001; Leow, 2015; Truscott & Sharwood Smith, 2011; VanPatten, 2004). However, more research is needed to examine these claims, and, of course, establishing whether and how much cognitive effort learners expend while processing the L2 input can be difficult to establish. Researchers have employed a variety of methods to do so, including concurrent data elicitation from think-aloud protocols (e.g., Leow et al., 2003) and pupillometry.

Pupillometry

While eye-tracking data, such as fixations and regressions, have increasingly been used to study the attentional processes involved in L2 learning, other eye-related data can be used to shed light on different cognitive processes beyond attention.[1] Pupillometry, which involves measuring changes in pupil dilation in response to different stimuli, has been extensively used in cognitive psychology as an index of cognitive effort and processing load (for an overview, see Sirois & Brisson, 2014) but has not, to our knowledge, seen much use in SLA (although, see Schmidtke, 2014).

The pupil is the open region of the iris which allows light to reach the retina, and the muscles controlling the pupil are sensitive to a wide variety of factors of interest to psychologists and SLA researchers, including cognitive effort (e.g., Kahneman & Beatty, 1966) and amount of mental activity (e.g., Wierda, van Rijn, Taatgen, & Martens, 2012). Kahneman (1973) described the validity of pupillometric measures of cognitive task demands and the use of pupillometry to capture variability in a person's effort both during a task and across tasks of varying challenge. Because increases in dilation are associated with higher levels of mental effort, dilation is often used to measure cognitive effort or load. For example, during an attentional blink task, which requires attention across a series of distractors, dilation increases significantly as the time between stimuli and number of distractors increases (Wierda et al., 2012). Cabestrero, Crespo, and Quirós (2009) used pupillometry as in index of mental effort and allocation of cognitive resources under several load conditions. Using a voice-specificity paradigm often used in recognition memory experiments, Papesh, Goldinger, and Hout (2012) found pupil dilation was greater when items were subsequently recognized with more confidence, relative to those recognized with less confidence or not recognized. The items successfully recognized with greater confidence were items which participants apparently expended greater cognitive effort during encoding.

Thus, because pupillary responses are so tightly linked to cognitive effort, pupillometry is ideally suited for assessing the role of cognitive effort in attention-related language learning phenomena.

The Present Study

The interactions among TE, attention, and deeper processing make for a complex picture that is in need of more investigation and clarification. Pupillometry is poised to assist in addressing this need. To that end, the aim of the present study was to begin investigating whether the efficacy of one type of input enhancement (textual enhancement) interacts with one learner-internal factor (cognitive effort), indexed by pupil dilation. We did so by focusing on the domain of incidental word form learning. In particular, this study aimed to address several related research questions:

RQ1: Does textual enhancement lead to better learning of and memory for novel word forms?
RQ2: Does cognitive effort, indexed by changes in pupil dilation, predict learning of and memory for novel word forms?
RQ3: Is there an interaction between the effects of textual enhancement and cognitive effort in predicting learning of and memory for novel word forms?

Given that the effects of input enhancement have yielded mixed results, we made no specific hypotheses regarding the first research question. Regarding the second research question, and following suggestions that deeper processing (e.g., Leow, 2001, 2015; Sharwood Smith, 1991) may be critical to the effectiveness of input enhancement and that involvement effort may be critical for incidental word learning (e.g., Hulstijn & Laufer, 2001), we hypothesized that greater cognitive effort during the training phase—as indexed by greater pupil dilation—would predict memory for the

TABLE 10.1 Biodata for participants by group

Group	Gender	Mean Age	Mean L2 Experience in Years (total)
+TE	10 females, 4 males	20.71 (19–23)	3.67 (2–5)
–TE	10 females, 2 males	20.58 (18–27)	3.25 (2–4)

Note: Ranges in parentheses.

new words at test. Regarding the third research question, which follows from using a factorial design with an interaction, we predicted that textual enhancement would interact with cognitive effort in predicting learning of and memory for novel words. We predicted an interaction on the expectation that the salience of a form (i.e., whether or not it is enhanced) should influence the probability that it gets processed further, and that word learning may depend on whether enhancement has this effect.

Methods

Participants

Thirty-six volunteer undergraduates participated in the experiment in exchange for extra credit in their introductory linguistics courses. Participants were randomly assigned to a group that received input with textual enhancement (+TE) or without textual enhancement (–TE). Data from 10 participants were unable to be used because of loss of pupil information (n = 8), for having uncorrected medical conditions involving the eye (n = 1), and for not being a native speaker of English (n = 1). This left 14 participants in the +TE group and 12 participants in the –TE group. All of the remaining participants reported having normal or corrected-to-normal vision and hearing.

Materials

Training Phase

The experimental task was programmed and displayed with E-Prime 2.0® (Schneider, Eschman, & Zuccolotto, 2012). Participants were visually presented with 30 English sentences (Table 10.2). Each sentence was presented twice, once for a control condition in which the sentence-final word was a normal English word and once for an experimental condition in which the sentence-final word was a target pseudoword. Presenting each sentence this way allowed us to control several factors, including angle of the target to the eye. It has been shown that measurement of pupil diameter can be influenced by gaze position as a participant's eyes move across the screen, even when the pupil itself remains the same size (Hayes & Petrov, 2016).[2] Presenting the same sentences twice, once in a control condition and once in a target condition, allowed us to rule out stimulus-eye angle as a confound between conditions.

TABLE 10.2 Sample sentences from the training phase

Sentence-final control word	Sentence-final target pseudoword
She could tell he was mad by the tone of his voice.	She could tell he was mad by the tone of his tolve.
After every meal it's good to brush your teeth.	After every meal it's good to brush your thrig.
His boss refused to give him a raise.	His boss refused to give him a septh.

The English sentences were taken from a set of sentences with reported cloze probability and completion norms made publicly available (Block & Baldwin, 2010). In order to keep participants' focus on meaning, we chose sentences with sentence-final words that had high cloze probabilities ($M = 0.87$, $SD = 0.08$) in order to make it easier to induce meaning from context even in the presence of a sentence-final pseudoword (e.g., *The bride smiled as she walked down the bealm*).

Pseudowords were produced via search queries to the English Lexicon Project website database (Balota et al., 2007). The search was aimed at retrieving pseudowords that were similar to control words in terms of their lexical characteristics. Control words were each monosyllabic, five letters long, with mean bigram (i.e., two-letter combinations) frequencies of 1400 ($SD = 488$). Therefore, the following search criteria were used: word length = 5 letters, syllables = 1, average bigram frequency = 1,000 to 3,000.[3]

To control for memorability, all possible pseudowords were normed using a recognition memory task. A sample of 13 students who did not participate in the main experiment was given one of two lists of 30 pseudowords (list A or list B). In the study phase, participants were instructed to remember as many pseudowords as they could. They were then given a recognition task that contained all the words from both lists in random order. Memory performance for list A ($M = 0.66$, $SD = 0.20$) was not significantly different from memory performance for list B ($M = 0.63$, $SD = 0.18$), $t(58) = 0.59$, $p = .55$. Since participants appeared to have no pre-existing bias making one list more memorable than the other, we assigned list A to be the target pseudowords in the training phase and list B to be the foil (new) words for the recognition memory test for the main experiment. In the final version of the stimuli, both control words and pseudowords all contained five letters and one (apparent) syllable. The difference in mean bigram frequency between control words ($M = 1400$, $SD = 488$) and pseudowords in the training phase ($M = 1285$, $SD = 280$) was not statistically significant, Welch's $t(46.31) = 1.11$, $p = .27$, $d = 0.29$, 95% CI [-92, 321].

In the training phase, all participants in both the +TE and −TE groups read the same exact sentences the same number of times, with the order of presentation randomized for each participant. The only difference in the stimuli between groups was the presence of textual enhancement, operationalized as yellow highlighting. Highlighting was achieved using the Visual Basic RGB function in E-Prime for yellow (255 red, 255, green and 0 blue). For the +TE group, both sentence-final control words and pseudowords were highlighted (so that any luminance effects from highlighting on pupil dilation would be balanced across control and target stimuli). The –TE group saw the sentences without any highlighting. All pupillometry measures came from changes to pupil diameter measured during this training phase.

Recognition Memory Task

After the training phase, participants were given a surprise recognition memory test for the pseudowords from the training phase. They were instructed that they would see 60 words presented in the middle of the computer screen. They were informed, correctly, that half the pseudowords occurred in the sentences from the training phase and that these should be classified as "old" while the other half of the pseudowords would be new ones that they had not yet seen. These should be classified as "new." Participants were instructed to make their old/new decision as quickly and as accurately as they could by pressing the computer keys corresponding to "old" and "new." Reaction times and accuracy were recorded.

Apparatus

Pupil size and other eye-tracking data were recorded with an Applied Science Laboratories ASL 6 eye-tracker, sampling at 60 Hz from participants' left eye, and stimuli were presented in in black print on a white background in Arial font size 24. Participants were seated so that their eyes were approximately 65 cm from the eye-tracker and such that the participants' gaze angle was less than 42° to the screen as recommended by the manufacturer.

Procedure

Participants were seated in a quiet, dimly lit room. They placed their chins in a chinrest that minimized head movement. A nine-point calibration of eye movement was performed at the beginning of the experiment for each participant. Each training phase trial began with a 250 ms fixation cross placed at the left edge of the screen where the first word of each stimulus sentence would appear. Then a stimulus sentence appeared for 2 seconds followed by a blank screen ISI of 1 second. Participants were told that the goal of the study was to understand how people process sentences for meaning via the use of eye-tracking technology. They were told that their task was to read each sentence in order to understand its meaning just like they "would read a book, a news article, or a blog." Participants were not informed that they would be tested, nor were they instructed to try to learn anything. In other words, participants were exposed to the target pseudowords under incidental learning conditions.[4]

Results

All statistical analyses were performed in the statistics program R (R Core Team, 2015) and figures were produced with the package ggplot2 (Wickham, 2009).

Accuracy and Reaction Time on the Recognition Task

The recognition memory task was first analyzed to establish whether any learning took place. We computed d' scores for each participant (Wickens, 2001). The d' measure is commonly used to assess recognition memory because it can discriminate between "signal" (e.g., memory for a target word) and "noise" (e.g., other factors that lead participants to make one kind of response over another) that jointly contribute to recognition judgments. Because we were most interested in memory for previously seen target pseudowords, and because participants may be expected to perform differently on target pseudowords (old items) and foil pseudowords (new items), we analyzed hits (correct classification of old items as old) and correct rejections (correct classification of new items as new) separately. Table 10.3 reports the descriptive results. Visual inspection of the descriptive statistics indicated opposite patterns of accuracy for hits and correct rejections between the +TE and −TE groups. Therefore, we conducted a mixed ANOVA with Group (2 levels: +TE, −TE) as a between-subjects factor and Item Type (two levels: hits, correct rejections) as within-subjects factor. The results of the mixed ANOVA revealed no significant effects of Group, $F(1, 24) = 0.02, p = .87, \eta_p^2 = 0.001$, or Item Type, $F(1, 24) = 0.18, p = .67, \eta_p^2 = 0.01$, but there was a significant Group*Item Type interaction, $F(1, 24) = 6.35, p = .02, \eta_p^2 = 0.21$. However, Bonferroni-adjusted post-hoc t-tests (revised p value = 0.025) did not show significant between group differences in accuracy on hits, $t(24) = 1.71, p = .09$, or on correct rejections, $t(24) = 1.92, p = .06$.

We analyzed participants' reaction times (RT) in the same fashion as their accuracy, focusing on RT for hits and correct rejections. A mixed ANOVA with Group (2 levels: +TE, −TE) as a between-subjects factor and Item Type (two levels: hits, correct rejections) as a within-subjects factor revealed a significant effect of Item Type, $F(1, 24) = 5.17, p = .03, \eta_p^2 = 0.18$, Group, $F(1, 24) = 4.24, p = .05, \eta_p^2 = 0.15$, and no significant Group*Item Type interaction, $F(1, 24) = 0.11, p = .74, \eta_p^2 = .004$. Bonferroni-adjusted post-hoc t-tests (revised p value = 0.025) did not show significant between group differences in RT for hits, $t(24) = 2.21, p = .03$, or for correct rejections, $t(24) = 1.83, p = .07$.

Taken together, the results indicate that both groups were accurate to similar degrees on the recognition task, but their patterns of accuracy differed. On the other hand, the RT data appeared to show that the +TE group was generally faster than

TABLE 10.3 Descriptive results for the recognition memory task

	+Textual Enhancement	−Textual Enhancement
Hit Accuracy	0.61 (0.13, 0.03)	0.69 (0.07, 0.02)
Correct Rejection Accuracy	0.71 (0.12, 0.03)	0.62 (0.10, 0.03)
d'	0.89 (0.50, 0.13)	0.83 (0.39, 0.12)
Hit RT	953 (294, 78)	1219 (318, 91)
Correct Rejection RT	1031 (367, 98)	1323 (443, 127)

Note: Standard deviations and standard errors are reported in parentheses, respectively. Reaction times (RT) are reported in milliseconds.

the −TE group at classifying items in the recognition task, regardless of whether those items were old or new.

Cognitive Effort as a Predictor of Recognition Task Performance

To investigate our second and third research questions, we built a series of regression models testing whether pupil diameter during the training phase predicted performance on the recognition memory test. Due to the interaction between groups and accuracy on old and new items at test, we built separate regression models[5] for hits and correct rejections and separate models for accuracy and RT. Models were fit with an outcome variable being predicted by main effects of the categorical predictor Group (two levels: +TE, −TE) and the continuous predictor of pupil dilation (measured during the training phase). The −TE group served as the reference level for all analyses. The regression model for accuracy on hits showed that pupil dilation during the training phase did not predict accuracy on hits for the −TE group, but

TABLE 10.4 Regression model results for accuracy for hits in the recognition test

	Estimate	SE	t-value
Intercept	1.032	0.221	4.677**
+Textual Enhancement	−1.172	0.440	−2.663*
Pupil Dilation	−0.008	0.005	−1.556
+Textual Enhancement × Pupil Dilation	0.027	0.011	2.499*

Note: **$p < .001$. *$p < .05$.

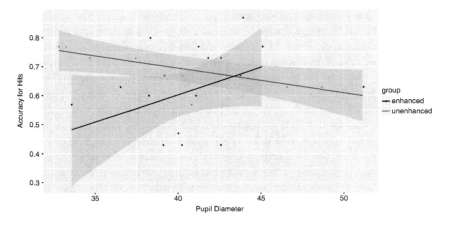

FIGURE 10.1 Scatterplot depicting relationships between recognition test accuracy for hits and mean pupil dilation in the training phase by group. Each dot represents a single participant. The gray region around the regression lines indicates the 95% confidence interval.

the significant interaction indicates that increased pupil dilation during the training phase predicted increased accuracy on hits for the +TE group (Table 10.4). Thus, cognitive effort predicted accuracy on hits for the +TE group, but not for the −TE group. This regression model was statistically significant, $F(3, 22) = 3.28, p = .04$, and it accounted for 21% of the variance in accuracy on hits. However, this model did not survive a Bonferroni correction for multiple comparisons ($p > .025$). Regression models for the other three outcome variables (accuracy for correct rejections, RT for hits, RT for correct rejections) were not statistically significant, all $ps > .17$.

Discussion

This study investigated three research questions. The first question asked whether textual enhancement lead to better learning of and memory for novel words. While the +TE group was faster than the −TE group at correctly classifying items in the recognition task, overall accuracy between the two groups on the recognition task was not significantly different. However, closer inspection of the accuracy data revealed that the −TE group outperformed the +TE group specifically on the recognition of novel words from the training phase (i.e., hits). Conversely, the +TE group was better than the −TE group at classifying new items that had not occurred in the training phase (i.e., correct rejections). What accounts for this pattern of results? One simple explanation is perceptual priming. Perceptual priming is a phenomenon whereby subsequent recognition or classification of a repeated stimulus is affected by its perceptual similarity to (or difference from) a previous stimulus. For example, presentation of "dog" followed by "dog" is more likely to result in perceptual priming than a presentation of "dog" followed by "***dog***." On this view, the visual similarity between training and test phase items may have been higher for the −TE group because the target pseudowords were unenhanced in both the training and recognition test phases. In this scenario, if participants used perceptual similarity as a response heuristic then this would lead to a response bias favoring more "old" judgments. That is, there would be more hits (correct classification of old items as old) and more false alarms (incorrect classification of new items as old). This pattern can be seen in the data (bearing in mind that false alarms = 1 − correct rejections). Relative to the −TE group, the similarity between highlighted target pseudowords from training and unenhanced words in the recognition task may have resulted in the opposite bias for the +TE group, namely, a response bias favoring more "new" judgments. That is, there would be more misses (incorrect classifications of old items as new) and correct rejections (correct classifications of new items as new). This was precisely the pattern of results found (again, bearing in mind that misses = 1 − hits). Thus, we propose that perceptual priming may account for these findings. Importantly, this perceptual priming account can easily be tested in future replication and extension studies by, for example, manipulating the perceptual modality of the stimulus items between training and testing.

Our second and third research questions asked whether cognitive effort during initial learning, as indexed by pupil dilation during training, predicted performance in the recognition task. Our results indicated that cognitive effort during training did not uniformly predict recognition task performance. Instead, there was an interaction whereby cognitive effort predicted accuracy for hits for the +TE group, but not the −TE group. That is, correct identification of previously seen words among participants who received textual enhancement depended on degree of cognitive effort (with greater cognitive effort, as indexed by pupil dilation, being related to increased accuracy). On the other hand, for those who did not receive textual enhancement, increased cognitive effort was not related to increased recognition accuracy. What explains this pattern of findings? Once again, we turn to the possibility of perceptual priming. It has been noted elsewhere (e.g., Jacoby & Dallas, 1981) that perceptual priming is insensitive to changes in levels of processing. If this holds for the current study, then increased reliance on perceptual similarity in the −TE group may account for the reduced influence of cognitive effort on recognition performance. Conversely, since the recognition task stimuli were perceptually less similar to the training stimuli, the +TE group may have been more likely to rely on other sources of information that might have benefited from increased cognitive processing during training. Moreover, it is also worth noting that the range of pupil dilation during training was larger for the −TE group. This large amount of individual variability coupled with our small sample sizes may have obscured the effects of cognitive effort in the −TE group.

Whatever the ultimate explanation for these results, our findings are consistent with the wider notion that the efficacy of input enhancement depends, at least in part, upon the depth of cognitive processing that learners engage in during initial encoding. Our results are consistent with several approaches that emphasize the importance of cognitive effort (e.g., Leow, 2015) and other processes beyond noticing in L2 learning (e.g., Sharwood Smith, 1991) and incidental vocabulary learning (e.g., Hulstijn & Laufer, 2001). Our results are also somewhat consistent with other eye-tracking studies on TE (Indrarathne & Kormos, 2016; Winke, 2013) in that we also found that participants' cognitive effort beyond noticing may have been a factor in their learning outcomes. These results suggest that cognitive effort after noticing may also play a role in learning beyond the well-established effects of attention on word learning (Godfroid et al., 2013). These results—particularly if they are replicated and extended in future research—may go some way toward improving our understanding of whether and how cognitive effort and deeper processing more broadly may moderate the effectiveness of TE. However, using the present results to shed light on the hitherto mixed findings on TE should be done with great caution. At the very least, one must bear in mind that our study focused on word form learning, which obviously limits its comparability to the majority of TE studies which have focused primarily on grammar and/or meaning comprehension.

Limitations

Several other limitations to our study warrant caution in generalization. First, there are obvious limitations in sample size, which might obscure the smaller effect sizes associated with pupillometry, increasing Type II error risk. Likewise, although we controlled for stimulus-level confounds in pupil dilation by presenting the target and control words in the exact same sentential context twice, this procedure could have led to larger variability in pupil dilation measurement because pupil dilation reflected differences that could have occurred due to other effects (e.g., repetition of the same sentential context). The study is also limited by the narrow, semi-artificial scope of our experimental design and materials. To some degree, these limitations were necessary due to the delicate nature of pupillometry itself. Although the use of recognition memory tasks and semi-artificial languages certainly have precedent in SLA research (e.g., Hamrick, 2014, 2015), they come with their own limitations and validity threats that necessitate future research using a range of complementary tasks and materials. This study was also limited in that it only investigated incidental learning conditions. Given the ample evidence that different learning conditions often result in different learning outcomes (for an overview, see Leow & Zamora, 2017) and that they may interact with different cognitive processes (e.g., Hamrick, 2015), it will be important for future research to investigate whether and how cognitive effort moderates the efficacy of input enhancement under different learning and instructional conditions.

Conclusion

The present study employed a novel methodology, pupillometry, for investigating the interaction between TE and participants' cognitive effort during training. The results suggest that it may be cognitive effort (or some other deeper mental processing) that plays an important role in moderating the effects of TE on word learning. If such results continue to be found—particularly if they are found across studies using a variety of different research methods—then it would suggest that salience—especially salience that is constructed by researchers and teachers in the form of TE—may be useful for language learners, but critically when it is accompanied by deeper processing (Leow, 2015), more elaboration or instruction (Sharwood Smith, 1991), or more cognitive effort.

Notes

1 Although traditional eye-tracking measures (e.g., fixations) may tap more than just attentional processing, for present purposes we assume that traditional eye-tracking measures tap distinct processes from pupillometry measures, which index cognitive effort—the focus of this study—more specifically.
2 We thank an anonymous reviewer for this point and reference.
3 This was the final set of parameters for our search. Several different mean bigram frequency ranges had to be tested multiple times during the search to establish a mean and standard deviation value that was comparable to the control words.
4 Incidental learning conditions were used to minimize the likelihood of ceiling effects (i.e., where performance is so high that no further gains can be made).
5 We avoided using mixed effects or multilevel models due to the fact that the sheer volume of data (over 6 million individual data points) was computationally too great.

References

Balota, D. A., Yap, M. J., Cortese, M. J., Hutchison, K. A., Kessler, B., Loftis, B., Neely, J. H., Nelson, D. L., Simpson, G. B., & Treiman, R. (2007). The English lexicon project. *Behavior Research Methods, 39,* 445–459.

Block, C., & Baldwin, C. (2010). Cloze probability and completion norms for 498 sentences: Behavioral and neural validation using event-related potentials. *Behavior Research Methods, 42*, 665–670.

Bowles, M. A. (2003). The effects of textual input enhancement on language learning: An online/offline study of fourth semester Spanish students. In P. Kempchinsky & C. Piñeros (Eds.), *Theory, practice, and acquisition: Papers from the 6th Hispanic Linguistic Symposium and 5th Conference on the Acquisition of Spanish and Portuguese* (pp. 395–411). Somerville, MA: Cascadilla Press.

Cabestrero, R., Crespo, A., & Quirós, P. (2009). Pupillary dilation as an index of task demands. *Perceptual & Motor Skills, 109*, 664–678.

Ellis, N. C. (2006). Selective attention and transfer phenomena in L2 acquisition: Contingency, cue competition, salience, interference, overshadowing, blocking, and perceptual learning. *Applied Linguistics, 27*, 164–194.

Gass, S. (1988). Integrating research areas: A framework for second language studies. *Applied Linguistics, 9*, 198–217.

Gass, S. (1997). *Input, interaction, and the second language learner*. Mahwah, NJ: Lawrence Erlbaum Associates.

Godfroid, A., Boers, F., & Housen, A. (2013). An eye for words: Gauging the role of attention in incidental L2 vocabulary acquisition by means of eye-tracking. *Studies in Second Language Acquisition, 35*, 483–517.

Godfroid, A., & Winke, P. (2015). Investigating implicit and explicit processing using L2 learners' eye-movement data. In P. Rebuschat (Ed.), *Implicit and explicit learning of languages* (pp. 325–348). Philadelphia: John Benjamins.

Hamrick, P. (2014). Recognition memory for novel syntactic structures. *Canadian Journal of Experimental Psychology, 68*, 2–7.

Hamrick, P. (2015). Declarative and procedural memory as individual differences in incidental language learning. *Learning and Individual Differences, 44*, 9–15.

Han, Z., Park, E. S., & Combs, C. (2008). Textual enhancement of input: Issues and possibilities. *Applied Linguistics, 29*, 597–618.

Hayes, T. R., & Petrov, A. A. (2016). Mapping and correcting the influence of gaze position on pupil size measurements. *Behavior Research Methods, 48*, 510–527.

Hulstijn, J., & Laufer, B. (2001). Some empirical evidence for the Involvement Load Hypothesis in vocabulary acquisition. *Language Learning, 51*, 539–558.

Indrarathne, B., & Kormos, J. (2016). Attentional processing of input in explicit and implicit learning conditions: An eye-tracking study. *Studies in Second Language Acquisition, 39*, doi: 10.1017/S027226311600019X.

Jacoby, L. L., & Dallas, M. (1981). On the relationship between autobiographical memory and perceptual learning. *Journal of Experimental Psychology: General, 110*, 306–340.

Kahneman, D. (1973). *Attention and effort*. Englewood Cliffs, NJ: Prentice-Hall.

Kahneman, D., & Beatty, J. (1966). Pupil diameter and load on memory. *Science, 154*, 1583–1585.

Lee, S. K. (2007). Effects of textual enhancement and topic familiarity on Korean EFL students' reading comprehension and learning of passive form. *Language Learning, 57*, 87–118.

Lee, S. K., & Huang, H. T. (2008). Visual input enhancement and grammar learning: A meta-analytic review. *Studies in Second Language Acquisition, 30*, 307–331.

Leow, R. P. (2001). Do learners notice enhanced forms while interacting with the L2? An online and offline study of the role of written input enhancement in L2 reading. *Hispania, 84*, 496–509.

Leow, R. P. (2015). *Explicit learning in the L2 classroom: A student-centered approach.* New York: Routledge.
Leow, R. P., & Zamora, C. (2017). Intentional and incidental learning. In S. Loewen & M. Sato (Eds.), *Routledge handbook of instructed second language acquisition*, pp. 33–49. New York: Routledge.
Leow, R. P., Egi, T., Nuevo, A. M., & Tsai, Y. C. (2003). The roles of textual enhancement and type of linguistic item in adult L2 learners' comprehension and intake. *Applied Language Learning, 13*, 1–16.
Leow, R. P., & Mercer, J. D. (2015). Depth of processing in L2 learning: Theory, research, and pedagogy. *Journal of Spanish Language Teaching, 2*, 69–82.
Loewen, S., & Inceoglu, S. (2016). The effectiveness of visual input enhancement on the noticing and L2 development of the Spanish past tense. *Studies in Second Language Learning and Teaching, 6*, 89–110.
Papesh, M. H., Goldinger, S. D., & Hout, M. C. (2012). Memory strength and specificity revealed by pupillometry. *International Journal of Psychophysiology, 83*(1), 56–64.
R Core Team. (2015). *R: A language and environment for statistical computing.* Vienna: R Foundation for Statistical Computing.
Schmidt, R. (1990). The role of consciousness in second language learning. *Applied Linguistics, 11*, 129–158.
Schmidtke, J. (2014). Second language experience modulates word retrieval effort in bilinguals: Evidence from pupillometry. *Frontiers in Psychology, 5*, 1–16.
Schneider, W., Eschmann, A., & Zuccolotto, A. (2012). *E-Prime user's guide.* Pittsburgh: Psychology Software Tools, Inc.
Sharwood Smith, M. S. (1991). Speaking to many minds: On the relevance of different types of language information for the L2 learner. *Second Language Research, 7*, 118–132.
Sharwood Smith, M. S. (1993). Input enhancement in instructed SLA. *Studies in Second Language Acquisition, 15*, 165–179.
Sirois, S., & Brisson, J. (2014). Pupillometry. *WIREs in Cognitive Science, 5*, 679–692.
Tomlin, R. S., & Villa, V. (1994). Attention in cognitive science and second language acquisition. *Studies in Second Language Acquisition, 16*, 183–203.
Truscott, J., & Sharwood Smith, M. S. (2011). Input, intake, and consciousness. *Studies in Second Language Acquisition, 33*, 497–528.
VanPatten, B. (2004). Input processing in second language acquisition. In B. VanPatten (Ed.), *Processing instruction: Theory, research, and commentary* (pp. 5–31). New York: Routledge.
Wickens, T. (2001). *Elementary signal detection theory.* Oxford: Oxford University Press.
Wickham, H. (2009). *ggplot2: Elegant graphics for data analysis.* New York: Springer-Verlag.
Wierda, S., van Rijn, H., Taatgen, N., & Martens, S. (2012). Pupil dilation deconvolution reveals the dynamics of attention at high temporal resolution. *Proceedings of the National Academy of Sciences, 109*, 8456–8460.
Winke, P. M. (2013). The effects of input enhancement on grammar learning and comprehension. *Studies in Second Language Acquisition, 35*, 323–352.

11
EFFECTS OF CONTEXTUAL AND VISUAL CUES ON SPOKEN LANGUAGE PROCESSING

Enhancing L2 Perceptual Salience Through Focused Training

Debra M. Hardison

Introduction

Previous research demonstrated that speech is a multimodal phenomenon. Neuroimaging studies revealed a relationship between visual input and activity in the auditory cortex during speech perception (e.g., Hickok, Buchsbau, Humphries, & Muftuler, 2003; Sams et al., 1991; Skipper, van Wassenhove, Nusbaum, & Small, 2007). Perception studies showed that visual cues from a talker's face provided a significant advantage in the accurate identification of speech sounds for a variety of populations, languages, and stimulus conditions. These include infants in their first language (L1) development (e.g., Meltzoff & Kuhl, 1994), the hearing impaired (e.g., Bergeson, Pisoni, & Davis, 2003; Walden et al., 1977), non-impaired listeners in ambient noise (e.g., Benoît, Mohamadi, & Kandel, 1994 for French; Summerfield, MacLeod, McGrath, & Brooke, 1989 for English), and individuals responding to the McGurk Effect (e.g., Hardison, 1999; McGurk & MacDonald, 1976)—a perceptual effect in which discrepant auditory-visual cues may result in an illusory percept (e.g., visual /ga/ and auditory /ba/ may produce the percept /da/).

For second language (L2) learners, salience (i.e., perceived strength of a stimulus) plays a critical role in perceptual learning and is influenced by the learner's L1. Focused training can increase the salience of speech cues. Training studies demonstrated that auditory-visual (AV) input from talkers' faces (e.g., lip movements) provided a significant advantage over auditory-only (A-only) input in the development of L2 perceptual accuracy of American English (AE) /r/, /l/, /f/, and /θ/ for Japanese and Korean speakers (Hardison, 2003), and earlier identification of words beginning with these sounds (Hardison, 2005a). AV input also facilitated the improvement of identification accuracy of L2 French nasal vowels for L1 English speakers (Inceoglu, 2016).

Those studies involved consonant-vowel (CV) syllables, minimal pairs, or isolated words. The question arises as to what effect the simultaneous presence of preceding context and visual cues might have on spoken word identification by L2 learners. Context has long been known to facilitate auditory word identification by native speakers (NSs) (e.g., Zwitserlood, 1989), and has been incorporated into bilingual auditory-input models (Dijkstra & van Heuven, 2002; FitzPatrick, 2007), and supported by event-related potential (ERP) experiments (e.g., van den Brink, Brown, & Hagoort, 2001). However, Zwitserlood found that members of the initial cohort of word candidates were activated even if they were inconsistent with semantic context, suggesting that context effects occurred after the initial bottom-up cohort activation.

In multimodal contexts, visual input can enter the word identification process early given the natural temporal precedence of the articulatory gesture over the associated acoustic signal (Munhall & Tohkura, 1998), assuming the gesture is salient and accurately identified; for example, labial closure in English represents three possible consonants /p, b, m/, which reduces the perceiver's initial cohort. These bilabial sounds constitute a visually homophenous category (i.e., sounds not visually discernible from one another). Speechreading studies on the confusability of consonants varied somewhat in their determination of homophenous groups; however, in general, visual categories included /p, b, m/, /f, v/, /θ, ð/, /ʃ, ʒ/, and /s, z, t, d, n, k, g/ based on studies using CV syllables with /ɑ/ (Binnie, Montgomery, & Jackson, 1974). Generally, /r/ and /l/ constitute separate visual categories (e.g., Binnie, Jackson, & Montgomery, 1976), but their discernibility is reduced if they occur in a cluster with bilabial (versus velar) stops or /f/ (Franks & Kimble, 1972), or in environments with rounded vowels. In fact, rounded vowels, especially /u/, obscure articulatory details because the rounding can spread up to four segments early (e.g., Benguerel & Pichora-Fuller, 1982). Like auditory intelligibility, visual discernibility is also influenced by talker variability (Kricos & Lesner, 1982), and both impact cue salience.

The current study explored the use of contextual and visual cues in the process of word identification by L2 learners and NSs of English in the United States, and the change for learners before and after segmental-level perception training. A particular focus was whether increased salience of speech cues following training would alter the influence of context on perceivers' decisions; in other words, if one cue source becomes more salient, does it impact the use of the other? For the word identification task, stimuli began with the following: bilabial /p/, labiodental /f/, /r/, /l/, and nonlabials /s, t, k/. Based on previous findings (Hardison, 2005a), each consonant was paired with high and low unrounded vowels and a rounded vowel as the initial CV sequence of a target word; these first two sounds are critical in initiating lexical access (Tyler, 1984). Although there is variability across talkers and speech styles (Hardison, 2005b), the articulatory characteristics of these sounds create salient gestures. For such cues to contribute to an accurate percept, they must also be identifiable (Ellis, 2006; Hardison, 2003); therefore, perception training for learners included the contrasts /p/-/f/ and /r/-/l/ in minimal pairs with feedback.[1]

Japanese and Korean learners of L2 English often struggle with /r/ and /l/. The AE /r/ is generally characterized by a lower third formant frequency that distinguishes it from /w/ and /l/ (Lindau, 1985). Japanese has a voiced dental/alveolar flap in utterance-initial and intervocalic positions. It does not appear adjacent to other consonants, but occurs in the environment of all Japanese vowels (Tsujimura, 1996). Korean has a voiced nonvelarized /l/ in syllable-final position and a voiced dental/alveolar flap intervocalically (or between vowel and glide) (Shin, Kiaer, & Cha, 2013). In addition, Korean learners often confuse AE /f/ with /p/; Korean does not have a labial fricative. Japanese has a weak bilabial fricative occurring in careful speech but it differs from AE /f/ (Vance, 1987).

There is a substantial literature on Japanese speakers' difficulty with AE /r/ and /l/ and the attempts to improve their identification accuracy through auditory training. The most successful studies in terms of robust perceptual category development involved multiple talkers producing multiple natural exemplars (e.g., Lively, Logan, & Pisoni, 1993)—now known as high variability perception training. A multimodal extension of this approach found that after three weeks of focused training, learners who received AV input (i.e., a talker's face and voice) showed significantly better results than those receiving A-only input (Hardison, 2003). Perceptual accuracy was also significantly influenced by the adjacent vowel, word position, and talker.

Such variable performance in light of stimulus and talker variability is compatible with episodic models for the encoding of speech in long-term memory. As between-category differences and within-category similarities are enhanced through training with feedback, whether AV or A-only, categorization accuracy of sounds improves (Hardison, 2012). Nosofsky (1986) referred to this as the stretching and shrinking of psychological space. Specifically, the relevant auditory and visual stimulus dimensions of each sound become more salient cues as learners come to associate them with the correct perceptual outcome. Similarly, the irrelevant dimensions (e.g., allophonic variants of AE /r/ or /l/) become less salient.

Successful perception training also resulted in earlier word identification by Japanese and Korean learners of English, especially with AV (versus A-only) input (Hardison, 2005a). In that study, the gating paradigm was used, which involves successive presentations of increasing amounts of a target word, each referred to as a *gate*. Initial studies using gating involved A-only input with NSs of English and showed effects of word length and context (e.g., Grosjean, 1980, 1996; Salasoo & Pisoni, 1985; Warren & Marslen-Wilson, 1988). With more constraining preceding contexts, target word length played less of a role (Grosjean, 1980). Monosyllabic words not identified before their acoustic offset (Grosjean, 1985) could be identified afterwards if facilitated by subsequent context (Bard, Shillcock, & Altmann, 1988). The paradigm was later adapted for AV presentation (e.g., Hardison, 2005a, 2005b; Moradi, Lidestam, & Rönnberg, 2013). In AV scenarios, information from both modalities (versus unimodal input) can be integrated over time to provide faster and more accurate identification as it is matched against stored lexical representations in long-term memory (e.g., Fort, Spinelli, Savariaux, & Kandel, 2010; Hardison, 2012). However, success depends on the salience of cues from the perceiver's perspective, and their accurate identification and integration into a unitary perceptual outcome. In the current study, word identification was also tested using the gating paradigm.

Given the temporal precedence of articulatory gestures over the acoustic signal (Munhall & Tohkura, 1998), auditory-visual speech can result in the initiation of a smaller, more precise cohort by enhancing identification of otherwise confusable sounds (e.g., auditory /p/ and /k/), and by tapping into the smaller lexical neighborhoods that represent the overlap between separate auditory and visual neighborhoods (Tye-Murray, Sommers, & Spehar, 2007). This approach resolves lexical competition and reduces the cognitive demands involved in the search process (Besle, Fort, Delpuech, & Giard, 2004; Skipper et al., 2007). Matching of input to stored lexical representations begins early and continues to be updated as more of the signal is processed. Evidence suggests that information from each modality contributes the most at different points in time. Using a gating task with synthetic speech and a virtual talker, Jesse and Massaro (2010) found that visual speech contributed more information at the beginning of a consonant (e.g., to clarify place of articulation), whereas the auditory modality's contribution tended to accumulate over time. Crucially, the salience of the cues and accuracy of their identification dictate the preciseness of the cohort of candidates.

During concurrent activation of candidates, selection of the correct one emerges from a process of competition among them. In this scenario, it is easy to see how early an L2 learner's word identification process could be derailed by the inability to identify a word-initial sound accurately, resolve initial ambiguity quickly, and/or integrate top-down (contextual) and bottom-up (perceptual) information.

Several research questions guided the current study: 1) Do stimulus condition (i.e., presence or absence of context) and modality of presentation (AV versus A-only) affect word identification accuracy? 2) How does cue integration differ between L2 learners and NSs? 3) How does segmental-level training affect word identification by learners? and 4) Is there a significant effect of the initial CV sequence of a target word? It was hypothesized that word identification would be earlier with two sources of input (i.e., contextual and visual cues) if learners were able to attend to both cues as the process unfolded. It was also hypothesized that the initial CV sequence of the targets would show an effect, especially for sounds such as /r/ and /l/, which are particularly challenging for Japanese and Korean speakers, and that focused training would increase the perceptual salience of these stimuli. Independent variables were modality of presentation (AV, A-only), stimulus condition (sentence, excised word), initial CV sequence of the target word, and—for learners—time (pre- and post-training).

Details for the L1 Japanese, Korean, and English speakers are presented in Experiments 1, 2, and 3, respectively. The chapter focuses on the results of the word identification (i.e., gating) tasks.

Experiment 1: Japanese Speakers

Method

Participants

A total of 72 L1 Japanese speakers participated in Experiment 1. They had met the English proficiency requirement for admission to a large Midwestern university in the United States, but still needed and wanted to improve their aural skills. They had started learning English in middle school, but were not receiving English instruction or tutoring at the time of the study. Data collection spanned several semesters. In each administration, those who participated had been in the United States less than six months. They reported corrected-to-normal vision and no hearing problems. Participants were assigned to one of four experimental groups (18 participants per group); that is, the AV and A-only groups for the gating tasks were each subdivided into sentence and excised-word conditions. Learners in AV groups received AV perception training; the others received A-only training. Control groups (for AV and A-only) participated in the gating tasks but received no training. Given that this study required a between-groups design, care was taken to ensure that each group included a range of individuals based on their Test of English as a Foreign Language (TOEFL) listening scores and L2 English use while in the United States (e.g., percentage of time spent interacting in English); biographical and language use data were obtained from a questionnaire.

Materials

Gating

Two parallel sets of materials (Sets A and B) were created for the word identification tasks to avoid potential carryover effects from the use of the same stimuli before and after training. Half the participants received Set A as pre-training and Set B as post-training; for the other half, the order was reversed.

Stimuli were bisyllabic content words with initial-syllable stress that began with the following: /p/, /f/, /r/, /l/, and /s, t, k/. The nonlabials (/s, t, k/) offered some baseline data because these sounds are typically not problematic for learners at this level—a status which also contributes to positive learner affect during the experiment. As noted earlier, each consonant was paired with three types of vowels chosen according to height and rounding, which are visually salient dimensions for vowels. This created a balanced design of 15 CV sequences (5 consonant categories × 3 types of vowels) each with 3 words (see Appendix for examples). Stimuli were chosen from a database that indicated they were frequent words in spoken English from relatively low density neighborhoods (i.e., fewer words with a similar phonetic structure). Identification is generally earlier for high-frequency words with few neighbors (e.g., Garlock, Walley, & Metsala, 2001).[2] In addition, subjective familiarity ratings were obtained prior to the study from learners with a lower proficiency than the study population. Selected targets were those that were rated as 6 or 7 on a 7-point familiarity scale (where 7 = *know the word and its meaning*).

Two stimulus conditions were created: 1) sentence condition with context preceding the target word, and 2) word condition in which the target was digitally excised from the recorded sentence. In doing so, the stimulus in the word condition differed only from its counterpart in the sentence condition by the absence of context. The contexts preceding the target words were carefully constructed to be relatively short, and appropriate syntactically, semantically, and pragmatically (see Appendix).

They suggested the possible word class of the target (e.g., noun), but did not contribute a substantial amount of information. To ensure that participants would not likely guess the target word without using any of its acoustic-phonetic (and visual) properties, the preceding contexts were distributed to two peer groups (native and non-native speakers of English) as a cloze task. They were asked to write the first word they thought of in a blank after each context to provide a measure of the predictability of the intended target (e.g., Marslen-Wilson & Welsh, 1978). If anyone guessed the target or provided a close synonym, a new context was constructed and tested. Additional considerations in stimulus selection included placement of sentence focal stress on the target, no rounded vowels in the preceding or subsequent word, and a relatively neutral lip position in the articulation of the end of the preceding word (e.g., *a*), which also facilitated editing. To avoid sentence-final effects on intonation, a prepositional phrase followed each target in recording, but was deleted in editing.

Stimulus sentences were recorded in a quiet studio by a female NS of English from the upper Midwest. Intelligibility of all stimuli, including the contexts, was confirmed prior to their use. Stimuli were digitally edited using AVID Media Composer to ensure precision. The researcher worked in conjunction with a professional video editor to develop the stimuli. In excising a target word from a sentence, care was taken to avoid including part of the preceding word. Based on previous studies (e.g., Hardison, 2005a) and concern for participant fatigue, a two-frame gate (about 66 ms) was used. Stimuli were randomized for presentation.

Summary of Materials: Perception Training

For AV and A-only perception training, stimuli were minimal pairs produced by five NSs of AE from the upper Midwest (three female, two male). There were 80 trials for /r/ and /l/ (6 words × 4 positions × 3 adjacent vowels: /i or ɪ/, /ɑ or aɪ/, and /u or o/; plus 8 words in intervocalic position), and 57 trials contrasting /p/-/f/ in initial singleton and cluster positions, and in final singleton with a variety of vowels (see Hardison, 2003, for details). Stimuli were digitally edited and presented on a computer screen. AV groups saw a life-sized image of the talker's head. Each trial was preceded by a warning tone, followed by the stimulus, and then 4 seconds of black for response. For AV training groups, the talker appeared on the screen about 1 second before and after each utterance. For feedback, all participants saw the correct word on the screen in 72-point Times black type on a 90% white background, and then the stimulus was repeated to increase the strength of the relationship between the auditory and/or visual cues and the correct choice.

Procedure

Gating

Participants were tested individually in a sound-attenuated room. They were seated comfortably in front of a 24-inch monitor and chose to listen through studio speakers versus headphones. The researcher observed all sessions to ensure that participants followed instructions. To familiarize them with gating, they were given 10 practice trials involving unrelated stimuli produced by a talker not used in the study, and were encouraged to ask questions. For the pre- and post-training gating tasks, they were instructed to write down the word they thought the talker was saying at each gate and not to change any previous responses. Based on earlier research with a comparable population (Hardison, 2005a), participants were given 4 seconds to respond after each gate. Each task took about 30 minutes, including a break.

In the sentence condition, the first presentation or pass included the sentence fragment (i.e., preceding context) up to the point before the target to allow for the possibility that a participant might predict the correct word. The second pass presented that context plus the first gate (two frames) of the target. Subsequent stimulus presentations provided the context, the first gate, plus an additional gate, and this continued until the acoustic offset of the target word. Studies have shown no significant effect of the successive presentation format on performance (e.g., Cotton & Grosjean, 1984). One warning tone signaled the next gate of the same stimulus, and two warning tones indicated a new trial. In the word condition, the first pass involved no stimulus input in order to correspond to the first pass in the sentence condition; the second pass presented the first gate (two frames) of the target word.

Following data collection, participants were asked to rate each stimulus on a 7-point scale to confirm its familiarity, and transcribe the preceding contexts to assure their intelligibility. The pre- and posttest gating tasks were separated by a three-week period of perception training.

Summary of Procedure: Perception Training

Training was conducted in the same setting as that described for the gating tasks. Individuals participated in small groups seated in front of a raised monitor. Those in AV groups were instructed to look at the screen when they heard the warning tone, and to circle the word on their response sheets that matched what the talker had said. Training sessions were also observed. The stimuli recorded by each of the five talkers were presented a total of three times over a period of 15 sessions (three weeks). Each session involved only one talker and took about 20–25 minutes, including a break.

Results and Discussion: Gating

The tabulation of data for the pre- and post-training gating tasks followed previous studies (e.g., Hardison, 2005a, 2005b; Moradi et al., 2013; Salasoo & Pisoni, 1985). The identification point for each target was determined by the gate at which the correct word was written with no subsequent changes; this was converted to a percentage of the word's total duration in gates to compensate for differences in the absolute duration of the stimuli, which ranged from five to eight gates. For analysis purposes, tabulations for targets not correctly identified by their acoustic offset were based on the total duration of the word plus one gate (producing percentages more than 100).

The experimental design involved the following fixed factors: modality (AV, A-only), condition (sentence, excised word), time (pre- and post-training) and CV sequence. Trials (three nested in each level of the CV factor) and participants (nested in the Modality x Condition interaction) were random factors. Discussion of results focuses on the significant findings, which involved only the experimental groups. Effect sizes are reported as omega-squared (ω^2). Planned comparisons, based on a priori hypotheses guided by the learners' L1 phonology and previous research, focused on words beginning with /f/, and /r/ and /l/.[3]

As shown in Figure 11.1a, each pair of columns represents the mean percentage of the target word that participants needed for accurate identification per modality and condition prior to and following focused perception training. Overall means (with standard deviations and 95% CIs in parentheses) for participants in each experimental group were as follows from earliest to latest identification point: AV sentence, pretest $M = 88.93$ ($SD = 11.25$; [82.70, 95.16]), posttest $M = 64.71$ ($SD = 7.74$; [60.42, 68.99]); A-only sentence, pretest $M = 99.86$ ($SD = 6.97$; [96.00, 103.73]), posttest $M = 76.23$ ($SD = 5.74$; [73.06, 79.41]); AV word, pretest $M = 100.48$ ($SD = 10.14$; [94.87, 106.10]), posttest $M = 76.85$ ($SD = 5.76$; [73.66, 80.04]); and A-only word, pretest $M = 107.61$ ($SD = 7.02$; [103.73, 111.50]), posttest $M = 85.31$ ($SD = 5.42$; [82.31, 88.31]). Note that the pre- and posttest means for A-only input with context (i.e., A-only sentence) were comparable to those for AV input without context (i.e., AV word).

There was a significant main effect of modality, $F(1, 31.30) = 27.07, p < .001$, $\omega^2 = 0.08$; condition, $F(1, 32.99) = 28.01, p < .001, \omega^2 = 0.07$; time, $F(1, 53.32) = 260.12, p < .001, \omega^2 = 0.42$; and CV sequence, $F(14, 31.66) = 3.41, p = .022, \omega^2 = 0.06$. Identification was earliest when participants had visual cues or context. Most notable, based on its effect size, was the influence of perception training. There was also a significant Modality × Time × CV sequence interaction, $F(14, 30) = 3.18$,

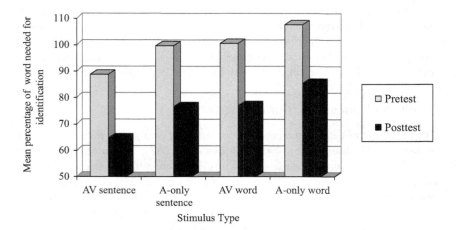

FIGURE 11.1A L1 Japanese: Mean percentage of target word needed for identification in pretest and posttest per modality (AV, A-only) and condition (sentence, excised word)

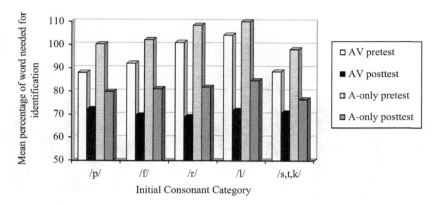

FIGURE 11.1B L1 Japanese: Mean percentage of target word needed for identification in pretest and posttest by modality and initial consonant category (collapsed across condition)

$p = .021$, $\omega^2 = 0.02$, indicating that for some levels of the CV factor, the advantage of AV over A-only input was more accentuated following training. In sum, following Cohen's (1988) guidelines, perception training had a very large effect on responses, accounting for 42% of the variance.[4] The remaining factors had a medium effect; in all, they accounted for about 63% of the variance. The two random factors accounted for an additional 7% (trials) and 5% (participants).

The variable responses across CV sequences are shown in Figure 11.1b, which breaks down the results by initial consonant category (averaged here across vowels). These data are collapsed across condition, as there were no significant interactions involving condition. The lower the percentage, the less information was needed for accurate word identification. The second column for each category represents the results for post-training AV input. This is the stimulus requiring the least amount of input for identification across categories. A planned comparison was significant, $F(1, 14) = 15.65$, $p = .002$ indicating that CV sequences involving /r/ and /l/ (collapsed across vowels) benefited more from AV (versus A-only) input following training compared to the other consonant categories (i.e., bilabial, labiodental, nonlabial). For words beginning with /r/ followed by an unrounded vowel, the amount of input needed for accurate identification declined from about 95% of the word in the AV pretest to 63% in the AV posttest presentations. In contrast, in the pretest A-only conditions, these words were not identified prior to their acoustic offset; however, following training, about 77% of the words were sufficient for identification. Words beginning with /r/ and a rounded vowel were not identified before their acoustic offset in the AV or A-only pretest, but this improved to identification based on about 80% (AV) or 90% (A-only) of the words in the posttest.

Figure 11.2 shows some of the candidates proposed by participants for two sample stimuli: *riot* (pretest word with unrounded vowel) and *robot* (posttest word with rounded vowel) in the AV and A-only sentence conditions. Recall that the same

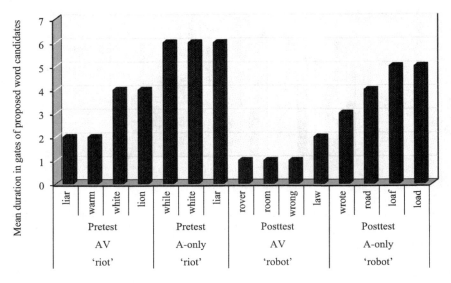

FIGURE 11.2 L1 Japanese: Mean duration in gates of word candidates proposed for stimuli *riot* (pretest) and *robot* (posttest) in AV and A-only sentence presentations

stimuli were not presented to the same learners in both pre- and posttests. In the pretest, candidates for *riot* began with /l/ or /w/ regardless of modality. Participants who were presented with this word in the posttest had little difficulty correctly identifying it; even incorrect candidates began with /r/ (e.g., "writer"). In the posttest, /r/-initial words followed by a rounded vowel (e.g., *robot*) were easier to identify, especially in the AV condition, but still tended to show candidates beginning with /l/, as shown in the figure (e.g., "law, loaf, load"). Some of the candidates (e.g., "liar, lion") proposed for the stimulus *riot* were possible given the context (*The story was about the ___*); however, in the case of *robot*, the candidates, with the exception of "rover," did not suggest an influence of context (*The student wants to design a ___*). In both the pre- and posttest A-only presentations, incorrect candidates persisted over more gates compared to AV. Note, however, that these candidates tended to reflect the correct vowel quality (/ɑ/ or /aɪ/ in the pretest, and /o/ in the posttest)—a finding that was consistent across responses.

Experiment 2: Korean Speakers

Method

Participants

A total of 88 L1 Korean speakers participated in Experiment 2. They were assigned to one of the experimental groups (22 participants per group) following the same guidelines as in Experiment 1: AV sentence, AV word, A-only sentence, and A-only word. Similar background information was obtained for Korean speakers as for the Japanese speakers in Experiment 1.

Materials and Procedure

Stimuli and procedures were the same as for Experiment 1.

Results and Discussion: Gating

The data were tabulated and analyzed as in Experiment 1. As shown in Figure 11.3a, less of a word was needed for accurate identification post-training and when AV input was present. Overall means (with standard deviations and 95% CIs in parentheses) for participants in each experimental group were as follows: AV sentence, pretest $M = 84.42$ ($SD = 9.88$; [78.95, 89.89]), posttest $M = 64.43$ ($SD = 6.92$; [60.59, 68.26]); A-only sentence, pretest $M = 100.01$ ($SD = 7.18$; [96.03, 103.98]), posttest $M = 78.03$ ($SD = 5.01$; [75.25, 80.80]); AV word, pretest $M = 96.31$ ($SD = 6.43$; [92.75, 99.87]), posttest $M = 74.90$ ($SD = 5.97$; [71.59, 78.21]); and A-only word, pretest $M = 104.36$ ($SD = 6.67$; [100.67, 108.06]), posttest $M = 84.77$ ($SD = 4.15$; [82.47, 87.07]).

There was a significant main effect of modality, $F(1, 29.33) = 34.23$, $p < .001$, $\omega^2 = 0.11$; condition, $F(1, 34.60) = 15.59$, $p < .001$, $\omega^2 = 0.06$; and time, $F(1, 50.06) = 260.18$, $p < .001$, $\omega^2 = 0.36$. Identification was earliest when participants had visual cues or context. As in Experiment 1, the greatest influence on identification performance came from perception training. Although CV sequence did not show a significant main effect, there were two significant interactions involving this factor: Modality x CV, $F(14, 402) = 4.93$, $p < .001$, $\omega^2 = 0.01$; and Time × CV, $F(14, 35.04) = 2.29$, $p = .011$, $\omega^2 = 0.02$. These interactions indicated that the effect of

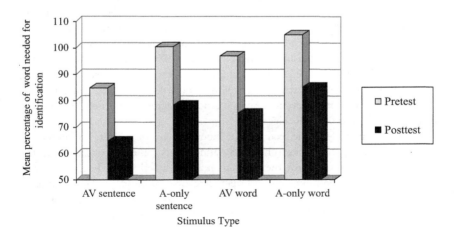

FIGURE 11.3A L1 Korean: Mean percentage of target word needed for identification in pretest and posttest per modality (AV, A-only) and condition (sentence, excised word)

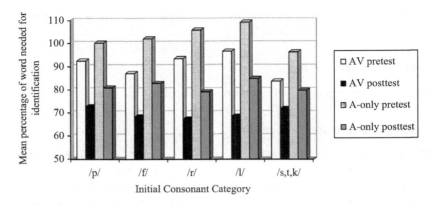

FIGURE 11.3B L1 Korean: Mean percentage of target word needed for identification in pretest and posttest by modality and initial consonant category (collapsed across condition)

modality and training varied according to the CV sequence. Planned comparisons pointed to the sequences involving /r/ and /l/ as benefiting more from AV input, $F(1, 14) = 5.91, p = .04$, and showing greater improvement from training, $F(14, 35.26) = 2.21, p = .011$.

Figure 11.3b breaks down the results by initial consonant category (averaged across vowels). These data are collapsed across condition; there were no significant interactions involving this factor. As in Experiment 1, the second column for each category represents the post-training AV presentation, which is the stimulus requiring the least amount of input for identification across categories. About 95% of the words beginning with /r/ or /l/ in the AV conditions were required for identification prior to training regardless of the adjacent vowel. In the posttest, this figure dropped to about 68%. In the A-only conditions before training, identification was not made prior to the acoustic offset of the words; however, following training, about 79% of the /r/-initial words and 84% of the /l/-initial words were needed for identification. In sum, perception training had a very large effect on responses, accounting for 36% of the variance. In all, the above factors accounted for about 53% of the variance in responses. The two random factors accounted for an additional 9% (trials) and 6% (participants).

Figure 11.4 provides some examples of incorrect word candidates proposed for *razor* (pretest) and *lighter* (posttest) in the AV and A-only sentence conditions. In the pretest, incorrect responses for the stimulus *razor* included words beginning with /w/ and /l/; those beginning with /l/ persisted over more gates. The candidates did not indicate an influence of context. In the posttest, incorrect responses for *lighter* generally began with /l/ except for one ("writer"), which occurred in both modalities. Some of these candidates (e.g., "letter," "library") were logical choices following the context (*He couldn't find the ___*). In addition, candidates in the AV pretest varied more in terms of the vowel compared to the posttest.

Effects of Contextual and Visual Cues **213**

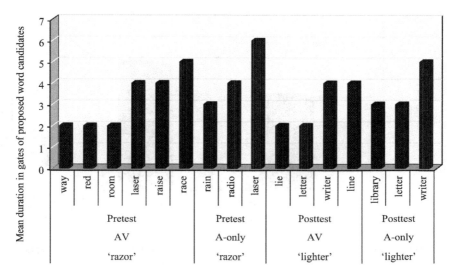

FIGURE 11.4 L1 Korean: Mean duration in gates of word candidates proposed for stimuli *razor* (pretest) and *lighter* (posttest) in AV and A-only sentence presentations

Experiment 3: Native Speakers of English

Method

Participants

A total of 66 NSs of AE from the upper Midwest participated in Experiment 3 and were randomly assigned to one of the four experimental groups: AV sentence (18), AV word (18), A-only sentence (15), and A-only word (15). They were graduate students or instructors at a large U.S. university. They reported corrected-to-normal vision and no hearing problems.

Materials and Procedure

Stimuli and procedures for gating were generally the same as in Experiments 1 and 2, except that stimuli in both Sets A and B were used and no perception training was involved. None of the participants was familiar with gating; therefore, the same practice trials were used.

Results and Discussion: Gating

The data were tabulated and analyzed as in Experiments 1 and 2, with the exception of the time factor which did not pertain to the NSs. As shown in Figure 11.5a, much less of a word (about 63%) was needed for accurate identification when both

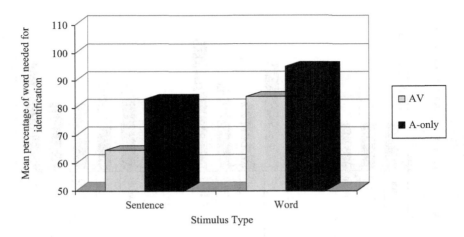

FIGURE 11.5A L1 English: Mean percentage of target word needed for identification per modality (AV, A-only) and condition (sentence, excised word)

AV input and sentence context were present. Overall means (with standard deviations and 95% CIs in parentheses) for participants in each experimental group were as follows, ranked from earliest to latest identification point: AV sentence $M = 62.91$ ($SD = 11.50$; [56.54, 69.27]); A-only sentence $M = 81.63$ ($SD = 13.08$; [74.39, 88.88]); AV word $M = 82.27$ ($SD = 8.43$; [77.60, 86.94]); and A-only word $M = 93.24$ ($SD = 9.58$; [87.93, 98.55]).

There was a significant main effect of modality, $F(1, 30) = 129.57, p < .001$, $\omega^2 = 0.14$; condition, $F(1, 30) = 134.54, p < .001, \omega^2 = 0.15$; and CV sequence, $F(14, 460) = 29.85, p < .001, \omega^2 = 0.18$. These effect sizes were fairly large. In contrast to the learners, there were significant interactions involving condition, most notably a Modality × Condition × CV interaction, $F(14, 406) = 2.65, p = .001, \omega^2 = 0.02$. The planned comparisons pointed again to the sequences involving /r/ and /l/ as benefiting more from AV input; however, this benefit was present only in the sentence condition, $F(1, 406) = 4.21, p = .037$.

Figure 11.5b breaks down the results by initial consonant category (averaged across vowels). The first column for each category represents the AV sentence condition, which is the stimulus requiring the least amount of input for identification. In this condition, words beginning with /r/ followed by high or low unrounded vowels required an average of 65% of the word for identification; whereas the sequences involving a rounded vowel required about 80%, perhaps due to the masking influence of the vowel. In the same condition, words beginning with /l/ were identified earlier regardless of vowel type, requiring on average 56% of the word. In sum, those factors accounted for about 47% of the variance in responses; the two random factors accounted for an additional 8% (trials) and 4% (participants).

In general, incorrect word candidates began with the correct consonant and continued for no more than two gates, especially with visual cues. When context

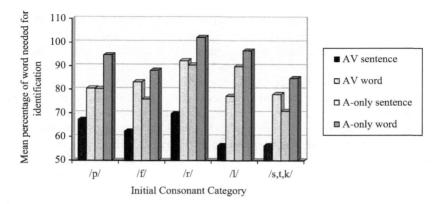

FIGURE 11.5B L1 English: Mean percentage of target word needed for identification per modality, condition, and initial consonant category

was also present, candidates represented logical sentence completions such as "raincoat" for the target *razor* following *Be sure to pack a___*. For the target *rescue* in the AV sentence condition, proposed candidates included "result," "rainstorm," and "record," which demonstrated perception of the target's initial CV sequence (with some vocalic variation), and were compatible with the context *We were surprised to see that ___*. However, in the A-only word condition (i.e., no contextual or visual cues), for some targets beginning with /r/ such as *rescue*, even L1 English participants proposed /l/- and /w/-initial words (e.g., "lesson" and "west"). In contrast to the learners' responses, ambiguity was resolved within two gates.

General Discussion

Returning to the research questions guiding this study, stimulus condition and modality of presentation significantly affected word identification for both L2 learners and NSs of English, and with medium-to-large effect sizes. Identification was earlier with AV (versus A-only) input and with preceding context, despite its deliberately unconstraining nature. For learners, the process was significantly facilitated by perception training, which alone accounted for 42% of the variance for the Japanese speakers and 36% for the Korean speakers. The percentage of a word needed for identification in the post-training AV sentence condition for both learner groups was similar to that for the NSs. In addition, the word-initial CV sequence influenced responses. Planned comparisons revealed that AV input and training resulted in significantly earlier identification of words beginning with /r/ and /l/ compared to other sequences. In all, the four main factors (modality, condition, time/training, CV sequence) accounted for about 63% of the variance in the L1 Japanese data and 53% in the L1 Korean data.

Although the data suggested that learners' word identification accuracy was somewhat comparable with either visual cues or context, the garden path data pointed to a greater dependence on perceptual than contextual cues to establish the initial cohort, consistent with Zwitserlood's (1989) scenario. This cohort was much less accurate before training and in A-only (versus AV) presentations. It is possible that perceptual and contextual cues vied for attention at various points in the word identification process, and this competition varied across trials and participants. It is not possible to determine more precisely when participants may have attended to or given a particular source of information more weight. The absence of a significant Modality × Condition interaction for learners indicates that overall the influence of one of the cue sources was not mediated by the other. For learners, garden paths created by cohorts, established on the basis of inaccurate perception, tended to persist despite the context. Although more constraining contexts might have produced different results, those in the current study were specifically designed following previous research to allow for the investigation of the influence of both perceptual and contextual cues when both are available.

The temporal precedence of the articulatory gesture over the associated acoustic cue gives the visual cue in an AV context the upper hand in dictating the perceptual information that guides the composition of the initial cohort (Skipper et al., 2007). In the current study, the salience of the perceptual cues was significantly enhanced following training, allowing these cues to contribute more to the outcome. The persistence of the initial cohort or a subsequent change in its composition depends on a variety of factors, including how well the context has been understood. For this reason, the present study also investigated the intelligibility of the contexts by the participants.

In contrast to the learner data, results for the NSs showed a significant Modality × Condition interaction. Much less (about 63%) of a word was needed for identification when both visual cues and context were present compared to about 82% for either the AV word or A-only sentence presentations, and 93% for the A-only word. Most incorrect word candidates in the sentence condition were compatible with the context. As with the learners, it is possible that the initial cohort on a given trial was based primarily on perceptual cues. Even for NSs, words beginning with /r/ and /l/ posed somewhat more of a challenge compared to other initial consonant categories in establishing a cohort of word candidates, compatible with findings of Hardison (2005b). However, for the NSs in the current study, ambiguity was resolved quickly as candidates beginning with an incorrect consonant did not persist beyond two gates.

For the learners, flawed initial cohorts (i.e., those established on the basis of misperception), especially in A-only presentations, lasted longer and delayed identification. In spontaneous interactions, although learners might experience delayed identification after a target's offset, the focusing of attention on a single extended word search with a decaying memory trace of the context might also cause them to lose track of the remaining discourse.

In conclusion, results suggested that segmental-level perception training can enhance the salience of multimodal cues, and thus, identification accuracy to facilitate spoken language processing for L2 learners by improving the preciseness of the initial cohort of word candidates.

Notes

1 Perception training also included the contrast /θ/-/s/ or /t/ (e.g., *think-sink*); however, there was an insufficient number of words meeting selection criteria to include /θ/-initial words in the word identification tasks.
2 Data on neighborhood density were obtained from the Speech Research Laboratory, Department of Psychological and Brain Sciences, Indiana University, Bloomington, IN 47405, USA. Following Hardison (2005b), low density in the current study was defined as no more than 15 neighbors. Density calculations served as guidelines; however, their validity for L2 learners is questionable much as it is for children (Garlock et al., 2001) as neighborhoods fluctuate throughout interlanguage development and are subject to L1 influence (both facilitative and inhibitory).
3 The large number of degrees of freedom in the CV factor made finding a significant effect by post-hoc tests highly improbable.
4 Cohen (1988) suggested effect size interpretations: "small" < 0.06; "medium" 0.06-0.15; "large" > 0.15.

References

Bard, E. G., Shillcock, R. C., & Altmann, G. T. M. (1988). The recognition of words after their acoustic offsets in spontaneous speech: Effects of subsequent context. *Perception & Psychophysics*, 44, 395–408.

Benguerel, A.-P., & Pichora-Fuller, M. K. (1982). Coarticulation effects in lipreading. *Journal of Speech and Hearing Research*, 25, 600–607.

Benoît, C., Mohamadi, T., & Kandel, S. (1994). Effects of phonetic context on audio-visual intelligibility of French. *Journal of Speech and Hearing Research*, 37(5), 1195–1203.

Bergeson, T. R., Pisoni, D. B., & Davis, R. A. O. (2003). A longitudinal study of audiovisual speech perception by children with hearing loss who have cochlear implants. *Volta Review*, 103(4), 347–370.

Besle, J., Fort, A., Delpuech, C., & Giard, M. H. (2004). Bimodal speech: Early suppressive visual effects in the human auditory cortex. *European Journal of Neuroscience*, 20, 2225–2234.

Binnie, C. A., Jackson, P. L., & Montgomery, A. A. (1976). Visual intelligibility of consonants: A lipreading screening test with implications for aural rehabilitation. *Journal of Speech and Hearing Disorders*, 41, 530–539.

Binnie, C. A., Montgomery, A. A., & Jackson, P. L. (1974). Auditory and visual contributions to the perception of consonants. *Journal of Speech & Hearing Research*, 17, 619–630.

Cohen, J. (1988). *Statistical power analysis for the behavioral sciences* (2nd ed.). Hillsdale, NJ: Lawrence Erlbaum Associates.

Cotton, S., & Grosjean, F. (1984). The gating paradigm: A comparison of successive and individual presentation formats. *Perception & Psychophysics*, 35, 41–48.

Dijkstra, T., & van Heuven, W. J. B. (2002). The architecture of the bilingual word recognition system: From identification to decision. *Bilingualism: Language and Cognition*, 5(3), 175–197.

Ellis, N. C. (2006). Selective attention and transfer phenomena in L2 acquisition: Contingency, cue competition, salience, interference, overshadowing, blocking, and perceptual learning. *Applied Linguistics*, 27(2), 164–194.

FitzPatrick, I. (2007). Effects of sentence context in L2 natural speech comprehension. *Nijmegen CNS, 2,* 43–56.
Fort, M., Spinelli, E., Savariaux, C., & Kandel, S. (2010). The word superiority effect in audiovisual speech perception. *Speech Communication, 52,* 525–532.
Franks, J. R., & Kimble, J. (1972). The confusion of English consonant clusters in lipreading. *Journal of Speech and Hearing Research, 15,* 474–482.
Garlock, V. M., Walley, A. C., & Metsala, J. L. (2001). Age-of-acquisition, word frequency and neighborhood density effects on spoken word recognition: Implications for the development of phoneme awareness and early reading ability. *Journal of Memory and Language, 45,* 468–492.
Grosjean, F. (1980). Spoken word recognition processes and the gating paradigm. *Perception & Psychophysics, 28,* 267–283.
Grosjean, F. (1985). The recognition of words after their acoustic offset: Evidence and implications. *Perception & Psychophysics, 38,* 229–310.
Grosjean, F. (1996). Gating. *Language and Cognition Processes, 11,* 597–604.
Hardison, D. M. (1999). Bimodal speech perception by native and nonnative speakers of English: Factors influencing the McGurk effect. *Language Learning, 49,* 213–283.
Hardison, D. M. (2003). Acquisition of second-language speech: Effects of visual cues, context, and talker variability. *Applied Psycholinguistics, 24,* 495–522.
Hardison, D. M. (2005a). Second-language spoken word identification: Effects of perception training, visual cues, and phonetic environment. *Applied Psycholinguistics, 26,* 579–596.
Hardison, D. M. (2005b). Variability in bimodal spoken language processing by native and nonnative speakers of English: A closer look at effects of speech style. *Speech Communication, 46,* 73–93.
Hardison, D. M. (2012). Second-language speech perception: A cross-disciplinary perspective on challenges and accomplishments. In S. Gass & A. Mackey (Eds.), *The Routledge handbook of second language acquisition* (pp. 349–363). London: Routledge.
Hickok, G. B., Buchsbau, B., Humphries, C., & Muftuler, T. (2003). Auditory-motor interaction revealed by fMRI: Speech, music, and working memory in area Spt. *Journal of Cognitive Neuroscience, 15*(5), 673–682.
Inceoglu, S. (2016). Effects of perception training on L2 vowel perception and production. *Applied Psycholinguistics, 37,* 1175–1199.
Jesse, A., & Massaro, D. W. (2010). The temporal distribution of information in audiovisual spoken-word identification. *Attention, Perception & Psychophysics, 72,* 209–225.
Kricos, P. B., & Lesner, S. A. (1982). Differences in visual intelligibility across talkers. *Volta Review, 84,* 219–225.
Lindau, M. (1985). The story of /r/. In V. A. Fromkin (Ed.), *Phonetic linguistics: Essays in honor of Peter Ladefoged* (pp. 157–168). Orlando, FL: Academic Press.
Lively, S. E., Logan, J. S., & Pisoni, D. B. (1993). Training Japanese listeners to identify English /r/ and /l/: II: The role of phonetic environment and talker variability in learning new perceptual categories. *Journal of the Acoustical Society of America, 94,* 1242–1255.
McGurk, H., & MacDonald, J. (1976). Hearing lips and seeing voices. *Nature, 264,* 746–748.
Marslen-Wilson, W., & Welsh, A. (1978). Processing interactions and lexical access during word recognition in continuous speech. *Cognitive Psychology, 10,* 29–63.
Meltzoff, A. N., & Kuhl, P. K. (1994). Faces and speech: Intermodal processing of biologically relevant signals in infants and adults. In D. J. Lewkowitz & R. Lickliter (Eds.), *The development of intersensory perception: Comparative perspectives* (pp. 335–369). Hillsdale, NJ: Lawrence Erlbaum Associates.

Moradi, S., Lidestam, B., & Rönnberg, J. (2013). Gated audiovisual speech identification in silence vs. noise: Effects on time and accuracy. *Frontiers in Psychology*, *4*, 1–13.

Munhall, K. G., & Tohkura, Y. (1998). Audiovisual gating and the time course of speech perception. *Journal of the Acoustical Society of America*, *104*, 530–539.

Nosofsky, R. M. (1986). Attention and learning processes in the identification and categorization of integral stimuli. *Journal of Experimental Psychology: Learning, Memory and Cognition*, *13*, 87–108.

Salasoo, A., & Pisoni, D. B. (1985). Interaction of knowledge sources in spoken word identification. *Journal of Memory & Language*, *24*, 210–231.

Sams, M., Aulanko, R., Hämäläinen, M., Hari, R., Lounasmaa, O. V., Lu, S.-T., & Simola, J. (1991). Seeing speech: Visual information from lip movements modifies activity in the human auditory cortex. *Neuroscience Letters*, *127*, 141–145.

Shin, J., Kiaer, J., & Cha, J. (2013). *The sounds of Korean*. Cambridge: Cambridge University Press.

Skipper, J. I., van Wassenhove, V., Nusbaum, H. W., & Small, S. L. (2007). Hearing lips and seeing voices: How cortical areas supporting speech production mediate audiovisual speech perception. *Cerebral Cortex*, *17*(10), 2387–2399.

Summerfield, Q., MacLeod, A., McGrath, M., & Brooke, J. (1989). Lips, teeth, and the benefits of lipreading. In A. W. Young & H. D. Ellis (Eds.), *Handbook of research on face processing* (pp. 223–233). Amsterdam: Elsevier.

Tsujimura, N. (1996). *An introduction to Japanese linguistics*. Oxford: Blackwell.

Tye-Murray, N., Sommers, M., & Spehar, B. (2007). Auditory and visual lexical neighborhoods in audiovisual speech perception. *Trends in Amplification*, *11*, 233–241.

Tyler, L. (1984). The structure of the initial cohort: Evidence from gating. *Perception & Psychophysics*, *36*, 417–427.

Vance, T. J. (1987). *An introduction to Japanese phonology*. Albany, NY: State University of New York Press.

van den Brink, D., Brown, C. M., & Hagoort, P. (2001). Electrophysiological evidence for early contextual influences during spoken-word recognition: N200 versus N400 effects. *Journal of Cognitive Neuroscience*, *13*, 967–985.

Walden, B. E., Prosek, R. A., Montgomery, A. A., Scherr, C. K., & Jones, C. J. (1977). Effects of training on the visual recognition of consonants. *Journal of Speech & Hearing Research*, *20*, 130–145.

Warren, P., & Marslen-Wilson, W. D. (1988). Continuous uptake of acoustic cues in spoken word recognition. *Perception & Psychophysics*, *43*, 21–30.

Zwitserlood, P. (1989). The locus of the effects of sentential-semantic context in spoken-word processing. *Cognition*, *32*(1), 25–64.

APPENDIX

Shown below are sample sentences from the study. The target word is shown in italics. Ellipses replace the final prepositional phrases, which were deleted for stimulus presentation.

They couldn't decide where to put the *picture*. . .	The student wants to design a *robot*. . .
I forgot to pick up the *package*. . .	We were told there was a *limit*. . .
The information came from the *poster*. . .	We did not expect the *laughter*. . .
The mistake was in the *figure*. . .	We looked in the store for the *lotion*. . .
That issue may be a *factor*. . .	You will need a *ticket*. . .
His friend suggested a *focus*. . .	She decided to order a *salad*. . .
They wanted to know the *reason*. . .	All they needed was a *sofa*. . .

PART IV
Salience in Context

12
SALIENCE OF NOUN–ADJECTIVE AGREEMENT IN L2 LATIN

John Sarkissian and Jennifer Behney

Introduction

A great deal of second language acquisition (SLA) research has found that second language (L2) learners do not process grammatical cues and inflectional markers, such as gender, number, case, and verbal morphology, in the same way that first language (L1) speakers do (Behney, Spinner, Gass, & Valmori, Chapter 5; Culman, Henry, & VanPatten, 2009; DeKeyser, Alfi-Shabtay, Ravid, & Shi, Chapter 7; Foote, 2015; Jackson, 2007; Keating, 2009; LoCoco, 1987; Simoens & Housen, Chapter 6; VanPatten & Borst, 2012a, 2012b; VanPatten, Collopy, & Qualin, 2012). L2 learners of languages more highly inflected than their own native languages tend to rely on lexical, pragmatic, or semantic cues or on L1 word order for meaning—especially at lower levels of proficiency—before they turn to grammatical cues in the input, even when these strategies lead to faulty interpretations of the L2 input (Bardovi-Harlig, 2000; N. Ellis, 2008; Larsen-Freeman, 1975, 2010; VanPatten & Cadierno, 1993). Various theories have been put forth to describe and account for learners' difficulty with processing of L2 inflection, such as Input Processing (VanPatten & Cadierno, 1993) and various formal approaches such as Missing Surface Inflection (Prévost & White, 2000) and the Failed Functional Features Hypothesis (Franceschina, 2005; Hawkins & Liszka, 2003). Similarly, instructed SLA research has investigated various methods of drawing learners' attention to grammatical cues in the input, such as Processing Instruction (VanPatten & Cadierno, 1993); explicit grammar instruction (Hulstijn & de Graaff, 1994; Terrell, 1991); Focus on Form (R. Ellis, 2012; see Norris & Ortega [2000] for meta-analysis on Focus on Form research); and Form-Focused Instruction (Spada, 1997). Lack of salience of the grammatical markings compounded by a limited processing capacity of lower level learners has been proposed as responsible for learners' lack of processing inflection (VanPatten & Cadierno, 1993; VanPatten et al., 2012). Various methods have been researched in terms of how to make such input more salient to the learner, such as textual enhancement through the use of different fonts or bolding and highlighting of text (Izumi, 2002; Leow & Martin, Chapter 9; Sharwood Smith, 1993; Winke, 2013), and some research has considered the role that the task itself plays in making the grammatical cues more salient to the learner (i.e., structured input activities in Processing Instruction [VanPatten & Cadierno, 1993; VanPatten et al., 2012; VanPatten & Oikkenon, 1996]).

In this eye-tracking study, the role of the task in making inflectional marking more salient to learners is considered. Two tasks were employed to capture L2 Latin learners' eye fixations as they read Latin sentences focused on the processing of case markings of nouns and adjectives: a translation task, which we argue was *low-salience* because of the degree to which it encouraged learners to notice case endings, and a forced choice adjective completion task, which we argue was *high-salience* because of the degree to which it encouraged learners to notice case endings. The study considers learner accuracy, dwell times, and awareness of form during stimulated recall sessions.

Background

L2 Processing of Inflectional Markers

Since the early days of the field of SLA, researchers have noted the difficulty that learners have in processing inflectional markers. The studies on developmental sequences of English morphemes tracked how L2 English learners moved from an initial lack of grammatical morphemes and a dependency on lexical items in order to communicate meaning through the well-documented stages of grammatical morpheme acquisition (e.g., progressive *-ing* early, third-person singular final *-s* late) (Goldschneider & DeKeyser, 2001; Larsen-Freeman, 1975. Bardovi-Harlig (2000) in her tense and aspect studies found that L2 learners moved from expressing time through pragmatic and lexical means before being able to make use of morphological and syntactic means.

Processing Instruction, first proposed by VanPatten and Cadierno (1993), describes how learners process (at times, incorrectly) input that they receive and what types of pedagogical activities can push learners to change their processing strategies. The model is composed of a collection of constraints such as the First Noun Principle and the Lexical Preference Principle. The First Noun Principle states that the first noun that learners encounter in the sentence is assigned the role of agent by learners. In English, assigning the role of agent to the first noun in the sentence is generally unproblematic, but this is not the case for learners of languages that, unlike English, are not always subject–verb–object (SVO), for example Spanish where L2 learners interpret *Lo ve María* (Him$_{\text{DirectObjectClitic}}$ sees Maria) as 'He sees Maria' because *lo* is the first (pro)noun that they encounter in the sentence, rather than the correct 'Maria sees him.' The Lexical Preference Principle states that learners process lexical items first (e.g., *yesterday*) before grammatical markers (i.e., past tense). VanPatten and colleagues have conducted various studies confirming the existence of the First Noun Principle and the Lexical Preference Principle and suggest the use of *structured input* activities which force learners to rely on grammatical cues, not word order, intonation, animacy, lexical cues, or event probabilities, in order to process meaning; the activity constrains the learner to understand who did what to whom through recognizing grammatical markers such as case (e.g., Henry, Culman, & VanPatten, 2009; VanPatten & Borst, 2012a, 2012b; VanPatten et al., 2012; VanPatten & Oikkenon, 1996). Structured input activities begin with *referential activities*, which are those that have a right or wrong answer (e.g., *The instructor sees the student* or *The student sees the instructor?*) identified through the use of pictures, for example, and then continue with *affective activities*, which are those that allow for more than one answer and encourage learners to reveal something about themselves, such as agreeing with opinions (e.g., *Lady Gaga idolizes Madonna*) while still forcing learners to process case endings (who idolizes whom?) (VanPatten et al., 2012).

The First Noun Principle has been investigated not only in Spanish, but also in other languages that are not restricted to SVO word order and that express who did what to whom through case marking—including German (Culman et al., 2009; Jackson, 2007; LoCoco, 1987; VanPatten, & Borst, 2012b) and Russian (Comer & deBenedette, 2010; VanPatten et al., 2012). Jackson (2007) and LoCoco (1987) found, for example, that L2 German learners do not use case markings to interpret who did what to whom; learners interpret both *Der Junge küsst die Frau* (The$_{Nom}$ boy kisses the$_{Nom/Acc}$ woman, SVO) and *Den Jungen küsst die Frau* (The$_{Acc}$ boy kisses the$_{Nom/Acc}$ woman, OVS) as 'The boy kisses the woman.' Many of these studies have dealt with the question of whether explicit information (i.e., explanation of the rule) is a necessary or beneficial component of Processing Instruction. Results have suggested that learners benefit from explicit information on the First Noun Principle for German nominative/accusative case differentiation before Processing Instruction treatment (Henry et al., 2009; VanPatten & Borst, 2012b), but that learners who received explicit information on Spanish clitic objects (Fernández, 2008; VanPatten & Borst, 2012a) and on Russian nominative/accusative case differentiation (VanPatten et al., 2012) performed no better than those who received no explicit information before treatment involving structured input activities. In the Spanish and Russian studies, learners performed similarly regardless of whether they had been instructed on the structures ahead of the Processing Instruction treatment. VanPatten et al. (2012) suggest that this difference in the facilitating role for explicit information in German but not in Russian case may be explained by differences between the Russian and German case systems. In German, nominative and accusative cases are marked by different articles only in the masculine singular (*der*$_{Nom}$ versus *den*$_{Acc}$) while the feminine and neuter singular nouns in the two cases carry the same articles, as do all plural nouns. In Russian, although masculine and feminine nouns in the nominative do not change endings, masculine nouns in the accusative have an -а or an -я ending and feminine nouns in the accusative have a -у or -ю ending. This Russian paradigm containing more forms may have simply been too complicated for the learners in the study to make use of the rule in real-time processing. So, even if the +explicit information group in Russian read the rule beforehand, they had no advantage over the −explicit information group who did not learn the rule before treatment. In fact, the German learners who had received the explicit information before treatment (Henry et al., 2009; VanPatten & Borst, 2012b) reported only looking for the difference between *den* and *der* during the following treatment, a simpler task than recognizing the more numerous Russian inflections and applying the explicit rule. Both the fact that in the case of the L2 Latin learners in the current study the L1 (English) is SVO and the fact that the most common word order in Latin is SOV, although any order may be encountered, as well as the complexity of the paradigm in Latin, led us to hypothesize that the learners will not process case in a nativelike manner (like the Russian L2 learners in VanPatten et al., 2012).

This facilitative aspect of explicit instruction in Processing Instruction is similar in many ways to various other SLA strands of research that focus on the need to draw learners' attention to grammatical forms that may not otherwise be salient to the learner. Hulstijn and de Graaff (1994) found that explicit instruction has a greater effect on highly inflected forms than moderately inflected forms because moderately inflected forms are more frequent than the highly inflected forms (they occur more frequently across the paradigm) and thus result in more individual item learning, rather than rule learning. Explicit instruction helps to make the rule clearer in these cases of highly inflected forms which are less salient because they are less frequent. Terrell (1991) also argued for explicit grammar instruction in helping learners make sense of the input (see also Gass, Svetics, & Lemelin, 2003).

And of course, a fruitful research domain in SLA is Focus on Form (FonF) studies (R. Ellis, 2012; Norris & Ortega, 2000) and Form-Focused Instruction (FFI) (Spada, 1997), both of which rely on drawing learners' attention to grammatical cues in the input in order to facilitate their acquisition of the forms.

Salience

Salience, or lack thereof, in the input has often been cited as a reason for learners not processing grammatical cues. Morphemes such as case endings tend to be short in terms of letters/phonemes and not stressed in speech, whereas lexical cues tend to be complete words and stressed in the input (e.g., compare the lexical cue to time meaning *yesterday* and the past tense *-ed* morpheme in *Yesterday he walked*). N. Ellis (2008) describes a cycle of language usage, language change, language perception, and language learning. Usage of the language leads to it being changed over time (e.g., through processes such as assimilation, lenition). Change in the language affects the perception of particular aspects, in that they become less salient to the perceiver/learner. Lack of salience makes forms more difficult to learn. Learning affects the usage. Emergentist theories of L2 acquisition claim that the limited end-state of L2 adult learners is due to this cycle. Grammatical functors (i.e., function words and inflectional endings) are highly used, and thus reduced phonologically (language usage→language change). Their reduction results in low salience and the fact that they have low contingency (i.e., one form does not always result in one function; for example, the allomorphs /s/, /z/, /ez/ can each result in one of three functions: plural *-s*, possessive *-s*, or third-person singular *-s*) makes them harder to perceive for the learner and thus harder to learn (language change → language perception). Since naturalistic learners can get by with learning the communicatively effective words (through content words, adverbials, and serialization) and since grammatical functors tend to have low salience and be redundant, naturalistic learners without form-focused instruction may develop an interlanguage with little grammatical complexity (language perception → language learning).

This lack of salience of many grammatical markings in the input has led to SLA research on textual enhancement, or manipulating the structure in question through highlighting, coloring, or changing of the font to make it more evident to the learner (Izumi, 2002; Leow & Martin, Chapter 9; Sharwood Smith, 1993). Processing Instruction does require tasks that draw learners' attention to the grammatical cues in the input, but the degree to which the task itself enhances salience has not been investigated. For ease of discussion, we will refer to *low-salience* and *high-salience* tasks with the understanding that we are referring to the degree to which the task enhances the salience of the forms. For example, a task that has a learner translate sentences from Latin into English, thereby not forcing a learner to actually use case marking productively, is quite different than a task in which a learner completes a Latin sentence with the correctly marked case form of the adjective. The former, we argue, is a low-salience task because the use of case markings is not being highlighted; the latter is a high-salience task because task completion is dependent on accurately using case markings. This is not unlike the claims made within the interactionist tradition in which Comprehensible Output (Swain, 1985, 2005) is highlighted precisely because producing language forces learners to focus on grammatical elements in a way that comprehension does not.

In order to better understand the learners' cognitive processes as they were completing the two tasks on the eye-tracker, we decided to use stimulated recalls (Gass, Behney, & Plonsky, 2013; Gass & Mackey, 2000). Stimulated recalls are a form of verbal report data that consist of questioning by the researcher of the participant about what the participant was thinking when completing a particular task. Stimulated recalls must be in concert with some type of stimulus to jog the participant's memory of the thinking during the task and should be conducted as soon as possible following the task (Gass et al., 2013). We played back video recordings of the participants' eye movements during the task, which served as the stimulus, and we completed the stimulated recalls immediately after the two tasks had been completed.

Latin as an L2

Latin as a second language is under-researched in SLA, although more recent research by N. Ellis and colleagues has started to use Latin as a language of inquiry—not with learners of the L2, but with participants with no previous study of the language (Cintrón-Valentín & Ellis, 2015; N. Ellis et al., 2014; N. Ellis & Sagarra, 2010a, 2010b, 2011). Rich in gender, case, number, and verbal morphology, L2 Latin may be informative for our understanding of learner processing of inflection. Carlon (2013) called for more research on how reading for content in Latin as opposed to just literal translation and grammatical analysis may expedite learning of Latin as an L2. Harrison (2010) called for L2 Latin exercises that focus on Processing Instruction where learners have to process syntactical markers, not just lexical markers. She noted Hulstijn and de Graaff's (1994) hypothesis about the teaching of highly inflected languages where explicit instruction is even more important.

Latin Nouns and Adjectives Used in This Study

Adjectives in Latin agree with the nouns they modify in case, number, and gender. Two factors add to the difficulty of identifying which noun in a sentence is modified by a particular adjective: 1) the adjective may occur either before or after the noun it modifies (in authentic Latin, particularly poetry, an attributive adjective may not even be contiguous with the noun it modifies), and 2) because in Latin there are five declensions to one of which each noun belongs (which convention identifies simply by the ordinal numbers: 1st, 2nd, etc.), each with its own set(s) of endings, and two groups of adjectives (1st-2nd declension and 3rd declension), the endings on adjectives often are not identical with the endings on the nouns they modify (see Tables 12.1 and 12.2). For this study, we limited ourselves to 1st, 2nd, and 3rd declension nouns and to 1st and 2nd declension adjectives, as the learners had not yet been introduced to other declensions.

As can be seen from the tables, when a noun is first or second declension, it is highly likely that the adjective that modifies it will have the same ending, but when the noun is third declension, the ending on the 1st-2nd declension adjective that modifies it will almost never have the same ending (the exception being neuter nominative and accusative plurals).

Considering the difficulties L2 learners have processing case endings and the rich morphological system of Latin, whether learners process the endings may be dependent on whether they are forced to do so by the task. In translating a sentence from Latin to English, there may be less need to process the case ending on nouns and adjectives, but when choosing which form of an adjective is appropriate to complete a sentence, learners are forced to pay attention to the case endings.

TABLE 12.1 Noun patterns

	1st Decl. (mostly F.)	2nd Decl. M.	2nd Decl. N.	3rd Decl. M. & F.	3rd Decl. N.
Nom. Sing.	puella	animus[a]	verbum	mīles[b]	tempus[b]
Gen. Sing.	puellae	animī	verbī	mīlitis	temporis
Dat. Sing.	puellae	animō	verbō	mīlitī	temporī
Acc. Sing.	puellam	animum	verbum	mīlitem	tempus[b]
Abl. Sing	puellā	animō	verbō	mīlite	tempore
Nom. Plur.	puellae	animī	verba	mīlitēs	tempora
Gen. Plur.	puellārum	animōrum	verbōrum	mīlitum	temporum
Dat. Plur.	puellīs	animīs	verbīs	mīlitibus	temporibus
Acc. Plur.	puellās	animōs	verba	mīlitēs	tempora
Abl. Plur.	puellīs	animīs	verbīs	mīlitibus	temporibus

Note: [a]Nouns whose base ends in -r do not add the -us ending.
[b]There is considerable variety in the nominative singular of 3rd declension nouns, and therefore also in the accusative singular of third declension neuter nouns.

TABLE 12.2 Adjective patterns

	Masculine 2nd Decl.	Feminine 1st Decl.	Neuter 2nd Decl.
Nom. Sing.	bonus[a]	bona	bonum
Gen. Sing.	bonī	bonae	bonī
Dat. Sing.	bonō	bonae	bonō
Acc. Sing.	bonum	bonam	bonum
Abl. Sing	bonō	bonā	bonō
Nom. Plur.	bonī	bonae	bona
Gen. Plur.	bonōrum	bonārum	bonōrum
Dat. Plur.	bonīs	bonīs	bonīs
Acc. Plur.	bonōs	bonās	bona
Abl. Plur.	bonīs	bonīs	bonīs

Note: [a] Adjectives whose base ends in -r do not add the -us ending.

The research questions in this study were:

RQ1: Do L2 learners of Latin process case markings on adjectives to assign them to the correct nouns that they modify during an online, low-salience translation task? We operationalize processing as the amount of time spent in an interest area. We predict that items for which learners accurately place the adjective with the correct noun will show longer dwell times on the modified noun ending than incorrect items.

RQ2: Do L2 learners of Latin assign the correct case markings to adjectives during an online, high-salience forced choice adjective completion task? We predict that they will spend more time fixating on noun endings for items in which they accurately choose an adjective ending, as compared to inaccurate items. We further predict that the accuracy rate on this forced choice adjective completion task will be greater than that of the translation task, as the learners will be forced to process the case endings by the nature of the task (i.e., they have to choose the correct form of the adjective to complete the sentence from various possible endings).

RQ3: Are L2 learners of Latin aware of the case markings on the adjectives, as measured through their comments in stimulated recall protocols? We predict that learners who were more successful on the tasks will be aware of the importance of case marking.

Method

Participants

The learners in this study were 17 students in their first semester of Latin study at a medium-sized Midwestern state university in the United States. They were all native speakers of English between the ages of 18–45 ($M = 24.6$, $SD = 7.35$). There were

10 females and seven males. Eleven of the learners reported having studied Spanish, four having studied French, two having studied Italian, and two having studied Latin in high school,[1] as well as three who had studied ASL, one German, and one both Chinese and Japanese. None of the participants indicated any functional proficiency in these previously studied L2s. All of the participants had been exposed to direct instruction on the Latin case system in their Latin class which met for 50 minutes a day, four times a week, and in their Latin textbook. The data reported here were collected during the twelfth week of a 15-week semester.

Materials

The materials for the translation task consisted of six Latin sentences (See Appendix A). The sentences were 4–6 words long and contained vocabulary that had been taken from the learners' first semester Latin textbook (Shelmerdine, 2013). Each sentence contained an adjective that could plausibly modify either of the two nouns in the sentence, but the case ending on the adjective constrained which noun it modified. Half of the adjectives appeared before the modified noun in the sentence and half followed the modified noun,[2] so that learners could not resort to word order strategies. Interest areas, indicated below with boxes, which were not visible to participants, captured all fixations on noun and adjective endings.

Example of translation task sentence (adjective-noun):

Cōnsul|ī|nov|um|imperi|um| dābimus.
consul$_{Dat}$ new$_{Acc}$ power$_{Acc}$ we will give
We will give new power to the consul.
*We will give power to the new consul.

The materials for the forced choice adjective completion task consisted of 16 Latin sentences that contained between 3–6 words, again with the vocabulary taken from the learners' first-year Latin textbook. A line appeared (a blank) where the adjective would appear in the sentence and the six adjective choices (representing different case-number endings, although only the correct gender) appeared below the sentence. An interest area, indicated below with a box which was not visible to participants, captured all fixations on noun endings.

Example of forced choice adjective completion task:

Cōnsulibus fām|ae| _____ sunt. The consuls have _____ reputations.
a. bonae   d. bonārum   a. good$_{GENsgDATsgNOMpl}$ d. good$_{GENpl}$
b. bonam   e. bonīs   b. good$_{ACCsg}$ e. good$_{DATplABLpl}$
c. bonā   f. bonās   c. good$_{ABLsg}$ f. good$_{ACCpl}$

Procedure

After signing a consent form and completing a background questionnaire, participants completed the eye-tracking task. The procedure was carried out on an EyeLink 1000 eye-tracker with a desk-mounted monocular eye-tracking camera, with chin and forehead rest, and a 19-inch computer screen. During the translation task, participants' eyes were tracked as they translated the Latin sentences into English, typing their responses onto a line provided below the Latin sentence on the screen. The sentences were written in Courier New font size 18 and were centered in the middle of the screen. As we were concerned with the learners' processing of the Latin noun–adjective inflections and not their vocabulary knowledge, a "cheat sheet" (a box in the upper right hand corner of the screen with dictionary translations of the words in English) appeared with each item. Following the translation task, learners completed the forced choice adjective completion task. Centered in the middle of the screen, learners found a Latin sentence with a blank where an adjective would appear in the sentence. Below the Latin sentence, six forms of the adjectives appeared listed in a column with various case and number endings. Learners chose the form of the adjective (a-f) with a mouse click and the experiment would proceed to the next item. All items in both tasks were randomized across participants. After the eye-tracking tasks, the participants engaged in a stimulated recall; the second author replayed the video of the learner's eye movements during the forced choice adjective completion task while asking her/him questions such as "Do you remember what you were thinking as you were doing this item?" A video camera caught the audio responses and was trained on the monitor of the eye-tracking computer so as to see the eye movement video as the participant completed the stimulated recall. The entire procedure including the stimulated recall protocol took approximately 1 hour, 15 minutes.

Data Analysis

Accuracy was determined in the translation task by whether the learners placed the adjective with the correct noun that it modified. For example, in the sentence *Cōnsulī novum imperium dābimus*, if the learner placed the adjective *novum* with the noun *imperium* ('new power') the item was marked as correct. If on the other hand, the learner translated the adjective with the noun *Cōnsulī* ('new consul') effectively ignoring the case ending on the adjective, it was marked as incorrect.

Accuracy on the translation task and on the forced choice adjective completion task was calculated. Mean dwell times were calculated for the interest areas around the endings of the nouns modified by the adjectives for each task. All dwell times faster than 120 ms were cut and those two standard deviations above the mean were replaced with the cutoff value, as is common in psycholinguistic research (Rayner & Pollatsek, 1989). As Shapiro-Wilk tests revealed the data in both tasks to be non-normally distributed, we conducted nonparametric Mann-Whitney U tests comparing the dwell times on modified noun ending interest areas of accurate responses with the dwell times on modified noun ending interest areas of inaccurate responses; dwell times in milliseconds were the dependent variable and accuracy was the independent variable. We also conducted Mann-Whitney U tests comparing overall dwell times on noun endings on the high-salience task with those on the low-salience task and comparing higher performing learners with lower performing learners; here the independent variables were task and learner group, respectively.

The video recordings of the stimulated recall sessions of the forced choice adjective completion task were transcribed and coded. Each item from each participant was coded as "Noun Ending Noted" if the participant specifically stated while watching the video playback of their eye movements during the reading of the item that they had decided on a particular adjective choice because of the ending on the noun in the sentence that it modifies (e.g., Participant 203: "I was focusing on the ending of *terram* to figure out the ending of the adjective.") or because of the case of the noun in the sentence that it modifies (e.g., Participant 207: "*Nomina*, that I think was accusative plural."). If the learner did not mention the modified noun or mentioned it only in terms of the meaning or some other irrelevant factor (e.g., Participant 217: "*Terram* is land."), the item was coded as "Not Noted."

Results

Translation Task

Overall accuracy on the translation task was 51.46% ($SD = 50.00$, Range from 0–100%, over six items). In four of the six sentences, the case ending on the adjective did not match letter by letter the equivalent case ending on the modified noun. When the case endings were the same (e.g., *fāmae bonae* 'good reputations'), the accuracy rate was 61.77% as compared to 45.59% when the case endings on the noun and adjective differed in spelling (e.g., *cīvitās bona* 'good state').

The mean dwell time in the interest areas around the noun endings on accurate items was $M = 2430$ ms ($SD = 2343$) and on inaccurate items it was $M = 3141$ ms ($SD = 2664$). The Mann-Whitney U test did not find this difference to be significant, $U = 773.50, p = .105$.

We also performed a Mann-Whitney U test on the dwell times on the noun endings comparing how long learners looked at the nouns when they were in sentences in which the modified noun preceded the adjective and those in which the noun followed the adjective (i.e., NounAdj versus AdjNoun). The learners looked significantly longer at the noun ending when the noun preceded the adjective (NounAdj: $M = 3784$ ms, $SD = 2728$) in the sentence than when it followed the adjective (AdjNoun: $M = 1429$ ms, $SD = 1324$), $U = 361.50, p = .000$.

Forced Choice Adjective Completion Task

In the forced choice adjective completion task, in half of the 16 sentences the ending on the adjective did not match that on the modified noun in terms of exact letters (because, while all the adjectives were 1st or 2nd declension, half of the nouns were 3rd declension). Not surprisingly, when the endings matched (e.g., *novum imperium* 'new power'), learners were much more successful in selecting the correct adjective form, with 71% accuracy on the items with matching endings as opposed to 32% on items in which the endings were not matching (e.g., *pax nova* 'new peace'). The overall accuracy on the forced choice adjective completion task was $M = 52.00\%$ ($SD = 22.99$, Range 12.5–100%). The numbers for each answer choice chosen can be seen in the item analysis (see Table 12.3).[3]

TABLE 12.3 Item analysis, forced choice adjective completion task

Item		Answer Choice	Times Selected	%	Average Score
Dīc dominō meō dē pecūniā.	a	meī	5	31.25	33.75
Tell my master about the money.	b	meō★	11	68.75	60.23
	c	meum	0	0	
	d	meōrum	0	0	
	e	meīs	0	0	
	f	meōs	0	0	
Fīliābus optāmus nōmina pulchra dare.	a	pulchrum	1	6.25	56.25
We want to give our daughters beautiful names.	b	pulchrī	1	6.25	12.5
	c	pulchrō	1	6.25	31.25
	d	pulchra★	12	75	58.33
	e	pulchrōrum	1	6.25	31.25
	f	pulchrīs	0	0	
Vīta est bona in cīvitātibus līberīs.	a	līberae	4	25	43.75
Life is good in free states.	b	līberam	4	25	46.875
	c	līberā	2	12.5	59.38
	d	līberārum	1	6.25	18.75
	e	līberīs★	4	25	79.6875
	f	līberās	1	6.25	12.5
Pāx nova nōbīs placet.	a	nova★	8	50	66.41
The new peace is pleasing to us.	b	novae	1	6.25	18.75
	c	novam	3	18.75	54.17
	d	novārum	0	0	
	e	novīs	2	12.5	37.5
	f	novās	2	12.5	21.88
Semper magnā cum virtūte labōrābās.	a	magnae	4	25	28.13
You always used to work with great virtue.	b	magnam	3	18.75	43.75
	c	magnā★	9	56.25	65.28
	d	magnārum	0	0	
	e	magnīs	0	0	
	f	magnās	0	0	
Dōna mātris tuae mihi placent.	a	tua	4	25	46.88
Your mother's gifts please me.	b	tuae★	3	18.75	60.42
	c	tuam	2	12.5	59.375
	d	tuārum	3	18.75	50
	e	tuīs	4	25	48.44
	f	tuās	0	0	
Verba hominis aegrī nōn audīre poteram.	a	aegrī★	4	25	70.31
I was not able to hear the sick man's words.	b	aegrō	1	6.25	50
	c	aegrum	4	25	48.44
	d	aegrōrum	3	18.75	31.25
	e	aegrīs	4	25	53.13
	f	aegrōs	0	0	

(Continued)

TABLE 12.3 (Continued)

Item		Answer Choice	Times Selected	%	Average Score
Nocēbitisne vestrīs ducibus?	a	vestrī	3	18.75	60.42
Will you harm your leaders?	b	vestrō	0	0	
	c	vestrum	4	25	45.31
	d	vestrōrum	2	12.5	31.25
	e	vestrīs★	6	37.5	62.5
	f	vestrōs	1	6.25	31.25
Lēgibus malīs nōn pārēre dēbētis.	a	malae	2	12.5	53.125
You should not obey bad laws.	b	malam	2	12.5	31.25
	c	malā	3	18.75	35.42
	d	malārum	1	6.25	68.75
	e	malīs★	7	43.75	62.5
	f	malās	1	6.25	50
Sapientiam patrum nostrōrum laudāmus.	a	nostrī	2	12.5	62.5
We praise the wisdom of our fathers.	b	nostrō	2	12.5	53.13
	c	nostrum	7	43.75	49.11
	d	nostrōrum★	1	6.25	100
	e	nostrīs	2	12.5	40.63
	f	nostrōs	2	12.5	37.5
Multī deōs vītam longam ōrant.	a	longae	0	0	
Many ask the gods for a long life.	b	longam★	13	81.25	58.17
	c	longā	1	6.25	18.75
	d	longārum	1	6.25	43.75
	e	longīs	0	0	
	f	longās	1	6.25	12.5
Cōnsulibus fāmae bonae sunt.	a	bonae★	12	75	57.81
The consuls have good reputations.	b	bonam	0	0	
	c	bonā	3	18.75	41.67
	d	bonārum	1	6.25	12.5
	e	bonīs	0	0	
	f	bonās	0	0	
Ad terram laetam nāvigābimus.	a	laetae	4	25	31.25
We will sail to the fertile land.	b	laetam★	10	62.5	65.63
	c	laetā	1	6.25	31.25
	d	laetārum	0	0	
	e	laetīs	1	6.25	18.75
	f	laetās	0	0	
Puerōs exemplīs multīs docēbō.	a	multum	1	6.25	37.5
I will teach the boys with many examples.	b	multī	0	0	
	c	multō	1	6.25	31.25
	d	multa	0	0	
	e	multōrum	1	6.25	43.75
	f	multīs★	13	81.25	55.29

Item		Answer Choice	Times Selected	%	Average Score
Nāvigāre in pontō altō timēbam.	a	altī	0	0	
I was afraid to sail on the deep sea.	b	altō★	11	68.75	61.36
	c	altum	3	18.75	31.25
	d	altōrum	2	12.5	31.25
	e	altīs	0	0	
	f	altōs	0	0	
Turbam movēbās verbīs miserīs.	a	miserum	2	12.5	31.25
You were moving the crowd with sad words.	b	miserī	3	18.75	60.42
	c	miserō	2	12.5	15.63
	d	misera	0	0	
	e	miserōrum	0	0	
	f	miserīs★	9	56.25	61.81

Note: ★ indicates correct answer choice.

The mean dwell time on interest areas around the noun endings for accurate responses was $M = 2649$ ms ($SD = 2507$) and for inaccurate items was $M = 2667$ ($SD = 2483$). The Mann-Whitney U test did not find a significant difference between the dwell times on noun endings in accurate items and noun endings in inaccurate items, $U = 7044, p = .778$.

Upon noticing the variety of accuracy scores across participants (Range = 12.5—100%, on 16 items), we decided to divide the learners into two groups; the High Group ($n = 9$) had a mean accuracy score of $M = 68.06\%$ ($SD = 16.07$, Range 50—100%) and the Low Group ($n = 8$) had a mean score of $M = 32.03\%$ ($SD = 11.30$, Range 12.5—43.75%). This difference in accuracy scores between the High and Low groups was found to be significantly different by an independent-samples t-test, $t(15) = 5.3, p = .000$. The High Group had longer dwell times on the noun endings, $M = 2493$ ms ($SD = 2403$), than the Low Group, $M = 2249$ ms ($SD = 2311$), but this difference was not found to be significant by a Mann-Whitney U test, $U = 19,127, p = .191$.

In order to measure differences in attention to the items in each task, we also ran a Mann-Whitney U test comparing the mean accurate dwell times on the Translation task ($M = 2430$ ms, $SD = 2343$) to the Forced Choice Adjective Completion task ($M = 2649$ ms, $SD = 2507$) to see if the learners spent more time looking at the noun ending in the high-salience task but the difference was not found to be significant, $U = 2466.50, p = .512$.

Stimulated Recalls

Of the 272 items across participants, there were 108 items which were coded as "Noun Ending Noted." Of these 108 items for which participants had mentioned the modified noun's ending or case as a factor in their adjective choice, 77 (71.30% of the 108 Noted items) were items which had been answered accurately and 31 (28.70% of the 108 Noted items) were items which had been answered inaccurately. Of the 108 Noun Ending Noted items, 60 were from participants in the High Group (51 of which were accurate items and nine of which were inaccurate items) and 48 of which were from participants in the Low Group (26 of which were accurate items and 22 of which were inaccurate items).

Discussion

The first research question asked whether learners would spend more time processing the noun endings in the sentences for which they accurately placed the adjective with the correct noun in their English translation than in the sentences for which they failed to do so. Learners did not spend a significantly different amount of time on those sentences to which they responded accurately. It was found, however, that learners spent significantly more time processing the noun endings when the noun appeared before the adjective that modified it than when it followed the adjective. This could indicate that learners are aware that adjectives often follow the noun that they modify in Latin (as well as in other Romance languages, as only one participant had not studied a Romance language previously to this Latin course), and they assumed that the adjective in the sentence to be translated appeared after the noun that it modified.

The second research question asked whether learners would spend more time looking at noun endings on items on which they accurately chose the adjective case ending than on items on which they chose the wrong adjective case ending. Also for this forced choice adjective completion task, the learners did not spend significantly more time on accurate items than on inaccurate items (in fact, in terms of descriptive statistics, they spent slightly more time on the inaccurate items, although this difference was not significant). A further analysis breaking the learners into high performers and low performers also failed to find any significant differences in terms of the amount of time that learners in each group spent fixating the noun endings. We had predicted that the accuracy rate on the high-salience forced choice adjective completion task which required learners explicitly to choose the correct case ending for the adjective would be greater than that of the low-salience translation task in which the learner's attention was not drawn to the agreement by the task, and this was the case. The absolute accuracy percentages for the two tasks are almost identical (51.56% on the translation task and 52% on the forced choice adjective completion task). However, when it is taken into account that there were only two choices on the translation task (i.e., the learner could translate the adjective as modifying one or the other noun between which the adjective had been placed) and that there were six choices in the adjective completion task, the results on the adjective completion task could be interpreted to be considerably better. In theory, a learner could have achieved 50% accuracy on the translation task just by guessing, whereas guessing on the adjective completion task would theoretically lead to only 16.67% accuracy. We may conclude therefore that the learners actually performed considerably better on the high-salience adjective completion task. We also ran a comparison of the overall dwell times that learners spent on the noun endings in the high-salience task as compared to those in the low-salience task to measure differences in attention to the items in each task; the times were longer on the high-salience task, but not significantly so.

The third research question asked whether the L2 Latin learners indicated awareness of the case agreement between nouns and adjectives in the Latin sentences. It was predicted that higher performing learners would be more likely to mention the noun ending or the noun case when choosing the correct form of the adjective to complete the sentence, and this was in fact the case. Not only were more of the items on which the noun ending was noted from higher performing participants, but the higher performing participants were also more likely to *accurately* choose the correct form of the adjective. It appears that in the cases of lower performing learners either the learners did not note the importance of the noun and its case at all in determining the form of the adjective (e.g., Participant 210: "I knew it was going to be *they* because of the ending on the verb.") or they knew that it was important but were not able to connect the noun case with the correct form of the adjective (e.g., Participant 204: "Since the *verbis* had an -*is* I didn't think it could have an -*is* too, it didn't look right to have the same ending.").

Several participants noted the ease with which they were able to choose the correct form of the adjective when the noun ending and the adjective ending were exactly the same (e.g., *famae bonae* 'good reputations') and the difficulty when the two endings were not exactly matching (e.g., *hominis aegrī* 'sick man'—Participant 201: "Now the endings don't always match which makes it a lot harder."). Many previous studies on L2 gender and number agreement have found that learners have less difficulty marking agreement on adjectives when the noun and adjective agree morphophonologically through the same endings (Bordag & Pechmann, 2008; Davidson, de la Fuente, Montrul, & Foote, 2011; Holmes & Segui, 2006; Oliphant, 1998). Here too with case, it appears that learners find the task of marking noun–adjective agreement easier when the agreement is transparent in the endings.

The learners from the Low Group who were aware of the need to mark case on the adjectives but were unable to do so are similar to the Russian learners in VanPatten et al. (2012). The Russian learners in that Processing Instruction study who had received explicit information on Russian nominative and accusative case before completing the structured input experiment fared no better than those participants who had only the structured input treatment without the benefit of explicit information on how case works in Russian. VanPatten, Collopy, and Qualin argued that the Russian learners did not benefit from direct instruction unlike the L2 learners of German in previous studies (Henry et al., 2009; VanPatten & Borst, 2012b) because the Russian case system is more complicated in terms of actual inflections than that of German, which indicates nominative and accusative case differences only in the masculine singular through the definite articles *der* and *den*, respectively. Here in the current study too the learners' task is complicated by the complexity of the case system of the language. Even knowing that the adjective must agree with the noun in case is not beneficial to the learner if the task is too burdensome: "the greater the amount of explicit information, the less likely it can be used during real-time processing." (VanPatten et al., 2012, p. 267). The fact that some of the learners in this study (the higher performing learners) were able to use their understanding of Latin case marking to make agreement with the adjectives and to verbalize it when describing what they were thinking during the stimulated recalls adds greater credence to the theory that the complexity of the Latin case system results in (at least some of) the learners not being able to make use of the rules in real time; individual differences in learners in terms of working memory or aptitude or familiarity with the paradigm (i.e., having studied what they were taught in class) are evident in their performance on the tasks. Future studies should examine the role that individual differences such as working memory play in Latin (and Russian) case agreement tasks and how these differences interact with the role of explicit information in Processing Instruction. A limitation of the current study is that we conducted the stimulated recall protocols only for the forced completion adjective task and not for the translation task so it was not possible to compare directly the learners' awareness of the endings in the two tasks through their responses to the stimulated recalls. Future studies should gather verbal report data for both high- and low-salience tasks in order to better compare how learners' awareness was drawn to case endings by the task.

There is clear evidence of the importance of structured input activities in changing learners' processing of L2 structures that conflict with their own inclinations such as processing the first noun as the agent of the sentence (First Noun Principle) or preferring lexical cues to grammatical ones (Lexical Preference Principle) (e.g., Henry et al., 2009; VanPatten & Borst, 2012a, 2012b; VanPatten & Cadierno, 1993; VanPatten et al., 2012). Although it is clear that explicit information is not always necessary for forcing learners to process case markings (VanPatten & Oikkenon, 1996), it may have "a facilitative effect in Processing Instruction" (VanPatten et al., 2012, p. 267), in particular for certain language structures (i.e., German case, Henry et al., 2009; VanPatten & Borst, 2012b; VanPatten et al., 2013). The results of the present study suggest that L2 Latin learners too would benefit from structured input activities with explicit information. That is, learners need to complete activities that push them to process the case markings on the nouns morphosyntactically and not just lexically:

> What is needed is to limit the exercise to focus on one or two related forms and to require the use of the meaning of the form in order to do the exercise. . . . to develop an automatic association of the form with the meaning, so that working memory is freed to work on other aspects.
> *(Harrison, 2010, p. 13)*

Conclusion

This eye-tracking study investigated the eye movements of learners of Latin as they completed a low-salience translation task and a high-salience forced choice adjective completion task. Although the learners did not spend more time looking at noun case inflection while marking adjective agreement on accurate sentences than inaccurate sentences and the longer dwell times on noun endings in the high-salience task were not significant, learners were more accurate on the high-salience task in which they were forced to notice case marking. Additionally, learners indicated an awareness of the need to mark case agreement on the adjectives during stimulated recall sessions even if they were not all able to do so accurately. Latin with its rich morphological system is a language rife with possibility for future research on learners' processing of L2 grammatical morphemes.

Notes

1 Out of concern that the two students who had studied two years of high school Latin may affect the results, we compared their results on the two tasks with those of the other participants. Participants 209 and 212 earned 66.67% and 50%, respectively, on the Translation task and 37.5% and 43.75%, respectively, on the Forced Choice Adjective Completion task. As their scores were by no means higher than the other participants (both placing in the Low Group), we argue that the high school Latin courses did not make them qualitatively different from the other participants, and we included them in the analyses.
2 The adjectives and modified nouns were contiguous in all of the sentences except for one Translation task item: *Rēx magnā cum virtūte regit* ('The king rules with great virtue.'). It was pointed out by a reviewer that in *magnā cum virtūte* the adjective is not in the same phrase as the noun. This particular combination (adjective *CUM* noun) is a common word order in Latin (e.g., *magnā cum laude*), but in retrospect, the sentence should have been written without *cum* (i.e., just *magnā virtūte*). Although it did not seem to make the item more difficult for the learners—accuracy on this item was actually higher (64.71%) than the overall average (51.46%)—it is a limitation of these materials that we recommend avoiding in future similar studies.
3 As a multiple-choice question on which the stronger students perform less well is suspect, it is important to examine the individual item analysis. But even in this small group, the average overall score of the students who chose the correct answer on any given item is higher than the average of any group who chose another answer. It has to be noted, however, that the choices played no role in item difficulty as those were determined by the possible endings available. Item difficulty was solely the result of the sentence (or maybe the word the adjective modified). Also, gender is not a factor here—only case and number—because the choices all were the correct gender.

References

Bardovi-Harlig, K. (2000). *Tense and aspect in second language acquisition: Form, meaning, and use*. Oxford: Blackwell.

Bordag, D., & Pechmann, T. (2008). Grammatical gender in translation. *Second Language Research, 24*, 139–166.

Carlon, J. M. (2013). The Implications of SLA research for Latin pedagogy: Modernizing Latin instruction and securing its place in curricula. *Teaching Classical Languages, 4*, 106–122.

Cintrón-Valentín, M., & Ellis, N. C. (2015). Exploring the interface. *Studies in Second Language Acquisition, 37*, 197–235.

Comer, W. J., & deBenedette, L. (2010). Processing instruction and Russian: Issues, materials, and preliminary experimental results. *Slavic and East European Journal, 51*(4), 118–146.

Culman, H., Henry, N., & VanPatten, B. (2009). The role of explicit information in processing instruction: An on-line study with German accusative case inflections. *Die Unterrichtspraxis, 42*, 20–32.

Davidson, J., de la Fuente, I., Montrul, S., & Foote, R. (2011). *Early language experience facilitates gender processing in Spanish heritage speakers*. Paper presented at the 35th Boston University Conference on Language Development, (BUCLD), Boston University, Boston, MA.

Ellis, N. C. (2008). The dynamics of second language emergence: Cycles of language use, language change, and language acquisition. *Modern Language Journal, 92,* 232–249.

Ellis, N. C., Hafeez, K., Martin, K. I., Chen, L., Boland, J., & Sagarra, N. (2014). An eye-tracking study of learned attention in second language acquisition. *Applied Psycholinguistics, 35,* 547–579.

Ellis, N. C., & Sagarra, N. (2010a). The bounds of adult language acquisition: Blocking and learned attention. *Studies in Second Language Acquisition, 32,* 553–580.

Ellis, N. C., & Sagarra, N. (2010b). Learned attention effects in L2 temporal reference: The first hour and the next eight semesters. *Language Learning, 60*(Suppl. 2), 85–108.

Ellis, N. C., & Sagarra, N. (2011). Learned attention in adult language acquisition: A replication and generalization study and meta-analysis. *Studies in Second Language Acquisition, 33,* 589–624.

Ellis, R. (2012). *Language teaching research and language pedagogy.* Oxford, UK: Wiley-Blackwell.

Fernández, C. (2008). Reexamining the role of explicit information in processing instruction. *Studies in Second Language Acquisition, 30,* 277–305.

Franceschina, F. (2005). *Fossilized second language grammars: The acquisition of grammatical gender.* Amsterdam: John Benjamins Publishing.

Foote, R. (2015). The production of gender agreement in native and L2 Spanish: The role of morphophonological form. *Second Language Research, 31,* 343–373.

Gass, S., Behney, J., & Plonsky, L. (2013). *Second language acquisition: An introductory course.* New York: Routledge.

Gass, S., & Mackey, A. (2000). *Stimulated recall methodology in second language research.* New York: Routledge.

Gass, S., Svetics, I., & Lemelin, S. (2003). Differential effects of attention. *Language Learning, 53,* 497–546.

Goldschneider, J. M., & DeKeyser, R. M. (2001). Explaining the "natural order of L2 morpheme acquisition" in English: A meta-analysis of multiple determinants. *Language Learning, 51,* 1–50.

Harrison, R. R. (2010). Exercises for developing prediction skills in reading Latin sentences. *Teaching Classical Languages, 2,* 1–30.

Hawkins, R., & Liszka, S. (2003). Locating the source of defective past tense marking in advanced L2 English speakers. In R. van Hout, A. Hulk, F. Kuiken, & R. Towell (Eds.), *The interface between syntax and lexicon in second language acquisition* (pp. 21–44) Amsterdam: John Benjamins.

Henry, N., Culman, H., & VanPatten, B. (2009). More on the effects of explicit information in processing instruction: A partial replication and response to Fernández (2008). *Studies in Second Language Acquisition, 31,* 359–375.

Holmes, V. M., & Segui, J. (2006). Assigning grammatical gender during word production. *Journal of Psycholinguistic Research, 35,* 5–30.

Hulstijn, J. H., & de Graaff, R. (1994). Under what conditions does explicit knowledge of a second language facilitate the acquisition of implicit knowledge? A research proposal. *AILA Review, 11,* 97–112.

Izumi, S. (2002). Output, input enhancement, and the noticing hypothesis: An experimental study on ESL relativization. *Studies in Second Language Acquisition, 24,* 541–577.

Jackson, C. (2007). The use and nonuse of semantic information, word order, and case markings during comprehension by German L2 learners. *Modern Language Journal, 91,* 418–432.

Keating, G. D. (2009). Sensitivity to violations of gender agreement in native and nonnative Spanish: An eye-movement investigation. *Language Learning, 59,* 503–535.

Larsen-Freeman, D. (1975). The acquisition of grammatical morphemes by adult ESL students. *TESOL Quarterly, 9,* 409–419.
Larsen-Freeman, D. (2010). Not so fast: A discussion of L2 morpheme processing and acquisition. *Language Learning, 60,* 221–230.
LoCoco, V. (1987). Learner comprehension of oral and written sentences in German and Spanish: The importance of word order. In B. VanPatten, T. R. Dvorak, & J. F. Lee (Eds.), *Foreign language learning: A research perspective* (pp. 119–129). Rowley, MA: Newbury House.
Norris, J., & Ortega, L. (2000). Effectiveness of L2 instruction: A research synthesis and quantitative meta-analysis. *Language Learning, 50,* 417–528.
Oliphant, K. (1998). Acquisition of grammatical gender in Italian as a foreign language. *The Canadian Modern Language Review, 54,* 239–262.
Prévost, P., & White, L. (2000). Missing surface inflection or impairment in second language acquisition? Evidence from tense and agreement. *Second Language Research, 16,* 103–133.
Rayner, K., & Pollatsek, A. (1989). *The psychology of reading.* Englewood Cliffs, NJ: Prentice-Hall.
Sharwood Smith, M. (1993). Input enhancement in instructed SLA: Theoretical bases. *Studies in Second Language Acquisition, 15,* 165–179.
Shelmerdine, S. (2013). *Introduction to Latin* (2nd ed.). Indianapolis, IN: Hackett Publishing.
Spada, N. (1997). Form-focused instruction and second language acquisition: A review of classroom and laboratory research. *Language Teaching Research, 30,* 73–87.
Swain, M. (1985). Communicative competence: Some roles of comprehensible input and comprehensible output in its development. In S. Gass & C. Madden (Eds.), *Input in second language acquisition* (pp. 235–253). Rowley, MA: Newbury House.
Swain, M. (2005). The output hypothesis: Theory and research. In E. Hinkel (Ed.), *Handbook of research in second language teaching and learning* (pp. 471–483). Mahwah, NJ: Lawrence Erlbaum Associates.
Terrell, T. (1991). The role of grammar instruction in a communicative approach. *Modern Language Journal, 75,* 52–63.
VanPatten, B., & Borst, S. (2012a). The roles of explicit information and grammatical sensitivity in the processing of clitic object pronouns and word order in Spanish L2. *Hispania, 95,* 270–284.
VanPatten, B., & Borst, S. (2012b). The roles of explicit information and grammatical sensitivity in processing instruction: Nominative-Accusative case marking and word order in German L2. *Foreign Language Annals, 45,* 92–109.
VanPatten, B., & Cadierno, T. (1993). Explicit instruction and input processing. *Studies in Second Language Acquisition, 15,* 225–243.
VanPatten, B., Collopy, E., Price, J. E., Borst, S., & Qualin, A. (2013). Explicit information, grammatical sensitivity, and the First-Noun Principle: A cross-linguistic study in processing instruction. *Modern Language Journal, 97,* 506–527.
VanPatten, B., Collopy, E., & Qualin, A. (2012). Explicit information and processing instruction with nominative and accusative case in Russian as a second language: Just how important is explanation? *The Slavic and East European Journal, 56,* 256–276.
VanPatten, B., & Oikkenon, S. (1996). Explanation versus structured input in processing instruction. *Studies in Second Language Acquisition, 18,* 495–510.
Winke, P. M. (2013). The effects of input enhancement on grammar learning and comprehension. *Studies in Second Language Acquisition, 35,* 323–352.

APPENDIX A

Translation Task Stimuli

Frātrēs meī mātrem amant.
My brothers love mother.

Rēx magnā cum virtūte regit.
The king rules with great virtue.

Cīvitās bona lēgibus nōn carēre potest.
A good state cannot be without laws.

Populō laeta lībertās erit.
Freedom will be happy for the people.

Cōnsulī novum imperium dābimus.
We will give new power to the consul.

Puerōs nōmina Rōmāna deōrum docēbō.
I will teach the boys the Roman names of the gods.

APPENDIX B

Forced Choice Adjective Completion Task Stimuli

Dīc dominō meō dē pecūniā.	Tell my master about the money.
Fīliābus optāmus nōmina pulchra dare.	We want to give our daughters beautiful names.
Vīta est bona in cīvitātibus līberīs.	Life is good in free states.
Pāx nova nōbīs placet.	The new peace is pleasing to us.
Semper magnā cum virtūte labōrābās.	You always used to work with great virtue.
Dōna mātris tuae mihi placent.	Your mother's gifts please me.
Verba hominis aegrī nōn audīre poteram.	I was not able to hear the sick man's words.
Nocēbitisne vestrīs ducibus?	Will you harm your leaders?
Lēgibus malīs nōn pārēre dēbētis.	You should not obey bad laws.
Sapientiam patrum nostrōrum laudāmus.	We praise the wisdom of our fathers.
Multī deōs vītam longam ōrant.	Many ask the gods for a long life.
Cōnsulibus fāmae bonae sunt.	The consuls have good reputations.
Ad terram laetam nāvigābimus.	We will sail to the fertile land.
Puerōs exemplīs multīs docēbō.	I will teach the boys with many examples.
Nāvigāre in pontō altō timēbam.	I was afraid to sail on the deep sea.
Turbam movēbās verbīs miserīs.	You were moving the crowd with sad words.

13
MEASURING LEXICAL ALIGNMENT DURING L2 CHAT INTERACTION

An Eye-Tracking Study

Marije Michel and Bryan Smith

Introduction

Written synchronous computer-mediated communication (SCMC or text-chat) is a pervasive means of communication in our globalized society, with many writing messages in the L2. From a Second Language Acquisition (SLA) perspective, text-chat interaction has been argued to be potentially facilitative of second language (L2) development. As Smith (2005) claims, written SCMC is "the ideal medium for students to benefit from interaction" (p. 34) because it affords greater opportunity to attend to and reflect on the content and form of incoming (as well as their own) messages.

There is a growing body of research exploring the questions of how and why SCMC might support L2 learning (cf. Chapelle, 2009; Kern, Ware, & Warschauer, 2008; Sauro, 2011; Ziegler, 2016). One recurring argument is that text-based SCMC increases "the visual saliency of certain forms . . . and the enduring as opposed to ephemeral nature of the turns" (Sauro, 2009, p. 96). Increased salience follows from the fact that during SCMC interlocutors have more time to process incoming messages, review earlier turns in the conversation, and monitor and self-correct their own output before hitting the enter (return) key. In addition, the salience of input and output, which is afforded by the permanence of the written message on the screen, has been said to contribute to noticing of form and meaning during text-chat (Schmidt, 2001; Smith, 2005).

The present study draws on this idea of increased salience during SCMC and explores how the specific modality of text-chat affects interactional alignment between peers chatting in L2 English. To define alignment, Costa, Pickering, and Sorace (2008, p. 530) explain that:

> Interlocutors construct mental models of the situation under discussion, and successful dialogue occurs when these situation models become aligned. . . .

In the interactive-alignment account, such alignment of situation models is linked to the tendency for interlocutors to repeat each other's choices at many different linguistic levels, such as words, sounds, and grammar.

The authors distinguish the mental alignment from the surface phenomenon of, for example, repeating the same words; this is called 'lexical entrainment.' Entrainment in turn is distinguished from the underlying psycholinguistic mechanism—that is, priming, which refers to a speaker's repeated production of a previously spoken or heard structure across successive utterances (Bock, 1995). To avoid terminological confusion in this chapter, we will consistently use 'alignment' to encompass all three aspects of the phenomenon under investigation, knowing that this represents a simplification. That is, we talk about alignment in all three cases: 1) when we refer to convergence of the mental model, 2) that manifests itself as lexical entrainment, and 3) is likely to be caused by the psycholinguistic mechanism of priming (see Costa et al., 2008, p. 531, for a discussion of the three concepts and the fact that alignment is "often loosely used to refer to observable behaviour"). In the following, we will review literature covering all these different angles given that they add to the understanding of the phenomenon under investigation in the present study.

The aim of the work presented in this chapter is to investigate instances of lexical alignment (or overlap) between chat interactants and use eye-tracking methodology to establish whether the repetition of exact lexical items of a partner's earlier utterance goes hand in hand with increased overt attention (i.e., higher fixation duration and fixation counts). This study is the first of its kind to explore alignment in SCMC using eye-tracking methodology. Apart from our theoretical goal to investigate whether L2 interactional alignment takes place in an SCMC context, we also aim at advancing the field by our methodological contribution on how to apply eye-tracking technology in SCMC research.

Salience in SLA and SCMC

One of the first studies that coined the notion of salience in SLA research was Bardovi-Harlig (1987), who defined it as the "availability of data" (p. 401). More recent work found that salience is based on perceptual physical features like stress or position in a phrase as well as categories affecting processing such as frequency and complexity of a structure (Ellis, 2006; Goldschneider & DeKeyser, 2001). Goldschneider and DeKeyser (2001) define salience as "how easy it is to hear or perceive a given structure" (p. 22). From an SLA perspective, salience has long been acknowledged as an important factor (Gass, 1988) that explains why some input becomes intake while other input remains unnoticed and therefore does not easily become integrated into the L2 learner's system. Salience is strongly related to noticing and attention, building on the idea that the more salient a feature is, the more likely it is to attract attention and be noticed. Attention and noticing—that is, "the conscious apprehension and awareness of input" (Schmidt, 2001, p. 26)—are key processes that support L2 learning. Schmidt's (1990) original strong version of the Noticing Hypothesis sees noticing as a necessary and sufficient condition for learning to happen. Later, in the weaker version Schmidt

(1994) assigns noticing only a facilitative role for SLA. Whether awareness is needed for learning or not remains a topic of debate (Ellis, 2006; Robinson, 1995; Tomlin & Villa, 1994). Most research seems to agree, however, that selective attention (with or without awareness) is needed for successful SLA and selective attention is more likely when a language feature is salient.

From a language pedagogic perspective, it has been claimed that the distinct characteristics of written SCMC increase the salience of the linguistic input during L2 chat, thereby guiding a learner's attention to linguistic form and supporting uptake and intake of L2 forms (Smith, 2005). First, most people type more slowly than they speak, which results in a slower pace of turn-taking during SCMC than in spoken interaction (Gurzynski-Weiss & Baralt, 2015), resulting in what Beauvois (1992) refers to as a "conversation in slow motion" (p. 455). Second, the output of a chat conversation remains visible on the screen, which also increases the potential salience of lexical items and grammatical structures. This "permanence" allows L2 users to reread and revisit information they might have missed or misunderstood at first instance or to get inspiration for their own contributions and, for example, appropriate parts their partner's language. In this sense, SCMC contrasts strongly with ephemeral spoken interaction where everything said is gone within seconds, or as soon as it leaves working memory. Third, SCMC allows L2 learners to monitor and edit their own writing before they transmit their message by hitting the enter key. Fourth, because intonation, gesture and facial expressions that often guide oral interaction are absent, SCMC pushes L2 learners to use language (e.g., pragma-linguistic forms) to express themselves (Sykes, 2005) as they encounter (and arguably) resolve gaps between what they want to say and what they are able to say (Swain, 2005).

Because of these distinct features of text-based chat, Sauro (2009, p. 96) argues that text-chat "holds particular promise for the learning of especially complex or low salient forms" because the modality has the potential of increasing salience. As such, SCMC could be used as a tool in L2 pedagogy as it implicitly guides attention to form. This is in accordance with Schmidt (2001) who stated that intentionally focusing attention (e.g., on non-salient forms), is an essential prerequisite for learning to happen. Empirical evidence for these claims comes from Lai and Zhao (2006), who did find more noticing during written SCMC than in oral interactions. Immediately relevant to the present study is that the characteristics of written SCMC suggest that it could be an ideal context for alignment where salience of and attention to a form might play a major role in eliciting aligned language. The following section will explain why alignment in the L2 is a phenomenon worth exploring.

Alignment: L1 and L2 Perspectives

Over the years, different scholarly fields have used a variety of terms to refer to the observational linguistic "unintentional and pragmatically unmotivated tendency to repeat the general (syntactic) pattern of an utterance" (Bock & Griffin, 2000, p. 177). In psycholinguistics, where the focus lies on investigating the underlying processing mechanism, researchers tend to use 'priming' or 'persistence' (Pickering & Ferreira, 2008). Sociocultural scholars tend to refer to 'alignment,' 'accommodation,' 'convergence,' or just 'repetition' (Atkinson, Churchill, Nishino, & Okada, 2007; Tannen, 1987) as they investigate the phenomenon as an aspect of successful dialogue (Costa et al., 2008). In this chapter, we draw on literature from these different fields and have chosen to use 'alignment' in order to avoid terminological confusion when we address the same basic phenomenon (i.e., the inclination of interlocutors to adopt each other's language). We chose 'alignment' because, firstly, it seems to encompass all levels of the phenomenon: the mental alignment of situational models, the linguistic manifestation of it (also called 'entrainment') as well as the underlying psycholinguistic mechanism of 'priming'. Secondly, alignment better reflects the context of the current investigation (i.e., naturally occurring repetition of linguistic forms in authentic conversation) in contrast to 'priming,' which seems to be most often used in situations where an intentional (experimental or pedagogical) design is aimed at eliciting lexical or structural repetition (cf. Branigan, Pickering, McLean, & Cleland, 2007). Please note that, when reviewing earlier work, we will use the term that is used by the respective authors.

Why do conversational partners align? According to Branigan et al. (2007), successful dialogue is the product of "collaborative effort" (p. 165) as interlocutors "come to share many aspects of their representations of the situation under discussion" (p. 164) and alignment of their mental models of the situation happens. Such situational alignment is known to influence linguistic alignment and vice versa (Pickering & Garrod, 2004). That is to say, over the course of authentic interaction, partners are likely to re-use each other's language patterns (Trofimovich, 2013) as they work towards a common ground of their mental model (Horton, 2005). In their comprehensive review of earlier work on alignment, Pickering and Ferreira (2008) state that alignment affects all levels of linguistic processing (i.e., morpho-syntactic, lexico-semantic, phonological, and pragmatic choices of production and perception). To give an example: when speaker A uses the sentence *'The chair was put next to the table,'* the interactional partner B will subsequently process words like *CABLE* and *DESK* faster and with greater ease because of the phonological and semantic overlap between these words and the prime *TABLE*. In addition, partner B will be more likely to also use passive voice in following utterances because the passive structure was activated.

Extensive lab-based psycholinguistic research suggests that syntactic alignment, in particular, is based on automatic and implicit processes that take place largely beyond the awareness and intentions of language users (Costa et al., 2008; Pickering & Branigan, 1999; Pickering & Ferreira, 2008), while lexico-semantic choices could be a result of more conscious decisions to maximize understanding (cf. Branigan et al., 2007).

In L2 pedagogy, empirical research has shown priming (as a pedagogical tool to elicit aligned language) to successfully trigger the use of a variety of structures, such as double-dative constructions (McDonough, 2006), passive voice (Kim & McDonough, 2008), question formation (McDonough & Chaikitmongkol, 2010; McDonough & De Vleeschauwer, 2012; McDonough & Kim, 2009; McDonough & Mackey, 2006), noun and verb morphology (Marsden, Altmann, & St Claire, 2013; McDonough & Fulga, 2015), pronunciation (Trofimovich, 2013; Trofimovich, McDonough, & Neumann, 2013), and others (see Trofimovich & McDonough's [2011] edited collection).

Even though this research as a whole tentatively supports the occurrence of primed production, effects are often small and the influence on different target structures is quite variable. For example, McDonough (2006) found evidence for primed production of prepositions but not of double object dative constructions. Similarly, Shin and Christianson (2012), who combined priming and explicit instruction, did find priming plus explicit instruction to elicit enhanced production of double datives in the short term, but priming only showed greater long-term effects. For phrasal verbs, the opposite picture emerged. Boston (2009) used pre-task priming to elicit passive voice and found no statistical differences between the experimental and control groups. As acknowledged by McDonough and De Vleeschauwer (2012), prompt frequency and individual differences may play a role. Similarly, context and interlocutor (e.g., interacting with a scripted L1 speaker versus classroom based peer interaction) seem to influence the success of priming (Kim & McDonough, 2008).

In contrast to L1 processes, there is some evidence that alignment in an L2 may not be entirely beyond awareness. For example, findings by Marsden et al. (2013) have shown that focusing an L2 user's attention to the morphological structure of a prime increases the size of subsequent processing gains attributed to priming. From a theoretical point of view Costa et al. (2008) further explain that in L2 conversation, "the degree of shared knowledge between the interlocutors may not be enough for automatic linguistic alignment to function in the same way it does when the two interlocutors are native speakers" (p. 537). In addition, alignment is thought to be resource-free and automatic between-speaker adaptive behavior (Pickering & Garrod, 2004), which is not something we associate with L2 processing, in particular, with regard to processes of formulation (lexical retrieval, morphosyntactic encoding) at a beginner or intermediate level (de Bot, 1992). Moreover, L2 speakers may not be able to align to a structure or word they lack in their interlanguage system. Costa et al. (2008) also point out that L2 learners may actively suppress alignment because they want to avoid a form they feel insecure about. Finally, processing limitations may interfere with alignment, either because the L1 of an L2 speaker is highly activated and L1 transfer overrules automatic alignment in the L2 or because slow speech rates, activated structures, and items have already decayed in working memory by the time an interactant reaches a possible context for alignment.

Whether alignment in an L2 is an implicit and automatic process or whether it is mediated by conscious strategic behavior of second language users is an empirical question. Moreover, even though there is a body of SLA research that provides evidence that priming is the underlying mechanism of alignment, this earlier work has looked only at spoken interaction. The aim of the present chapter is to explore alignment in the context of written synchronous computer-mediated communication (SCMC or text-chat).

Alignment in SCMC

So far, very little research has looked at alignment in an SCMC context. Reviewing L1-L2 text-chat interactions from a sociocultural perspective, Uzum (2010) concludes that by scrolling back and forth through earlier statements, "participants aligned their language use and choice of grammatical structure and words to that of their partners" (p. 144). Michel (in press) performed an SCMC study in a high school classroom among British girls learning German. Her chatlog analyses of the peer interaction revealed several instances of alignment at the lexical and syntactic level. Accompanying focus-group interviews supported these findings, as the L2 learners reported taking their partner's writing as a model for their own chat contributions. In a corpus-based study comparing L1 interactions to elicited L2 interactions in a classroom, Collentine and Collentine (2013) explored 'convergence'. Their study targeting the use of subjunctive mood in Spanish showed that L2 peers displayed even greater convergence than L1-L1 partners. Finally, the authors ask about the use of "structural convergence as a learning mechanism" in an SCMC environment (p. 185). The present study pursues exactly this goal—that is, to examine aligned production during written SCMC in an instructed setting. At this point, our aim is not so much to explore whether learning might occur as a result of alignment. In the first place, we wish to examine whether alignment during L2 SCMC is related to overt attention as a prerequisite for noticing and eventually learning. The novelty of this study lies not least in its methodological approach, which includes eye-gaze measurement.

Eye-Tracking SCMC

Until recently (and continuing on today, unfortunately), many SCMC studies relied solely on chat transcript logs—a very static approach to explaining a dynamic process (e.g., O'Rourke, 2008; Smith, 2010). O'Rourke (2008) suggests that reliance on such "impoverished data" is quite dangerous as researchers may be quick to assume that because a particular tool has certain affordances, that learners actually make use of these affordances. Some studies have now started to use screen-recording methodology to capture the dynamicity of the process (Gurzynski-Weiss & Baralt, 2015; Sauro & Smith, 2010).

Smith (2010, 2012) argued that on top of screen capturing, eye-gaze data may help to inform some of the contentious debates in SLA (e.g., is noticing a prerequisite for learning?) and that gaze tracking may be employed as a robust supplemental measure when triangulating findings based on other established methodologies (e.g., stimulated recall and think-alouds). Indeed, as pointed out by Godfroid, Housen, and Boers (2010), eye-tracking as a data collection technique seems less likely than, say, think-aloud to interfere with the participants' cognitive processing (see also Godfroid & Spino, 2015).

For example, Smith (2010) showed that learners noticed about 60% of the intensive recasts they received. He found that lexical recasts were much easier than grammatical recasts for students to notice, retain, and accurately produce on a written posttest. Of particular relevance to the current study, learners were also better able to productively use the recast targets during subsequent chat interactions. Smith (2012) found eye-tracking to be a reliable technique for measuring what learners attend to (along with stimulated recall) in written corrective feedback from a native speaker interlocutor. Semantic and syntactic targets were more easily noticed by learners than were morphological targets. Smith and Renaud's (2013) learners focused on about 75% of teacher recasts. Of these recasts, up to one-third were retained as measured by a delayed posttest one week later. A suggestive positive effect was established for fixation count (number of fixations on a target) and posttest success, while total fixation duration and posttest success were not related. A small-scale study on learner-teacher interactions by Örnberg Berglund (2012, 2013) revealed that all of the teacher's comments were seemingly noticed, though at times long after they were posted (up to several minutes later). In her study, writers focused on their own writing and read the teacher's contributions only once they had finished with their own composition and had hit the enter key. This confirms O'Rourke's (2012, p. 319) pattern of "post-send monitoring" during written SCMC and suggests that some learners do not engage in two other common patterns: "simultaneous monitoring" or "pre-send monitoring."

The question of how salience affects L2 learning during text-based SCMC is just one of the open questions regarding attentional processes in this medium. Eye-tracking methodology can be a fruitful approach to tap into these issues.

The Present Study

In the present study, we investigate lexical alignment by L2 peers during task-based SCMC performance. Besides our aim to increase our understanding of whether alignment takes place during L2 peer interaction via SCMC, we also wish to make a methodological contribution. By broadening our approaches to measuring eye-gaze behavior in SCMC research we address the question of how we can code and analyze linguistic content and targets that are creative and dynamic in nature.

Research Questions

RQ1: To what extent do L2 peers align at the lexical level when interacting via text-based SCMC during task-based interaction?

RQ2: Can eye-tracking technology help us disentangle explicit, overt attention to an interlocutor's output from implicit processes of aligned production?

Method and Design

Participants

Given the study's explorative nature, only six participants were recruited for this study (Table 13.1 summarizes their characteristics). All participants were L2 users of English with various L1 backgrounds and were studying in an MA TESOL or Applied Linguistics program in the United Kingdom or the United States. They had a mean age of 26.3 years ($SD = 5.0$) and had studied English for an average of 11.1 years ($SD = 3.3$). At the time of the study they had resided in an English-speaking country for a mean of 5.7 months ($SD = 4.6$). Their self-rated

TABLE 13.1 Participant characteristics

Participant/ Country of residence	Age	Gender	L1	Years of studying English	Months in L2 country	Self-rating for writing (CEFR)	Proficiency out of 150 (%)[a]
1 / UK	23	female	Chinese	10	2	C1	142 (85)
2 / UK	35	female	Nepali	14	1	C1	128 (85)
3 / UK	22	female	Chinese	10	13	C1	141 (94)
4 / USA	23	female	Taiwanese/Chinese	15	8	B2	137 (91)
5 / USA	26	male	Arabic	12	3	B2	137 (91)
6 / USA	29	male	Arabic	6	8	B2	128 (85)

Note: [a] www.transparent.com/learn-english/proficiency-test.html

writing proficiency in English was at B2 to C1 of the Common European Framework of Reference for Languages (CEFR; Council of Europe, 2001), which was supported by their scores at the higher end of a general test of English proficiency (www.transparent.com/learn-english/proficiency-test.html). Students signed up on a voluntary basis.

Materials

Students were paired up—one in the UK and one in the USA, P1 and P6; P2 and P5; P3 and P4—for a total of seven chat sessions that each lasted 45 minutes. The first session was dedicated to getting to know each other and to familiarize themselves with the chat environment. For this purpose, partners used the written chat function in Skype to ask and answer a couple of questions targeting their individual characteristics and knowledge of CALL (see Appendix). In the following weeks, students participated in six experimental sessions. In each session, they received an abstract from a published CALL study that was divided into three parts (beginning, middle, ending), two parts of which were available in full text. The third part was presented as a bullet-point summary (cf., Figure 13.1). Their task was to construct a full version of the bulleted section so that the abstract was complete.

Participants were asked to first discuss with each other how to reconstruct the bullet-point text during 20 minutes of chat interaction. Afterwards, as a post-task they had 15 minutes to write their individual reconstructions. Each week, students worked on a different study and abstract. The experimental sessions focused on the beginning (sessions 1 and 2), middle (sessions 3 and 4) and ending (sessions 5 and 6) parts of the abstract respectively (cf., Figure 13.2).

In order to ensure the content of the tasks was relevant yet largely unfamiliar to the participants, abstracts for all tasks were taken from a major CALL journal. We also included the post-task reconstruction activity in order to frame their chat interaction as a meaningful preparation for the individual writing task.

252 Michel and Smith

Beginning	This study investigates L2 attainment in asynchronous online environments, specifically possible relationships among anonymity, L2 motivation, participation in discussions, quality of L2 production, and success in L2 vocabulary learning. It examines, in asynchronous discussions, (a) if participation and (b) motivation contribute to L2 vocabulary learning, (c) if motivation is related to level of participation in anonymous versus non-anonymous discussions, and (d) if a student's quality of L2 use varies in anonymous vs. non-anonymous discussions.

	Basic Design & Method	Participants	Analysis & Measures
Middle	• **Independent Variables** anonymity, L2 motivation (e.g., introjected and identified regulation), participation in online discussions, quality of L2 production • **Dependent variable** L2 vocabulary learning	• N=87 • High school students • Spanish level 2 **Tasks** Asynchronous computer-mediated communication (ACMC; discussion forums)	• Pre-test cloze activity • Post-test cloze activity • Receptive vocabulary test • Transcripts of interaction • L2 motivation survey

Ending	Results revealed that students who participated in the asynchronous discussions received significantly higher scores on the post-test than those who did not. In terms of level of participation, non-anonymous forums may have a comparative advantage over anonymous ones for learners with high levels of *introjected regulation*, whereas for learners with high levels of *identified regulation*, both forums are advantageous. *Introjected regulation* was the only significant predictor of success in learning L2 vocabulary. Finally, non-anonymous forums seem to generate higher quality L2 production than anonymous ones.

FIGURE 13.1 Example experimental task: reconstruct middle part of an abstract

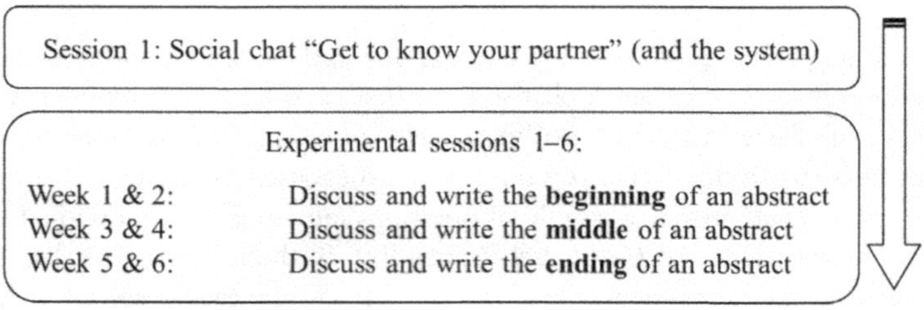

Session 1: Social chat "Get to know your partner" (and the system)

Experimental sessions 1–6:

Week 1 & 2: Discuss and write the **beginning** of an abstract
Week 3 & 4: Discuss and write the **middle** of an abstract
Week 5 & 6: Discuss and write the **ending** of an abstract

FIGURE 13.2 Design of the study

Apparatus

Eye-Tracking and Screen-Recording

Eye movements of the UK participants were recorded with a Tobii TX300 integrated eye-tracking system using dark pupil tracking (sampling rate of 300Hz) on a 23-inch TFT screen. The experiment was presented with Tobii Studio 3.0.9 software (Tobii Technology, n.d.[1]) and standardized criteria for the procedure (e.g., nine-point calibration of each eye) and position of the participants (e.g., about 60 cm from screen) were followed.

Eye movements of the U.S. participants were recorded with a portable TM3 eye-tracker (sampling rate 60Hz) from EyeTech Digital Systems using Gaze Tracker 10.0

Data analysis software. The TM3 was attached to a 21-inch monitor. This system also uses dark pupil, single or binocular tracking. Nine-point calibration was used with a 60 cm operating distance.

We used the in-built screen-recording feature of the eye-tracking software to capture the entire experimental session. In addition to allowing a playback of each learner's eye-gaze during the entire recording, the software records the location and duration of each eye fixation (among many other aspects of learners' eye-gaze).

Chat Interactions

Student partners used the written chat function of Skype to interact with one another. This program allowed us to set the font size to 24 so there would be enough space between words and lines to pinpoint eye-gaze behavior. Chat partners each received an anonymous Skype name and login. During the testing sessions, the task and chat window were presented side by side on the same screen (cf. Figure 13.3). For the post-task abstract reconstruction, students worked individually in Microsoft Word.

Procedure

Participants were tested during individual sessions at each end (UK and United States) in the eye-tracking lab. Because of the time difference between the two testing locations, these were scheduled between 5 and 7 pm (UK) and 10 am and 12 noon (United States) for seven weeks in a row on Wednesdays. Before the students arrived, the researchers had established Skype contact with the respective user names. Upon arrival, participants were seated at approximately 60 cm from the screen in a comfortable position that allowed them to use the keyboard and the mouse. After calibration, they spent about two minutes reading the instructions and task sheet. They then signaled to their chat partner that they were ready and were allowed 20 minutes to discuss the content of the bullet-point summary of the abstract for the specific week.

Coding and Analysis[2]

The coding and analysis of the data consisted of three steps: 1) identifying lexical overlap of 3–10 multi-word units between the two chat partners; 2) manual coding of these possible sources for alignment in the eye-tracking data, as well of baseline gaze behavior; and 3) qualitative and quantitative analyses comparing baseline data to gaze behavior on possible primes. The following sections provide details on each of these steps.

N-Gram Analysis to Identify Lexical Overlap

Chatlogs for each participant pair and each task were copied from Skype into plain text documents. An automatic spelling checker identified unknown words (e.g., vocabulrary) and manual corrections were made of typos (e.g., "vocabulrary" to "vocabulary"). Using R, each chat partner's corrected contributions were then

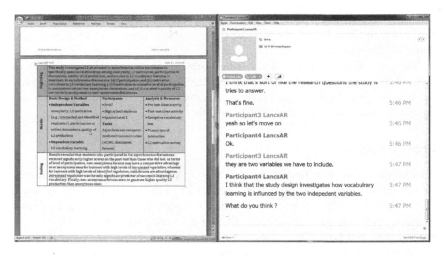

FIGURE 13.3 Experimental setup showing the task (reconstruct the middle part of an abstract) on the left and chat window of the interaction between participants 3 and 4 on the right

TABLE 13.2 Example chatlog of participants 2 and 5 interacting on the beginning of an abstract in the experimental session 1

Turn	Time	Participant	Text
10	18:28	P5	what do you think
11	18:28	P2	i think we can start by mentioning the main objective *of the study*
12	18:28	P5	in the beginning *of the study* i think we may introduce what the study is all about [. . .]
[. . .]			
30	18:31	P2	*what do you think* about the background of the learners

Note: Coding shows two *PSLA*s: The 4-gram 'what do you think,' first mentioned by P5 in turn 10 and later repeated by P2 in turn 30. The 3-gram 'of the study' was used first by P2 and repeated by P5 in the contingent turn 12.

divided into multi-word units of 3–10 words (n-grams) and a comparison between the two partners' n-gram lists identified exact lexical overlap[2]. Restricting ourselves to 3–10-grams allowed us to work with a meaningful set of target constructions. That is, while 2-grams could consist of function words only (e.g., "of the") 3-grams and larger units would always include at least one content word, which was seen as the basis of lexical alignment. A further benefit of this restriction was that the resulting set of target constructions was of a manageable size to allow manual coding of the eye-gaze data. We named the extracted n-grams 'possible source of lexical alignment' (*PSLA*). Those identified *PSLA*s were then located in the chatlogs and we determined which chat partner had used the n-gram first (see example in Table 13.2).

Manual Coding of Eye-Gaze Data

Using the eye-tracking software we replayed the chat interactions until the *PSLA* (as written by learner A) appeared on the screen of learner B. For example, the 3-gram 'of the study' was identified as a *PSLA* in the interaction between participants 2 and 5. Participant 2 (learner A) used it first. In the screen-recording of participant 5 (learner B), we found the time stamp when 'of the study' appeared in learner B's chat window; that is, as soon as participant 2 had finished writing this unit and had hit the enter key. We drew an Area of Interest (*AoI*) around this *PSLA*. An *AoI* is a type of box that the eye-tracking software uses to keep track of eye-gaze behavior in a specific location on the screen. As soon as one of the partners hit the enter key again, the target would move up to its new position in the chatlog window. The original *AoI* was deactivated and a new *AoI* was drawn at the new location. This procedure was repeated until the *PSLA* was off the screen or until the participant (learner B in this case) used the same lexical n-gram productively, whichever came first. Finally, all *AoI*s that belonged to the same *PSLA* (e.g., all for 'of the study') were grouped, and the statistics tools in the respective software packages were used to retrieve the Total Fixation Duration and Fixation Count for each group of *AoI*s corresponding to one specific *PSLA*.

To enable a comparison with normal gaze behavior during chat interactions, a recording of one full chat session for each participant was used to establish a baseline (Godfroid, Boers, & Housen, 2013). In each case, participants served as their own controls. This time, *AoI*s around each complete turn of the chat partner were drawn following the process described previously. Total Fixation Duration and Fixation Count metrics for each baseline turn were retrieved from the software.

Finally, metrics were normalized for the size of each *AoI*. That is, as *AoI*s were of different length, such as 'what do you think' (17 characters including three spaces) versus 'of the study' (12 characters including two spaces), it was expected that larger *AoI*s would receive longer and more fixations. Therefore, we standardized our measures by establishing the number of characters including spaces for each *AoI* and dividing the gaze metrics by this number (cf., Indrarathne & Kormos, 2016).[3]

Results

Qualitative Examples

When qualitatively reviewing eye-gaze data of our SCMC participants, we found examples of overt attention to lexically aligned text, that is, instances that suggested a participant was drawing on the input of their chat partner when writing their own contribution. We found these instances concerning single words and multi-word units as well as re-use of structural patterns. For example, in the first task, participants 2 and 5 discussed the use of vocabulary. Participant 5 consistently uses 'vocab' and provides three models over a course of several turns (40, 41, and 48), which eventually is picked up on by participant 2, who uses 'vocab' in turn 60 (cf. Table 13.3).

Exploring the eye-gazes on this specific instance indeed showed that participant 2 fixated 17 times on P5's 'vocab' during a total of 3.645 seconds.

256 Michel and Smith

TABLE 13.3 Use of 'Vocab' by both participants 2 and 5

Turn	Time	Participant	Text
40	6:36:52	P5	maybe how do learners acquire **vocab**
41	6:37:19	P5	or what is the most effective way to teach **vocab** to learners of different levels
[...]			[...]
48	6:39:28	P5	but i think this study is not only concerned with how learners learn **vocab**
[...]			[...]
60	6:43:01	P2	i think multimedia and **vocab** learning

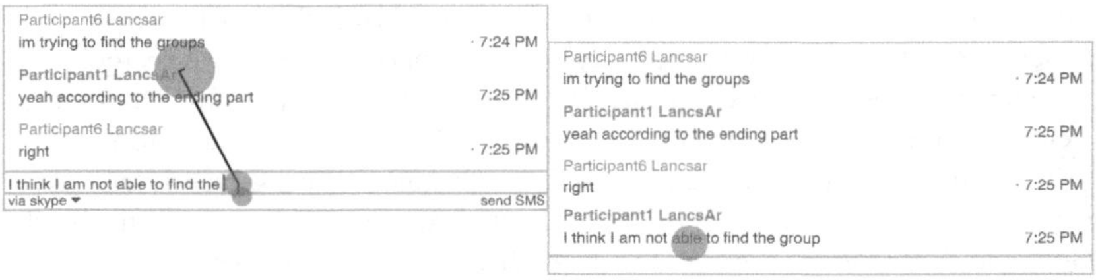

FIGURE 13.4 Screenshot of participant 1 paying attention to participant 6's earlier writing of 'to find the groups' while writing herself 'to find the group' (left) as demonstrated by the screenshot seconds later with the output of both partners (right)

Note: Gray dots represent eye fixations (the larger, the longer).

Similarly, we established overt attention to larger units of overlapping text between partners. For example, Figure 13.4 shows the eye-gaze of participant 1 conversing with participant 4 during the fourth experimental session. On the left, we see attention to the multi-word unit 'to find the groups' participant 6 wrote at time 7:24 p.m., while participant 1 is writing the same words herself at 7:25 p.m., as demonstrated by the screenshot on the right.

Finally, at a more abstract level, eye-gazes also attested overt attention to reproduced structures. As shown in Figure 13.5 where participants 3 and 4 interact, we see repeated eye-gazes of participant 3 on the expression 'you want to add to our discussion' contributed by participant 4 during the third experimental chat session. A few turns later, participant 3 writes 'we have to add this in our middle', which has the same underlying syntactic structure 'SUBJ VERB$_{finite}$ *to add* PREP *our* OBJ' including partial lexical overlap of 'to add' and 'our'.

While these kinds of examples were found in all participants' recordings, one aim of this study was to evaluate just how frequently such overt attention to aligned text occurred. In the next section, we will present data on the total fixation duration and number of fixations in a quantitative analysis.

Lexical Alignment During L2 Chat **257**

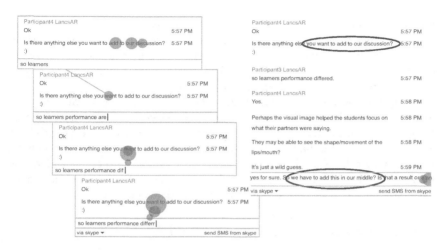

FIGURE 13.5 Example of multiple instances of overt attention to model structure (left) aligned to a few turns later (right)

Descriptive Data: Baseline Turns and PSLA N-Grams

Overall, the three pairs produced a total of 8,759 words ($M = 2{,}920$, $SD = 586$, per pair) for all six experimental chat conversations. We identified 82 instances of exact lexical overlap of 3–10-grams of two chat partners, where we could draw *AoI*s. Output of the eye-tracking software revealed that at least one eye fixation was recorded in 58 *PSLA*s (47 × 3-grams, 10 × 4-grams and 1× 5-gram). For baseline data, we analyzed 135 turns of the six participants that had received at least one eye fixation. Table 13.4 summarizes the descriptive statistics on the gaze behavior (Total

TABLE 13.4 Descriptive baseline and *PSLA*

Participant	Baseline, Mean (SD)			PSLA, Mean (SD)		
	N	TFD/char	FC/char	N	TFD/char	FC/char
1	15	0.074 (0.085)	0.369 (0.383)	11	0.084 (0.084)	0.353 (0.362)
2	42	0.176 (0.204)	0.844 (0.872)	12	0.199 (0.306)	0.867 (1.108)
3	43	0.114 (0.152)	0.565 (0.638)	12	0.151 (0.134)	0.746 (0.516)
4	16	0.036 (0.449)	0.163 (0.127)	9	0.147 (0.313)	0.700 (1.389)
5	11	0.031 (0.021)	0.187 (0.114)	2	0.037 (0.008)	0.307 (0.080)
6	8	0.041 (0.043)	0.159 (0.107)	12	0.068 (0.061)	0.285 (0.218)
Mean	22.5	0.079 (0.057)	0.381 (0.277)	9.7	0.114 (0.061)	0.543 (0.257)
Per word		0.360	1.743		0.523	2.483

Notes: PSLA = Possible Source for Lexical Alignment; N = Number of observations; TFD/char = Total Fixation Duration/character; FC/char = Fixation Count /character; per word = hypothetical value calculated on the basis of average of 4.57 characters per word in *PSLA*

Fixation Duration/number of characters including spaces = TFD/char; Fixation Count/number of characters including spaces = FC/char) for our six participants on the baseline turns and the *PSLA* n-grams. Baseline data average the gaze behavior over one full chat session per participant. *PSLA* data summarize the gaze times and counts for the 58 *PSLA*s that had received gaze attention.

Comparisons reveal that for all participants, *TFD/char* was longer on *PSLA*s than on baseline data even though differences are very small. The same holds for all participants but number 1 for *FC/char*. This time, differences are more pronounced, particularly for the U.S. participants (4, 5, 6), but also for UK participant 3. Mean scores on both measures reflect this general impression, which is even more apparent when looking at the value calculated for average gaze behavior per word. Data further show large individual differences substantiated by high standard deviation values.

Comparing Baseline versus Alignment Data

Given the relatively small dataset, we looked at each individual *PSLA* and identified those that received higher (mean plus 1 SD) and substantially higher (mean plus 2 SD) gaze attention than the baseline data for that participant. As shown in Table 13.5, out of 11 *PSLA*s we identified only two instances for participant 1 that had received higher ('the last part') and substantially higher ('non-anonymous and anonymous') values than the baseline. The latter *PSLA* only showed a substantially higher total fixation duration but not fixation count in comparison to the baseline.

By repeating this procedure for all six participants we found the list of *PSLA*s listed in Table 13.6 and renamed them *Identified* Sources for Lexical Alignment. What

TABLE 13.5 Higher values than baseline plus 1 (bold) or 2 (bold italics) SD for participant 1

PSLA	# char	TFD	TFD/char	FC	FC/char
I think we should	17	0.077	0.005	1	0.059
better than online	18	0.083	0.005	1	0.056
not better than	15	2.149	0.143	9	0.600
you think about the	19	0.460	0.024	2	0.105
I don't think we	16	1.493	0.093	7	0.438
I think we	10	0.473	0.047	2	0.200
the last part	13	2.516	**0.194**	10	**0.769**
non-anonymous and anonymous	26	6.772	***0.260***	25	**0.962**
see you next week	17	0.283	0.017	1	0.059
to find the group	17	0.786	0.046	3	0.176
Im not sure	11	1.036	0.094	5	0.455

Notes: PSLA = Possible Source for Lexical Alignment; # char = number of characters; TFD/char = Total Fixation Duration/character; FC/char = Fixation Count/character; **bold** = higher value than baseline plus 1 SD (TFD/char = .158; FC/char =.752); ***bold italics*** = higher value than baseline plus 2 SD (TFD/char = 0.243; FC/char = 1.135).

TABLE 13.6 Identified Source of Lexical Alignment (ISLA) based on baseline comparison for all participants

ISLA		# char	TFD	TFD/char	FC	FC/char
P1	the last part	13	2.516	0.194	10	0.769
	non-anonymous and anonymous	26	6.772	*0.260*	25	0.962
P2	oral cmc and ftf	16	6.138	0.384	26	1.625
	oral cmc and ftf	16	17.918	*1.120*	67	*4.188*
P3	written synchronous cmc	23	6.418	0.279	24	1.043
	written synchronous cmc	23	10.751	*0.467*	45	*1.957*
P4	the written synchronous	23	1.587	0.069	9	0.391
	L2 vocabulary learning	22	1.606	0.073	10	*0.478*
	as a measure	12	1.116	0.093	6	*0.500*
	I am not	8	7.824	*0.978*	35	*4.375*
P5	But I think	11	0.462	0.042	4	0.364
P6	nice to meet	12	1.608	*0.134*	4	0.333
	better than online	18	2.322	*0.129*	12	*0.667*
	It is asynchronous	18	3.798	*0.211*	14	*0.777*
	The rest of	11	0.407	0.037	3	0.273
	it is OK	8	0.720	0.090	3	*0.375*

Notes: ISLA = Identified Source for Lexical Alignment; # char = number of characters; TFD/char = Total Fixation Duration/character; FC/char = Fixation Count/character; *italics* = higher value than individual baseline plus 2 SD for each participant

is apparent in this list is the low frequency of some of the Identified Sources for Lexical Alignment (e.g., non-anonymous and anonymous) in contrast to others that reveal high frequent expressions (e.g., I am not). Furthermore, two 3-grams (oral cmc and ftf; written synchronous cmc—referring to oral computer-mediated communication and face-to-face and written synchronous computer-mediated communication, respectively) were identified twice for the same participants. As we have seen before, large individual differences exist. For example, we identified only one such expression for participant 5 but five instances for participant 6. Finally, it is worth noting that from the initial 82 *PSLAs*, only 16—that is, 5.1% (or 27.6% of the 58 *PSLA* with gaze data)—were identified as having received higher fixation duration and/or counts than baseline reading behavior would expect.

Quantitative Analysis

Using inferential statistics, we tried to further identify the value of our two predictor variables (*TFD/char* and *FC/char*) to identify sources of lexical alignment. The binomial response variable was alignment (yes = 1/no = 0) where overlapping n-grams (*PSLAs*) based on the chat transcripts were coded as 1. All baseline text was coded as zero. Because of the difference in hardware and software used by the UK and U.S. groups, statistical analysis of the two groups' performance was kept separate.

TABLE 13.7 Relationship between fixation count and alignment (U.S. group)

	B	S.E.	Wald	Df	p	Exp(B)
FC/char	−4.4598	2.0131	4.9079	1	0.026	86.472
constant	−1.4179	0.5138	7.6167	1	0.005	0.242

TABLE 13.8 Identified Source of Lexical Alignment (ISLA) based on statistical analysis (U.S. group)

	ISLA	#char	TFD	TFD/char	FC	FC/char
P4	L2 vocabulary learning	22	1.1606	0.073	10	0.478
	as a measure★	12	1.116	0.093	6	0.500
	I am not★	8	7.824	0.978	35	4.375
P6	better than online	18	2.322	0.129	12	0.667
	It is asynchronous	18	3.798	0.211	14	0.777
	It is OK	8	0.720	0.090	3	0.375

Notes: ★ = containing only K1 words; ISLA = Identified Source for Lexical Alignment; # char = number of characters; TFD/char = Total Fixation Duration/character; FC/char = Fixation Count/character

A separate regression analysis was run on the combined baseline ($n = 135$) and PSLA ($n = 58$) observations for each group (UK and U.S.) with *TFD/char* and *FC/char* as predictor variables and alignment as the (binominal) single criterion variable. For the UK group, neither variable returned a significant result. That is to say, neither variable discriminated very well between the PSLAs and baseline behavior. Likewise, *TFD/char* was non-significant for the U.S. group. However, the *FC/char* measure was a significant predictor of PSLA for the U.S. participants. We ran a second regression for the U.S. group alone with *FC/char* as the sole predictor variable. As shown in Table 13.7, results suggest that the standardized fixation count is a powerful predictor of alignment. For each unit increase in the index (*FC/char*), coding the respective target as "alignment" (rather than no alignment) was over 86 times more likely (Exp(B) = 86.472).

Based on this procedure six cases of the 23 PSLA in the U.S. data were identified as sources of lexical alignment. A concordance program was used (Cobb, n.d.) to examine the actual text of these phrases. Table 13.8 shows that in four of the six targets, 'off list' words were present (i.e., words that were not K1, K2, or academic words, according to the corpus). These include words like 'asynchronous,' 'L2,' 'FTF,' and 'online.' In the remaining two instances, all words in the aligned text were K1 words (1,000 most common).

Discussion

This chapter is a theoretically and methodologically explorative study into using eye-gaze measurement as an indicator of lexical alignment during SCMC among peers in their second language. Our first research question asked to what extent L2 peers align at the lexical level when interacting via text-based SCMC during task-based interaction. Our second research question inquired whether eye-tracking technology can help us disentangle explicit, overt attention to an interlocutor's output from implicit processes of aligned production. Chatlogs of six task-based 20-minute chat interactions were compared for exact lexical overlap of 3–10-grams. Out of the nearly 9,000 words, 82 instances of shared text were coined Possible Sources for Lexical Alignment (*PSLA*) and eye-tracking software was used to extract eye-gaze measurements (standardized Total Fixation Duration and Fixation Count) on those targets as they moved on the screen during the dynamic text-chat interactions. Comparisons between gaze data on baseline and experimental data identified 16 instances of lexical overlapping n-grams as sources for lexical alignment (identified source for lexical alignment). This is 28% of those *PSLA*s that had received at least one eye fixation. A regression analysis on part of the data identified fixation count (*FC/char*) but not total fixation duration (*TFD/char*) as a strong predictor for *PSLA*s when compared to baseline data. Six out of 23 (i.e., 26%) *PSLA*s were identified due to higher fixation counts. Together with qualitative screenings of the data that showed clear examples of visual attention to aligned text, our data do give some support for lexical alignment based on overt attention to the partner's language. However, the majority of lexical overlap did not go hand in hand with increased overt visual attention or noticing (as operationalized by Godfroid et al., 2013).

Methodologically, this study shows that eye-gaze measurement can support attempts to tease apart which cases of potential alignment are linked to more overt attentional behavior. Even though we worked with a small dataset, the results partially confirm earlier work by Smith and Renaud (2013), who suggest that fixation count (rather than total fixation duration) is a good indicator of what learners attend to during task-based SCMC interactions. For part of our data, the fact that *FC/char* was a predictor of alignment over baseline text suggests more overt attention to aligned text than baseline text, as measured by *FC/char*.

In the present study, there were many cases of potential alignment for which fixation count was under the required threshold. In these cases, there are two possible explanations. First, these could be simply coincidental occurrences that appear as overlap on the chat transcript. In this case, our findings would suggest that earlier work in this field—which relied on chatlog analyses (Collentine & Collentine, 2013; Michel, in press)—might overestimate the actual alignment taking place.

A second option is that these cases indeed reflect alignment, but they are not going hand-in-hand with overt attention. This could be interpreted as an indication that the L2 alignment is more implicit in nature, which is consistent with the theory behind L1 alignment (Pickering & Garrod, 2004). Yet, as the current study did not measure awareness (e.g., by means of stimulated recall), we cannot draw any firm conclusions in this respect.

For our data, it might be that the increased salience of SCMC conversation frees attentional capacity as it decreases the need to rely on working memory. In this context, 'normal' as opposed to excessive gaze behavior could be enough to activate and appropriate the same lexical items. In our data, alignment may occur in L2 speakers because their processing limitations—in comparison to L1 speakers (Costa et al., 2008)—are mediated by the medium of SCMC.

Branigan et al. (2007) suggest that lexico-semantic alignment is thought to be more conscious than alignment at the morphosyntactic level because of conversation strategies that help us to avoid nonunderstandings. Yet, most of our participants' alignment seems not to follow exceptional overt attention to their partner's output. In fact, at least one of our participants demonstrated a habit of only rarely reading what the partner wrote. Most of the reading focused on reviewing her own contributions in the chatlog and monitoring and editing her own messages before sending them, which is typical behavior during SCMC (O'Rourke, 2012; Örnberg Berglund, 2012, 2013). Another reason why our participants might not show much overt excessive attention to their partner's output could be the fact that they were conversing with a peer. Kim and McDonough (2008) found that target language partners tended to elicit more primed production in learners than peers. Other contextual factors (e.g., prompt frequency, McDonough & De Vleeschauwer, 2012) are likely to have played a role too. Following Marsden et al. (2013), this study could imply that for alignment to become pedagogically useful, it might be important to explicitly teach language learners to benefit from the increased salience during SCMC and instruct them to review their partner's contributions as a source for their own messages. As a whole, our study is in line with earlier work in both pedagogic L2 priming and eye-tracking SCMC as we yielded some support for overt attention to aligned text—be it to a limited extent only.

Finally, a noteworthy methodological contribution of this paper is the use of n-gram analyses in alignment research. We have shown that limiting automatic search for overlapping text to multi-word units of at least three words allowed us to work with a meaningful set of target structures that was manageable in terms of the further manual coding of the eye-gaze data. We would encourage that future research follows this same approach.

Limitations and Directions for Future Research

The most obvious limitation to this study was our modest sample size ($n = 6$). Each location in this study had one eye-tracker, which meant that participants' eye-gaze was tracked one dyad at a time. Practical constraints prohibited including more participants with the time available. Second, although we attempted to sculpt a series of highly relevant academic tasks for this study, in the final analysis, we are left with one task type—namely, a sort of information-gap task. This may have affected the nature of learner eye-gaze captured. The dual site nature of the study creates another layer of complexity. First, two different types of hardware and software were used for data collection and analysis. This surely limits the ability to consider the data as a whole. Similarly, the time difference between the UK and the southwestern United States may have reflected a difference in learner fatigue as data collection commenced in the late evening in the UK.

In our data collection and analysis, we employed 3–10-gram strings of lexical overlap as our basis for determining alignment. Future studies may wish to look at structural overlap. Though we did observe some syntactic alignment, this was not the focus of this paper. A careful analysis of syntactic alignment may reveal a different picture in terms of the nature of alignment during task-based SCMC.

Finally, the choice of using total fixation duration and fixation count is somewhat arbitrary. Nevertheless, we feel that these two measures are reasonable given the nature of the text (SCMC) being eye-tracked. Future studies may wish to incorporate another layer of data elicitation such as stimulated recall.

Conclusion

Text-based SCMC interaction has been argued to enhance the visual salience of forms, which promotes noticing. This, coupled with the persistence of the input and reduced conversational tempo in this modality, combine to make input more salient to learners during text-based SCMC and, therefore, create conditions facilitative for language learning. Indeed, the visual and orthographic nature of SCMC input may lead to stronger long-term memory traces than acoustic, phonological forms, as found in speech. Viewed another way, salience in the SCMC environment may be the result of differences (an increase) in noticing opportunities.

Capitalizing on these affordances of text-based SCMC, the current study has employed eye-tracking technology in an attempt to disentangle overt attention to (and noticing of) an interlocutor's output from implicit processes of aligned production. Though the current dataset is too small to present any robust conclusions, the present study has made some theoretical and methodological contributions to the investigation of lexical alignment during text-based peer SCMC in an L2 and the use of eye-tracking methodology in a text-chat environment. First, it seems that only a small amount of lexically aligned text goes hand-in-hand with heightened overt visual attention, which suggests that alignment in an L2—like in L1—might be the result of subconscious implicit processes rather than strategic explicit behavior; second, our data indicate that it is fixation count (rather than fixation duration) that might reflect the increased salience of an interlocutor's input and therefore predict noticing during text-based SCMC; and third, combining corpus-based n-gram analyses of chatlogs and measurement of eye-gazes during SCMC has shown to be a fruitful methodology to investigate how the salience of the interlocutor's contribution might influence L2 use by a chat partner. Finally, it must be acknowledged that due to large individual differences in gaze behavior, any generalizations are difficult to make based on the current findings.

Notes

1 Retrieved May 16, 2017 from www.tobii.com.
2 We thank Mark McGlashan—Lecturer at City University Birmingham, UK—for his help with the programming in R for the n-gram analysis. We also thank Michelle Chow, Isabelle Morley, and Pucheng Wang at Lancaster University for help with data coding and

the statistics helpdesk, School of Mathematical and Statistical Sciences at Arizona State University for statistical advice. Also thanks to Joe Collentine.

3 In contrast to the study cited, we decided to use the number of characters rather than the number of syllables as a divisor for the standardization. The rationale is multi-fold. First, this study involved purely text-based interaction. Second, many of our targets included abbreviations (e.g., CMC, FTF) for which we would not know whether or how our participants, being L2 speakers of English, would sound out those letter combinations.

References

Atkinson, D., Churchill, E., Nishino, T., & Okada, H. (2007). Alignment and interaction in a sociocognitive approach to second language acquisition. *The Modern Language Journal*, *91*(2), 169–188.

Bardovi-Harlig, K. (1987). Markedness and salience in second—language acquisition. *Language Learning*, *37*(3), 385–407.

Beauvois, M. H. (1992). Computer-assisted classroom discussion in the foreign language classroom: Conversation in slow motion. *Foreign Language Annals*, *25*(5), 455–464.

Bock, K. (1995). Sentence production: From mind to mouth. In J. Miller & P. Eimas (Eds.), *Handbook of perception and cognition, Vol. 11: Speech, language and communication* (pp. 181–216). San Diego: Academic Press.

Bock, K., & Griffin, Z. M. (2000). The persistence of structural priming: Transient activation or implicit learning? *Journal of Experimental Psychology: General*, *129*(2), 177–192.

Boston, J. S. (2009). Pre-task syntactic priming and focused task design. *ELT Journal*, *64*(2), 165–174.

Branigan, H. P., Pickering, M. J., McLean, J. F., & Cleland, A. A. (2007). Syntactic alignment and participant role in dialogue. *Cognition*, *104*(2), 163–197.

Chapelle, C. A. (2009). The relationship between second language acquisition theory and computer-assisted language learning. *The Modern Language Journal*, *93*, 741–753.

Cobb, T. Web VP Classic v.4 [computer program]. Retrieved from www.lextutor.ca/vp/eng/.

Collentine, J., & Collentine, K. (2013). A corpus approach to studying structural convergence in task-based Spanish L2 interactions. In K. McDonough & A. Mackey (Eds.), *Interaction in diverse educational settings* (pp. 147–165). Philadelphia: John Benjamins.

Costa, A., Pickering, M. J., & Sorace, A. (2008). Alignment in second language dialogue. *Language and Cognitive Processes*, *23*(4), 528–556.

Council of Europe. (2001). *Common European framework of reference for languages*. Cambridge: Cambridge University Press.

De Bot, K. (1992). A bilingual production model: Levelt's 'speaking' model adapted. *Applied Linguistics*, *13*, 1–24.

Ellis, N. C. (2006). Selective attention and transfer phenomena in L2 acquisition: Contingency, cue competition, salience, interference, overshadowing, blocking, and perceptual learning. *Applied Linguistics*, *27*(2), 164–194.

Gass, S. M. (1988). Integrating research areas: A framework for second language studies. *Applied Linguistics*, *9*(2), 198–217.

Godfroid, A., Boers, F., & Housen, A. (2013). Gauging the role of attention in L2 vocabulary acquisition by means of eye-tracking. *Studies in Second Language Acquisition*, *35*(3), 483–517.

Godfroid, A., Housen, A., & Boers, F. (2010). A procedure for testing the noticing hypothesis in the context of vocabulary acquisition. In M. Pütz & L. Sicola (Eds.), *Cognitive processing in second language acquisition* (pp. 169–197). Amsterdam: John Benjamins.

Godfroid, A., & Spino, L. A. (2015). Reconceptualizing reactivity of think-alouds and eye tracking: Absence of evidence is not evidence of absence. *Language Learning, 65*(4), 896–928.

Goldschneider, J. M., & DeKeyser, R. M. (2001). Explaining the "natural order of L2 morpheme acquisition" in English: A meta-analysis of multiple determinants. *Language Learning, 51*(1), 1–50.

Gurzynski-Weiss, L., & Baralt, M. (2015). Does type of modified output correspond to learner noticing of feedback? A closer look in face-to-face and computer-mediated task-based interaction. *Applied Psycholinguistics, 36*(6), 1393–1420.

Horton, W. S. (2005). Conversational common ground and memory processes in language production. *Discourse Processes, 40*(1), 1–35.

Indrarathne, B., & Kormos, J. (2016). Attentional processing of input in explicit and implicit conditions. *Studies in Second Language Acquisition, 39*.

Kern, R., Ware, P., & Warschauer, M. (2008). Network-based language teaching. In N. Hornberger (Ed.), *Encyclopedia of language and education* (pp. 1374–1385). New York: Springer Science+Business Media, LLC.

Kim, Y., & McDonough, K. (2008). Learners' production of passives during syntactic priming activities. *Applied Linguistics, 29*(1), 149–154.

Lai, C., & Zhao, Y. (2006). Noticing and text-based chat. *Language Learning and Technology, 10*(3), 102–120.

McDonough, K. (2006). Interaction and syntactic priming: English L2 speakers' production of dative constructions. *Studies in Second Language Acquisition, 28*(2), 179–207.

McDonough, K., & Chaikitmongkol, W. (2010). Collaborative syntactic priming activities and EFL learners' production of wh-questions. *Canadian Modern Language Review, 66*(6), 817–841.

McDonough, K., & De Vleeschauwer, J. (2012). Prompt-type frequency, auditory pattern discrimination, and EFL learners' production of wh-questions. *Studies in Second Language Acquisition, 34*(3), 355–377.

McDonough, K., & Fulga, A. (2015). The detection and primed production of novel constructions. *Language Learning, 65*(2), 326–357.

McDonough, K., & Kim, Y. (2009). Syntactic priming, type frequency, and EFL learners' production of wh-questions. *The Modern Language Journal, 93*(3), 386–398.

McDonough, K., & Mackey, A. (2006). Responses to recasts: Repetitions, primed production, and linguistic development. *Language Learning, 56*(4), 693–720.

Marsden, E., Altmann, G., & St Claire, M. (2013). Priming of verb inflections in L1 and L2 French: A comparison of "redundant" versus "non-redundant" training conditions. *International Review of Applied Linguistics in Language Teaching, 51*(3), 271–298.

Michel, M. (in press). Practising online with your peers: The role of text-chat for second language development. In C. Jones (Ed.), *Practice in second language learning*. Cambridge: Cambridge University Press.

Örnberg Berglund, T. (2012). Corrective feedback and noticing in text-based second language interaction. In L. Bradley & S. Thouësny (Eds.), *CALL: Using, learning, knowing, EUROCALL Conference, Gothenburg, Sweden, 22–25 August 2012, Proceedings* (pp. 234–239). Research-publishing.net.

Örnberg Berglund, T. (2013). Text-based chat and language learning. Opportunities and challenges. In A. Sundberg, C. Rosén, & P. Simfors (Eds.), *ASLA 2012 Proceedings* (pp. 139–149). Uppsala: ASLA.

O'Rourke, B. (2008). The other C in CMC: What alternative data sources can tell us about text-based synchronous computer mediated communication and language learning. *Computer Assisted Language Learning, 21*(3), 227–251.

O'Rourke, B. (2012). Using eye tracking to investigate gaze behaviour in synchronous computer-mediated communication for language learning. In M. Dooly & R. O'Dowd (Eds.), *Researching online interaction and exchange in foreign language education: Methods and issues* (pp. 305–341). Frankfurt am Main: Peter Lang.

Pickering, M. J., & Branigan, H. P. (1999). Syntactic priming in language production. *Trends in Cognitive Sciences, 3*(4), 136–141.

Pickering, M. J., & Ferreira, V. S. (2008). Structural priming: A critical review. *Psychological Bulletin, 134*(3), 427–459.

Pickering, M. J., & Garrod, S. (2004). Toward a mechanistic psychology of dialogue. *Behavioral and Brain Sciences, 27*(2), 169–226.

Robinson, P. (1995). Attention, memory, and the "noticing" hypothesis. *Language Learning, 45*(2), 283–331.

Sauro, S. (2009). Computer-mediated corrective feedback and the development of second language grammar. *Language Learning and Technology, 13*(1), 96–120.

Sauro, S. (2011). SCMC for SLA: A research synthesis. *CALICO Journal, 28*, 369–391.

Sauro, S., & Smith, B. (2010). Investigating L2 performance in text chat. *Applied Linguistics, 31*(4), 554–577.

Schmidt, R. (1990). The role of consciousness in second language learning. *Applied Linguistics, 11*, 129–158.

Schmidt, R. (1994). Implicit learning and the cognitive unconscious: Of artificial grammars and SLA. In N. Ellis (Ed.), *Implicit and explicit learning of languages* (pp. 165–209). London: Academic Press.

Schmidt, R. (2001). Attention. In P. Robinson (Ed.), *Cognition and second language instruction* (pp. 3–32). New York: Cambridge University Press.

Shin, J., & Christianson, K. (2012). Structural priming and second language learning. *Language Learning, 62*(3), 931–964.

Smith, B. (2005). The relationship between negotiated interaction, learner uptake, and lexical acquisition in task-based computer-mediated communication. *TESOL Quarterly, 39*(1), 33–58.

Smith, B. (2010). Employing eye-tracking technology in researching the effectiveness of recasts in CMC. In F. M. Hult (Ed.), *Directions and prospects for educational linguistics* (pp. 79–98). New York: Springer.

Smith, B. (2012). Eye-tracking as a measure of noticing: A study of explicit recasts in SCMC. *Language Learning and Technology, 16*(3), 53–81.

Smith, B., & Renaud, C. (2013). Using eye tracking as a measure of foreign language learners' noticing of recasts during computer-mediated writing conferences. In K. McDonough & A. Mackey (Eds.), *Teaching second language interaction in diverse educational contexts* (pp. 147–166). Amsterdam/Philadelphia: John Benjamins.

Swain, M. (2005). The output hypothesis: Theory and research. In E. Hinkel (Ed.), *Handbook of second language teaching and learning* (pp. 471–483). Mahwah, NJ: Lawrence Erlbaum Associates.

Sykes, J. M. (2005). Synchronous CMC and pragmatic development: Effects of oral and written chat. *CALICO Journal, 22*(3), 399–431.

Tannen, D. (1987). Repetition in conversation: Toward a poetics of talk. *Language, 63*(3), 574–605.

Tomlin, R. S., & Villa, V. (1994). Attention in cognitive science and SLA. *Studies in Second Language Acquisition, 16*(2), 183–203.

Trofimovich, P. (2013). Interactive alignment: A teaching-friendly view of second language pronunciation learning. *Language Teaching, 49*(3), 411–422.

Trofimovich, P., & McDonough, K. (Eds.). (2011). *Applying priming methods to L2 learning, teaching and research: Insights from psycholinguistics.* Amsterdam/Philadelphia: John Benjamins.

Trofimovich, P., Mcdonough, K., & Neumann, H. (2013). Using collaborative tasks to elicit auditory and structural priming. *TESOL Quarterly, 47*(1), 177–186.

Uzum, B. (2010). An investigation of alignment in CMC from a sociocognitive perspective. *CALICO Journal, 28*(1), 135–155.

Ziegler, N. (2016). Taking technology to task: Technology-mediated TBLT, performance, and production. *Annual Review of Applied Linguistics, 36,* 136–163.

APPENDIX

Week 1: Getting to Know Your Partner

Task 1

Try to collect the following information from your partner. In turn, you will be asked to chat a bit about yourself and your studies. You have 15 minutes to get to know your partner.

A. Name:

B. Age:

C. Gender: male/female

D. Mother tongue/cultural background?

E. How long has your partner been in the UK/USA?

F. What is your partner studying?

G. Has your partner ever learned a language through CALL (computer-assisted language learning)?

H. Ask some more details about this experience, e.g., what did your partner like or dislike about it?

I. Does your partner have experience with online teaching?

J. Ask some more details about this experience, e.g., what did your partner like or dislike about it?

K. Anything else you want to know and ask. . .

14

TASK MODALITY, NOTICING, AND THE CONTINGENCY OF RECASTS

Insights on Salience From Multiple Modalities

Nicole Ziegler

Introduction

The Role of Noticing in SLA

The importance of noticing for second language acquisition (SLA) is well-attested, with a number of scholars proposing different frameworks to explain the role of attention and awareness of L2 learning and development. Schmidt's Noticing Hypothesis (Schmidt, 2001), for example, posits that noticing, defined as attention plus awareness, is a necessary condition for SLA, stating that "noticing requires of the learner a conscious apprehension and awareness of input" (p. 26). In other words, although second language (L2) learning without intention or understanding is possible, awareness at the level of noticing—in which learners consciously register a form—is necessary for L2 development to occur. Robinson (1995, 2003) also suggests that noticing is a necessary condition for SLA, but extends the operationalization to include detection plus rehearsal in short-term memory, in which activation due to the allocation of attentional resources takes place. Similarly, Gass (1997) highlighted the role of apperception as the first stage in processing input, in which "the apperceived input is that bit of language which is noticed by the learner because of some particular features" (p. 202), and then consciously relating this to "some prior knowledge" (p. 201). These processes are what facilitate the transformation of input into intake, allowing for internalization and the restructuring of a learners' interlanguage (IL).

In addition, the construct of noticing has featured prominently in the interaction approach to SLA (e.g., Long, 1996; Gass & Mackey, 2007), playing a critical role in terms of negotiation and feedback as part of the interaction-driven L2 learning process (Mackey, 2012). For example, receiving feedback and participating in negotiation may support learners' L2 development by providing both positive and negative evidence, which as Gass and Mackey (2006) point out, can aid learners in noticing their erroneous utterances and focusing their attention on the target language, thereby preparing learners to be more observant regarding future instances of linguistic input and the testing of their linguistic hypotheses. In addition, production of output may also promote noticing, by offering learners opportunities to reflect on their and their interlocutors' language. Furthermore, forms that are more salient—that is, more visually, auditorily, or communicatively prominent—may be more likely to be noticed and acquired over more non-salient forms or features (Leeman, 2003). However, as Leeman (2003) points out, the salience of a form does not ensure that it will be noticed by learners, nor do learners attend to only salient forms. The degree to which learners actively attend to—or direct their cognitive resources to—features in the input is affected by a wide range of factors, including developmental readiness (Mackey, 2012), task conditions (e.g., Robinson, 1995; Skehan, 1996), and individual differences (e.g., Long, Inagaki, & Ortega, 1998; Mackey & Sachs, 2012). Previous research has suggested that corrective feedback, such as recasts, may enhance the salience of target forms by juxtaposing a learner's erroneous utterance with the correct utterance (the recast) (Leeman, 2003), facilitating learners' noticing and possibly leading to restructuring of their interlanguage and subsequent L2 development (Schmidt & Frota, 1986).

Recasts, Salience, and Noticing

Recasts can be defined as the reformulation of all or part of a learner's immediately preceding utterance in which one or more nontarget-like item(s) are replaced by the corresponding target form, and where the focus is on meaning rather than form or object (Long, 2007). Research has shown that recasts may facilitate L2 development as they enhance the salience of the target feature and direct learners to contrast their erroneous utterances with their interlocutors' reformulations (Doughty & Varela, 1998; Goo & Mackey, 2013; Leeman, 2003; Long, 1996, 2007), thereby focusing learners' attentional resources on the target form. Research also suggests that recasts may be more salient for adult learners due to their increased cognitive capacity for linguistic analysis and more intentional approach to learning (Muñoz, 2010). However, research has also demonstrated that the salience of recasts—specifically the extent to which they are consciously attended to and noticed by learners (Mackey, 2012), and thus the impact of recasts on learning—may be affected by a variety of factors, such as target feature (Egi, 2007), setting (Oliver, 2000), and task characteristics (Révész, Sachs, & Mackey, 2011). For example, studies indicate that the salience of the target linguistic feature may mediate the positive benefits associated with recasts, as learners' attention and uptake of L2 forms may be mediated by the relative communicative importance of those forms in expressing and interpreting meaning (VanPatten, 1996). Drawing on theories of associative learning, N. Ellis (2006) outlines how experience attending to common non-redundant linguistic cues to make meaning may lead learners to overlook other cues which may be relevant to utterance interpretation. In terms of corrective feedback, including recasts as well as negotiation, learners might more readily recognize feedback that targets more salient forms (e.g., lexis and phonology) compared to less salient features (e.g., morphosyntax) (Mackey, 2012; Mackey, Gass, & McDonough, 2000). Recasts may also be provided more often in response to the erroneous production of non-salient forms (morphosyntax), despite the contention that they may not always constitute sufficient negative evidence (e.g., Mackey et al., 2000; Nicholas, Lightbown, & Spada, 2001; Leeman, 2003). Furthermore, some scholars have questioned how frequently learners correctly recognize recasts as feedback and integrate the correction into their own language output (Lyster & Ranta, 1997). In other words, because recasts are thought to fall on the more implicit end of the continuum of explicitness (Mackey, 2012), recasts as a form of corrective feedback may be less salient to learners than other forms, such as metalinguistic feedback. Despite these potential challenges with the salience of recasts, Long (2007) advocates that recasts are beneficial regardless of error type, arguing instead that it is their contingency and juxtaposition to non-targetlike utterances that drives their efficacy.

The importance of contingency has also been highlighted by other scholars (e.g., Gass, 2003; Lai, Fei, & Roots, 2008; Saxton, 1997), with research suggesting that the corrective potential of negative evidence is affected by the "proximity of the response to an error" (Saxton, 1997, p. 145). For example, according to Saxton's Direct Contrast Hypothesis, when a child produces an erroneous utterance that is immediately responded to with the correct form, the child may then perceive this form as being in contrast with the previously uttered and deviant form. Recognition and awareness of this contrast may then form the foundation for the child to understand the provided form as the correct alternative to the original form. As Gass (2003) points out, this is similar to the idea of learners 'noticing the gap' between their erroneous production and the target form. Similar to the role of contingency in the development of a child's first language (L1), the adjacency of the correct and incorrect forms is thus helpful in creating a conflict or contrast, thereby drawing the learner's attention to the erroneous form. Because this contrast can be enhanced using corrective feedback, such as recasts, contingency may play a substantial role in the salience of feedback (Lai et al., 2008).

Overall, although some studies have found that recasts may be unlikely to lead to acquisition (e.g., Lyster, 2004; Lyster & Ranta, 1997), research has empirically demonstrated the effectiveness of recasts on learners' L2 development (see Mackey and Goo [2007] for a review). However, despite the growing interest in technology and tasks (Ziegler, 2016a), few studies have empirically examined the extent to which the salience and noticing of recasts are affected by modality (Gurzynski-Weiss & Baralt, 2015; Lai et al., 2008).

The Impact of Computer-Mediated Communication on Salience and Noticing

A growing body of research has proposed advantages for salience and noticing, and thus subsequent L2 development, in interaction in computer-mediated contexts (e.g., Smith, 2004, 2010). For example, researchers have argued that because text-chat provides learners with a written record of their interactions, they are afforded more opportunities to reflect on the discourse (Beauvois, 1992), to notice new target items as well as the gaps in their IL (Kelm, 1992), and enhance incidental noticing

(Warschauer, 1997), than might be found in traditional face-to-face (FTF) environments. For instance, Pellettieri (2000) argues that the additional time for monitoring and processing in synchronous computer-mediated communication (SCMC), in which learners interact in real time through text, video, or multimodal chat, facilitates learners' noticing, thereby enabling their L2 development. Numerous scholars have argued that the unique characteristics of SCMC, specifically within the written mode of text-chat, provide learners with enhanced salience in terms of input and feedback, as learners are provided with additional chances to review the output of both interlocutors and longer processing times than might be found in FTF interaction (Smith, 2004). These potential benefits may then lead to increased opportunities for learners to focus on form, providing improved chances for L2 development (Salaberry, 2000). In their study examining the relationship between learners' verbalizations, gestures, and scrolling, Smith and Gorsuch (2004) found an increased attention to form, while Smith's (2010) study used eye-tracking technology to examine the relationship between recasts, noticing, and uptake, providing tangible evidence of what learners attended to in the input and feedback. In addition, Payne and Whitney (2002) found that learners reported noticing their mistakes more frequently in SCMC chat environments than in FTF interaction, suggesting that mode may have played a role in improving noticing and self-monitoring.

In particular, text-chat has been argued to enhance the salience of target forms and corrective feedback (e.g., Long, 2007; Smith, 2004, 2010; Yilmaz, 2012), with research demonstrating advantages for computer-mediated contexts. For example, the results of Yilmaz and Yuksel (2011) indicate improved L2 development following recasts provided in SCMC contexts compared to FTF contexts. More recently, Yuksel and Inan (2014) compared SCMC and FTF, finding that learners noticed negotiation for meaning more often in the SCMC condition than in FTF, suggesting that modality may have played a role in enhancing noticing and the salience of feedback. Seeking to provide empirical evidence for the hypothesis that SCMC supports enhanced salience and greater opportunities for noticing, Lai and Zhao (2006) employed stimulated recall (SR) protocols, finding that learner-learner interaction in text-chat promoted noticing more than in FTF contexts, particularly in regards to learners' monitoring and noticing of their own errors.

In addition to the noticing of corrective feedback, research has examined the relationship between noticing and modified output, a critical component for L2 development as it allows for the comparison of structures and deeper processing than might be found in only receptive learning (Swain, 2005). Gurzynski-Weiss and Baralt (2015) investigated the relationship between learners' noticing of corrective feedback, production of modified output, and communication mode. Results demonstrated that there were no significant differences across mode in terms of noticing feedback or the target of feedback. However, after accounting for error type, findings indicated that partial modified output resulted in greater noticing in the SCMC condition, suggesting that modality may have helped to make target forms more salient for the learners than in the FTF condition. Not all research indicates positive benefits for technology, however. For example, Gurzynski-Weiss and Baralt (2014) found significantly fewer opportunities for learners to modify output and significantly less modified output produced in text-chat when compared to FTF, suggesting that there may be fewer available opportunities for noticing and its subsequent developmental benefits. However, little research has addressed the relationship among feedback, modified output, noticing, and modality (although see Baralt, 2010; Gurzynski-Weiss & Baralt, 2014, 2015; Smith, 2010). In addition, the majority of the research has focused on the (dis)advantages of written text-chat, highlighting the need for further research examining the role of other modalities, particularly oral SCMC (Pellettieri, 2000; Smith, 2003; Toyoda & Harrison, 2002; Ziegler, 2016b).

In addition, although results regarding the enhanced salience of feedback in computer-mediated contexts are encouraging, scholars have highlighted the possible negative impact of non-contingent recasts provided during split negotiation routines on salience (e.g., Lai et al., 2008; Smith, 2012), a common occurrence in CMC. For example, because the juxtaposition of non-targetlike utterances and corrective feedback may occur multiple turns apart, thereby potentially reducing the contrast between forms (Saxton, 1997), the salience of the feedback may be reduced (Sauro, 2009). Empirical evidence demonstrating that learners notice contingent recasts significantly more often than non-contingent recasts (Lai et al., 2008) seems to support these claims. Importantly, because the developmental benefits associated with recasts are thought to stem from their ability to enhance the salience of target forms (Leeman, 2003), further research examining whether there are indeed negative impacts on salience due to the contingency of recasts is needed.

Research Questions

The current research aims to address these gaps in the literature by investigating the following research questions:

RQ1: What are the effects of modality (FTF, text-chat, video-chat) on learners' noticing of recasts?
RQ2: What impact does the contingency of recasts have on learners' noticing?
RQ3: What is the relationship between mode, modified output, and learners' noticing?

Methodology

Participants

Participants in the study were 14 intermediate-advanced learners of English enrolled in two sections of an advanced listening and speaking course within an English for Academic purposes program at a large Pacific university in the United States. The average TOEFL score of the participants was 83.9 ($SD = 9.0$) out of a possible score of 120. Considering that the minimum TOEFL score required for admittance to many English-speaking universities is usually in the 60–80 score range, learners in this study were considered to be at an advanced level of proficiency. The L1 backgrounds of the participants included Chinese (n = 7), Japanese (n = 6), and Vietnamese (n = 1). All had an average of 10.9 (SD = 2.42) years of experience studying English in foreign language contexts. The activities in the course typically consist of small group and pair interaction, and all participants had prior exposure to the type of information-gap task used in the study. The average length of residence in years of the participants was 1.01 (SD = 1.41 years), with little other prior experience living in or visiting English-speaking countries, indicating that most had recently had their first major exposure to the L2 learning context (though two participants had been living in the United States for approximately three years each). Participants also reported high familiarity and comfort with using technology on a daily basis, though none of the participants reported previous experience using SCMC for English language learning purposes.

The interlocutor was a researcher assisting with the project, a 28-year old L1 English PhD student at the university whose research focus was task-based language teaching and interaction, and who had more than five years of foreign and second language teaching experience with young adults, university-aged students, and non-university adults. The researcher-interlocutor was comfortable using technology for language teaching purposes, and at the time of the project, had more than three years of experience conducting private English lessons using video-conferencing and text-chat.

Materials

Materials in the study included three versions of a spot-the-difference task, chosen because of its potential to provide the ideal conditions for negotiation of meaning and opportunities for feedback to occur (Pica, Kanagy, & Falodun, 1993). Each version contained two pictures containing at least 10 differences. Though participants were familiar with this type of task, they were nevertheless reminded that the goal of the task was to find as many differences as possible. The pictures selected for the study were specifically chosen to be balanced in terms of scene familiarity (a kitchen, park, or hill scene), number of elements, distribution of differences, and visual density (number of elements per quarter of the picture). All three tasks were counterbalanced for both version (A or B) and scene (kitchen, park, or hill), and evenly delivered across the FTF, video-chat, and text-chat modes. The tasks were piloted with participants from the same class sections that were not part of the current research project in order to determine how long each task took. Both the FTF and video-chat conditions took approximately 8 minutes while the text-chat took approximately 17 minutes. These times were used as guidelines for completion of the tasks in order to minimize fatigue and boredom, and to make sure the entire session was completed within a reasonable time frame (approximately 45–50 minutes). Similar to Gurzynski-Weiss and Baralt (2014), the extra time in the text-chat mode was not assumed to lead to differential amounts of feedback, given that the participants were observed to take this extra time to formulate and prepare their descriptions, as well as review their output prior to message transmission.

Stimulated Recall Protocol

To measure the salience and noticing of recasts provided across the three modes, the current study adopted stimulated recall protocols (SR), a commonly used retrospective measure of cognitive processes (Gass & Mackey, 2000, 2017) in which participants are presented with stimuli (in the case of this study) via video (i.e., their task performance) and asked to comment on their thought processes during the original interaction, either at specific points pre-selected by the researcher or whenever they felt it was pertinent to do so (see the upcoming "Procedure" section for more information). Specific questions were adapted from Gurzynski-Weiss and Baralt (2014), and were designed to elicit the participants' introspective thoughts at the time of the interaction. Following Gass and Mackey (2000), care was taken during the protocols not to "lead" the participants into analyzing past actions in the present; rather, through a series of prompts (e.g., *"What were you thinking about your participation at that time?"; "What were you thinking about the interaction between you and your partner?"*; Gurzynski-Weiss & Baralt, 2014, p. 37) participants were encouraged to verbalize their thoughts during the interaction itself, focusing on the time of the recall. Additionally, at the end of the stimulated recall, participants were encouraged to report on their preference of mode, the relative advantages/disadvantages they saw in each, and other comments related to task-based performance across modes.

Background and Exit Questionnaire

A two-part questionnaire (background and exit) was administered to the participants before (background) and after (exit) the task-based interaction. The background questionnaire contained questions asking about computer use habits/comfort, native language, language learning experience, length of residence in English-speaking countries, standardized test scores, and time spent using English with native/non-native speakers in their daily life. To obtain information regarding students' perceptions of the benefits/drawbacks of each mode, an exit questionnaire examined which mode was more enjoyable, preferred, perceived to be more beneficial for learning, and which mode was most difficult. However, because much of this information was also addressed during the SRs, the results of the exit questionnaire are not reported in this paper.

Procedure

Each participant met with the researcher-interlocutor in a quiet office to conduct the three interactive tasks. Following an explanation of the purpose of the research, participants signed consent forms and filled out the background information questionnaire. The participants then proceeded to complete the interactional tasks with the researcher-interlocutor. The FTF tasks were conducted with the researcher-interlocutor and participant seated facing each other in desk-matching chairs. Neither the researcher-interlocutor nor participant showed the other their picture during the task, but the close-quarters FTF interaction did allow for gestures to be used to help communicate meaning. Feedback was provided in a variety of ways by the researcher-interlocutor (including negotiation triggers, explicit correction, and recasts) wherever it seemed natural and appropriate, addressing a range of errors including lexis, morphosyntax, phonology (in FTF and video-chat), and orthography (unique to text-chat). Both the video-chat and text-chat were completed on separate PCs in separate rooms (with the researcher-interlocutor moving to a separate office) using the Skype video-conferencing software. The FTF interaction and video-chat interactions were recorded using a Sony PCM-M10 audio recorder and Sony Handycam CX-160 positioned over the shoulder of the researcher-interlocutor (FTF) and participant (video-chat). The text-chat was recorded via the open-source screen capture program ShareX. These videos were subsequently used as the stimulus input for the stimulated recalls. Following the tasks, the participants completed the exit questionnaire. Within 24 hours, the participants returned to the same quiet research office and met with the researcher to participate in the stimulated recall protocols. The SRs were conducted in the same order in which the tasks were administered to maintain consistency. The participants were told that the purpose of the video-watching procedure was to understand what the participants were thinking while performing a task in different modes. They were then informed that the researcher would be stopping the video recording at various points to elicit commentary, but that the participants were free to pause the video and comment at any time. In order to avoid listener fatigue and to complete the SR session within a reasonable time frame (approximately 60 minutes), the text-chat video was viewed at 2x speed, and the participants were instructed to inform the researcher if the video was progressing too fast for them to process; no learners reported having any problems with the increased speed of the video.

Coding and Analysis

The dataset for the current study consisted of the recorded interaction in all three modes (FTF, text-chat, video-chat) and comments from the stimulated recalls. The interaction data were transcribed and then examined in terms of the nature/type of student errors (morphosyntax, lexis, phonology, and orthography); interlocutor feedback (recasts); contingency of recasts (following Lai et al., 2008); opportunities for modified output (MOO); and actual modified output (MO). The stimulated recall data were coded in terms of noticing.

Error Type/Recasts

Participant errors were coded for morphosyntax and lexis (in all modes), phonology (in FTF and video-chat), and orthography (text-chat). Examples and definitions of each error type are provided in Examples 1–6.

Lexical Errors

Lexical errors we operationalized as the inappropriate use of a word in a given context, or words directly transferred over from their L1 and misapplied to L2 use. An example (1) of a lexical error is given below:

(1) Lexis   *And he might have been bitten by a bee.*

Error: Use of 'bitten' instead of 'stung.'

Morphosyntax Errors

Morphosyntax errors were operationalized as the incorrect inflection of verbs for tense, possession, plurality, etc.; the omission/inappropriacy of article use, prepositions, etc.; and errors in word order. An example (2) of a morphosyntactic error is given below:

(2) Morphosyntax   *I have her in left side.*

Error: Incorrect use of preposition (in → on).

Phonological Errors

Phonological errors were operationalized as the non-targetlike pronunciation in terms of segmental errors including stress placement and non-targetlike consonant/vowel sounds and clusters. An example (3) of a phonological error is given below:

(3) Phonological   *And wear a [sleɪpər]*.*

Error: Incorrect vowel sound in the word 'slipper.'

Orthographic Errors

Orthographic (or spelling) errors occurred uniquely in the text-chat mode (the only written mode). They were distinguished from lexical errors when it was evident that the participant knew the correct word but provided the correct spelling, often (but not always) a phonological transfer of L1-influenced pronunciation of the word into the written mode. Example (4) illustrates this:

(4) Orthographic   *So there is a CD hanging from a ramp?*

Error: 'lamp' misspelled as 'ramp'; participant was L1 Japanese, which has notable difficulty with the /r-l/ contrast in speech.

Recasts

Following previous research (e.g., Gurzynski-Weiss & Baralt, 2014), recasts were provided wherever and whenever it seemed natural and appropriate to do so, with an overall priority on maintaining communicative flow; as such, not every error produced by the participants were subject to corrective feedback. Recasts were coded in accordance with the oft-referenced operationalization found in the task-based language teaching and focus-on-form literature. According to Long (2007), recasts are:

> reformulation(s) of all or part of a learner's immediately preceding utterance in which one or more non-targetlike items is/are replaced by the corresponding target language form(s) and where, throughout the exchange, the focus of the interlocutors is on meaning, not language as object.
>
> (p. 77)

A distinction was not made between partial and full recasts in this study. Full recasts were defined as a reformulation of the entire preceding utterance, error, while partial recasts were coded as instances where the native-speaking interlocutor provided a reduced recast which only contained some of the information in the preceding utterance, specifically the targetlike reformulation of the erroneous error segment (Loewen & Philp, 2006). Two examples (5, 6) of recasts are given below:

Full Recast

(5) Participant: *So (.) the left bottom part.*
Researcher: *The bottom left part, okay*

Partial Recast

(6) Participant: *On the right corner there are a man and a woman.*
Researcher: *In the right corner, yeah.*

In coding the transcripts, each recast was reviewed in reference to the video-records in order to: 1) ensure that recasts were coded that addressed a form-based (not meaning-based) problem; and 2) distinguish them from confirmation checks, a common signal used to indicate comprehension difficulty and initiate negotiation for meaning in interaction (Pica, 1987). In addition, recasts were coded as being contingent or non-contingent (non-contingent recasts were coded as those which were separated from non-targetlike utterances by discussion or comment about a different point or element of the picture, and which were non-adjacent; see Lai et al., 2008). An example of each of these is presented below in (7) and (8).

Contingent

(7) Participant: *What is the color of the chair which the man sit on?-*
Researcher: *That the man is sitting on? Red.*

Non-Contingent

(8) Participant: *A man taking a picture* → error
Participant: *A bird in front of his camera*
Researcher: *There is a man taking a picture?* → non-contingent recast (separated by meaning and position)

Modified Output Opportunities/Modified Output (MOO/MO)

Following Gurzynski-Weiss and Baralt (2015) and Oliver (2000), MOO was operationalized as instances following recasts when there was time and space for learners to produce modified output in the turn following the feedback. Affirmative and negative opportunities for output are shown in examples (9) and (10):

(9) Participant: *Yeah and gl- (1.0) old man wear glasses?*
    Researcher: *He's wearing glasses?* → + MOO
    Participant: *Yeah*

(10) Participant: *What is the color of the chair which the man sit on?*
     Researcher: *That the man is sitting on* → − MOO
     Researcher: *It's red*
     Researcher: *How about the empty chair*

MO was coded binarily: as either the presence or absence of modified output (+/− MO). Following standards in SLA research, MO was operationalized as a participant's complete or partial correction of the error identified in their non-targetlike utterance in the preceding turn, which could be more or less targetlike; this decision was made given the importance ascribed to the psycholinguistic *processes* behind as opposed to the linguistic *product* of MO (e.g., McDonough & Mackey, 2006). Examples of +/− MO are shown in examples (11) and (12).

(11) Participant: *There is a man (.) hurting? hurting: his feet?*
     Researcher: *Holding his foot?*
     Participant: *Yeah (.) holding both his feet- Uh one- left feet- left foot* → + MO

(12) Participant: *Yeah uh biting the pen and*
     Researcher: *Yeah she's holding a paintbrush in her mouth*
     Participant: *Uh huh* → − MO

Noticing in Stimulated Recalls

The stimulated recall comments were coded by the researcher binarily according to whether or not they reported conscious awareness of their error in response to the researcher-interlocutor's feedback. An example of noticing is found in example (13):

(13) P4   Mmm, there are two (.) uh there are one (2.0) old man?
     R1   Mmm
     P4   And also there is a one elderly- elder woman
     R1   Yep, one elderly woman
     P4   Yeah and also . . .

   SR Comment

   Researcher: *What do you remember thinking of our interaction at this?*
   Participant: *Yeah I said "elder woman" but that's not- that's incorrect so he corrected me.* → + Noticing

In contrast, comments which were classified as not noticing generally related to the participants' perception of the interaction between themselves and the researcher-interlocutor as being due to a *meaning* not *form* problem; a lack of any specific thoughts about that point in the interaction; or other comments not related to perception of one's own error. Example (14) demonstrates an example of non-noticing:

(14) P1   So like a uh ceiling there's a-
     R1   Mhmm
     P1   -a light, and has a CD like hang there
     R1   So on the ceiling there's a light and there's a CD hanging from it?
     P1   Yeah

SR Comment

Researcher: *So what were you- what were you thinking at this time.*
Participant: *At this time?*
Researcher: *Yeah*
Participant: *I was just describing what I see. [The research-interlocutor] was just listening to me and what I said, trying to figure out differences.* → − Noticing

Analysis

Because salience refers to a psychological construct, it can be difficult to define and measure. In order to facilitate a quantitative analysis, this paper follows Mackey's (2012) suggestion that salience depends on a learner's level of noticing. Thus, the primary dependent variable of interest in the current study was participants' (binary) noticing. Independent variables and analysis differed based on the research question. For RQ1, examining learners' noticing across mode, a repeated-measures design was adopted with three levels (FTF, text-chat, video-chat). For RQ2, examining the contingency of recasts and noticing, logistic regression was run with contingency as the independent variable. For RQ3, examining the relationship between mode, modified output, and noticing, multiple regression analysis was conducted, with mode and modified output as predictor variables for learners' noticing of feedback. Finally, descriptive statistics on error type according to noticing and mode are presented to provide a more detailed picture of how noticing varies according to linguistic target of feedback in FTF, text-chat, and video-chat interactions.

Results

RQ1: *What are the Effects of Modality (FTF, Text-Chat, Video-Chat) on Learners' Noticing of Recasts?*

To examine the effects of different modes of interaction on learners' noticing of recasts, the proportional scores (the frequencies of noticing divided by the number of received recasts) across three modes of interaction were analyzed using a one-way

TABLE 14.1 Descriptive statistics for noticing, mode, and recasts

N = 14	FTF	Video	Text
Total recasts provided	74	74	87
Total recasts noticed	24	32	30
Mean (SD) % noticing	0.29 (0.26)	0.39 (0.27)	0.37 (0.31)
Mean (SD) recasts provided	5.29 (2.40)	5.29 (2.49)	6.21 (1.78)
Mean (SD) recasts noticed	1.71 (1.62)	2.29 (2.19)	2.14 (1.60)

repeated measures ANOVA after checking for all the statistical assumptions. The results indicate that there was no statistical difference across the three modes ($F(2, 26) = .443, p = .647, \eta^2 = 0.33$), suggesting that learners' noticing of recasts is not modulated by the modes of interaction. Descriptive statistics for noticing levels across modality are presented in Table 14.1.

RQ2: *What Impact Does the Contingency of Recasts Have on Learners' Noticing?*

To examine the claim that the noticing of recasts in text-based SCMC may be mediated by their contingency with the triggering error (Lai et al., 2008), the text-chat transcripts were examined in further detail. Results indicate that the vast majority of recasts delivered by the researcher-interlocutor (89.7%) were contingent. A total of 78 such recasts were identified, 28 of which (36%) were reported as being noticed in the SR protocols. Only nine instances of non-contingent recasts could be identified in the transcripts, however—two of which (22%) were noticed. Because there was a marked difference between the number of contingent and non-contingent recasts provided overall, inferential analyses were not conducted due to violations of variance. Rather, descriptive statistics are reported in Table 14.2.

RQ3: *What is the Relationship Between Modality, Modified Output, and Learners' Noticing?*

First, to ensure that the amount of modified output was not influenced by the number of modified output opportunities (MOO) following interlocutor feedback, opportunities were coded and compared across all three modes. Results of a one-way repeated measures ANOVA revealed no significant differences between the amount of MOO provided in FTF ($M = 5.36, SD = 2.62$), video-chat ($M = 5.29, SD = 2.58$), or text-chat ($M = 4.43, SD = 2.38$) conditions ($F(2, 26) = 0.476, p = .627$). After checking the statistical assumptions, a logistic regression was performed to examine the relationship between learners' modified output and noticing of recasts

TABLE 14.2 Descriptive statistics for noticing and contingency

	Total number	Percent of total	Number noticed	Percentage Noticed
Contingent RC	78	89.7%	28	36%
Non-contingent RC	9	10.3%	2	22%

across the three modes of interaction (FTF, video-chat, and text-chat). The data were set up in such a way that the participants' binarily-coded MO and noticing were respectively combined for each mode. In doing this, individual participants were discarded as the focus of the analysis, and emphasis was placed on individual recasts; thus, the total number of cases of both MO and noticing in each mode was equal to the total number of recasts delivered in that mode (74 for FTF and video-chat, and 87 for text-chat). In other words, for each participant and for each recast, we coded both MO and noticing as either 0 (−) or 1(+), and aligned them in vertical columns according to mode. These data were then submitted to logistic regression analysis.

Results indicate that for the face-to-face interaction, the logistic regression model was statistically significant, $\chi^2(1) = 23.51, p < .01$. The output modification explained approximately 40% (Nagelkerke R^2) of the variance in the participants' noticing of recasts and correctly classified 77.5% of cases. In other words, when learners modified their output it was 17.55 times more likely that they accurately noticed recasts than when they did not modify their production following the provision of feedback (odds ratio = 17.55). Similarly, the logistic regression model was also statistically significant in the video-chat with $\chi^2(1) = 15.07$, odds ratio = 8.5, $p < .01$. In other words, when learners in the video-chat condition produced modified output, they were 8.5 times more likely to notice recasts. The variance in learners' noticing can be 25.6% explained by their modified output (Nagelkerke $R^2 = 0.256$), and the model correctly classified 73.2% of cases. Thus, for FTF and video-chat, the results suggest that modified output was significantly predictive of learners' noticing. However, the relationship between modified output, recasts, and noticing in the text-chat interaction was less clear, with results indicating that the model was not statistically significant, $\chi^2(1) = 3.68$, odds ratio = 3.37, $p > .05$, and Nagelkerke $R^2 = 0.058$. Table 14.3 provides detailed descriptive information on mode of interaction, modified output, and noticing.

TABLE 14.3 Learner noticing in relation to modified output and mode

	Modified Output		
	− MO	+ MO	Totals
	FTF (74 recast episodes)		
− Notice	40 (80.0%)	10 (20.0%)	**50**
+ Notice	4 (16.6%)	20 (83.4%)	**24**
Totals	44 (59.5%)	30 (40.5%)	**74**
	Video-chat (74 recast episodes)		
− Notice	39 (92.9%)	3 (7.1%)	**42**
+ Notice	15 (46.9%)	17 (53.1%)	**32**
Totals	54 (73.0%)	20 (27.0%)	**74**
	Text-chat (87 recast episodes)		
− Notice	53 (91.4%)	4 (8.6%)	**58**
+ Notice	23 (76.7%)	7 (23.3%)	**30**
Totals	76 (87.4%)	11 (12.6%)	**87**

The table is binarily organized according to two categories: provision of modified output (+/− MO), and presence of noticing (+/− Notice). Numbers in the cells of the table indicate the frequencies of co-occurrences of the two categories, with the numbers in parentheses dictating the proportion of a cell's contents in relation to the total number of recasts provided. Descriptive information in the table corroborates the statistical analysis, in that there was comparatively more noticed-modified output in the FTF and video-chat conditions compared to the text-chat condition. It should also be noted here that the FTF condition seemed to have a relatively greater amount of noticed-modified output compared to the video-chat condition as well.

Discussion

The present study investigated the role of mode of interaction in influencing the salience and noticing of recasts in task-based interaction. Using SR protocols, the analysis investigated the noticing reports of fourteen participants interacting in FTF, video-chat, and text-chat. Results indicate that in terms of noticing according to mode of interaction, there were no significant differences in proportion of noticing across any of the modes, indicating that there were no substantial differences in terms of noticing of recasts across FTF, video-chat, and text-chat interaction conditions, suggesting that the proposed advantages of text-chat, in particular, did not result in enhanced salience of target features or feedback. This result partially corresponds to previous research demonstrating a lack of differences in the noticing of recasts in FTF and text-based SCMC (Lai & Zhao, 2006). These findings seem to run counter to the claim that because of the slower-paced, permanent nature of text-based SCMC, the cognitive burden on learners may be reduced to a sufficient degree that more attention can be directed towards attending to language form, and specifically interlocutor feedback (Pellettieri, 2000; Yilmaz & Yuksel, 2011). However, there were some notable differences between the present study and previous empirical work on noticing in SCMC environments that may have influenced the current results. First, it is important to note that previous work has included different operationalizations of feedback, measures of noticing, and overall modes of interaction. For example, the positive benefits for SCMC found in Lai and Zhao (2006) were primarily realized in the form of learner self-corrections or noticing in response to negotiation sequences. The focus of the current study, on the other hand, was the salience, noticing, and contingency of recasts, and the production of modified output as variables of interest. Thus, the definition of what constitutes noticing and salience might vary across these studies, making direct comparisons more challenging.

In addition, recasts have been differentially operationalized across previous research. For instance, recasts were defined in Smith (2012) as "always sentence-length and often involved more than one linguistic change" (p. 62), and were thus labeled "explicit" recasts. The recasts delivered in the present study consisted of both partial and complete reformulations of learner utterances, which may have been less explicit, and thus less salient to learners, than those in Smith (2012). As highlighted in previous research (e.g., Mackey et al., 2000; Sheen, 2004), the varied nature of the recasts delivered in the present study may have had an influence in triggering the participants' awareness that a correction had actually occurred, given that partial reformulations may be mistaken for non-corrective repetitions naturally occurring in interaction, thus impacting both the noticing and salience of the feedback.

Although no statistically significant differences for noticing were found across modalities, qualitative data from the SRs provides support for learners' perceptions of the positive benefits of SCMC for L2 learning, particularly in terms of whether this might have enhanced the salience of target forms or recasts for learners. Analysis of interview questions at the end of the SRs indicate that learners perceived text-chat as enhancing the salience, and thus subsequent noticing, of recasts, with several participants commenting on the affordances of text-chat and its utility for checking corrections (Excerpt Set 1):

Excerpts 1

1a. P2 (SR): "In technology (referring to text-chat) you can have like a record, you can go back and to review the text you type and maybe find there are some errors."
1b. P8 (EQ): "Best aspect: We can check in the history."
1c. P11 (SR): "Typing you can see exactly what he want to say."
1d. P15 (SR): "Maybe I learned most from the text because he corrected my mistakes many times."

Furthermore, although previous research has highlighted these potential benefits for text-chat (e.g., Pellettieri, 2000; Smith, 2012), it is interesting to note the slightly greater amounts of noticing in the video-chat condition, an area of SCMC which has received relatively little research attention (Parlak & Ziegler, 2016; Yanguas, 2010, 2012). Both of these oral modes involve aural/oral processing abilities, and to some extent a potentially similar reliance on non-verbal cues to assist in negotiation of meaning (Faraco & Kida, 2008). Indeed, comments from the SRs and interviews reveal that learners perceived little to no difference between these two modes (Excerpt Set 2):

Excerpts 2

2a. P1 (EQ): "It's similar to face to face. You could see the other person and talk to him/her."
2b. P6: (SR): "It's similar to face to face, there is no big difference between face to face and video."

Importantly, although L2 development was not investigated in the current study, several comments made by the participants regarding the differential affordances of the FTF and video-chat modes indicate that there might be unique characteristics of video-chat that may support L2 learning. For example, two commonly recurring themes regarding video-chat (in a negative sense from the view of the participants) was that the audio quality was worse in the video-chat mode compared to FTF, and that the ability to use non-verbal cues for communication was limited due to the constrained field of view of the video-conferencing tool (for all sessions, participants only saw the upper bust and head of the researcher-interlocutor in the video-chat window). Comments pertaining to these points are presented in Excerpt Set 3:

Excerpts 3

3a. P3: (SR): "I prefer face-to-face . . . because the communication was most smooth and the voice was more clear than Skype."
3b. P4 (EQ): "I couldn't hear [his] voice clearly compared to face-to-face."
3c. P2 (SR): (About video-chat) "You can see each other but you cannot recognize or aware the facial expression, cannot see."
3d. P9 (SR): "I think Skype is hardest. Compare to face to face, I feel- I think we use Skype just like use the phone, we don't see each other, we don't use body language to describe things."

Due to the lack of non-verbal information from gestures and the diminished audio quality, learners may be directed to attend more carefully to their interlocutors' speech, thereby potentially increasing the salience of corrective feedback (i.e., recasts). Yanguas (2012), who compared two modes of oral CMC (audio and video) with traditional FTF interaction for their potential to enhance L2 Spanish vocabulary development, proposes similar effects for oral SCMC. Results indicate that the audio CMC group outperformed the video CMC group (but not the FTF group) in terms of listening comprehension, although no benefit was found for production or vocabulary measures. Yanguas (2010) posits that the lack of visual support during the interaction encouraged learners to allocate attention to language form, with learners self-reporting a greater focus on language use in both oral and written CMC modes compared to FTF interaction. SRs revealed similar results for the current research, suggesting that the reduced quality of speech and access to visual support may have led to increased attentional focus and greater salience in terms of target features and feedback (Excerpt 4):

Excerpt 4

4a. P4: (SR): "Also, if we use video sometimes the voice is not clear, so I also focused on listening to what [he] was saying in the video."

The second research question related to contingency of recasts and noticing in text-based interaction, in particular. Results indicated that the majority of recasts were delivered contingently (89.7%), a finding that stands in contrast to previous research and predictions (e.g., Lai et al., 2008; Smith, 2008). One explanation for these conflicting results may be that the researcher-interlocutor completing the task in the current study was highly experienced and comfortable with teaching and performing interactive tasks via text-chat. As such, in the delivery of recasts in a "natural" and "appropriate" manner, the researcher-interlocutor likely defaulted to entrenched feedback patterns which center around providing feedback as immediately as possible to ensure its relevance to the interaction. This corresponds with observations made by Gurzynski-Weiss (2016) on how prior teaching and context experience can exert a strong influence on in-the-moment feedback decisions. Additionally, the slow-paced nature of the text-based interaction, characterized by slow, methodical typing out of complete descriptions by the participants of their picture, provided ample time for the researcher-interlocutor to prepare for feedback provision. This notion supports previous findings by Ziegler and Smith (2016), which indicated that experienced teachers reported having plentiful time to respond to their interlocutor in text-based SCMC interactions, treating the interaction as a "turn-taking exercise."

The last research question sought to deepen our understanding of the relationship between modified output, recasts, and noticing across FTF, video-chat, and text-chat. Supported by the fact that there were no significant differences in terms of modified output opportunities across modes, thus adding support to the findings of Lai and Zhao (2006), results indicate that when modified output was produced, learners were significantly more likely to have noticed the preceding recast. This finding, however, was not consistent across text-chat, a finding that corresponds to previous research demonstrating that learners tend to produce less MO (and especially fully-formed MO) under SCMC conditions (Baralt, 2010; Gurzynski-Weiss & Baralt, 2015). Although Long (2007) highlights the potential for text-chat to increase the salience of feedback, and thus potentially the usability of the feedback in terms of leading to modified output and subsequent L2 development, the current results do not seem to support this hypothesis. However, the current study did not differentiate between fully and partially MO, a factor that may have affected the findings given that previous research has suggested that partially MO is predictive of noticing in both FTF and SCMC environments (Gurzynski-Weiss & Baralt, 2015). In other words, the relationship between type of modified output and mode may need further exploration at a more nuanced level in order to further develop our understanding of the role of text-chat in supporting (or not) enhanced salience and noticing. Finally, the lack of a significant relationship between noticing and modified output in the text-chat condition may have been impacted by learners' perceptions of the necessity in producing MO in SCMC interactions. For example, Gurzynski-Weiss and Baralt (2015) suggest that MO—particularly full MO—may be produced for social rather than developmental reasons. In text-chat, in which there is a written record of the contrast between the original erroneous form and the corrected form already available on screen, the production of MO may serve more as an acknowledgement of feedback rather than evidence of noticing or deeper levels of processing. Rather, learners might produce MO to explicitly indicate that they were aware of receiving a correction, regardless of whether the salience of the target form was enhanced or whether it was accurately noticed (Gurzynski-Weiss & Baralt, 2015).

Limitations and Future Research

Overall, the current results seem to suggest a complex relationship among salience, noticing, production of modified output, and mode of communication. In contrast to previous research suggesting that the additional processing time of text-chat, as well as the more permanent nature of the feedback, would result in increased salience and noticing (e.g., Lai & Zhao, 2006), the current results indicate no significant advantages for text-chat when compared to FTF or video-chat interactions. However, due to the small sample size of the current research, these results should be interpreted cautiously. More research drawing on larger samples of learners, as well as with learners in diverse contexts, is needed. Results also indicated that modified output was a significant predictor of noticing in FTF and video-chat, potentially due to modified output serving more social rather than attention-related functions (Gurzynski-Weiss & Baralt, 2015), suggesting that modality does affect the interaction and the potential benefits learners may derive from feedback. Future research should seek to further investigate the role of modality on the salience and noticing of feedback, particularly in terms of controlling for type and explicitness of recasts provided. In addition, the current research focused on contingency as a binary variable. In order to obtain a more nuanced understanding of the role of contingency on the salience of corrective feedback, future research should examine the effects of distance between learners' errors and the feedback response, particularly in SCMC conditions. Furthermore, the current study did not discriminate between different types of modified output, providing a broad rather than narrow perspective. Future research might address different types of modified output, as well as conduct further qualitative investigations, in order to obtain a more nuanced understanding of how modality might affect the developmental benefits available to learners in traditional and different computer-mediated contexts. Lastly, the current research relied on SRs to investigate learners' noticing and the salience of feedback and target features. Future research should consider using additional methodologies, such as eye-tracking, in order to obtain a more comprehensive understanding of the relationships among recasts, noticing and salience, modified output, and mode of communication.

References

Baralt, M. (2010). *Task complexity, the Cognition Hypothesis, and interaction in CMC and FTF environments* (Unpublished doctoral dissertation). Georgetown University, Washington DC.

Beauvois, M. H. (1992). Computer-assisted classroom discussion in the foreign language classroom: Conversation in slow motion. *Foreign Language Annals, 25*, 455–464.

Doughty, C., & Varela, E. (1998). Communicative focus on form. In C. Doughty & J. Williams (Eds.), *Focus on form in classroom second language acquisition* (pp. 114–138). Cambridge: Cambridge University Press.

Egi, T. (2007). Recasts, learners' interpretations, and L2 development. In A. Mackey (Ed.), *Conversational interaction in second language acquisition: A collection of empirical studies* (pp. 249–267). Oxford: Oxford University Press.

Ellis, N. C. (2006). Selective attention and transfer phenomena in L2 acquisition: Contingency, cue competition, salience, interference, overshadowing, blocking, and perceptual learning. *Applied Linguistics, 27*(2), 164–194.

Faraco, M., & Kida, T. (2008). Gesture and the negotiation of meaning in a second language classroom. In G. Stam & S. G. McCafferty (Eds.), *Gesture: Second language acquisition and classroom research* (pp. 280–297). New York: Routledge.

Gass, S. M. (1997). *Input, interaction and the second language learner*. Mahwah, NJ: Lawrence Erlbaum Associates.
Gass, S. M. (2003). Input and interaction. In C. J. Doughty & M. H. Long (Eds.), *The handbook of second language acquisition* (pp. 224–255). London: Wiley-Blackwell.
Gass, S. M., & Mackey, A. (2000). *Stimulated recall methodology in second language research*. Mahwah, NJ: Lawrence Erlbaum Associates.
Gass, S. M., & Mackey, A. (2006). Input, interaction and output: An overview. *AILA Review*, *19*, 3–17.
Gass, S. M., & Mackey, A. (2007). Input, interaction, and output in second language acquisition. In B. VanPatten & J. Williams (Eds.), *Theories in second language acquisition: An introduction* (pp. 175–199). Mahwah, NJ: Lawrence Erlbaum Associates.
Gass, S. M., & Mackey, A. (2017). *Stimulated recall methodology in applied linguistics and L2 research*. New York: Routledge.
Goo, J., & Mackey, A. (2013). The case against the case against recasts. *Studies in Second Language Acquisition*, *35*, 127–165.
Gurzynski-Weiss, L. (2016). Factors influencing Spanish instructors' in-class feedback decisions. *The Modern Language Journal*, *100*(1), 1–55.
Gurzynski-Weiss, L., & Baralt, M. (2014). Exploring learner perception and use of task-based interactional feedback in FTF and CMC modes. *Studies in Second Language Acquisition*, *36*(1), 1–37.
Gurzynski-Weiss, L., & Baralt, M. (2015). Does type of modified output correspond to learner noticing of feedback? A closer look in face-to-face and computer-mediated task-based interaction. *Applied Psycholinguistics*, *36*(6), 1393–1420.
Kelm, O. R. (1992). The use of synchronous computer networks in second language instruction: A preliminary report. *Foreign Language Annals*, *25*, 441–454.
Lai, C., Fei, F., & Roots, R. (2008). The contingency of recasts and noticing. *CALICO Journal*, *26*, 70–90.
Lai, C., & Zhao, Y. (2006). Noticing and text-based chat. *Language Learning & Technology*, *10*(3), 102–120.
Leeman, J. (2003). Recasts and second language development. *Studies in Second Language Acquisition*, *25*, 37–63.
Loewen, S., & Philp, J. (2006). Recasts in the adult L2 classroom: Characteristics, explicitness and effectiveness. *The Modern Language Journal*, *90*, 536–556.
Long, M. H. (1996). The role of the linguistic environment in second language acquisition. In W. C. Ritchie & T. K. Bhatia (Eds.), *Handbook of language acquisition, Vol. 2: Second language acquisition* (pp. 413–468). New York: Academic Press.
Long, M. H. (2007). *Problems in SLA*. Mahwah, NJ: Lawrence Erlbaum Associates.
Long, M. H., Inagaki, S., & Ortega, L. (1998). The role of implicit negative feedback in SLA: Models and recasts in Japanese and Spanish. *The Modern Language Journal*, *82*, 357–371.
Lyster, R. (2004). Differential effects of prompts and recasts in form-focused instruction. *Studies in Second Language Acquisition*, *26*, 399–432.
Lyster, R., & Ranta, L. (1997). Corrective feedback and learner uptake: Negotiation of form in communicative classrooms. *Studies in Second Language Acquisition*, *19*, 37–67.
McDonough, K., & Mackey, A. (2006). Responses to recasts: Repetitions, primed production, and linguistic development. *Language Learning*, *56*, 693–720.
Mackey, A. (2012). *Input, interaction, and corrective feedback in L2 learning*. Oxford: Oxford University Press.

Mackey, A., Gass, S., & McDonough, K. (2000). How do learners perceive interactional feedback? *Studies in Second Language Acquisition, 22*, 471–497.

Mackey, A., & Goo, J. (2007). Interaction research in SLA: A meta-analysis and research synthesis. In A. Mackey (Ed.), *Conversational interaction in SLA: A collection of empirical studies* (pp. 408–452). New York: Oxford University Press.

Mackey, A., & Sachs, R. (2012). Older learners in SLA research: A first look at working memory, feedback, and L2 development. *Language Learning, 62*, 704–740.

Muñoz, C. (2010). On how age affects foreign language learning. In A. Psaltou-Joycey & M. Mattheoudakis (Eds.), *Advances in research on language acquisition and teaching: Selected papers* (pp. 39–49). Retrieved from www.enl.auth.gr/gala/14th/index_en.html

Nicholas, H., Lightbown, P. M., & Spada, N. (2001). Recasts as feedback to language learners. *Language Learning, 51*, 719–758.

Oliver, R. (2000). Age differences in negotiation and feedback in classroom and pairwork. *Language Learning, 50*, 119–151.

Parlak, O., & Ziegler, N. (2016). The impact of recasts on the development of primary stress in a synchronous computer-mediated environment. *Studies in Second Language Acquisition, 39*, doi: 10.1017/S0272263116000310.

Payne, J. S., & Whitney, P. J. (2002). Developing L2 oral proficiency through synchronous CMC: Output, working memory, and interlanguage development. *CALICO Journal, 20*, 7–32.

Pellettieri, J. (2000). Negotiation in cyberspace: The role of chatting in the development of grammatical competence. In M. Warschauer & R. Kern (Eds.), *Network-based language teaching: Concepts and practice* (pp. 59–86). Cambridge: Cambridge University Press.

Pica, T. (1987). Second-language acquisition, social interaction, and the classroom. *Applied Linguistics, 8*, 3–21.

Pica, T., Kanagy, R., & Falodun, J. (1993). Choosing and using communication tasks for second language instruction. In G. Crookes & S. M. Gass (Eds.), *Tasks and language learning* (pp. 9–34). Clevedon, UK: Multilingual Matters.

Révész, A., Sachs, R., & Mackey, A. (2011). Task complexity, uptake of recasts, and second language development. In P. Robinson (Ed.), *Second language task complexity: Researching the cognition hypothesis of language learning and performance* (pp. 203–238). Amsterdam: John Benjamins.

Robinson, P. (1995). Attention, memory, and the "noticing" hypothesis. *Language Learning, 45*, 283–331.

Robinson, P. (2003). Attention and memory during SLA. In C. J. Doughty & M. H. Long (Eds.), *Handbook of second language acquisition* (pp. 630–678). Oxford: Wiley-Blackwell.

Salaberry, M. R. (2000). L2 morphosyntactic development in text-based computer-mediated communication. *Computer Assisted Language Learning, 13*, 5–27.

Sauro, S. (2009). Computer-mediated corrective feedback and the development of L2 grammar. *Language Learning and Technology, 13*, 96–120.

Saxton, M. (1997). The contrast theory of negative input. *Journal of Child Language, 24*, 139–161.

Schmidt, R. (1990). The role of consciousness in second language learning. *Applied Linguistics, 11*, 206–226.

Schmidt, R. (1995). Consciousness and foreign language learning: A tutorial on the role of attention and awareness in learning. In R. Schmidt (Ed.), *Attention and awareness in foreign language learning* (pp. 1–63). Honolulu: University of Hawaii Press.

Schmidt, R. (2001). Attention. In P. Robinson (Ed.), *Cognition and second language instruction* (pp. 3–32). Cambridge, UK: Cambridge University Press.

Schmidt, R., & Frota, S. (1986). Developing basic conversational ability in a second language: A case study of an adult learner of Portuguese. In R. R. Day (Ed.), *Talking to learn: Conversation in second language acquisition* (pp. 237–326). Boston, MA: Newbury House.

Sheen, Y. (2004). Corrective feedback and learner uptake in communicative classrooms across instructional settings. *Language Teaching Research, 8*(3), 263–300.

Skehan, P. (1996). A framework for the implementation of task-based instruction. *Applied Linguistics, 17*, 38–62.

Smith, B. (2003). Computer-mediated negotiated interaction: An expanded model. *The Modern Language Journal, 87*, 38–57.

Smith, B. (2004). Computer-mediated negotiated interaction and lexical acquisition. *Studies in Second Language Acquisition, 26*, 365–398.

Smith, B. (2008). Methodological hurdles in capturing CMC data: The case of the missing self-repair. *Language Learning & Technology, 12*(1), 85–103.

Smith, B. (2010). Employing eye-tracking technology in researching the effectiveness of recasts in CMC. In F. M. Hult (Ed.), *Directions and prospects for educational linguistics* (pp. 79–97). Heidelberg: Springer.

Smith, B. (2012). Eye tracking as a measure of noticing: A study of explicit recasts in SCMC. *Language Learning and Technology, 16*, 53–81.

Smith, B., & Gorsuch, G. (2004). Synchronous computer mediated communication captured by usability lab technologies: New interpretations. *System, 32*, 553–575.

Swain, M. (2005). The output hypothesis: Theory and research. In E. Hinkel (Ed.), *Handbook of research in second language teaching and learning* (pp. 471–483). Mahwah, NJ: Lawrence Erlbaum Associates.

Toyoda, E., & Harrison, R. (2002). Categorization of text chat communication between learners and native speakers of Japanese. *Language Learning & Technology, 6*, 82–99.

VanPatten, B. (1996). *Input processing and grammar instruction: Theory and research*. Norwood, NJ: Ablex.

Warschauer, M. (1997). Computer-mediated collaborative learning: Theory and practice. *Modern Language Journal, 81*, 470–481.

Yanguas, I. (2010). Oral computer-mediated interaction between L2 Learners: It's about time! *Language Learning & Technology, 14*(3), 72–93.

Yanguas, I. (2012). Task-based oral computer-mediated communication and L2 vocabulary acquisition. *CALICO Journal, 29*(3), 507–531.

Yilmaz, Y. (2012). The relative effects of explicit correction and recasts on two target structures via two communication modes. *Language Learning, 62*, 1134–1169.

Yilmaz, Y., & Yuksel, D. (2011). Effects of communication mode and salience on recasts: A first exposure study. *Language Teaching Research, 15*, 457–477.

Yuksel, D., & Inan, B. (2014). The effects of communication mode on negotiation of meaning and its noticing. *ReCALL, 26*(3), 333–354.

Ziegler, N. (2016a). Taking technology to task: Technology-mediated TBLT, performance, and production. *Annual Review of Applied Linguistics, 36*, 136–163.

Ziegler, N. (2016b). Synchronous computer-mediated communication and interaction: A meta-analysis. *Studies in Second Language Acquisition, 38*, 553–586.

Ziegler, N., & Smith, G. (2016, September). *Teacher individual differences: A first look at the role of working memory on the provision of corrective feedback*. Paper presented at the 35th annual meeting of the Second Language Research Forum, New York.

AFTERWORD

The Role of Salience in Second Language Research

Patti Spinner, Jennifer Behney, and Susan M. Gass

As discussed in Chapter 1, the concept of salience has played a prominent role in the L2 literature as well as in a wide range of related disciplines. The goal of this volume was to take a broad view in order to get as full a picture as possible of how salience fits into current thinking. The chapters approach the topic from a variety of perspectives, included a range of L1s and L2s, and used innovative research methods. Position papers include a usage-based approach (Chapter 2: Ellis), an emergentist processing-based approach (Chapter 4: O'Grady, K. Kim and C.-E. Kim) and a generativist approach (Chapter 3: Lardiere). There are also review articles (Chapter 9: Leow & Martin; Chapter 8: McDonough & Trofimovich) as well as empirical studies, with some chapters falling into more than one of these categories.

Types of Salience

As we noted in Chapter 1, salience is a difficult concept to pin down. The basic notion is that something "stands out" from its environment in some way, but the specifics of how this occurs—and how to clearly define it—are complex and controversial. The contributors to this volume took different perspectives, with approaches that sometimes diverged but more often overlapped.

In delineating salience, Ellis described three main types: psychophysical, association, and surprisal. Psychophysical salience (which we often refer to as perceptual salience) refers to the fact that some sensations are experienced as more intense than others; association refers to the fact that based on our experience some pieces of information in the world are more important to us than others, and surprisal refers to the fact that we are drawn to pay more attention when our expectations for the world are not met.

DeKeyser, Alfi-Shabtay, Ravid, and Shi (Chapter 7), on the other hand, divided views of salience into narrow, medium, and wide. The narrow view of salience is what we might describe as perceptual salience, including the number of phones, sonority, stress, and so on. The medium view begins with perceptual salience but also includes issues of meaning, including "clarity of meaning and transparency of form-meaning mapping" (p. 133). For instance, under this analysis, plural marking in English is considered to have relatively low salience because of the complexity of form/meaning mappings: -*s* is associated with a variety of different meanings in English (for instance, plural, possessive, and third person singular) and also is realized with various allomorphs ([s], [ɪs], [z], [ɪz]). The wide view moves beyond linguistic issues to encompass psychological and physical contexts (and perhaps social ones, as well).

Another way to think of types of salience is to focus on whether attention to language is driven by bottom-up or top-down mechanisms. For instance, qualities of stress, sonority and so forth (i.e., perceptual salience) may draw attention because of their presence in the input, attracting the attention of bottom-up mechanisms. However, attention can also be guided by top-down mechanisms—for instance, the intentions of the language user in response to the demands of a particular task (Chapter 6: Simoens, Housen, & De Cuypere). These top-down mechanisms are relevant for what Ellis refers to as the salience of association.

In this volume, many of the chapters focused on perceptual salience (similar to DeKeyser et al.'s "narrow view"), which is presumably accessible to bottom-up mechanisms (Simoens et al.). For example, Lardiere focused on perceptual prominence in her discussion of salience in relation to the interpretability of features. Similarly, O'Grady et al. focused on acoustic/perceptual salience and argued that expanding the definition to include factors beyond this is not helpful for explaining the facts of linguistic development. Several of the empirical studies also focused on perceptual salience. Simoens et al., for example, compared the acquisition of two morphemes in a semi-artificial language; one of them, -*olp*, is more perceptually salient than the other, -*u*, because of its length. Examining eye-tracking data, they found that learners skipped over -*olp* less frequently and thus attended to it more, although there was also an effect of task type. Behney, Spinner, Gass, and Valmori (Chapter 5) also investigated the salience of morphological marking, specifically past tense marking in Italian. They concluded that the length of past tense marking in Italian made it relatively easy for English-speaking learners to detect; thus, even learners at an intermediate level were sensitive to the marking.

Moving into the "wide" view of salience, a number of papers in this volume investigated what we referred to as "constructed salience" (Leow refers to it as "externally induced salience"). This type of salience is particularly relevant to second language acquisition and particularly learning in a classroom context. Specifically, the contributions focused on the efforts of instructors to direct learners' attention to particular language features. For example, both Ryan, Hamrick, Miller, and Was (Chapter 10) and Leow and Martin discussed how textual enhancement can affect attention and learning. Additionally, the contributions in the section entitled "salience in context" took this wider view and examined the ways learners' attention to various aspects of the target language change depending on a variety of factors. For instance, Ziegler (Chapter 14) examined the ways that recasts direct learners' attention to target language features and how these effects can change depending upon the modality and contingency of recasts. McDonough and Trofimovich took a broad view of salience and considered it from three quite different perspectives: salience as input distribution; salience as learner-internal factors (especially L1 influence); and salience as learning context, including the effects of including different tasks.

These varying approaches make it clear that salience is not a monolithic construct but rather takes on different meanings depending on the views and goals of the researcher. We note that the researchers here have attempted to outline exactly what aspect of salience they are referring to, and emphasize that this is a crucial feature for future research as well.

Is Salience an Important Factor in L2 Acquisition?

The central question regarding salience in this volume is: to what extent does salience (of any kind) affect the ways that second language learners acquire and use language? Most of the contributions to this volume took the position that salience is a factor in second language acquisition; specifically, that greater salience leads to greater perception of and attention to target forms and ultimately to greater learning. On the other hand, items with low salience are a challenge to acquire. As Ellis wrote, "the low psychophysical salience of grammatical functors contributes to L2 learners' difficulty in learning them" (p. 26). DeKeyser et al. similarly argued for a strong role for salience in the acquisition of various grammatical functors; however, they argued that salience is particularly relevant for explicit learning. They claimed that because adult L2 learners rely on explicit learning in ways that children do not, salience is a major factor for adult learners only. Note that Simoens et al. made arguments that are similar in some respects: that is, they argued that perceptual salience makes learning more successful for second language learners because learners may need to have their attention drawn to particular features of language; however, their focus is on implicit learning:

> Without salience, L2 learners easily gloss over the language feature, thereby failing to attend and, consequently, to learn it. This is especially the case in implicit learning contexts, where learners are left to their own devices to pick up regularities from the input.
>
> (p. 107)

However, not all the contributors agreed that salience is an important factor in second language acquisition. Noting that progress in the field of SLA is often made by determining what does not have explanatory value rather than what does, O'Grady et al. wrote about salience, "Our conclusion, put simply, is that it has little impact, if any. Hopefully, time and further research will clarify this matter," (p. 83). Similarly, Lardiere focused on the detection of features (such as case marking or grammatical gender) in second languages and concluded, "detectability of grammatical feature contrasts is not limited to, and is likely only peripherally related to, the notion of perceptual salience if, by 'perceptual', we mean 'how easy it is to hear or perceive a given structure'" (p. 57). For each of these researchers, there is another factor that outweighs any possible effects of salience. For O'Grady et al., that factor is processing costs, and for Lardiere, that factor is the necessity of reassembling L1 features to the L2 configuration.

Findings differed also on whether various attempts to create constructed salience are useful or effective. Hardison (Chapter 11) demonstrated that segmental-level perception training can increase the salience of speech cues and the accuracy of word identification. On the other hand, both Ryan et al. and Leow and Martin argued that textual enhancement might be effective, but probably not in a straightforward way. As Leow and Martin put it (p. 182): "Given the revelations of the TE [textual enhancement] literature, teachers should be aware that making L2 grammatical data more salient does not necessarily lead to robust learning." They noted that tasks that encourage deeper processing of target forms seem to be more effective. Given the variety of ways that salience can be enhanced in the classroom—including textual enhancement, training, and recasts, among others—it is clear that this is a fruitful area for further research.

When is Salience Relevant?

Salience, in particular perceptual salience, is often invoked in research on inflectional morphology. As we noted in the introduction, discussions of salience played a role in the morpheme order studies dating back to the 1970s. Even now, much of the discussion about salience involves morphological endings, often with the argument that they are not particularly salient. In this volume, too, inflectional morphology received a good deal of attention; for instance, Behney et al., Simoens et al., Sarkissian and Behney (Chapter 12), and DeKeyser et al. all investigated morphological issues such as tense and case marking. Ellis pointed out previous work showing that grammatical functors such as inflectional morphology are typically shortened over time, and thus become less salient. However, this is not a universally accepted idea; O'Grady et al. argues that there is no reason to assume that the difference between *know* and *knows* is more difficult to perceive than the difference between *no* and *nose* (which is not known to be particularly difficult) (p. 75).

Perceptual salience is not generally considered to be an issue with the acquisition of open-class words such as nouns and adjectives or longer phrases such as idioms. However, these issues may be investigated with regard to constructed salience. For instance, Ryan et al. considered the effects of textual enhancement on word form learning, while Michel and Smith (Chapter 13) investigated whether learners would notice and use particular phrases (n-grams) that their peers used. In this volume there was also a contribution that investigated phonological acquisition with regard to constructed salience: Hardison investigated whether training would improve learners' word identification accuracy with segments such as /r/ and /l/.

Interacting Factors

The unifying factor among these varying types of salience studies is the assumption that salience (whether natural or constructed) promotes attention to something in the L2. However, it is important to note that attention is not sufficient; it is what happens after attention has been drawn that determines the learning outcome. A number of studies in this volume demonstrated that other factors interact with salience. Sarkissian and Behney showed the importance of task type as an interacting factor, as did McDonough and Trofimovich. McDonough and Trofimovich also included input distribution, learner characteristics, and learning context as variables that interact with salience. Importantly, both Ryan et al. and Leow and Martin noted that attention in and of itself is not enough to promote acquisition; rather, processing and the effort that is expended in processing are crucial. For DeKeyser et al., the effects of salience are moderated by the age of the acquirer, with adult learners benefitting from high-salience linguistic features; aptitude also plays a role. Ziegler investigated the way that salience might be different in face-to-face, video-chat, or text-chat interactions. These studies demonstrate that in addition to being a complex construct with different roles in various aspects of language, salience also interacts in complex ways with non-linguistic factors.

In sum, the chapters illustrate the complexities of salience. It is not a uniform construct, but one that can only help us understand how L2 learning takes place if we take a broad perspective and consider how salience works as it interacts with other more familiar and more established constructs.

How Can Salience Be Investigated?

The studies in this volume include a number of empirical studies using a variety of methodologies, including grammaticality judgments, stimulated recall, and pupillometry. Eye-tracking was employed in a significant number of the studies. The data-elicitation and measurement tools used by studies in this volume are shown in Table A.1.

TABLE A.1 Data used in the empirical studies in this volume

Author	Data Type
Behney, Spinner, Gass, & Valmori	Eye-tracking
Simoens, Housen, & De Cuypere	Eye-tracking
DeKeyser, Alfi-Shabtay, Ravid, & Shi	Grammaticality judgment task
	Aptitude test
Ryan, Hamrick, Miller, & Was	Eye-tracking
	Pupillometry
Hardison	Audio-visual training and gating
Sarkissian & Behney	Eye-tracking
	Stimulated Recall
Michel & Smith	Eye-tracking
	SCMC/text-chat
	Video-conferencing
Ziegler	SCMC/text-chat
	Video-conferencing
	Stimulated Recall
	Face-to-face interaction

A number of researchers noted that their approach was relatively new. For instance, Ryan et al. noted that pupillometry has not been used much in second language studies, despite its frequent use in cognitive psychology studies to measure cognitive effort and processing load. Michel and Smith commented that their use of eye-tracking for text-based peer interaction is unique and could serve as a model for future studies. Other studies combined more traditional data-elicitation methods (e.g., stimulated recall) with newer methods (e.g., eye-tracking), in an attempt to obtain a more complete overall picture of learner behavior. A variety of approaches will be necessary moving forward to investigate the complex nature of salience.

Eliciting data on salience is not always easy, but one way to simplify an investigation is to adopt and possibly modify existing tools. Many of the tools used by authors in this collection have been uploaded to the IRIS database, where they can be freely downloaded by researchers interested in empirically investigating salience (iris-database.org) (cf. Mackey & Marsden, 2015).

Where Do We Go from Here?

One of the fundamental questions still remains: is salience a relevant factor in second language acquisition? Fortunately, we believe the field is moving past the point of primarily using salience as a post-hoc explanation for research findings (see Carroll, 2012); rather, the time has come to precisely investigate the contributions that salience makes in the acquisition of grammar, lexis, and other aspects of language. This process will also involve determining when salience is not a factor. As O'Grady et al. note in the conclusion to their contribution in this volume:

> The literature abounds with examples of apparent salience effects, a number of which receive attention in the other chapters of this volume. It remains to be seen to what extent these effects might lend themselves to reanalysis in terms of processing-related factors.
>
> (p. 82)

Another important part of determining the contributions of salience will be clarifying the terminology. The term *salience* can refer to many different things—ease of perception, unexpectedness, and highlighted text, to name a few—that it is important to state clearly which aspect is meant when research is conducted. In time, perhaps a kind of classification for types of salience and its effects in SLA could be developed.

For specific research ideas, one needs only to turn to many of the contributions to this volume. For instance, for future work in perceptual salience, DeKeyser et al. suggested research on morphologically rich target languages such as Arabic or Japanese, a recommendation we agree with, especially because so much salience research is conducted with English. They also suggested moving beyond morphology to include syntax in investigations of salience. Behney et al. wondered if the importance of salience in relation to the specific morphological area they investigated (tense marking) would also hold for other morphological areas. For future work in constructed salience, Leow and Martin suggested research that uses methodology such as eye-tracking and think-aloud protocols to investigate learners' processing and processes beyond the simple measurement of attention.

As is often the case with research, we are left with as many questions as answers. To some extent, the works in this volume point the way forward by demonstrating how little is clearly established about the role of salience in second language acquisition. Happily, though, they have helped to lay out research directions for work that is to come.

References

Carroll, S. E. (2012). When is input salient? An exploratory study of sentence location and word length effects on input processing. *International Review of Applied Linguistics in Language Teaching, 50*, 39–67.

Mackey, A., & Marsden, E. (2015). *Advancing methodology and practice: The IRIS repository of instruments for research into second languages.* New York: Routledge.

INDEX

Note: *Italic* page references indicate figures and tables.

Abrahamsson, N. 132
accessibility hierarchy 68–9
acoustic prominence 65, 80
Adverb Pretraining 29
affective activities 225
affix position 81
age of acquisition (AoA) 131–3, 135
age-salience interaction 135–8, *137*
agreement: in English language 75–7; gender 45–7; manual versus non-manual 4; subject–verb 8, 44–5
Alarcón, I. V. 46
Alfi-Shabtay, I. 291–2
alignment in synchronous computer-mediated communication 248–9
allomorphs 27, 41, 50, 226, 292
American Sign Language (ASL) 4
animacy 47
Applied Science Laboratories ASL eye-tracker 193
Archibald, J. 52–3
Area of Interest (AoI) 255, 257
associations, salient 22, 291
attention: input enhancement and 187; learned 28–31; lexical alignment during second language chat interaction and 255–6, *256*, *257*, 261–2; salience and 4, 187, 245, 294–5; in second language acquisition 187; target structure and 8
attentional perception 111

auditory-visual (AV) input 201
auxiliaries 3
awareness 10, 109–11

Baralt, M. 272–3, 275, 278, 286
Barcroft, J. 110
Bardovi-Harlig, K. 9–10, 224
"Basic Variety" of interlanguage 24–5, 28, 33
Bates, E. 75
Beard, R. 56
Becker, A. 33
Behney, J. 12, 14, 292, 294–5, 296
Benati, A. 6–7
Berko, J. 81
Bertram, R. 117
Bever, T. 80–1
Bialystok, E. 168
Birdsong, D. 43–4, 52
blocking 28–31
Bock, K. 245
Boers, F. 249
Boston, J. S. 248
bottom-up salience 2, 108–9, 124, 292
Bowles, M. 179–80
Branigan, H. P. 247, 262
British Sign Language 4
Brooks, P. J. 159
Brown, P. 81
Brown, R. 12, 25, 27–8, 51, 64, 75, 82
Burt, M. 8–9

Cabestrero, R. 190
Cadierno, T. 224
Cameron-Faulkner, T. 2
Caras, A. 90
Carlon, J. M. 227
Carroll, S. E. 6, 10–11, 58, 110
Carter, D. M. 26
case: detectability in feature reassembly and 47–8, 53, 58; in English language 47–8; in German language 225, 230, 237, 238; in Korean language 77–80; in Latin language 224, 226, 227–238; in object–subject–verb language 78–80; in Russian language 237; salience and 78; in subject–object–verb language 78–9; in Turkish language 48, 53, 58, 80–1
Casillas, G. 56
Cazden, C. 75
Cerezo, L. 90
chat interactions 253
chatlogs 253, *254*
child language 2–3
Chinese speakers 8, 93–4; *see also* Italian language tense, participants in study
Chomsky, N. 41
Cho, S. W. 78
Christianson, K. 248
Cintrón-Valentín, M. 32, 93–4
Clackson, K. 67
Clahsen, H. 67
clitics 26
co-argument antecedent 65
"cocktail party effect" 10
cognition: context and 22; evolutionary role of 22; linguistics and 23–4; salience and 5; second language acquisition and 187; surprise and 22; usage-based second language acquisition and 22
cognitive effort and word learning: depth processing and 189–90; overview 13, 198, 292; as predictor of recognition memory task performance 195–6, *195*; pupillometry and 13, 138, 189–90; recognition memory task and 193–5, *194*; textual enhancement and 13, 187–8; *see also* textual enhancement study
cognitive linguistics 23–4
cognitive salience 5
Collentine, J. 249
Collentine, K. 249
Collins, L. 9
Common European Framework of Reference for Languages (CEFR) 251
Competition Model 29, 76
Comprehensible Output 227
Comrie, B. 69
Conditioned Stimulus (CS) 22–3
conditioning 22–3
conflated input enhancement (CIE) 168, 170–1, 182
congruency 99–102
Conroy, A. 68
consciousness-raising 8, 168–9
consonants, unvoiced 109
consonant-vowel (CV) syllables 201–2
constructed salience: attention-drawing techniques and 8; future research 296–7; occurrence of 7–8; overview 13–14, 292–3; second language acquisition and 7, 292; studies 8–9; subject–verb agreement in Italian, acquisition of 8; *see also* cognitive effort and word learning; contextual and visual cues on spoken language; input enhancement
Construction Grammar 23–4
constructionism 24
context and salience 14–15; *see also* lexical alignment during second language chat interaction; noun–adjective agreement in Latin as second language; task modality, noticing, and contingency of recasts
Contextual Complexity Hypothesis 56
contextual and visual cues on spoken language: advantage of 201; audio-visual input and 201; between-category differences and 203; conclusion of studies 216–17; consonant-vowel syllables and 201–12; event-related potential (ERP) experiments and 202; focused training and 14, 201, 203–4; Japanese speakers experiment 202–10; Korean speakers experiment 202–13, 210–2, *213*; native English speakers experiment 202, 213–5, *214*; native speakers and 202; overview 13–14, 294; perception training and 203, 206–7; research questions for studies 204, 215–17; visual input and 202; within-category similarities and 203
contingency 26–7, *26*
contingent recast 278, 292–3
co-occurrence conditions 52–7
Costa, A. 244–5, 248
Crespo, A. 190
criteria-list approach 5

critical period hypothesis (CPH) 132
cue-outcome reliability 27
Cutler, A. 26, 81

dative alternation 10
de Graaff, R. 226–7
DeKeyser, R. 9, 12–13, 27, 44, 51–2, 55, 58, 64–5, 93, 110, 132–5, 138, 150, 245, 291–2, 293–6
Dekydtspotter, L. 46
de León, L. 81
depth processing 189–90
de Saussure, F. 33
detectability in feature reassembly: case and 47–8, 53, 58; co-occurrence conditions and 52–7; features on different lexical items and, different 53–8; gender agreement and 45–7; inflectional morphology and uninterpretability and 50–2; Interpretability Hypothesis and 45, 48, 51–2, 55; interpretable features and 42, 58; overview 11, 57–8; subject–verb agreement and 44–5; uninterpretable features and 42–52, 58; *wh*-movement and 48–50
De Vleeschauwer, J. 248
dialect contact 4–5
dialogue, successful 247
Dick, F. 76
Diessel, H. 73
Dietrich, C. 3
Direct Contrast Hypothesis 271
Doughty, C. 8, 32
Dulay, H. 8–9
Dutch speakers 112; *see also* inflectional morphology, participants in study

Ellis, N. 9, 11–12, 24, 28–32, 89–91, 93, 95–7, 110, 149–51, 226, 270, 291, 293–4
Elman, J. 76
English language: agreement in 75–7; auxiliaries in 3; case in 47–8; indefinite objects in 53–4; multi-word negation in 2–3; plural in 27, 41, 49–50, 292; relative clauses in 68–75, *69, 70, 71, 72*; *-s* suffix in 27, 41, 49–50, 292; as subject–verb–object language 69; *see also* second language acquisition (SLA)
English as a second language (ESL) 28; *see also* English language; second language acquisition
Englishti language 12, 112–15

enhancing input to promote salience *see* input enhancement
entrainment 30–1, 245, 247
entrenchment 30–1
Esperanto transitive constructions 15, 148–50, 153–61
event-related potential (ERP) experiments 202
experimental approach 5
explicit grammar instruction 223
explicit learning 31, 111
eye-fixation times 116, 123
eye-gaze data 156, 161, 249, 255, 260–1
EyeLink 1000 eye-tracker 97, 230
EyeLink II 116
EyeTech Digital Systems 252–3
eye-tracking: learned attention and 30; lexical alignment during second language chat interaction and 245, 261; Michel and Smith study using 14, 244–5; sample picture used for *68*; screen-recording and 252–3; synchronous computer-mediated communication 249–50, 261; in verbal marking 94; *see also* inflectional morphology, processing second language; Italian language tense, second language acquisition of; noun–adjective agreement in Latin second language; textual enhancement study; video-chat modalities

face-to-face (FTF) interaction 274, 276, 282–3
Failed Functional Features Hypothesis 223
feature assembly 41–2; *see also* detectability in feature reassembly
Felser, C. 67
Fernald, A. 46
Ferreira, V. S. 247
Field, J. 28
first fixation duration (FFD) 120–1, *120*, 123–4
first language acquisition 24
First Noun Principle 224–5, 238
first run dwell time (FRDT) 120–1, *120*
focused training 14, 201, 203–4
Focus on Form (FonF) method 32, 223, 226
forced choice adjective completion task 232, *233–5*, 235, 243
Form-Focused Instruction (FFI) method 32, 223, 226

fossilization 24
Fox, N. 4
Franceschina, F. 45–6
full recast 278, 283

Gass, S. 2, 7, 10, 90, 93, 101, 269–71, 275, 292
gating: in Japanese speakers experiment 205–10; in Korean speakers experiment 211–12; in native English speakers experiment 213–16
Gaze Tracker 10.0 Data analysis software 252–3
Gebhardt, L. 56
gender agreement 45–7
German language 47–8, 225
Gilligan, G. 81
Giora, R. 9
Godfroid, A. 249
Goldberg, A. E. 147–8, 158
Goldinger, S. D. 190
Goldschneider, J. 9, 27, 44, 51–2, 55, 58, 64–5, 93, 110, 134–5, 150, 245
Goo, J. 32
Gorsuch, G. 272
grammatical constructions in second language acquisition 24–5, 41
grammatical cues 223
grammatical functors 25–6, 226
grammaticality judgments 117
grammaticalization 33
grammatical sensitivity 111
Grammatical Sensitivity Index (GSI) 115–17, 119–22, *120*, *121*
Granena, G. 32, 132
Greek language 7, 48, 53–4
"grounded" salience 7
Grüter, T. 46
Gürel, A. 54
Gurzynski-Weiss, L. 272–3, 275, 278, 286

Hamrick, P. 13, 292, 294–6
Hardison, D. M. 13–14, 216, 294
Harley, H. 56–7
Harris, M. 4
Harrison, R. R. 227
Hattori, H. 42, 49–50
Hawkins, J. 69, 81
Hawkins, R. 42, 49–50, 56
Haznedar, B. 54
Hebrew morphology 13
Hebrew as second language: age and 131–3, 135; age-salience interaction and 135–8, *137*; critical period hypothesis and 132; further analysis 138; future research 139; GJT and 135, *138*; implications of study 138–9; instruments in study 134; methodology of study 134–5; model with interaction 145; model without interaction 145–6; overview 12–13, 291–2; participants in study 134; procedure in study 135; results of study 135–8; salience in second language acquisition and 133–4; structures in test 135–6, 142, *143–4*
Hickey, R. 12
hierarchy effects 65, 69, 74, 75
high salience 124, 224, 227
Hollich, G. 3
homophony 27
Hopp, H. 46–8
Housen, A. 249
Hout, M. C. 190
Huang, H.-T. 171, 188
Hulstijn, J. H. 226–7
Hwang, S. H. 43, 56–7
Hyltenstam, K. 132

Identified Sources for Lexical Alignment 258–9, *259*
implicit learning 31, 111
Inan, B. 272
Inceoglu, S. 179, 188
incongruency 99, 101–3
indefinite objects 53–4
Indonesian language 81
Indrarathne, B. 179–81, 188
inflection: agreement in English language and 75–7; case in Korean language and 77–80; challenges of, further 80–2; in linguistic development 75–82, *79*
inflectional markers 223–6
inflectional morphology, processing second language: awareness and 109–11; bottom-up salience and 108–9, 124; discussion of study 123–4; Englishti language and 12, 112–15; eye-fixation times and 116, 123; eye-tracking and 12, 107; first fixation duration (FFD) 120–1, *120*, 123–4; first run dwell time (FRDT) 120–1, *120*; grammaticality judgments and 117; Grammatical Sensitivity Index and 115–17, 119–22, *120*, *121*; instructions in study 114–15; interaction effect 121–2, *121*; materials in study 112–15; measures in study 115–18;

method of study 112–19; overview 12, 124–5; participants in study 112; perceptual salience and 51, 107–8, 123–5; procedure in study 118–19; processing load measure and 116; rereading times (RRT) 122–4; research questions 110–11; results of study 119–23, *119*, *120*, *121*; retrospective interviews and 117–18; retrospective verbal reports and 122–3; salience and learning and 107–12; skipping rate and 119–20, *119*; target language in study 112; target morphemes in study 113; testing phase of study 114; top-down salience and 108, 111–12, 123–4; training phase in study 113–14; uninterpretability and 50–2; unvoiced consonants and 109
input distribution of salience 158–9
input enhancement: attention and 187; conflated 168, 170–1, 182; consciousness-raising and 8, 168–9; defining 8; external manipulation perspective 167; future research 181–2; instructed second language acquisition and 167, 169–71, 181, 183; internal input perspective 167; non-conflated 168, 171, *172–8*, 182; overview 13, 182–3; results of study 171, *172–8*, 179–81, *179*; summary of studies 171, *179*; teaching implications of study 182; textual enhancement and 168–71; theoretical underpinning of 168–9
Input Processing (IP) theory 29, 223
input salience-creation 8
instructed second language acquisition (ISLA) 167, 169–71, 181, 183, 223
Interpretability Hypothesis 45, 48, 51–2, 55
interpretable features 42, 58
IRIS database 296
Issa, B. 179
Italian language tense, second language acquisition of: analysis of study 98; compound past tense 12; congruency and 99–102; descriptive statistics and 99, *100*; discussion of study 101–3; dwell times and 98; incongruency and, present versus past 99, 101–3; materials in study 96, *97*; method of study 95–8; mixed model analysis and 99, *101*; morphology acquisition and 91–3; overview 12, 103, 292; participants in study 95–6; procedure in study 96–8; regressions and 98; results of study 98–101, *100*, *101*; salience and past tense 7; tense and 94–5, *94*; verbal marking and 93–4

Jackson, C. 225
Japanese language 49
Japanese speakers experiment: gating 205–10; materials 205–6; method 204–5; overview 202–3; participants 204–5; perception training 206–7; procedure 206–7; results 207–10, *208*, *209*, *210*; target words 205–6, 220
Jesse, A. 204
Johnson, V. 77
Jusczyk, P. 75

Kahneman, D. 190
Keating, G. D. 92
Kecskes, I. 9
Keenan-Comrie hierarchy 72
Keenan, E. 69
Kerswill, P. 5, 10
Kim, C.-E. 69, 73, 74
Kim, K. 79–80
Kim, Y. 262
Korean language: case in 77–80; plurals 43, 57–8; relative clauses in 68–75, *69*, *70*, *71*, *72*; as subject–object–verb language 69; *wh*-movement and 49
Korean speakers experiment: gating 211–12; materials 211; method 210–11; overview 202–3; participants 210–11; procedure 211; results 211–12, *211*, *212*, *213*
Kormos, J. 179–81, 188
Krashen, S. 168
Kwak, H.-Y. 65

Lai, C. 246, 272, 283
language change 5–6, 33–4
language consciousness raising 8, 168–9
language knowledge 24
language learning *see* second language acquisition (SLA); *specific language*
language teaching 31–3
Lardiere, D. 11, 43–4, 47, 49, 51, 56–7, 293–4
Larsen-Freeman, D. 8
Latin morphology 93–4
Latin as second language 227; *see also* noun–adjective agreement in Latin as second language
learnability theory 169

learned attention 28–31
learner-internal factors as salience 159–60
learner, salience as property of 154–6
learning: contingency and 26–7; explicit 31, 111; implicit 31, 111; learned attention and 28–9; psychophysical salience and 25–6; salience and 22–3, 107–12; *see also* second language acquisition
learning context as salience 160–1
learning environment, salience as property of 156–7, *157*
Lee, E. 56–7
Lee, M. 65
Leeman, J. 270
Lee, O.-S. 65
Leeser, M. 92, 124
Lee, S.-K. 171, 188
Legendre, G. 77
Lemelin, S. 93
Lenneberg, E. H. 131
Leow, R. 13, 90, 168, 170–1, 179–82, 189, 292, 294–5, 297
Lew-Williams, C. 46
lexical alignment during second language chat interaction: alignment in synchronous computer-mediated communication and 248–9; attention and 255–6, *256*, *257*, 261–2; dialogue and, successful 247; entrainment and 245, 247; eye-gaze data and 156, 161, 249, 255, 260–1; eye-tracking and 245, 261; eye-tracking synchronous computer-mediated communication and 249–50, 261; first and second language acquisition perspectives and 246–8; Identified Sources for Lexical Alignment and 258–9, *259*; mental model 245; overview 14, 263, 294; priming and 245, 247–8; psycholinguistic mechanism and 245; salience in second language acquisition and 245–6; salience in synchronous computer-mediated communication and 245–6; *see also* video-chat modalities
lexical constructions in second language acquisition 24–5
lexical cues 226
lexical errors 276
lexical gender assignment 46
lexical overlap 253–4
Lexical Preference Principle 29, 224–5, 238

Liceras, J. 51
Lidz, J. 68
Likert scale 96
linguistic development: inflection 75–82, *79*; overview 11, 82–3; questions at heart of linguistics and 64; reflexive pronouns 65–8; relative clauses 68–75, *69*, *70*, *71*, *72*; salience in *79*, 226
linguistics: cognition and 23–4; constructions and 25–6; cycle 33; questions at heart of 64; streamlining of 34
LoCoco, V. 225
Loewen, S. 7, 93, 179, 188
Long, M. 32, 132, 277, 286
low salience 224, 226–7, 292
Lyster, R. 8

McDonough, K. 14–15, 248, 262, 293, 295
Mackey, A. 269–70, 275, 280
MacLeod, B. 5
MacWhinney, B. 76
McWhorter, J. 33–4
Malay language 81–2
manual coding of eye-gaze data 255
manual versus non-manual agreement 4
Marsden, E. 248, 262
Martin, A. 13, 292, 294–5, 297
Massaro, D. W. 204
Mayan languages 81
medium view of salience 133, 291–2
Mercer, J. D. 189
Michel, M. 14, 249, 294, 296
Miller, G. 22
Miller, R. T. 292, 294–6
Missing Surface Inflection theory 223
Modern Language Aptitude Test 132
modified output opportunities/modified output (MOO/MO) 278–9, 281–2, *282*
morphemes: acquisition of 292; high-salient 124; lexical cues versus 226; perception of 111; studies of 135–6; target 113
morphology: Chinese learning Latin 93–4; English multi-word negation 2–3; Hebrew 13; Italian 94–5, *94*; Latin 93–4; perceptual salience and 107, 124–5; salience in 8, 91, 95, 102–3, 138, 292; second language acquisition of 91–3, 107; Spanish language 90–3; usage-based learning and 31; *see also* inflectional morphology
morphosyntax errors 277
multi-word negation 2–3

narrow view of salience 133, 137, 291–2
native English speakers experiment:
gating 213–16; materials 213; method 213; overview 202; participants 213; procedure 213; results 213–15, *214*, *215*
n-gram analysis 253–4, 257–8, 262
non-conflated input enhancement (NCIE) 168, 171, *172–8*, 182
non-contingent recast 278
Norris, J. 32
Nosofsky, R. M. 203
noticing: computer-mediated communication and 271–3; recasts and 270–1, 280–1, 284; salience and 270–1, 283; in second language acquisition 269–70; in stimulated recalls 279–80; synchronous computer-mediated communication and 272; *see also* task modality, noticing and contingency of recasts
Noticing Hypothesis 10, 31, 109, 245–6, 269
noun–adjective agreement in Latin as second language: adjectives accurately placed and 236–7; affective activities and 225; analysis of study 231–2; case marking and 229, 236–8; discussion of study 236–8; forced choice adjective completion task and 232, *233–5*, 235, 243; inflectional markers and 224–6; Latin as second language and 227; materials in study 230; method of study 229–32; nouns and adjectives used in study 228–9, *228*, *229*; overview 14, 238–9, 294; participants in study 229–30; procedure in study 230–1; referential activities and 225; research questions 229, 236–7; results of study 232–6; salience and 226–7; stimulated recalls and 235–6; structured input activities and 224–5; translation task and 232, 242
Novella, M. 32
novel second language pattern learning: analysis of study 153; challenge of 147–9; discussion of study 157–61; Esperanto transitive constructions and 15, 148–51, 153–61; eye-gaze data and 156, 161; input distribution as salience and 158–9; learner-internal factors as salience and 159–60; learning context as salience and 160–1; materials in study 152–3; method of study 152–7;

object–verb–subject language and 148, 153–4, *154*, *155*, 156–8, *156*, 160; overview 14–15, 161; participants in study 152; procedure in study 152–3; results of study 153–7; salience and 149–51; salience as property of learner and 154–6, *155*; salience as property of learning environment and 156–7, *157*; salience as property of stimulus and 153–4; stimulus-learner-context complex and 151; subject–object–verb language and 153

object–subject–verb (OSV) language 53, 78–81
object–verb–subject (OVS) language 148, 152–4, *154*, *155*, 156–8, *156*, 160
O'Donnell, M. B. 24
O'Grady, W. 11, 64–6, 69, 73, 74, 292, 294, 296
Oliver, R. 278
Örnberg Berglund, T. 250
O'Rourke, B. 249–50
Ortega, L. 32
orthographic errors 277

Panchronic principles 33
Papadopoulou, D. 55
Papesh, M. H. 190
Parodi, T. 44
partial recast 278, 283
Pavlovian conditioning 22–3
Pellettieri, J. 272
Penfield, W. 131
perception training 203, 206–7
perceptual salience: attention-drawing techniques and 8; focus on 292; inflectional morphology and 51, 107–8, 123–5; manual versus non-manual agreement and 4; morphology and 107, 124–5; overview 11–12; relevance of 294; second language acquisition and 7–9; *see also* Hebrew as a second language; inflectional morphology, processing second language; Italian language tense, second language acquisition of; novel second language pattern learning
Pfeiler, B. 81
Phillips, C. 68
Philp, J. 93
phonetic accommodation 5
phonological distinctions 3

phonological errors 277
phonology 4
Pickering, M. J. 244–5, 247
plurals: in English language 27, 41, 49–50, 292; in Korean language 43, 57–8
polysemy 27
possible source of lexical alignment (PSLA) 254–5, *254*, 257–8, *257*, *258*, 261
Preference for Nonredundancy Principle 29
priming 245, 247–8
Processing Instruction method 223–4, 226, 238
processing load measure 116
prosodic prominence 58, 81
pseudowords 192
psychological salience 21–2
psychophysical salience 21–2, 25–8, 291, 293
pupillometry 13, 138, 189–90
Pye, C. 81

quantified analysis 259–60
Quirós, P. 190

Rácz, P. 4–7
Rational Analysis of Cognition 22
Ravid, D. 7, 291
Rebuschat, P. 31
recasts: contingent 278, 292–3; defining 277–8, 283; full 278, 283; modality and 280–2, 292–3; modified output and 278–9, 281–3, *282*, 286; non-contingent 278; noticing and 270–1, 280–1, 284; partial 278, 283; salience and 270–1, 283–4; varied nature of 283–4; *see also* task modality, noticing and contingency of recasts
recognition memory task 193–6, *194*, *195*
referential activities 225
reflexive pronouns 65–8
Reinder, H. 7
relative clauses (RCs) 8, 10, 68–75, *69*, *70*, *71*, *72*
Renaud, C. 46, 250, 261
rereading time (RRT) 122–4
Rescorla, R. A. 22–3
Rescorla-Wagner equation 28
Ritter, E. 56–7
Roberts, L. 131
Robinson, P. 24, 111, 269
Roland, D. 76
Römer, U. 24

Russian language 225–6, 237
Russian speakers 134; *see also* Hebrew as second language, participants in study
Ryan, K. 13, 292, 294–6

Sagarra, N. 29–31, 96–7
salience: acquisition of lexus as 3; age and 135–8, *137*; approaches to 9–10; associations 22, 291; attention and 4, 187, 245, 294–5; awareness and 10; bottom-up 2, 108–9, 124, 292; case and 78; cognition and 5; complexity of 291, 295; computer-mediated communication and 271–3; context and surprise account of 22, 151; defining 1; dimensions of 1; Ellis's framework of 22, 89–91, 149–50, 291, 293; empirical data 295, *295*; future research 296–7; "grounded" 7; high 124, 224, 227; importance of 293–4; input distribution of 158–9; interacting factors and 294–5; investigating, methods of 295–6, *295*; lack of 226–7; in language change 33–4; learner-internal factors as 159–60; learning and 22–3, 107–12; learning context as 160–1; in linguistic development 79, 226; as linguistic property 12; low 224, 226–7, 292; medium view of 133, 291–2; in morphology 8, 91, 95, 102–3, 138, 292; narrow view of 133, 137, 291–2; noticing and 270–1, 283; noun–adjective agreement in Latin second language acquisition 226–7; novel second language pattern learning and 149–51; origins of term 1–2; as outcome of learning 10; as property of learner 154–6, *155*; as property of learning environment 156–7, *157*; as property of stimulus 153–4; in psychology 21–2; psychophysical 21–2, 25–8, 291, 293; recasts and 270–1, 283–4; reflexive pronouns and 66–7; relevance of 294; in second language acquisition 1–2, 6–7, 9, 108–12, 133–4, 201, 245–6, 291–7; surprisal 22, 291; in synchronous computer-mediated communication 245–6, 273; top-down 2, 108, 111–12, 123–4, 292; types of 291–3; verbal marking and 93–4; in video-chat modalities 245–6; wide view of 133, 137, 291–2; *see also* constructed salience; perceptual salience

salience-raising 94
salient input 8
salient phonetic variation 3
Sarkissian, J. 14, 294–5
Sauro, S. 246
Saxton, M. 271
Schachter, P. 75
Schmidt, R. 31, 108–9, 245–6, 269
second language acquisition (SLA): age and 131–3, 135; attention in 187; blocking in 29–31; child language 2–3; cognition and 187; constructed salience and 7, 292; grammatical constructions in 24–5, 41; grammatical cues and 223; "grounded" salience and 7; inflectional markers and 223; language change 5–6; learned attention in 29–31; lexical constructions in 24–5; of morphology 91–3, 107; noticing in 269–70; overview; perceptual salience and 7–9; psychophysical salience in 27–8; salience in 1–2, 6–7, 9, 108–12, 133–4, 201, 245–6, 291–7; sign language 4; sociolinguistics/dialect contact 4–5; text-chat and 244; transfer phenomena and 30–1; of uninterpretable features 42–52; usage-based approaches to 24; *wh*-movement and 49–50; *see also specific language*
second language acquisition (SLA) theory 10–11; *see also* detectability in feature reassembly; linguistic development; usage-based second language acquisition
semantic prominence 11
Sharwood Smith, M. 8, 109, 167–70, 187–8
ShareX program 276
Shea, C. 58
Shin, J. 248
sign language 4
Simoens, H. 12, 292–4
single-factor models 3
Sinnemäki, K. 151
situational alignment 247
skipping rate 119–20, *119*
Slobin, D. 81
Smith, B. 14, 244, 249–50, 261, 272, 283, 294, 296
Smith, G. 286
Smith, S. 8, 109, 167–9, 170, 187–8
sociolinguistics 4–5
Soderstrom, M. 75
Sony Handycam CX-160 276

Sony PCM-M10 audio recorder 276
Sorace, A. 244–5
Spada, N. 32
Spanish language 7, 90–3, 95, 224
Spinner, P. 292
-s suffix in English language 27, 41, 49–50, 292
stimulated recall (SR) 235–6, 272, 275, 279–80
stimulus-learner-context complex 151
stimulus, salience as property of 153–4
structured input activities 224–5
subject–object–verb (SOV) language 53, 69, 78–9, 80, 152–3
subject–verb agreement 8, 44–5
subject–verb–object (SVO) language 69, 73, 148
surprisal salience 22, 291
Svenonius, P. 47
Svetics, L. 93
synchronous computer-mediated communication (SCMC): alignment in 248–9; eye-tracking 249–50; Michel's study 249; noticing and 272; salience in 245–6, 273; use of 14, 244–5; *see also* video-chat modalities
syntactic alignment 247

Takahashi, E. 68
target form 270, 284
task modality, noticing and contingency of recasts: analysis of study 276–80; coding data in study 276–80; computer-mediated communication and 271–3; contingent recast and 278; descriptive statistics and 281, *281*; discussion of study 283–6; error type/recasts and 276–7; exit questionnaire and 275; full recast and 278, 283; future research on 287; lexical errors and 276; limitations of study 286–7; materials in study 274–5; method of study 273–80; modified output opportunities/modified output (MOO/MO) and 278–9, 281–2, *282*; morphosyntax errors and 277; non-contingent recast and 278; noticing and 270–1; noticing in second language acquisition and 269–70, 281–3; noticing in stimulated recalls and 279–80; orthographic errors and 277; overview 15, 292–3; partial recast and 278, 283; participants in study 273–4; phonological errors and 277; procedure

in study 275–6; research questions 273, 280–3, *281*; results of study 280–3; salience and 270–1; stimulated recall protocols and 272, 275; target form and 270; *see also* noticing; recasts
Terrell, T. 226
Test of English as a Foreign Language (TOEFL) 205, 273
text-chat 14, 244–6, 248–9, 272–3; *see also* video-chat modalities
textual enhancement (TE) 8, 13, 168–71, 187–8
textual enhancement study: discussion 196–7; eye-tracking apparatus 193; limitations 197–8; materials 190–3; methods 190–3; participants 190, *190*; procedure 193; pseudowords 192; recognition memory task 193–6, *194*, *195*; research questions 190–1, 196–7; results 193–6; training phase 190–3, *192*
Thai language 81–2
Theakston, A. 3
theoretical approaches 10–11; *see also* detectability in feature reassembly; linguistic development; usage-based second language acquisition
Thompson, R. 4
TM3 eye-tracker 252–3
Tobii TX300 integrated eye-tracking system 252
Tomasello, M. 73
Tomita, Y. 32
top-down salience 2, 108, 111–12, 123–4, 292
transfer phenomena 30–1
translation task 232, 242
Trofimovich, P. 14–15, 293, 295
Truscott, J. 109
Turkish language 48, 53–5, 58, 80–1
Type II error risk 197

Unconditioned Stimulus (US) 22–3
uninterpretable features 42–52, 58
Universal Grammar 64
unvoiced consonants 109
usage-based second language acquisition: approaches to first and second language acquisition 24; "Basic Variety" of interlanguage and 24–5, 28, 33; blocking and 28–31; cognition and 22; cognitive linguistics and 23–4; construction contingency and 27; Construction Grammar and 23–4; contingency and learning and 26–7, *26*; entrenchment and 30–1; fossilization and 24; grammatical constructions and 24–5; grammaticalization and 33; language change and 33–4; language teaching implications and 31–3; learned attention and 28–31; learning and salience and 22–3; lexical constructions and 24–5; linguistic cycle and 33; morphology and, acquiring from 31; overview 11; psychological salience and 21–2; psychophysical salience and 21–2, 25–8; salient associations and 22; transfer phenomena and 30–1
Uzum, B. 248–9

Valmori, L. 292
VanPatten, B. 6–7, 92, 102, 110, 224–5, 237
Veenstra, T. 33
verbal marking 93–4
verb-grammar instruction (VG) 32
Verb Pretraining (VP) 29, 32
verb salience with textual enhancement (VS) 32
Veronique, D. 33
video-chat modalities: analysis of study 253–5; Area of Interest and 255, 257; baseline data and 257–8, *257*; chat interactions 253, *254*; chatlogs 253, *254*; coding in study 253–5; comparing baseline versus alignment data and 258–9, *259*; descriptive data and 257–8; design of study 251, *252*; discussion of study 260–2; eye-gaze data and 156, 161, 249, 255; eye-tracking apparatus 252–3; eye-tracking synchronous computer-mediated communication and 249–50; face-to-face interaction 274, 276, 282–3; Fixation Count and 255, 258, 260, *260*; future research 263; getting to know partner and 251, 268; Identified Sources for Lexical Alignment and 258–9, *259*; lexical alignment and 246–8; limitations of study 262–3; manual coding of eye-gaze data and 255, *256*, *257*; materials in study 251–3, *252*; method of study 250–5; n-gram analysis and 253–4, 257–8, 262; overview 15, 263, 294; participants in study 250–1, *251*; possible source of lexical alignment and 254–5, *254*, 257–8, *257*, *258*, 261; procedure in study 253–5; qualitative examples 255–6, *255*,

256; quantitative analysis and 259–60; research questions 250; results of study 255–60; salience in 245–6; screen-recording 252–3, *254*; synchronous computer-mediated communication alignment and 248–9; Total Fixation Duration and 255, 258
Vigliocco, G. 4
Vinson, D. 4
visual cues *see* contextual and visual cues on spoken language
visual input 202

Wagner, A. R. 22–3
Was, C. A. 13, 292, 294–6
Wexler, K. 75
Whittle, A. 8
wh-movement 48–50

wide view of salience 133, 137, 291–2
Williams, A. 5, 10
Winke, P. 93, 179, 188
WordGen 114
word identification *see* gating
word learning *see* cognitive effort and word learning
word length and position in sentence 10

Yanguas, I. 285
Yilmaz, Y. 32, 272
Yuksel, D. 272

Zhao, Y. 246, 272, 283
Ziegler, N. 15, 286, 292–3, 295
Zipf, G. K. 25
Zobl, H. 51
Zwitserlood, P. 202, 216